AF506021

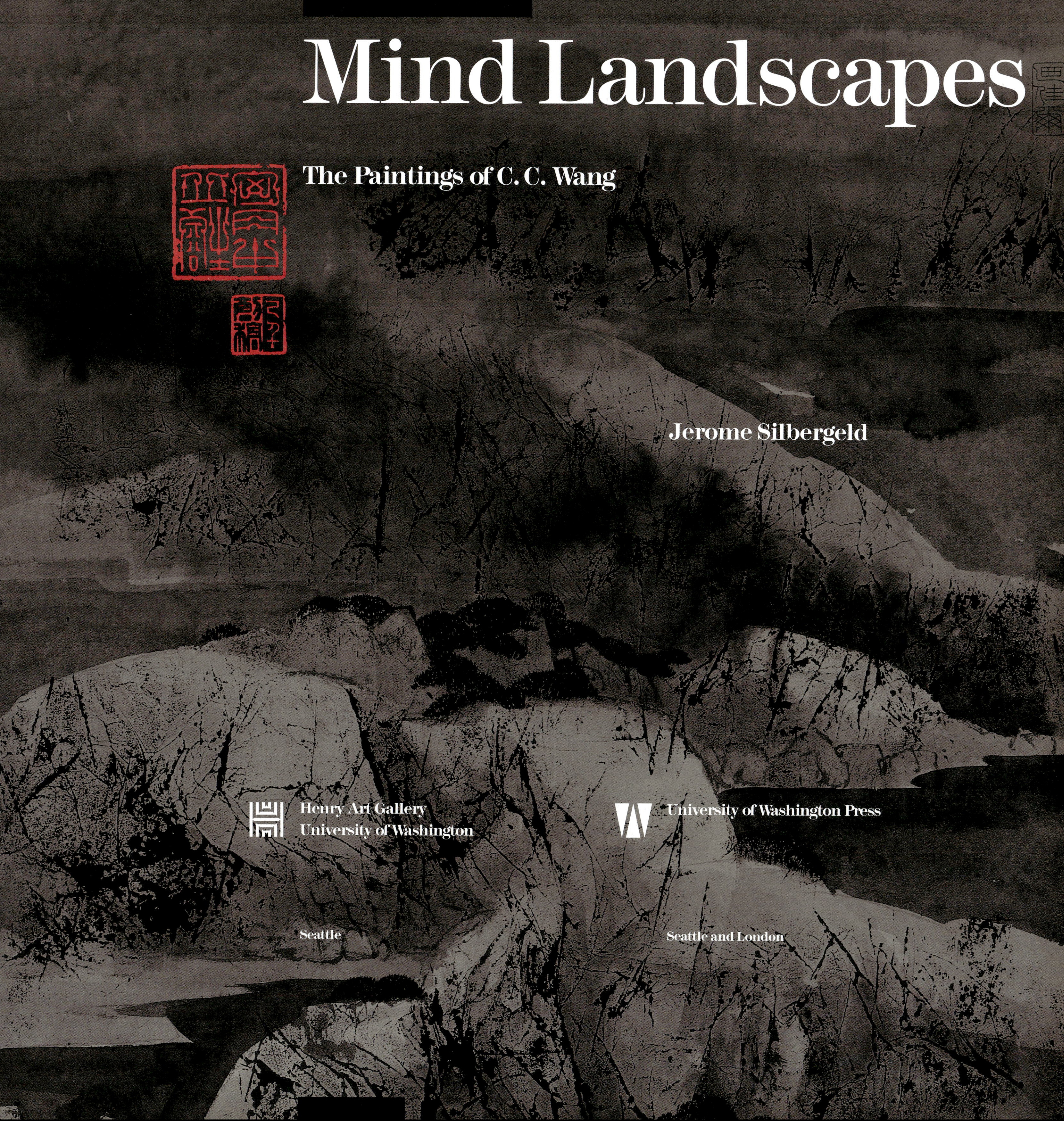

Mind Landscapes

The Paintings of C. C. Wang

Jerome Silbergeld

Henry Art Gallery
University of Washington

University of Washington Press

Seattle

Seattle and London

Library of Congress Cataloging-in-Publication Data
Silbergeld, Jerome.
    Mind landscapes.

    Bibliography: p.
    Includes index.
    1. Wang, Chi-ch'ien—Exhibitions. 2. Landscape painting, Chinese—20th century—Exhibitions.
3. Expatriate painters—New York (State)—Exhibitions.
I. Wang, Chi-ch'ien. II. Henry Art Gallery. III. Title.
ND1049.W18A4 1987   759.951   87-20788
ISBN 0-295-96521-5
ISBN 0-295-96520-7 (pbk.)

Edited by Joseph N. Newland
Designed by Douglas Wadden

Text type set in Baskerville and display type set in Modern 216 by Paul O. Giesey/Adcrafters, Portland, Oregon
Chinese set by Chinese Post and Typesetting, Seattle
Printed on 157 gsm Satin Kin-Fuji and bound with Muse Coton endpapers by Nissha Printing Co., Ltd., Kyoto, Japan
Edition: 2,000 hardbound, 1,000 softbound

All works reproduced are by C. C. Wang unless noted otherwise.

Cover:
Landscape Number 419, 1982. See figure 56, page 99.

Published with the assistance of the J. Paul Getty Trust

Photo Credits
Art Institute of Chicago, figure 3
Asian Art Photographic Distribution, 16
Chin Lem, 18, 28, 31, 32, 44, 50, 53
Frank Cho, 7, 24, 46
Chris Eden, 1
Metropolitan Museum of Art, 8, 23
Peter Neaman, 13, 21, 22, 29, 38, 39, 45, 48, 52, 55, 56, 57, 58, 62, 63, 64, 65, 66, 67, 68, 69
Otto Nelson, 2, 4, 5, 9, 10, 11, 12, 14, 15, 17, 19, 25, 27, 59, 60, 61
Phoenix Art Museum, 49
Jeffrey L. Riggenback, Photopia, 26
James Soong, 54
University Art Museum, Berkeley, 30, 33
Wettstein & Kauf, Reitberg Museum, 6, 34, 35
Steven J. Young, cover

Foreword

Like most worthwhile endeavors, this book and the exhibition we have mounted in conjunction with its publication have arisen from a confluence of planning and providence. Jerome Silbergeld, professor of Chinese art history at the University of Washington, became passionately interested in the art of Wang Chi-ch'ien, or C. C. Wang as he is known in the West, as well as in the artist himself. He began a book with the purpose of conveying to an unknowing audience the tremendous beauty, and in his view, the historical significance of C. C. Wang's painting. Jerome's enthusiasm was contagious, and when he approached the Henry Art Gallery, an exhibition was born, envisioned as a companion to the book. We are proud to be able to offer the first major retrospective of C. C. Wang's lengthy and productive career, which will travel to the Chinese Culture Center in San Francisco, to the Spencer Museum of Art at the University of Kansas, Lawrence, and in an abbreviated form to The China Institute in New York.

Having assumed the directorship of the Henry Art Gallery well after this project was underway, I am especially indebted to the members of our staff, who had the foresight to undertake it and the energy to carry it to a successful conclusion. Joan Klausner, assistant director (then acting director), Joseph Newland, editor of publications, Chris Bruce, curator of exhibitions, and Judy Darlene Sourakli, curator of collections, each deserve special mention for their efforts. Blair Rice, Paul Cabarga, and Jill Clark each contributed to the success of the project as well. Douglas Wadden, the catalogue designer, deserves special mention for this handsome and elegant publication.

Our accomplishments are due to the support of many individuals and organizations. The Henry Gallery Association, under the leadership of Gilbert C. Powers and Mrs. John E. Z. Caner, have given the Gallery the means to carry out this project, as they have so often in the past, and to the Association we offer our heartfelt gratitude. The book has been made possible by a grant to the Association from Seattle's PONCHO, a long-time and much valued supporter of many Henry Art Gallery publications, and by a grant to the University of Washington Press from the J. Paul Getty Trust, which has taken on an increasingly important role in sponsoring art historical research throughout the country. The exhibition in Seattle has been funded in part with a generous grant from the Kreielsheimer Foundation, a consistent supporter of the Henry Art Gallery in recent years. They have enabled our museum to achieve ambitious goals, for which we are deeply grateful. To each of these goes our thanks.

I am particularly pleased that we have benefited so richly from the resources of the University of Washington. Of course, it is art history faculty member Jerome Silbergeld who has been the driving force behind this project. It is fitting that a university art museum such as ours serve as a laboratory for ideas, and Jerome's ideas have added to those of a very productive museum staff. In addition, the University of Washington Press, under the leadership of Don Ellegood, has enthusiastically supported the publication of this book. We are hopeful that this kind of collaboration is only the first of many such ventures in the years to come.

Michael Komanecky
Director
Henry Art Gallery

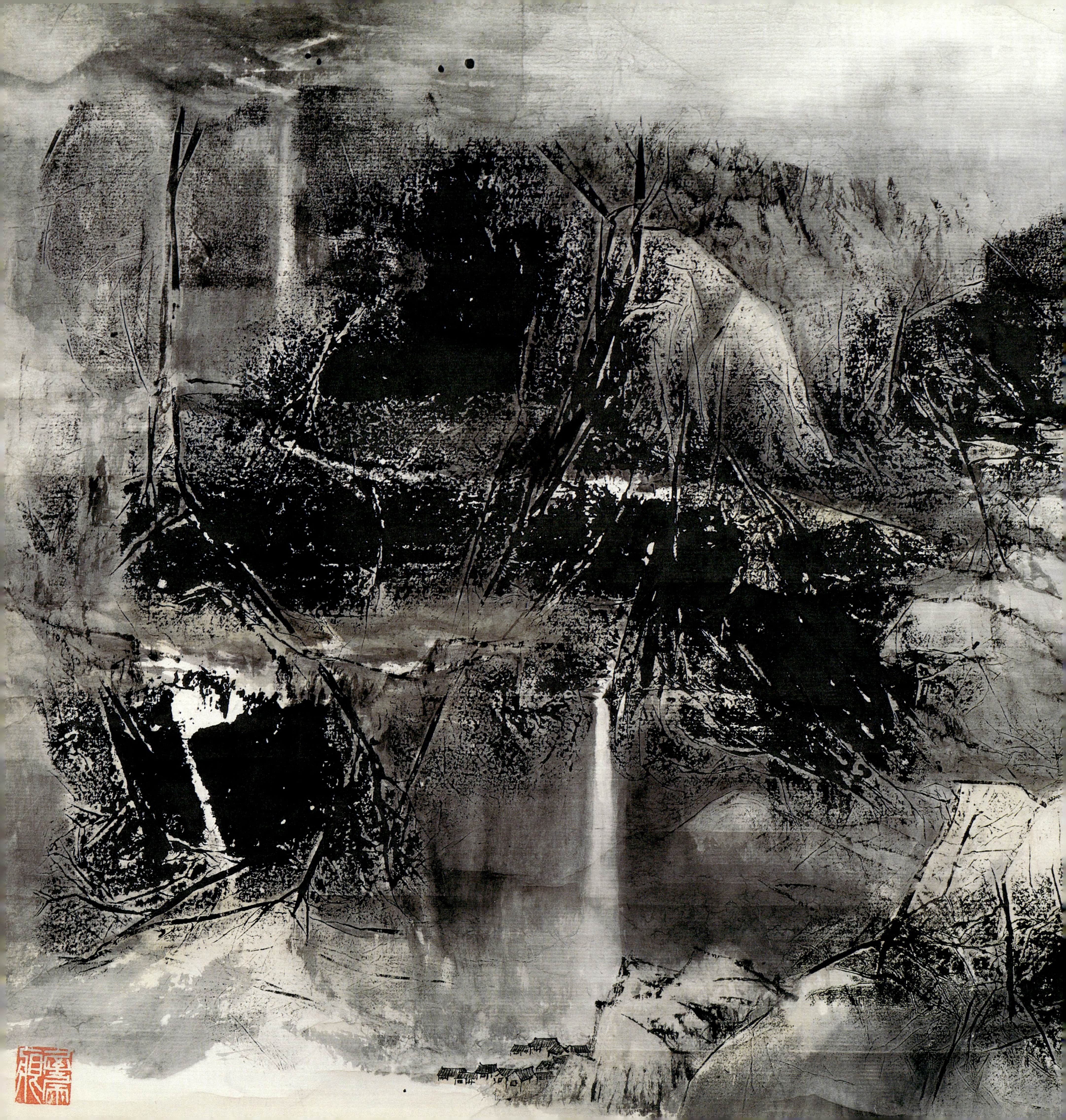

Preface

As an historian of ancient Chinese art, with no more of the art critic in me than is normal for an art historian, the task of writing about a contemporary artist seems appropriate only because I regard the subject, Wang Chi-ch'ien or C. C. Wang, as a Chinese artist of considerable historical significance. My view of his significance is twofold, the first of which *is* art critical: namely that the high quality of his work should suffice to earn him a lofty place in the history of 20th-century Chinese painting, indeed even in a broader history of later Chinese art. This is particularly true, in my opinion, of his painting from 1981 to the present, which at the time of this writing has scarcely been exhibited in America. It remains to be seen, of course, whether future generations will find his work all that outstanding or worthy of emulation—so far, C. C. Wang is a geographical isolate who has had no great impact on Chinese painters of the younger generation. Secondly, and of greater importance, I feel that his work merits an historian's attention because it is so deeply steeped in the history of Chinese painting, because it can only be fully appreciated and evaluated in that context and has so much to say about the potential fate of that great but threatened tradition.

It has been a great privilege to prepare this book, which was done with the full cooperation of the artist. An historian's work is conditioned by no more inescapable fact than the inability to communicate with his subject, to have his conclusions thereby validated or denied. It is therefore both a treat and a challenge to escape this condition in dealing with a living, articulate artist. C. C. Wang has been generous enough to provide unlimited time for interviews, which formed much of the basis of my research and writing. Because it is the subject and not his chronicler who is important, I hope that readers will find the rather high proportion of his own words to mine acceptable, indeed of lasting value. Since there are few available documentary sources on C. C. Wang outside of the artist's own possession, his wholehearted participation in this project has been of inestimable value. At the same time, as an historian, I remain well aware of the potential problems in relying so heavily on the subject as a major source, running afoul of the so-called intentional fallacy, and of the need to draw independent conclusions which might well differ from those that the subject would draw about himself. I am also particularly grateful to the artist for granting me unrestricted access to his paintings, the bulk of which remain in his own collection, making his generosity in this regard equally indispensable.

In writing this essay, I am indebted to several scholars who preceded me in evaluating C. C. Wang the artist and his work, beginning with Joan Stanley-Baker (Hsü Hsiao-hu), and continuing with Lois Katz, and Professor James Cahill of the University of California, Berkeley. I have frequently drawn on their insights.

Also of great help have been three of C. C. Wang's friends: Frank Cho (Cho Fu-lai), who became a student of Wang's in the early 1950s; Arnold Chang, a more recent student of Wang's who is now a vice president of Sotheby's New York auction house and director of their Chinese painting section; and Walter Hahn, a New York area artist. All three provided comments on drafts of the text and generously shared their valuable perspectives and insight. The artist's daughter, Mrs. Yien-koo Wang King, who in recent years has managed her father's professional activities, has been of enormous assistance in numerous practical ways, always responding cheerfully and promptly to my frequent calls for aid. Her daughter, Lynn King, provided most of the impressions of the painter's seals illustrated in this volume. In my many hours at work in the artist's apartment, Mrs. Wang has always been the perfect hostess.

The tireless efforts of Joseph Newland, editor of publications at the Henry Art Gallery, and Lynn Caddey Schweber, editorial assistant and indexer, have made this text immeasurably more readable. Douglas Wadden's design and production supervision have skillfully integrated text and illustrations and helped to convey the beauty of C. C. Wang's original works. To them, as well as to Don Ellegood and Naomi Pascal—director and editor-in-chief at the University of Washington Press, who gave this work enthusiastic support from its inception—I am most indebted. I would also like to express my gratitude to the many individuals and institutions who have allowed the reproduction of their paintings here and to those who have assisted in obtaining photographs. I would like to join Michael Komanecky in thanking the Henry Art Gallery staff for their diligent efforts in organizing and circulating the exhibition of C. C. Wang's painting.

To my family—Michelle, Emily, and David—who have endured lengthy absences during the research and writing of this book, I would like to reaffirm my interest and devotion. This book is dedicated to the memory of my parents.

It is more than a standard disclaimer to assert that this is but a general essay and hardly a thorough work of research. That kind of research, which would involve extensive travel and a more dispassionate approach and which would illustrate and examine a broader spectrum of the artist's work than appears in this book, is historically merited by the significance of C. C. Wang's painting and will surely be carried out, but remains a project for future years. It is much too soon to be definitive about an artist who, at the age of 80, is now at the height of creativity, at the peak of a long and varied career. But I hope that this essay, and particularly the artist's own words recorded here, will be of assistance to those who carry out that future task.

Jerome Silbergeld
Seattle
March 1987

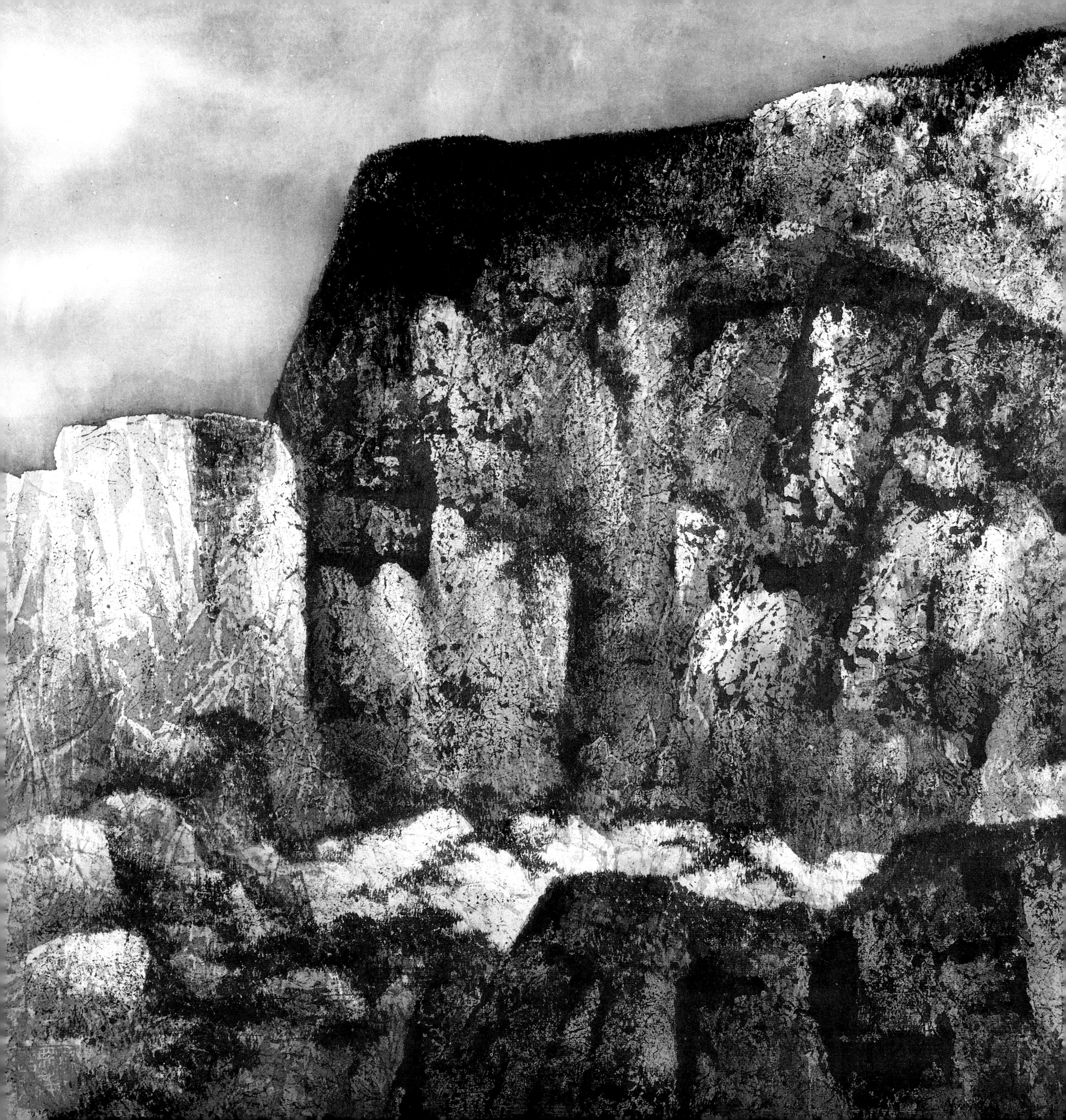

Detail of *Landscape No. 503*. Reproduced in full in
fig. 68, page 113.

Table of Contents

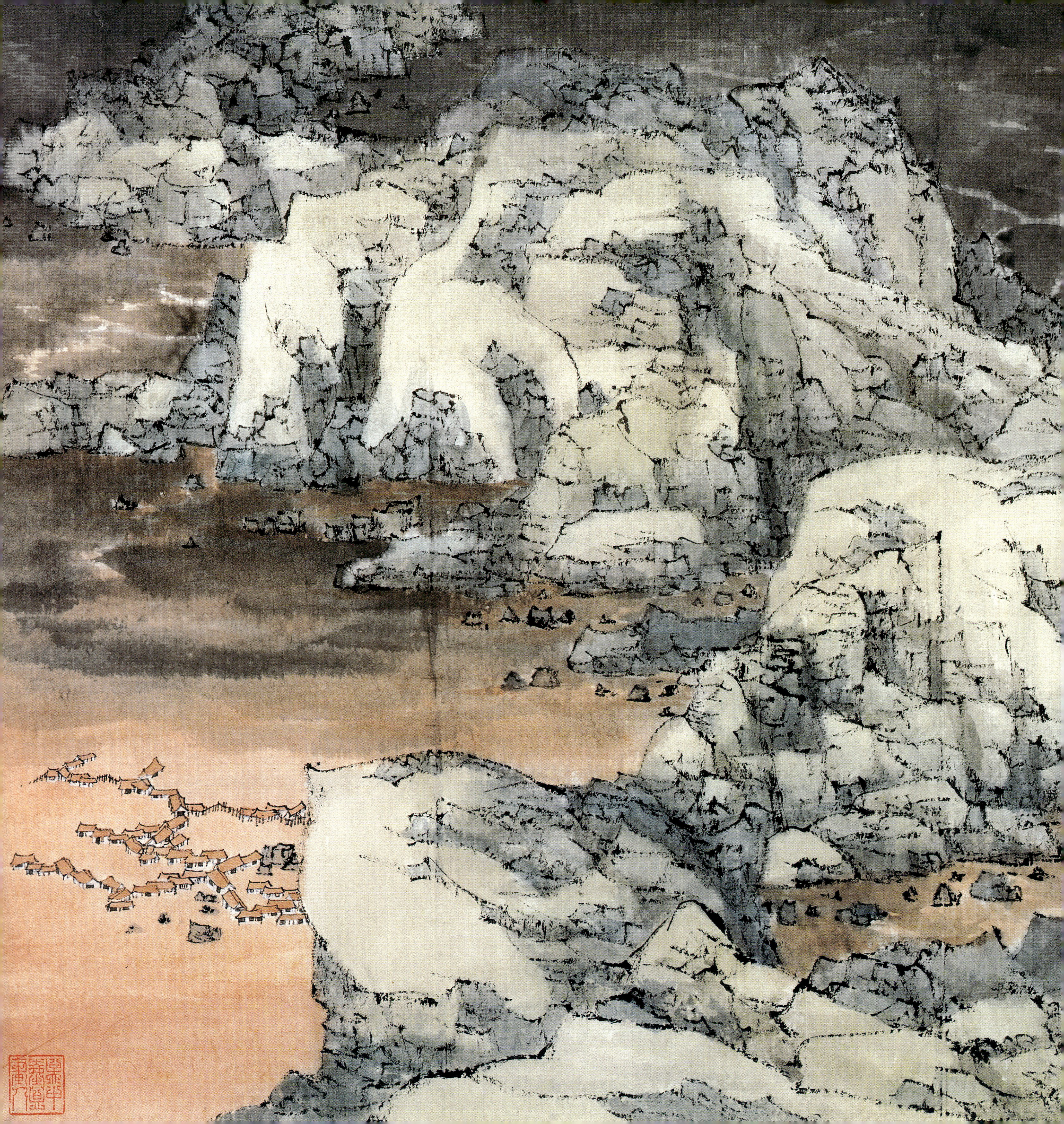

Inscription by C. C. Wang, 1987.

1. Tung Ch'i-ch'ang, *Hua-chih* (*Hua-lun ts'ung-k'an* edition) (Hong Kong: Chung-hua shu-chü, 1977), *shang*, p. 71.

2. Meredith Weatherby, ed., Hsü Hsiao-hu [Joan Stanley-Baker] et al., *Mountains of the Mind: The Landscape Painting of Wang Chi-ch'ien* (New York: Walker/Weatherhill, 1970); Lois Katz and C. C. Wang *The Landscapes of C. C. Wang: Mountains of the Mind* (New York: AMS Foundation, 1977).

Detail of *Landscape No. 450.* Reproduced in full in fig. 13, page 46.

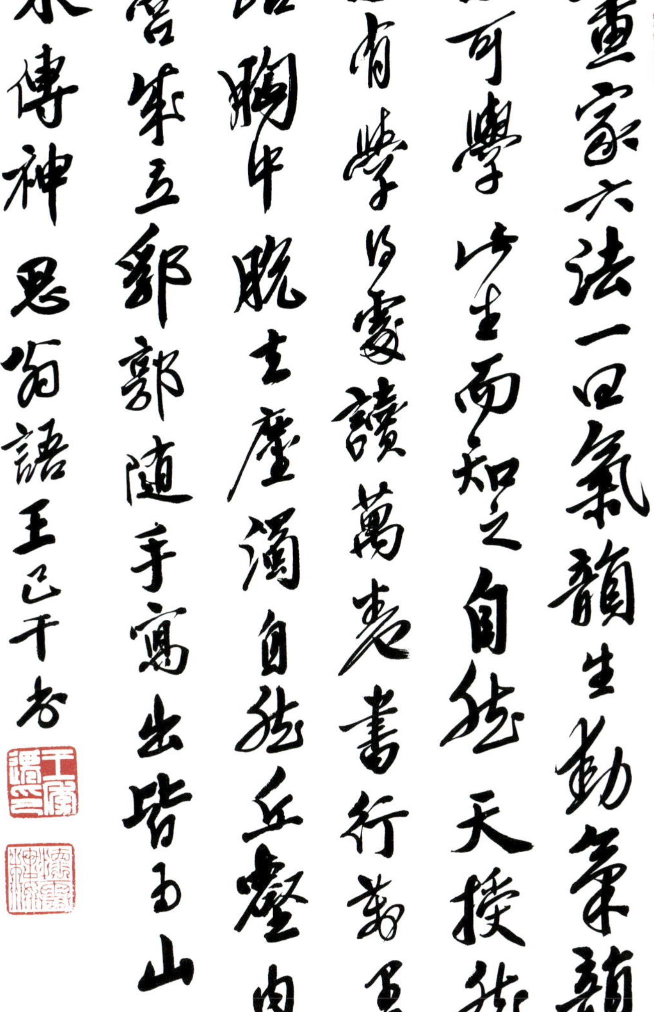

The ancient Chinese term "mind landscape" or "mountains of the mind" is one that C. C. Wang loves to apply to his own landscape paintings. Literally, "mountains and valleys in the breast" (*hsiung-chung ch'iu-ho*), this term is carved on one of his seals and impressed on some of his paintings, and it has already provided the title for two previous books about his art.[2] This ancient phrase refers to a state of mind that is completely natural, though difficult to obtain: a mind that is spontaneous and creative, as varied and inexhaustible in its generation of ideas and images as nature is in generating landscapes. Great Chinese artists—painters, poets, musicians: cultural exemplars of a society immersed in the reverence of nature—possessed in their minds the living spirit of the landscape itself and thus were able to convey this spirit in their art.

The best known discussion of the mind landscape occurs in the writing of Tung Ch'i-ch'ang (1555-1636), one of the artists most deeply admired by C. C. Wang. Tung's discussion is concerned with how the artist can best attain this state of mind. Tung's method of generating mountains within the mind— study and travel—is significant for its dualism, making it a comprehensive rather than a singular approach. He sought in theory, and somewhat attained in his art, a "Grand Synthesis" (*Ta-ch'eng*) of all the best ideas and images that appeared before him, not prescribing any single, narrow path leading toward some extreme but advocating a middle way with room enough to accomodate a large following of artists. To travel ten thousand miles means to acquire a personal knowledge of nature and in the end to merge with it, thus perfecting one's inner nature; it represents the artist's individual creativity. The study of ten thousand volumes refers to the historical element of art, art learned from art, to the artist as transmitter of traditions. According to Tung Ch'i-ch'ang, the great painter was a well rounded student of both past art and nature itself, a connoisseur as well as a painter, a preserver as well as a creator. True to his creed, Tung was the last great example in traditional China of the artist-collector and a well-traveled statesman as well.

Like Tung Ch'i-ch'ang's, the values, the life, and the art of C. C. Wang represent a "Grand Synthesis." Not only a painter of increasing renown, C. C. Wang's reputation as a traditionally-trained connoisseur of Chinese painting is matched by only one or two other living men, while his private collection of Chinese paintings is the equal or superior of any other in the world today (more will be said of this later). Bred and educated in China, he matured artistically in the West. Although growing up among the last generation of traditional mandarin families, he has forever sought out "the modern," the individualistic. As a connoisseur, he has perhaps had the opportunity to view more Chinese paintings than any man in history, and his travels have taken him farther than Tung Ch'i-ch'ang could have imagined. He has seen more than enough landscapes, both painted and real, for them to become well entrenched as mountains and valleys within his mind. His painted landscapes are mental images, rarely representing real places. They are a blend of both past and modern styles, of certain carefully selected stylistic traits and their associated cultural values. They merge aspects of earlier and later Chinese painting traditions (historically divided, roughly, around 1300 A. D.) and further combine these with aspects of Western art—particular aspects that often turn out to correspond quite closely to traditional Chinese taste and values. C. C. Wang combines an appreciation of disciplined composition with a love of accidental effects of brushwork; he achieves great skill but more deeply admires naïveté. His works have managed to become increasingly more modern and more traditional at the same time. As with Tung Ch'i-ch'ang, C. C. Wang's synthetic vision represents no mere eclectic assemblage, no measured recipe, but a true synthesis, a unique vision that surpasses the sum of its ingredients.

Tung Ch'i-ch'ang's description of "mind landscapes" was written in circumstances which, in significant ways, parallel the modern Chinese art historical environment of C. C. Wang. Both artists were born in periods of artistic tension and profound uncertainty about the future of their tradition. By the time Tung Ch'i-ch'ang reached artistic maturity, more than a half-century had passed since China last produced a great artist, if one includes Wen Cheng-ming; or if one discounts Wen, as Tung sometimes did, almost two centuries had elapsed since the great generation of the late Yüan dynasty, in the third quarter of the 14th century. Tung saw those around him either as individualists who lacked historical discipline or as historical sycophants lacking individual creativity. Combining the virtues of discipline and individualism was his goal, and his success at this helped usher in a generation or two that represented Chinese painting history's last triumphant moment. From that time on, roughly from the middle 18th century until the 20th, Chinese painting went into a long decline as meaningful creativity succumbed to suffocating traditionalism, even among those who saw themselves as followers of Tung Ch'i-ch'ang. In the 20th century, artists who still practice this ancient art have faced a most difficult task, not only of reviving this art after centuries of slumber but of making it relevant in a modern world which threatens to overrun altogether the last remnants of China's cultural traditions and render them obsolete.

Relevance, once defined in terms of the past, has in this century and particularly since 1949, come to be defined in terms of the new, summed up from time to time in phrases and movements like those of the New Society, the Great Leap Forward, and the Four Modernizations. The "new," to many Chinese artists, is largely now defined by reference to Western art. James Cahill has described this situation most lucidly:

Chinese painting today reflects the central problem of contemporary Chinese culture as a whole: how much of it is really viable in our world, adaptable and useful to present-day circumstances and sensibilities? Examples are plentiful to prove that holding on to the past for the sake of holding on is stultifying. Leading diametrically away from this wrong road is another, equally wrong if one is determined to preserve one's Chinese identity: letting go altogether, merging with the "international mainstream" (decidedly a muddied and disorienting current these days), relinquishing the sustenance of one's cultural heritage. How can artists remain Chinese without compromising their independence and originality, or their status as twentieth-century people? The question may sound somewhat artificial, but it troubles Chinese people today. Many of them, living in China, Hong Kong, Taiwan, the U.S., and elsewhere, have found personal solutions to this dilemma, solutions ranging in efficacy from barely workable to brilliant. Among these, Wang Chi-ch'ien's stands out as notably successful.[3]

The "notable success" of C. C. Wang's paintings lies, in part, in characteristics that make them visually satisfying or compelling, giving them artistic value apart from their place and time. But because of their place in history, because of their success in a period of widespread artistic frustration and experimentation, and because the timely solutions that underlie their artistic success represent fundamental solutions to the basic problems faced by this tradition, his paintings take on notable significance for other painters and for the modern history of Chinese art as a whole.

C. C. Wang is scarcely alone among contemporary Chinese painters in consciously facing the question of how to create relevant, successful art, of how once again to imbue landscape paintings with a "spirit-consonance" that seems alive and moves people. Traditional artists like Ch'i Pai-shih (1863-1957), Huang Pin-hung (1863/65-1955), Fu Pao-shih (1904-1965), and Chang Ta-ch'ien (1899-1983) also brought new life to the old tradition, yet even their work has not quite succeeded in leading 20th-century Chinese painting as a whole into the arena of modern world art. Throughout much of this century, from Kao Chien-fu (1878/79-1951), a Cantonese who studied Western painting in Japan shortly after the 1911 Revolution, to Hsü Pei-hung (1895/96-1953) and Liu Hai-su (b. 1895/96), who studied oil painting in Paris during the 1920s and 1930s, there have been various influential artists familiar with the Western traditions. Yet the shortcoming of many Western-trained painters has been the shallowness of their traditional skills. Major and minor painters alike continue to engage in Western studies and pursue a synthesis of Western and traditional means. Perhaps it is too soon to tell whether an infusion of international stylistic

3. James Cahill et al., *C. C. Wang: Landscape Paintings* (Hong Kong: Hsi An T'ang, 1987), p. 9.

4. Cf. Arnold Chang, *Painting in the People's Republic of China: The Politics of Style* (Boulder: Westview Press, 1980); Hugh Moss, *Some Recent Developments in 20th Century Chinese Painting: A Personal View* (Hong Kong: Umbrella, 1982).

5. Arnold Chang, "The Landscape Painting of Wang Jiqian [Chi-ch'ien]: A Modern Dialogue with the Ancients," *Orientations* 14, no. 1 (January, 1983), p. 39.

6. In Arnold Chang and Brad Davis, *The Mountain Retreat: Landscape in Modern Chinese Painting* (Aspen: The Aspen Art Museum, 1986), p. 72.

influence is truly needed to revitalize Chinese landscape painting. One strand running through much of the critical Western literature on Chinese painting since the 1950s is that the most effective and progressive Chinese landscape painters have been "expatriates" in Hong Kong and America and a few in refuge in Taiwan, places where international avant-garde culture has been relatively available. Correspondingly, less artistic success is seen in the People's Republic of China, where high quality Western art and taste was long inaccessible and still remains somewhat remote, where political dictates, the imposition of "popular" standards on artists, and the guaranteed income of painters in China's artists' associations have blunted artistic imagination and creativity.[4] This is a view which C. C. Wang shares:

There are many good painters in China. They're skillful, and they have the talent. They could be great, but they aren't. I don't think they can achieve greatness because they have such a limited environment. Too much is demanded by the public, whose standard is very low. Everybody wants to be popular. I haven't seen any mainland Chinese artist who still has the eremetic idea of the past, who doesn't care about popularity, who lives in the mountains and paints for himself. There are some, but they are just minor painters.

Arnold Chang, who feels that C. C. Wang is perhaps the most successful of all the overseas Chinese painters, asserts that this derives from the unique biographical fact of his having lived in the great art capitals of both China (Suchou and Shanghai) and America (New York, since 1949):

The attempts on the part of many recent Chinese artists at a synthesis of Chinese and Western art have often resulted in superficial and contrived combinations of Western subject-matter and Chinese technique or vice versa. Wang's best works, on the other hand, represent a genuine synthesis because the artist is himself a blend of Chinese and Western culture, having lived for most of the last three decades in the United States.[5]

Yet C. C. Wang is not simply the *most* Westernized of modern Chinese painters, being decidedly more traditional than a painter like the marvelously inventive Ch'en Ch'i-k'uan (b. 1921). If his paintings have anything to say about what it takes to revitalize Chinese landscape painting, it is not "the more modern, the more Western, the better." Rather, the particular vitality of C. C. Wang's works lies in their remarkable richness in both elements, traditional Chinese and modern Western, and in the means he has found to render compatible his traditional brushwork and love of landscape with a particularly subtle understanding of Western art and what it has to offer to Chinese painting today. Brad Davis has written that C. C. Wang "has exposed himself to the western artistic tradition in the largest measure, while still remaining a disciple of the most conservative of literati brushwork."[6]

It is beyond the scope of this book to accurately compare and contrast C. C. Wang's art with that of his peers. He may well lack the flair of Chang Ta-ch'ien, the versatility of Ch'en Ch'i-k'uan, or the modernity of Liu Kuo-sung (b. 1932). He is, in fact, more deeply conservative than any of these artists. He has chosen, like a traditional Chinese artist, to bring all of his insights gained and lessons learned to bear on a more singularly personal style, increasingly working within a self-defined and intentionally self-limiting range. Yet his achievements within that range, the chief subject of this essay, are undisputably of the highest order. And it may be precisely because of his greater traditionalism that what he, more than any of the others, has accomplished will contribute most directly to the extension of the Chinese painting tradition.

Whether the artistic achievements of C. C. Wang and others interested in the blending of Chinese with Western artistic values will usher in a major late 20th-century artistic revival, as Tung Ch'i-ch'ang did a 17th-century revival, remains to be seen. And whether this view of the role to be played by Western art and semi-Westernized artists is wholly accurate or not, it suggests that C. C. Wang's painting must be understood in terms of the specific alternatives that time and place have offered the artist as well as of the particular opportunities that he has sought out. This necessity for understanding his art historically, in turn, suggests the value in first providing a biographical sketch of the artist's life, from the days of the youth named Wang Chi-ch'üan, spent among the final generation of traditional Chinese scholars, to the days of C. C. Wang, the modern mandarin painting in uptown Manhattan.

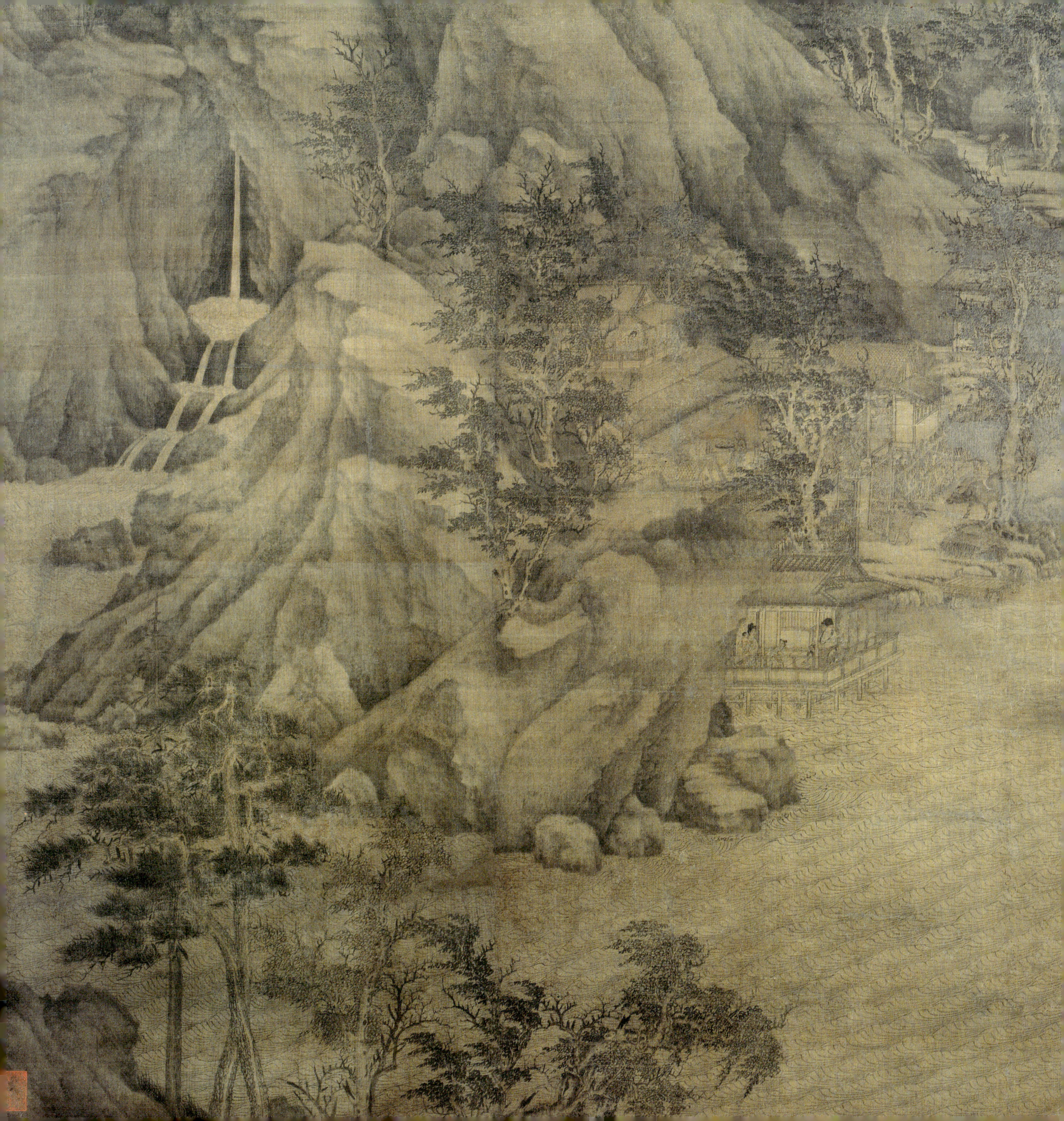

1

Detail of Tung Yüan, attributed to, *The Riverbank*. Late 10th century. Reproduced in full in fig. 9, page 40.

1. Throughout the text, all quotations by C. C. Wang not cited otherwise come from interviews recorded, transcribed, and edited by the author between June 1986 and March 1987.

2. Impressions, transliterations, and translations of these seals can be found in the appendix to this book.

3. Lois Katz and C. C. Wang, *The Landscapes of C. C. Wang: Mountains of the Mind* (New York: AMS Foundation, 1977), p. 3. (Page numbers for this unpaginated book have been provided for the introductory material; catalogue numbers are used for quotes regarding specific paintings.)

C. C. Wang was born into a family that traces its ancestry back to the Sung dynasty (960-1279), as only a distinguished scholar-class family could. The most famous of his ancestors, brother to his direct lineal ancestor fourteen generations ago, was Wang Ao (1450-1524), who became prime minister of China. Wang Ao was an outstanding calligrapher and a friend of Suchou's foremost painters, Shen Chou and Wen Cheng-ming, and of Wu K'uan, the distinguished scholar and calligrapher. Although not a painter himself, Wang Ao was a collector of some significance. His collection was never catalogued, and by the late Ming it was already dispersed. But the quality of the collection can be judged from Wang Ao's seals that survive on extant paintings. C. C. Wang calls it "good but not great" by Suchou's high standards.[1] Only a single painting has been handed down since that time, a landscape handscroll by Wang Ao's contemporary, T'ang Yin, entitled *Planting Bamboo in the Mountains*, plus a few letters by Wang Ao and one to him by Wu K'uan. In Wang Ao's time, the family home was located at Shih-ch'iao-ts'un, Stone Bridge Village, on the East Tung-t'ing peninsula that stretches into Lake T'ai near Suchou. Shih-ch'iao-ts'un is still regarded as the ancestral home, and in C. C. Wang's youth, the Wang family still had a garden there. The pride which C. C. Wang takes in this distinguished ancestor and the humble respect felt toward him are recorded in some of the seals stamped on his paintings: *Wen-ko i-sun* and *Wen-ko Kung hou-jen*, both meaning "Descendant of Wen-ko," or Wang Ao; *Shih-ts'ao-ts'un li jen-chia*, "From the family of Shih-ch'iao Village" *Chen-tse shih-chia*, "From Chen-tse's family of distinguished officials" (Chen-tse being another name for Lake T'ai).[2]

By the 17th century, the Wang family had moved its home from East Tung-t'ing to metropolitan Suchou, which for many centuries had been China's elite city of scholar-officials and the nation's cultural capital. Wealthy and beautiful, Suchou was the home of countless painters since the 12th century, and association with it was a source of mixed pride and humility for artists, as reflected in one of C. C. Wang's seals, carved *Wu-chung i hua-jen*, "One painter from Wu" (Wu being the classical name for the Suchou region), a humble recognition of his being just another painter in the midst of Suchou's many distinguished artists. But as a practical matter, so many of C. C. Wang's ancestors had maintained successful political careers at the imperial court that a family home was kept up in Peking and the family often dwelt away from Suchou for long periods of time.

C. C. Wang's father and grandfather helped sustain the mandarin tradition. His grandfather, Wang Jen-pao (1840-1917; style name Ku-ch'in), was an official at the Manchu court; his father, Wang I-sheng (1865-1915), was the mayor of a small northern city. By the time of C. C. Wang's birth, both his grandfather and father had retired from the failing Manchu administration and returned to Suchou, purchasing land and a house whose care were entrusted to C. C. Wang's father.

C. C. Wang was born on 14 February 1907 (by the Western calendar). He had two elder half-brothers and was the only son

A Biographical Sketch of C. C. Wang

of his father's second wife, who was surnamed Yeh. Although C. C. Wang's father and grandfather were no longer in government service, they retained their mandarin ideals and the boy was originally named Chi-ch'üan—the name *Chi* 季 being shared by all the males of his generation, the *ch'üan* 銓 meaning "selected." This *ch'üan* was derived from the expression, *ch'ing-ch'üan wan-hsüan* 青銓萬選 , roughly meaning "to get one good official from the youths, select from among ten thousand." His style name or *hao*, Hsüan-ch'ing 選青 , "Selected Youth," was also derived from this. "My father hoped for me to become a government official," C. C. Wang recalls, "but I didn't like that." By 1932, when seriously pursuing a career in art rather than in government service, he changed his name. "I didn't want to be a government official, so I changed it. I changed it to Wang Chi-ch'ien 季遷 , which has no meaning at all." Wang says he liked this character for *ch'ien* because it reminded him of the great historian Ssu-ma Ch'ien, who wrote his name with this character; he did not yet totally abandon the use of *ch'üan*. Still later, after he came to America, he twice changed the generational character used for *Chi* in Chi-ch'ien, each time substituting a simpler form "because it was good for inscriptions." In the early 1960s, he began writing 紀 , also reducing the *ch'ien* to 千 , meaning "one thousand" but chosen merely for simplicity's sake; then in 1970 he changed this *Chi* to 己 .

Before the age of fourteen, C. C. Wang was given a classical education, as his "old-fashioned" grandfather did not want his grandsons going to a Western style school. Instead, he was provided with a traditional home education, beginning at about the age of five under the tutelage of his father, who taught him writing. From the age of seven until about eleven, he studied with a private tutor. Painting was never a topic he discussed with his father, a subject that didn't interest him until he was fourteen and exposed to a Western style education. But his father did initiate him into the art of the brush through calligraphy, and beyond that to the basic Chinese ideals of artistic training. As he recounts,

I had studied calligraphy even before I started to paint. I first learned calligraphy from my father when I was about four or five years old. I had to trace in, in black ink, characters which were printed in red on sheets of paper. This was the way children always learned. Every day we had to write, and usually a certain specified amount. My parents would always give me a little reward if I wrote more than was required of me. I usually practiced one hour a day, but often two. Later, my tutor also encouraged the practice of calligraphy and it was one of my courses in high school. I eventually began to copy rubbings of the calligraphy of master calligraphers. In studying calligraphy, you begin by copying other people's writing and then gradually develop your own style.[3]

(Today, C. C. Wang still frequently copies old rubbings, routinely filling thick Manhattan telephone directories with pages of copied characters.)

C. C. Wang remembers little of his father. In 1915, when his son was only eight, Wang I-sheng suddenly died at the age of fifty-one. Wang Jen-pao, his grandfather, was left in charge of two younger generations. Two years later, in 1917, Wang Jen-pao also died. During the next eight years, with no clear cause, the entire remaining male population of the family except C. C. Wang himself passed away, so that within the decade from 1914 to 1924, his father, grandfather, two elder half-brothers and his younger nephew were all lost. Surviving were three widows and the teenaged C. C. Wang. The cause of these successive losses can be described by C. C. Wang today only as "a mystery." Each loss increased his responsibilities, until he was the sole male member of the family at the age of seventeen.

No sooner had his grandfather died than Wang began to seek his mother's permission to attend a Western style school, in place of his traditional home education, and he soon prevailed. At the age of fourteen, he graduated from primary school. Six years in Suchou's middle school followed. In 1924, the year that his young nephew died, C. C. Wang was seventeen, only halfway through middle school, and beginning to take over management of the family properties. The same year that he completed middle school, 1927, he entered Suchou University, established by the American Methodist Church. There he took a Western style general curriculum that included history, mathematics, physics, chemistry, and even athletics. Yet within a year, C. C. Wang, too, had fallen seriously ill. He was obliged to quit school and poor health kept him out for two years, but there was increasing pressure on him to pursue a practical career in public service, and in 1930 he finally returned to Suchou University. He enrolled in the pre-law program, which he completed in 1932. Around this time he adopted a literary name that reflected his loneliness at being left with no family but his mother: Shuang-wu, or Crow in the Frost, a traditional Chinese image, the crow being a symbol of filial piety and a wintry crow symbolizing orphanage (he used this name in the title of an album from 1932, his oldest surviving work, figs. 2, 25).

During these years in Suchou, C. C. Wang began to study painting with a number of teachers. The only significant painter in his ancestry was Wang Wu (1632-1690), known primarily for his flowers and birds although he also painted landscapes; his father's mother is also said to have painted well,

but C. C. Wang has never seen her works, so he can hardly be said to have had any particular familial disposition toward painting. His studies began at age fourteen with a middle school teacher, Fan Hao-lin (b. 1880, *hao* Shao-yin), who taught both traditional landscape and Western art techniques.

He was the first to teach me landscape painting techniques. I also studied flower and bird painting and bamboo painting. I was his best student so he talked to me about painting and recommended the Mustard Seed Garden Manual of Painting *to me for study. We had some paintings in our own collection inherited from our family, but I had never bothered to look at them until then. [Then] I started to practice from the* Mustard Seed Garden Manual *and to look at the paintings in our family collection.*[4]

He also studied flower painting with Ch'en Mo (dates unknown, *tzu* or literary name Chia-an).

C. C. Wang's most important teacher in Suchou was Ku Lin-shih (1865-1933). Ku, who was related to C. C. Wang's grandfather, owned what was regarded by some as China's second-finest private collection of ancient paintings, inherited from his grandfather, Ku Wen-pin (1811-1889). In Ku's Kuo-yün Lou, The Hall of Passing Clouds, paintings were said to be spread before the eyes of their owner and his friends like the endless flow of beautiful clouds. The opportunity to see paintings of great antiquity and high caliber was priceless in a society that as yet had virtually no public museums for this purpose. But like many collectors of his generation, the elderly Ku Lin-shih kept most of his finest works secret, lest they attract public attention and risk confiscation, as had frequently happened in imperial times and in the years of the warlords. Ku showed the young student mostly "late" (Ming and Ch'ing) paintings. C. C. Wang remembers being shown a Yüan period Ch'ien Hsüan painting, but his teacher made only about a third of his collection available and his pre-Ming works remained mostly hidden from view. As a student, C. C. Wang copied many of the landscapes painted by Ku Lin-shih himself. Later, in the 1930s and 1940s, C. C. Wang acquired many of Ku's landscapes for his collection, but he lost them all in departing from China.

Under Ku Lin-shih's tutelage, C. C. Wang's art quickly developed to the point where could begin to teach painting to others. His first position, held while he was but a young student, was at the Suchou Fine Arts School (Suchou Mei-shu Hsüeh-hsiao).

In 1928, C. C. Wang was married by arrangement to Cheng Yüan-su. Madame Cheng came from rural West Tung-t'ing (an island in Lake T'ai, not to be confused with the Wang family home at East Tung-t'ing). She was known to the family because her sister had already married one of Wang's relatives. Cheng Yüan-su was also a fine young painter, specializing in flower paintings that included bright colors and required considerable technical expertise. When they married, C. C. Wang was twenty-one and his bride was seventeen. Their eldest daughter, Yien-chen, was born a year later. Within the next decade there

1

Wu Hu-fan (1894-1968), "Spring," painted in the style of Huang Kung-wang, detail of *Handscroll in the Style of Four Yüan Masters.* 1933. Handscroll, ink and color on paper. 5 1/2 x 46 3/4 in (14.0 x 118.6 cm). C. C. Wang Family Collection.

2

Landscape After Mi Fu, from *Ink-play by Shuang-wu.* 1932. Album leaf, ink on paper. 6⅛ x 9⁹⁄₁₆ in (15.5 x 23 cm).
Collection of Mr. Chen-hua Lee.

Inscribed
"Mi Hai-yüeh worshipped clouds and mist. This is a copy from memory of part of a painting now in the collection of Mr. Wang of T'ai-ts'ang [Wang Shih-min or Wang Chien]. But I haven't captured one ten-thousandth of the original."

Artist's Seal
Wang Chi-ch'ien (upper left; not illustrated)

4. Ibid., pp. 1, 3.

5. Ibid., p. 3.

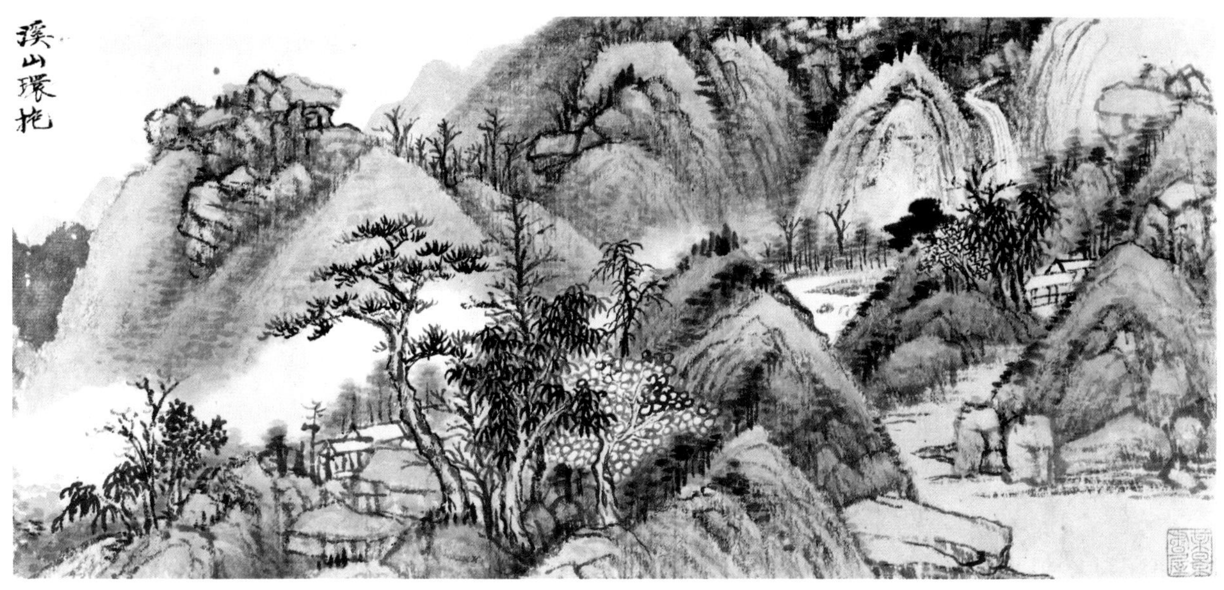

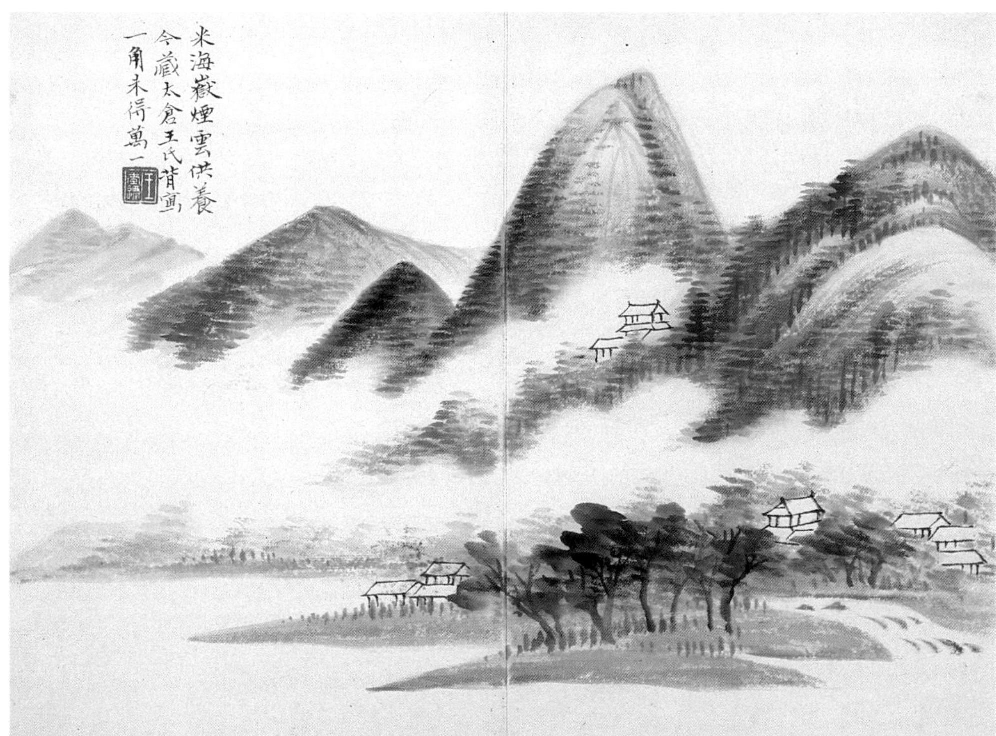

followed a son, Shou-k'un; a second daughter, Yien-ming; and twin daughters, Yien-yung and Yien-koo, the former of whom died of wartime malnutrition while still an infant. Two of these children shared their parents' artistic inclination: Yien-chen (now deceased) becoming a student of China's most famous 20th-century painter, Ch'i Pai-shih (1863-1957), and later, in America, practicing commercial design; Yien-koo becoming a fine ceramicist.

In 1932, at the age of twenty-five, C. C. Wang left Suchou for nearby Shanghai. His purpose was twofold. One was to continue his law studies. The arrival of each new child added to the practical pressure that he establish his career. The Suchou Law School was located in Shanghai, where it attracted a fine faculty. C. C. Wang completed its program in three years with an LL.B. His second purpose was to undertake painting studies with the artist Wu Hu-fan (1894-1968), although this had yet to be arranged by the time of his departure. Of this teacher-to-be, he recalls:

I had seen the work of one of the Shanghai painters in a mounter's shop in Suchou. His name was Wu Hu-fan. There were no good museums in China at that time and you couldn't see the work of a contemporary painter in a museum or gallery. But since all paintings had to be mounted or remounted, they could be seen in mounter's shops. Suchou was famous for its mounters. They would paste the paintings to be mounted on the walls of their shops and if you walked around every few days, you could always see new paintings. I learned a lot from this. Many of the paintings I saw were from famous collectors and were by early Chinese masters, but there were also paintings by contemporary artists. That's how I discovered Wu Hu-fan and I wanted very much to learn from him.[5]

Wu Hu-fan was also originally from Suchou. A grandson of the famous high official, archaeologist, calligrapher, and art collector Wu Ta-ch'eng (1835-1902), Wu Hu-fan had inherited his grandfather's famous collection of paintings, rubbings, and ancient bronzes. C. C. Wang had first met Wu Hu-fan in Suchou, introduced with the aid of a friend, the painter P'an Hou (1904-1943, literary name Po-shan), who was Wu's nephew. But Wu wanted no students at that time, and not until after C. C. Wang had moved to Shanghai did Wu agree to accept him. Thus, by moving to Shanghai, C. C. Wang satisfied two needs at one time. Attending Suchou Law School let him advance toward his ordained profession, and it also enabled him to study with Wu Hu-fan. Asked which of these two alternatives more strongly dictated his move from Suchou to Shanghai, C. C. Wang smilingly points to the law school's limited lecture hours, 5:00 to 8:00 p.m., which left him free most of the time to live a painter's life. Wu Hu-fan was to play a far greater role in C. C. Wang's life than the law.

C. C. Wang describes Wu as "a very emotional person. He was like an old-time scholar. He never had any degree, never even graduated from middle school." In training as a painter, says Wang, Wu "never copied any paintings. He just looked at them. He was a genius, really. Wu Hu-fan had the best brushwork after the K'ang-hsi period [1662-1722]." Placing him in historical context, C. C. Wang says,

I learned from different teachers, but I admired Wu Hu-fan the most. Better than anyone else, he knew how to handle the brush in Chinese landscapes like Ni Tsan [fig. 5] or the other Yüan masters. If he had lived earlier, he would have been one of the Yüan masters, I'm quite sure.

During his early years in Shanghai, C. C. Wang's family—his mother, wife, and children—remained in Suchou, and he commuted back and forth every weekend. In their absence, a personal bond developed between C. C. Wang and Wu Hu-fan, who was far closer in age to C. C. Wang (only thirteen years difference) than the elderly Ku Lin-shih, and he finally became as much a friend as a teacher.

Since Mr. Wu was very pleased with my work and thought I was worth teaching, he let me live in his home in Shanghai. I couldn't afford to live in a separate place because Shanghai was very expensive. In exchange for living with him, I helped him with some work at home.[6]

It is well known that Wu Hu-fan used opium before it was outlawed in 1949, and C. C. Wang discovered that "he painted only very late in the night, after he smoked opium. I slept at his place. I couldn't smoke—I tried it once and it made me dizzy. Otherwise I would have been an opium smoker too." Wu stayed up nights painting, then often slept until noon. His student stayed up with him, without the benefit of the drug which kept the master active and with law books waiting in the morning.

Over the years, Wu Hu-fan had more than twenty students, but C. C. Wang feels that only he and one other pupil grasped the meaning of Wu's brushwork. That fellow student was Hsü Pang-ta (b. 1911), who is now the senior connoisseurial consultant to the Palace Museum in Peking. Today, these fellow pupils of fifty years ago are regarded by many as the world's two foremost traditionally-trained connoisseurs of Chinese painting. But as fellow students, they did not receive the kind of training one expects from "teachers" in the West, nothing like the carefully supervised student activities that C. C. Wang became used to in Methodist-run Suchou University. He recalls:

My teachers never taught. They never taught me, never asked me to do anything. I learned by watching. I saw some of their paintings, borrowed some of their paintings, copied some of their paintings. I watched them painting, then tried to figure it out by myself. By the time I'd watched Wu Hu-fan paint a few times, I already knew what he was doing. Altogether, I watched him maybe a hundred times [over a period of nearly two decades]. There was no need for us to talk. He never

watched me paint. I didn't even want to show him how I painted. He never said anything good or bad when I did a painting and showed it to him. He just said, "Good." Or, "Very good." Or made no comment. He never said this tree is wrong, or that tree wasn't wrong. Never. I corrected myself gradually. He never told me what to copy. He never acted as a teacher, but was like a friend.

Perhaps most of what are referred to as teaching relationships in Chinese literati painting history resembled this: the student observed the teacher's practice, silently, assuming that his own youthful work was not worth the teacher's time and attention. Students shared more openly with each other, Wu's students meeting every month to discuss issues in painting, "something like what the scholar-painters of the past had done." The student was, largely, a copyist, relying on his teacher's own work and his teacher's collected works, while the teacher's comments on collected works were listened to intently. C. C. Wang never produced a painting in his teacher's presence, which typifies the role of the student. The teacher's role—at least toward a favored student—is demonstrated by a pair of handscrolls that Wu Hu-fan painted for C. C. Wang in 1933 and which are still in his collection, each scroll done in a succession of Yüan dynasty styles with a sequence of seasonal views—the first scroll done after Huang Kung-wang's clearing mists (a spring scene), Wu Chen's mountains in clouds (summer), Wang Meng's autumnal mountain ranges, and Ni Tsan's wintry mountains; the second painting done in the styles of Chao Meng-fu (spring), Kao K'o-kung (misty summer mountains), Ch'ien Hsüan (autumn hills and foliage), and Sheng Mou (a snowy winter scene).

In this traditional mode of education, the student's copying was challenged and limited by the quality of the teacher's collection. Although by the 1940s C. C. Wang had become a follower of the late Yüan masters, particularly Ni Tsan (fig. 5) and Huang Kung-wang of the 14th century, his student copywork was for a long time limited to post-Yüan models, especially the 17th-century painter Tung Ch'i-ch'ang (fig. 10) and his followers, the so-called Four Wangs: Wang Shih-min (see fig. 26), Wang Chien, Wang Yüan-ch'i (fig. 23), and Wang Hui. Ku Lin-shih had usually guarded the Yüan paintings in his collection from outside view, and Wu Hu-fan's collection offered no Yüan paintings during C. C. Wang's first years with him in Shanghai. When Wu Hu-fan finally began to collect Yüan paintings, Wang still resisted borrowing them: "The old important masters [Sung or Yüan] I wouldn't borrow from him. It was too risky. They were too expensive, too precious."

6. Ibid., p. 4.

Instead, he mostly borrowed the Four Wangs or Shen Chou and Wen Cheng-ming of the early 16th century. Later on, photographic reproductions of famous early paintings began to play a role in both his copywork and in his connoisseurial discussions with Wu Hu-fan, and Wang claims to have learned a great deal from such pictures.

The importance that access to private collections held for the serious artist in China can hardly be overestimated.

For me, as well as for scholar-painters of the past, friendships with other painters and collectors were extremely significant. Each new meeting might mean a new collection to see. In those days private collections were never publicly displayed. To see a particular painting you had to know the owner.[7]

Friendship with Wu Hu-fan provided C. C. Wang access to the painting collection that was often called China's greatest private collection, belonging to P'ang Yüan-chi (c. 1865-1949). P'ang came from a wealthy Chekiang family of salt merchants who had moved to Shanghai, and Wu Hu-fan was a relative of his. P'ang—also distantly related to C. C. Wang—was already in his late sixties when Wang first met him, but despite his age P'ang was "quite generous" with young people, whom he "loved to educate," inviting four to five guests every single afternoon to view paintings. He had a group of younger artists living at his home as if it were an academy, teaching them to copy paintings. C. C. Wang visited P'ang Yüan-chi almost every week for a long period of time. P'ang's collection was gathered up on a grand scale. He purchased only paintings on paper and no Sung paintings or types of painting that tended to be done on silk; Yüan paintings were his preference. P'ang published a catalogue of his collection, the *Hsü-chai ming-hua lu* or *Catalogue of Famous Paintings in The Studio of Vacuity,* known as "a model of clarity, consistency and thoroughness" among traditional Chinese painting catalogues.[8] The first edition in 1909 recorded 557 scrolls and albums, and in 1924 and 1925 supplements were published which included about 200 additional paintings. Wang first knew the collection in the mid-1930s and remembers it then as including more than 140 paintings by Wang Hui, about 120 by Wang Yüan-ch'i, and fifteen to twenty paintings by Wu Li.

He [P'ang] had more than one thousand scrolls and albums, and as I recall, the Freer Gallery in Washington, D. C., bought many paintings from him. Mr. P'ang would sometimes tell me what he had sold to them and that often what he thought was very good, they didn't like. Usually they preferred Sung paintings and not the Yüan paintings which he liked. Since I always had the chance to see this old man, he showed me a few paintings a day, twice a week.[9]

In addition to these private collections, one further resource existed for C. C. Wang to view a still broader selection of early Chinese paintings: opposite Wu Hu-fan's house (not coincidentally) was the largest antique shop in all China, Chi-pao Chai or The Hall of Gathered Treasures. Its manager, Sun Po-yüan, "always brought paintings in to show Mr. Wu, to get his opinion of them. This gave me the opportunity of seeing the top collections from both Suchou and Shanghai, and I had the chance of seeing many paintings come up for sale." C. C. Wang estimates that by the time he left Shanghai he had already had the opportunity to study between sixty and seventy percent of the paintings in private ownership there.

The most remarkable of all his opportunities for viewing ancient Chinese paintings came to C. C. Wang in 1935. In response to Japan's unrelenting military advances in north China, the best of the Palace Museum's art collection was sent south to Shanghai and Nanking for security. Using this opportunity to gain still greater safety for the art and to encourage Western support for the Chinese cause, the government arranged to send a vast exhibition of the Imperial Palace collection to Burlington House in London. C. C. Wang was appointed an advisor on painting to the London Exhibition Committee, and during three months in the winter of 1935-36 he examined the entire group of paintings, helping to authenticate and select the best works for exhibition. Together with a few fellow advisors, he patiently unrolled and rolled up every single scroll in the collection, working all day long, nearly every day, for three months. He enjoyed, at the age of twenty-eight, an experience that was more than rare: no private citizen in China had *ever* had this opportunity before. His viewing included much of what the emperors from Sung to Ming had liked the best and taken for their courts, beginning with dozens of paintings from the T'ang, Five Dynasties, Sung and Yüan. "I had the chance to look at the entire painting collection, one by one, at close range and leisurely."[10] Twice again he was able to enjoy this rare opportunity, first in the late 1950s and then in 1963.[11]

Shanghai offered numerous other opportunities for artistic contact. While his hometown of Suchou had served effectively as China's painting capital for hundreds of years, especially from the 14th through 16th centuries, the young commercial port of Shanghai, with its lack of traditional constraints and its direct cultural contact with the West, surged to the forefront of artistic centers attempting to reverse the decline of the Chinese painting tradition in the late 18th and 19th centuries. On the one hand, the city's new commercial wealth stimulated the rapid growth of art collections, eventually making it the best endowed community for viewing ancient paintings in private collections, to the advantage of Shanghai's more traditional artists. On the other hand, its bankers and brokers created a clientele for artistic styles more popular and less restrained than those preferred by more traditional patrons of the literati, while the relationship between artists and patrons became increasingly commercialized. Shanghai painting in the 1930s offered no unified leadership, no single direction, but rather

7. Ibid., p. 4.

8. Hin-cheung Lovell, *An Annotated Bibliography of Chinese Painting Catalogues and Related Texts* (Ann Arbor: Center for Chinese Studies, University of Michigan, 1973), p. 88.

9. Katz and Wang, *Landscapes,* p. 4.

10. Katz and Wang, *Landscapes,* p. 5.

11. Wang's second viewing was with Professor James Cahill, then curator of Chinese art at the Freer Gallery. His third viewing, undertaken with Cahill and Laurence Sickman of Kansas City's Nelson Gallery of Art-Atkins Museum, took place on the occasion of a photographic project that made high quality illustrations of the collection publicly available for the first time, through the Asian Art Photographic Distribution service at the University of Michigan. In 1963, C. C. Wang took a complete set of notes on his observations, which he had not done on previous viewing. As yet unpublished, these notes offer considerable insight into his connoisseurship and into the imperial collection itself.

a broad spectrum of individualistic initiatives ranging from followers of the stylized and somewhat sensational style of Jen Po-nien (1840-1895) and the popular, decorative flower-and-bird paintings of Chao Chih-ch'ien (1829-1884) and Wu Ch'ang-shih (1844-1927)—three "Shanghai school" painters who threw off more traditional influences in favor of the eccentric styles of Ming and early Ch'ing artists such as Hsü Wei, Ch'en Hung-shou, Tao-chi, and Chu Ta—to those who sought out Western influence either through Japanese channels or directly through European travel, such as the teacher Chou Hsiang, who founded the Sino-Western Painting Academy (Chung-hsi T'u-hua Hsüeh-hsiao), and Chou's pupil Liu Hai-su. Many of these figures, even including Jen Po-nien, Chao Chih-ch'ien, and Wu Ch'ang-shih, were not Shanghai natives but were attracted there by its new artistic possibilities, and throughout the early decades of the 20th century other major Chinese artistic figures like Hsü Pei-hung also came and went, greatly enriching Shanghai's artistic environment.[12] Wu Hu-fan—and C. C. Wang—represented the most conservative wing of the Shanghai artistic scene, closest to the old Suchou traditions and least affected by Shanghai's cosmopolitan modernism.

After the Japanese launched their general military offensive in north China in 1937, C. C. Wang moved for safety to the French concession and brought his family there from Suchou. The foreign concessions were thronged with artists, some of whom, in time, came to be major representatives of this era. Wu Hu-fan's home was nearby. Next door lived Huang Pin-hung, who had been head of Shanghai's Academy of Literature and Fine Arts (Wen-i Hsüeh-yüan) and also taught at Jinan University and the Hsin-hua Art Academy. Although regarded today as one of the outstanding 20th-century masters of traditional Chinese landscape, Huang's vigorous brush style was then considered too studiously individualistic to interest Wu Hu-fan and his students. Also living nearby was Liu Hai-su, who helped bring China its first view, through reproductions, of modern European artists such as Cézanne, Matisse, Gauguin, and Picasso. Liu was still in his mid-teens in 1912 when he founded the Shanghai Art Academy (Shanghai Mei-shu Yüan, later undergoing much splintering and various name changes including Shanghai School of Fine Arts, Shanghai Mei-shu Chuan-men Hsüeh-hsiao). Soon after, in 1917, with his use of draped female models and later, in 1924, with his exhibition of painted nudes, he outraged the authorities, earning for himself the name of "renegade artist."

Once, like Western *plein air* artists, he and his pupil Wang Chi-yüan went out to paint directly from nature, although after hours of walking in search of an excellent site they finally abandoned their effort.[13] The Western art which Liu showed to C. C. Wang aroused his curiosity but also much puzzlement, and even in the environment of westernized Shanghai nothing would come immediately from this exposure. Yet another neighbor was Hsieh Chih-liu (b. 1910), who now advises the Shanghai Museum and who is regarded as one of the few great traditionally-trained connoisseurs of Chinese painting, along with C. C. Wang and Hsü Pang-ta. But Wang and Hsieh seldom met, because Hsieh was associated with the painting group of Chang Ta-ch'ien, who in the West today is probably the best known Chinese landscape painter of this century. Also dwelling close by was the painter Chu Ch'i-chan (b. 1891/92), now at the Shanghai Chinese Painting Academy (Shanghai Chungkuo Hua-yüan).

C. C. Wang knew all of these painters. And yet the fragmentation of Shanghai painting into different groups, like China itself, seemed to offer irreconcilable alternatives, each group firmly adhered to by its immediate followers with little tendency for artists to "cross over." Liu Hai-su's group was interested in Western oils and watercolors. Chang Ta-ch'ien's group, from Wang's point of view, was "wild but actually not wild," meaning to him that even if they did their best to be wild according to Chinese standards, they were so tame by international measures that they came across as little more more than provincial. Wu Hu-fan's point of view was strictly "orthodox," interested in conservative Chinese painters like the so-called Four Masters of the late Yüan, Tung Ch'i-ch'ang, and the Four Wangs of the late Ming–early Ch'ing. P'ang Yüan-chi and Hsü Pang-ta, both living in Shanghai's English concession, shared this taste. So did another of Wang's friends, Chang Heng (or Chang Ts'ung-yü, 1915-1963), a well known calligrapher. Like P'ang Yüan-chi, Chang came from a family of wealthy salt merchants and used his wealth to develop a prominent collection of paintings, known as the Yün-hui Chai, The Studio of Hidden Glories. Other neighbors of C. C. Wang at that time followed Wu Ch'ang-shih, like Ch'i Pai-shih's group in Peking painting brushy versions of flowers and other small genre scenes with displays of virtuosity—"expressive" in intent yet often too conventionalized to allow much truly individualized expression. None of these groups except his own meant much to C. C. Wang: "We didn't talk. We didn't bother with each other. When Chang Ta-ch'ien had an exhibition of his own work, we usually didn't pay attention to it. We weren't very interested. We thought he wasn't like a major opera, but more like an operetta."

All of these groups were deeply influenced by art from other sources, whether the works of Ming and Ch'ing eccentrics, of Western painters, or more traditional Chinese artists. The early, traditional paintings that C. C. Wang was able to see were of such fine quality, particularly as compared with 19th-century and contemporary art, that they had a deep and lasting impact on his own art. They molded his sense of values. They

12.   See Mayching Kao, "China's Response to the West in Art: 1898-1937," Ph.D. diss., Stanford University, 1972; James Han-hsi Soong, "A Visual Experience in Nineteenth Century China: Jen Po-nien (1840-1895) and the Shanghai School of Painting," Ph. D. diss., Stanford University, 1978; and Chu-tsing Li, *Trends in Modern Chinese Painting (The C. A. Drenowatz Collection)* (Ascona: Artibus Asiae, 1979), pp. 31-34.

13.   Kao, "China's Response," p. 92.

monopolized his adulation. They were the sole basis of his study, which was founded on the belief that long years of selfless study precedes the emergence of a personal style. And when C. C. Wang first attempted to develop his own style, the weight of the past and the years of imitative training thwarted his efforts; the strong presence of past artists dominated his painting to a degree he did not fully recognize at the time:

During this time I really began to understand paintings, how to create them, and how to achieve a greater growth in my own paintings. I wasn't only copying now, I was painting in what I thought was my own style. I worked very hard, but I couldn't quite satisfy myself. I was, as I can see now with hindsight, too much influenced by tradition and it was not really a period in which I was expressing myself.[14]

In his years of copywork, C. C. Wang developed a formidable expertise at handling the brush, yet the imitative mentality that underlay this traditional practice delayed for a long period the emergence of a truly personal style. Before he left China, a typical painting by the artist might still be done as literal copywork: one such landscape done in the 1940s (fig. 4), splices together a composition from the top of one early painting and the bottom of another, both by Wang Meng of the 14th century, the originals of which were then both in the collection of his friend, Chang Ts'ung-yü.[15]

By the mid-1930s, C. C. Wang had already begun to sell his paintings—or at least some. While his clientele was among the most conservative in their tastes, his sales methods hardly complied to any traditional standards, since China's scholar-painters by tradition were amateurs or at least did their best to avoid a money-based relationship with their patrons.

Selling my paintings in Shanghai was not what you may think. I sold them through an agent—actually, a paper company which sold fans and paper, like a stationery store in this country. They charged ten to fifteen percent as a commission and took orders for my paintings from their customers. That's how I got work from different people.... The paper company gave me the measurements and type of painting requested, something like, "Please paint a painting with a flower on a scroll 3-feet by 2-feet."[16]

Profits from the sale of his own paintings were quickly used for his buying of others. "With the money I received," he says, "I started to buy paintings to study, and gradually built up a small collection of my own. I was still young—less than thirty—and, naturally, I couldn't afford to collect anything important. Mostly Ming and Ch'ing paintings."[17] It did not take long, however, for him to acquire Ming and Ch'ing paintings of real significance, including one of Tao-chi's finest albums (figs. 11, 19) and Kung Hsien's great masterpiece, *A Thousand Peaks and Myriad Ravines* (fig. 6), the latter lost to him only through the ruse of a Western collector in Shanghai who was undeterred by Wang's refusals to sell it, borrowed it from the unsuspecting Madame Wang in her husband's absence and then negotiated a price for the captured painting. Paintings by artists such as Tung Ch'i-ch'ang, Wang Yüan-ch'i (fig. 23), and eventually by earlier artists like Ni Tsan (fig. 5) became part of a rapidly expanding collection.

The earliest endeavors at collecting came about at the same time as C. C. Wang the artist won his independence from C. C. Wang the lawyer. After receiving his LL.B. from Suchou Law School in Shanghai in 1935, the artist says, "I had to earn a living, so I worked for a lawyer for two years and continued to paint for my own pleasure."[18] But in 1937, he decided to become completely free to study and practice his art:

It was only after I graduated from law school...that I realized I was interested in the theory of law but not the practice of it.... I found that even if I could make money practicing law, it was not something I could do for my entire life. I decided to quit law and concentrate on painting.[19]

Still needing to supplement the meager income from his paintings, he now began to sell stocks and real estate, which left him more independent than working in a law office. In one regard, he says, he did not simply put the law and its influence behind him: "Because I studied law, I have a logical mind. Otherwise my paintings would never be so clear. Everything logical that I do has a relationship to my study of law."

The first demonstration of C. C. Wang's "modern" sense of logic grew out of a friendship with Victoria Contag, wife of the German consul in Shanghai, when the two of them were serving as advisors to the London Exhibition Committee in 1935-36. Together, they decided to continue the viewing process begun with the Imperial Palace painting collection and to try to see as many of the major paintings in China as possible. They would determine which of these were authentic and photograph reliable artists' and collectors' seals on these works and then publish them in book form, thus helping to systematize the connoisseurial study of Chinese painting. Knowing that seals were forged as frequently as paintings were, Wang concluded that authentication had to be based on the paintings themselves in order to produce a reliable set of authentic seals. The authentication process, however, remained highly personal, drawing on C. C. Wang's diligent training, his impressive breadth of viewing experience, and his increasingly sharp instincts. So the book actually systematized the results of C. C. Wang's connoisseurial study, but not the process (something which, he now says, can only be learned by studying painting with him).

14. Katz and Wang, *Landscapes,* p. 4.

15. See Chapter 3 for a discussion of this painting and Wang Meng's originals.

16. Katz and Wang, *Landscapes,* p. 6.

17. Ibid., p. 4.

18. Ibid.

19. Ibid., pp. 4-5.

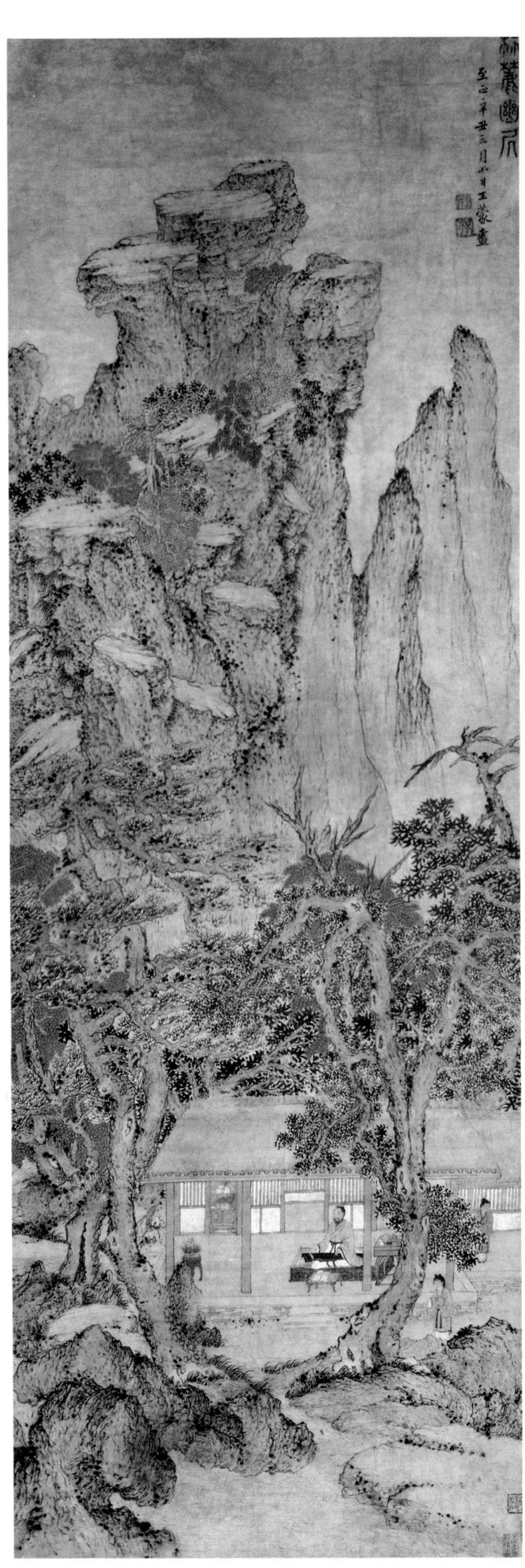

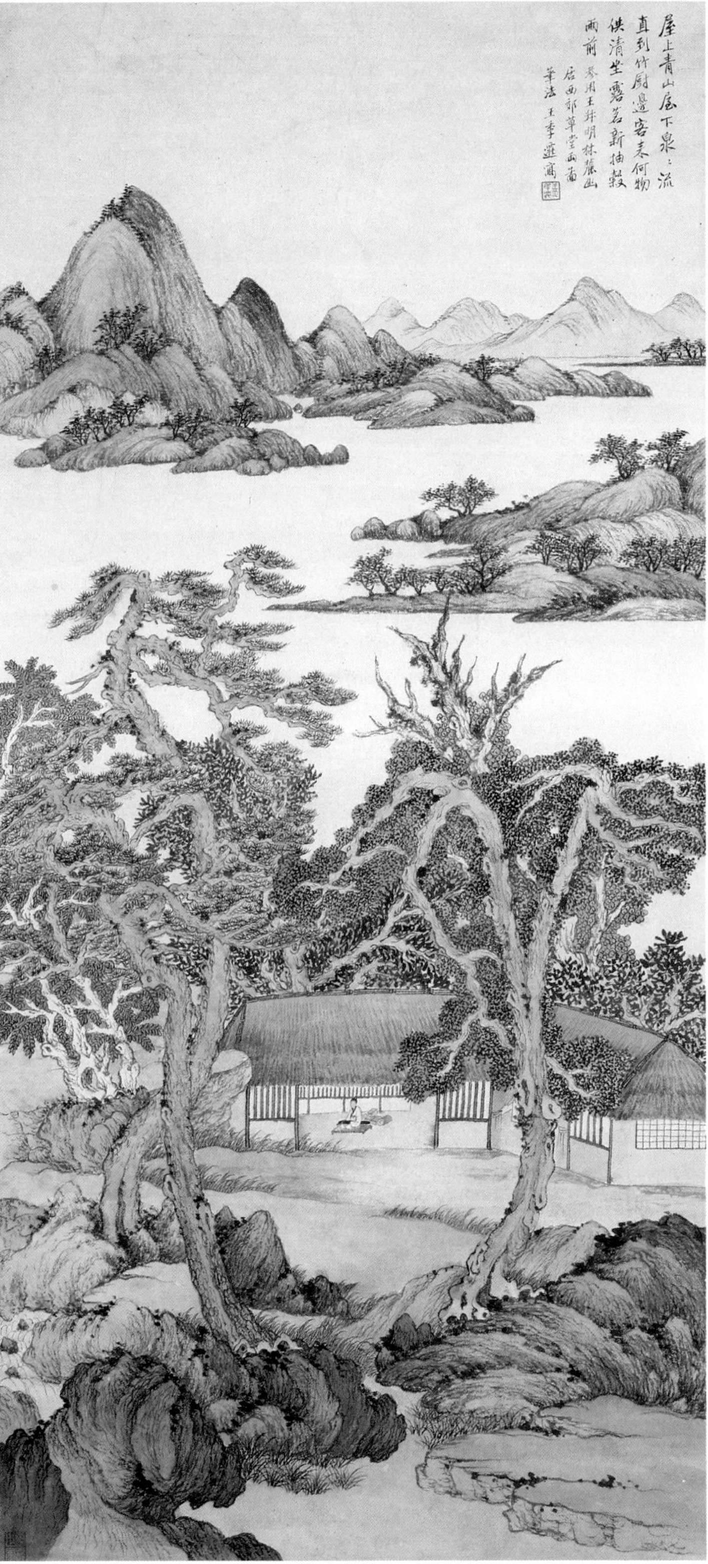

3

Wang Meng (1301-1385), A Quiet Life in a Wooded Glen. 1361. Hanging scroll, ink and colors on paper. 60 x 25³⁄₁₆ in (152.4 x 64.1 cm). Art Institute of Chicago, Kate S. Buckingham Fund.

4

Landscape After Wang Meng. 1940s. Hanging scroll, ink and color on paper. 42 x 19¾ in (106.7 x 50.2 cm). Collection of Arnold Chang.

Inscribed
" 'Above the studio, green mountains, below it a stream. / The stream flows right past the bamboo kitchen. / When guest comes, what will contribute to our pure meditation? / *Lu* tea, newly picked, should be set before the two of us.' I have combined here the brush-manner of two paintings by Wang Shu-ming [Wang Meng] *Quiet Life in a Wooded Glen* and *Thatched Hut in the Western Suburbs.* Written by Wang Chi-ch'ien."

Artist's Seals
Wang Chi-ch'ien yin ("Seal of Wang Chi-ch'ien"; not illustrated); *Chen-tse shih chia* (lower left)

Published
Chang, "Landscape," fig. 2

The project was begun in 1935-36 with photographs made of seals on paintings in the Palace Museum collection, then continued for three more years. Beginning in 1937, the two authors traveled to many parts of China despite the wartime difficulties, and they managed to view most of the public and private collections in the land. With Contag using a small fingerprint camera, Wang provided carefully disguised cues about which seals to photograph and which not, as owners and curators looked on unaware of the judgments on authenticity taking place. In 1940, in Shanghai, they published more than 9,000 halftone illustrations in a book that was meticulously organized, arranged by the names of painters and collectors of the Ming and Ch'ing periods (with a short additional section on the Sung and Yüan), providing names of the paintings and modern collections where these were found, and including various cross-indexes. With parallel texts in both German and Chinese, the book was titled *Maler- und Sammler-Stempel aus der Ming- und Ch'ing-Zeit, Ming Ch'ing hua-chia yin-chien*. In 1966, an English edition, *Seals of Chinese Painters and Collectors of the Ming and Ch'ing Periods*, was published in Hong Kong, supplemented by additional work begun in 1952 by Contag and Wang on paintings in European and American collections and by photos from the files of A. G. Wenley, the late director of the Freer Gallery of Art in Washington, D. C.[20] This book might well be said to have begun the modern study of authenticating Chinese painting. Even so, in his preface, Wang concludes that "seals are useful only as aids in the work of authentication. They must not be relied upon alone and the most important factors in judging a painting remain brushwork and calligraphy."[21] Indeed, more than providing a secure means to further authentication, these seals are his testimony of the authenticity of the works from which they are derived, judged primarily on factors other than seals themselves.

C. C. Wang had yet another reason for undertaking this enterprise:

If we hadn't done this book, it would have been very difficult to arrange to see the paintings in private collections around the country. You might be able to see one or two paintings but never the whole collection of a private collector. But since we were doing a book, they always showed us the whole collection…. After three years of this, we had seen about ninety percent of all Chinese paintings in public and private collections in the country.[22]

In his conquest of Chinese painting collections, C. C. Wang first advanced down private avenues in Suchou and Shanghai, which opened at least large portions of the collections of Ku Lin-shih, Wu Hu-fan, P'ang Yüan-chi, and others. Beginning in 1935, he gained access to the Imperial Palace collection and began to pursue other major collections scattered about the country. In addition, he energetically took advantage of the early public exposure of this private world through exhibitions and illustrated publications. By 1940, while still in his thirties and before seeing any Western collections, C. C. Wang had probably seen as much of China's best painting as any man in history.

At this same time, in his travels from one collection to another, C. C. Wang, the landscape painter, also came to view some of China's finest scenery. "I even managed to travel to many parts of China, to study its mountains and rivers—its landscapes. This, too, was in the tradition of scholar-painters of the past."[23] By the end of this period, he had come close to exhausting the collections and the landscapes in China. His interests, then his travels, would next lead him in the opposite direction, toward the West and the "modern" world.

In the early 1930s, while still a law student in Shanghai, Wang taught for two years at the Shanghai School of Fine Arts, whose director, Liu Hai-su, helped introduce Cézanne, Gauguin, Matisse, van Gogh, and Picasso to China and to C. C. Wang. This encounter aroused a curiosity in him, at first puzzling, later obsessive. In 1944-45, Wang studied sketching for a year with a French watercolor painter whom he knew only by his Chinese name, Chang Tsung-jen, an experience he found stimulating but not satisfying. Finally, after the war, in 1947, C. C. Wang made his first trip to America,

to find out whether what Liu Hai-su told me—that Matisse and Picasso are so great—was true. I thought there must be something important to be found outside of China. But I had only read books and had never seen original paintings.

Leaving his family behind in Suchou, he began his year abroad with several months of visiting public and private art collections in Japan. His interest there was primarily in Chinese paintings, which the Japanese had been collecting in earnest since the 15th century. Because of a distinctive Japanese taste for some aspects of Chinese culture which the Chinese had themselves long ago rejected, Japanese collectors were able to introduce him to the art of Ch'an (Zen) Buddhist painters such as Shih K'o and Liang K'ai of the 10th and 13th centuries, and he found himself better able to understand the spontaneous styles of 17th-century "individualists" such as Tao-chi (figs. 11, 19), Chu Ta (fig. 17), and Hung-jen. (Earlier in the decade, out of "prejudice," he had passed up the opportunity to purchase Hung-jen's foremost masterpiece, *The Coming of Autumn*, now in The Honolulu Academy of Arts.[24])

20.   Victoria Contag and Chi-ch'üan Wang, *Maler-und Sammler-Stempel aus der Ming- und Ch'ing-Zeit, Ming Ch'ing hua-chia yin-chien* (Shanghai: Commercial Press, 1940). Translated, with supplement added, as *Seals of Chinese Painters and Collectors of the Ming and Ch'ing Periods* (Hong Kong: Hong Kong University Press, 1966).

21.   Contag and Wang, *Seals*, p. xiv.

22.   Katz and Wang, *Landscapes*, p. 7.

23.   Ibid., p. 6.

24.   Illustrated in Laurence Sickman and Alexander Soper, *The Art and Architecture of China* (Baltimore: Penguin Books, 1971), pl. 241.

5

C. C. Wang was limited in Japan by his lack of spoken Japanese, but in America language was no great problem. He had studied English at Suchou University, and he had even taught English at a primary school while living in Shanghai. In the United States, he spent most of his time in New York, although he also managed to visit collections in Chicago and other cities, mostly in the east. With his connoisseurial reputation, he was able to obtain work at the Metropolitan Museum of Art, recommended to them by the well-known New York Oriental art dealer, Alice Boney. He served as consultant to curator Alan Priest, judging Chinese paintings in the museum's newly purchased A. W. Bahr Collection, acquired for the once-large sum of $300,000. C. C. Wang's judgment was that in this collection of about 170 paintings, only ten to fifteen works could be considered authentic. Despite the severity of this judgment, C. C. Wang thinks of himself as "on the bright side" as an authenticator, by Chinese standards; Hsü Pang-ta, he feels, sees "the darker side" and might have given a still harsher evaluation. C. C. Wang's judgment, which has certainly passed the test of time, helped instill in American museums' Orientalists a desire for stricter standards of evaluation, closer to those of China's most experienced connoisseurs. The Metropolitan Museum soon ceased all significant purchasing of Chinese painting for well over two decades, until 1973, when a new era began for them with the purchase of a group of paintings from C. C. Wang. At the same time as he advised the museum on the Bahr Collection, he put his own standards up for public display, assuring the authenticity of a group of paintings from Chang Ts'ung-yü's collection that was exhibited in the New York sales gallery of C. T. Loo and lending his name to the catalog.[25]

His year in America also provided political culture shock for C. C. Wang, at a time when politics, more than art, was about to restructure his entire life. By 1947, China was torn between the politics of privilege and the politics of leveling. C. C. Wang had grown up with privilege, but he had never been comfortable about it.

Always, when I was young, although not a Communist, I was the type of person who had the idea that everyone should be equal. When I was living with my family, I always thought of the servants and why should they live so poorly, why should they earn so little. I judged people only by good or bad, never judged them by money, never judged by class. There is no class among human beings.

Neither the Nationalists nor the Communists inspired him. In Shanghai, he had remained totally unaware of the left-wing woodblock print movement, begun there in 1929 by China's great satirical writer, Lu Hsün (1881-1936), who gave China its first and probably its finest socialist art. Despite having been a lawyer, or perhaps because of it, Wang took the attitude, "I don't trust the government, no matter who." America seemed a positive, "open-minded" alternative.

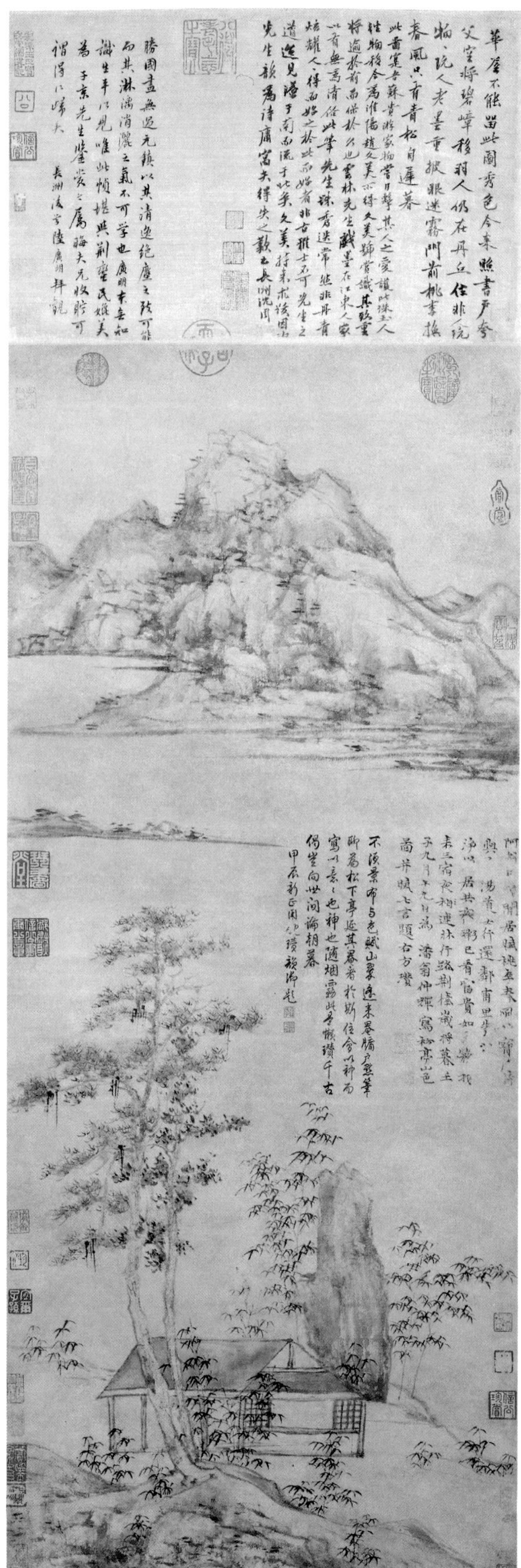

Ni Tsan (1301-1374), Pine Pavilion, Mountain Scenery. 1372. Hanging scroll, ink on paper. 40 x 17¼ in (101.6 x 43.8 cm). C. C. Wang Family Collection.

25. C. C. Wang, *Authenticated Works from the Collection of Chang Ts'ung-yü* (New York: C. T. Loo and Co., 1948).

The details of politics remained remote to C. C. Wang, who gave up law for art, but their larger implications for his life could not be ignored and he acted decisively. Although politics would never directly enter his art, his art was about to be shaped in a broader sense by the politics that led him from the East to life in the West and eventually to a meeting of East and West in his art. Although his artistic amalgamation of Orient and Occident was not fully realized until many years later, in the early 1960s, the historical process that carried it forward was now set in motion. In 1948, C. C. Wang returned to China for one last year.

This was a hectic and dangerous year. It was a period of devastating inflation and the artist relied heavily on his skills as a lawyer and broker, hurriedly exchanging family properties for stocks, for paintings in Hong Kong art shops, and for investments that could easily and legally be transported out of the country or else did not have to be. At the end of a year, C. C. Wang and his family managed to board one of the last planes out of Shanghai. His mother was unwilling to leave, so his son was left to care for her; this was expected to be a temporary arrangement, perhaps a year long, but Wang Shou-k'un was not permitted to leave China until 1980. Most of the artist's collection of paintings had to be left behind. He carried only two early paintings of any real significance, including one by Ni Tsan (fig. 5). His Tung Ch'i-ch'angs were abandoned. The one Wang Hui painting he brought with him, he later realized, was a forgery. He managed to bring only one pair of handscrolls by his teacher, Wu Hu-fan (fig. 1), and none by Ku Lin-shih. Virtually all of the landscapes he himself had painted were lost to him at that time. Some of his collected paintings were locked in a room in Suchou that, remarkably, remained sealed and untouched until the artist's first return in 1980. But the bulk of his collection was seized by public institutions, and many other works were destroyed without leaving any record.

The Wang family's exit was made through Hong Kong. Once in the United States, C. C. Wang was unable to leave the country until he received his citizenship, in 1956. These must have been his loneliest years. One of the seals he has impressed on his paintings reads *Hai-wai i-min*, roughly, "Overseas exile."

Once in New York, C. C. Wang and his family "lived poorly." He painted works for sale, but an initial American exhibition of his landscape paintings at the Warren E. Cox Galleries in 1950 was singularly unsuccessful, and he was soon obliged to turn to more decorative subject matter. His eldest daughter, Yien-chen, had studied with Ch'i Pai-shih, an artist of humble origins whose painting featured simple, popular, often humorous themes—flowers-and-birds, shrimps, and genre paintings in the Chinese sense of the term: quaint figures, mice nibbling away at scholars' books by candlelight, and the like—and brushwork so simple that its remarkable strength and poise might never be fully appreciated by the uninitiated viewer. The art dealer Alice Boney, fond of paintings by Ch'i Pai-shih and the Shanghai flower-and-bird painter Wang Yün (1887/91-1934/38), had requested C. C. Wang's assistance in acquiring original works by them for her to sell, making him aware of the marketability of this style in America.

Flowers and small genre subjects (figs. 7, 24, 30), with their heightened emphasis on calligraphic brush activity, also brought his work closer to the styles of Abstract Expressionism then dominant in New York—as other Chinese artists in America had already discovered—even as Wang remained frustrated throughout the 1950s at not knowing how to adjust his landscape style to accommodate contemporary American influence. Throughout most of his first decade in America, C. C. Wang had to curtail his painting of landscapes, producing "some, but not too many."

Although his scrolls of flowers done in the technically demanding manner of Ming and Ch'ing masters such as Hsü Wei and Chu Ta, his bamboos in a style reminiscent of that of the late Yüan artist Chao Yung, and his genre subjects in the manner of Ch'i Pai-shih (figs. 7 and 30) document a remarkably successful transition from landscape painting to other subjects and styles, these, too, could not effectively earn an adequate living. So Wang began hand-painting Chinese style wallpaper for the Gracie Company and other interior decoration firms, all of his work consisting of flowers and bamboo except for one large landscape commissioned by an art teacher. Flowers could be done fast and brought "easy" money. He even painted bamboo designs on ceramic lamps. The whereabouts of these works is unknown today, although some perhaps still exist. After about seven years of painting for home interiors, he was finally obliged to quit because of more recently arrived Hong Kong and Japanese painters willing to work for lower wages.

He also began to teach Chinese painting privately, mostly to
young Chinese girls who wanted to study flower painting, with
only a few more earnest students of landscape. It should be
observed that to serious landscape painters like C. C. Wang,
flowers were usually considered a trivial subject and the
technical skills they required were held to be superficial. "I can
paint flowers," he says, "but I have no patience to play with the
colors. Flowers are decorative, not too subtle, not deep enough
for me." Yet in order for him to earn a living, his art was often
pushed in directions far from his central concern with
landscapes, his mountains of the mind. This did, though,
provide his major source of income, however limited. Anxious
to broaden his opportunities for employment, C. C. Wang also
went to a trade school, learning how to produce photographic
prints, but he only completed one year of a two-year program.
He further supplemented his income by selling real estate, as
he had done in China after quitting the practice of law.

What income there was was often turned back into art. "Old
paintings," Sung and Yüan, were purchased mostly from Hong
Kong at a time when many works were making their way from
China's best private collections into the shops of Hong Kong
dealers. Although C. C. Wang might well have made purchases
at historically depressed prices, such purchases produced no
new income for him because he had no interest in reselling
them. Only occasionally, out of necessity, did he sell an older
painting to an American museum or collector. Such selling was
unpleasant for a collector who struggled to avoid the role of
dealer:

*I really was not too interested in selling paintings. Those who
understood them might not wish to buy them, while I felt too
uncomfortable when I tried to persuade those who didn't understand
them that they should buy them. I tried to be a businessman to persuade
them to buy, but really this was not my type of work. I'm not a dealer.
Besides, the paintings I love most, I don't want to sell. I buy because I
want to learn, not because I want to sell.*

Purchasing was rendered more risky by his inability to leave
the United States, which obliged him to select many paintings
by photograph:

*People said, "How can you dare to buy from photographs? It may be a
copy." I said, "I can see it." I made only one mistake.*

Moreover, the American government would no longer allow
the importation of items thought to have originated in China,
so importation from Hong Kong, while legal, was always
suspect.

The early 1950s was a peculiar period for the collector of
Chinese paintings. Chaos in China had flooded the Oriental
markets, yet most American museums had been frightened off
by the difficulties of authenticating early paintings. There were
plenty of opportunities for private collectors to acquire major
early works, and there were just as many opportunities for
making serious mistakes. Wang's purchasing brought him

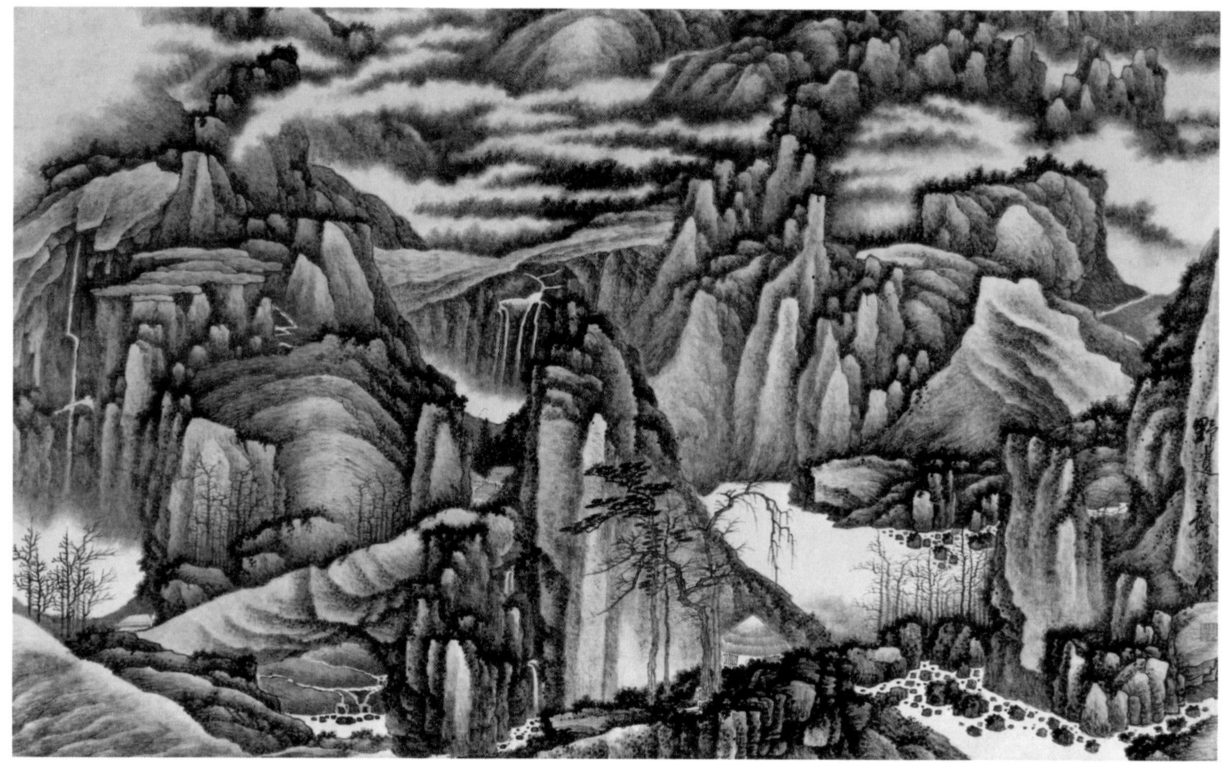

Kung Hsien (c. 1618-1689), A Thousand Peaks and Myriad Ravines. c. 1670. Hanging scroll, ink on paper. 24⁷⁄₁₆ x 39⅜ in (62 x 100 cm). Rietberg Museum, Zürich, Charles A. Drenowatz Collection. (Formerly in the C. C. Wang Family Collection.)

26.   This work is discussed and a detail of it is illustrated, together with a defense of its authenticity by C. C. Wang, in Richard Barnhart, *Along the Border of Heaven: Sung and Yuan Paintings from the C. C. Wang Family Collection* (New York: Metropolitan Museum of Art, 1983), pp. 52-53, 185-86, fig. 13. For a connoisseurial discussion by Hsü Pang-ta of this painting and the two other versions of it (in the Hsü Pei-hung Memorial Hall, Peking, and the Metropolitan Museum), see *Wen-wu*, February, 1956, p. 57.

directly into contact with the most outstanding group of forgeries ever produced. His expertise guided him to purchase, from originals in their midst, two of the finest paintings to enter his collection, but not without making his own mistake. The forgeries spoken of here were commissioned by a young man whom C. C. Wang remembers as a bright, wealthy Shanghai playboy who had begun to collect paintings during the war with the advice of C. C. Wang's friend, Chang Ts'ung-yü. He managed to acquire some of the early paintings in the collection of China's last emperor after P'u I was deposed as the puppet ruler of Manchukuo at the end of World War II, and by the end of the 1940s his collection included numerous important works. While conducting negotiations for the sale of some of his paintings to a major New York Oriental art dealer, he devised a scheme to have forgeries made of about twenty of them and to intersperse the forgeries with authentic paintings, hoping to minimize suspicion. The forgeries are described by Wang as being "really first-class good fakes" and unmatched in Chinese history as a large group of forgeries painted with the intent to deceive. The sale was concluded, forgeries mixed with authentic paintings, and the originals of the forged works were retained in Shanghai. In the wake of the Communist victory of 1949, the young man fled to Hong Kong, taking with him most of the originals he had retained. One day, a woman driving him around Hong Kong in his own car hit and killed a pedestrian. Fearing scandal or worse, he panicked and sold all these paintings in less than three days.

From among these works, C. C. Wang came to purchase two 14th-century masterpieces, Chao Meng-fu's *Twin Pines, Level Distance* and Chao Yüan's *Farewell by a Stream on a Clear Day.* (Both paintings are now in the Metropolitan Museum of Art; the forged version of the first of these is now in an American museum, while that of the latter is in a private Hong Kong collection.) He also bought a Sheng Mou painting from the same period. At the time of the purchase, Wang did not suspect the existence of forgeries. It came as a surprise when he saw duplicates of his recent acquisitions hanging at the New York gallery. Reexamining his works, he affirmed the authenticity of his Chao Meng-fu and Chao Yüan paintings, but he realized that his Sheng Mou was a copy. Moreover, he had recently sold the Sheng Mou to the Smithsonian Institution's Freer Gallery of Art. C. C. Wang remembers offering to buy back the painting but being told by the gallery director, John Pope, that the Freer assumed responsibility for faulty purchases; Wang was able only to return part of the purchase price, reducing it to the fair price of a study piece. All this was not without injury to his ego as a connoisseur.

Subsequently, Wang bought as an inexpensive study piece another work from the group which by then he knew to be a copy, made from the great painting *Quails and Sparrows in an Autumn Scene* by Wang Yüan, dated 1347; the original was in the collection of Chang Ts'ung-yü before becoming available for forging and had already been authenticated by C. C. Wang for the exhibition at C. T. Loo's gallery in 1948 (it is now in the Cleveland Museum of Art).

This case demonstrates well that the conditions for collecting Chinese painting in the 1950s were not so simple as to favor anyone with money and an interest in purchasing art. Building a great collection was a challenging and often controversial exercise that required critical acumen, conviction, perseverance, and a willingness to learn from error.

Trading paintings often served as a substitute for purchasing, a practice common among the literati in China. C. C. Wang's favorite painting among those now in his collection was acquired in this fashion. A long handscroll of eighty-seven Taoist immortals in procession before the King of Heaven, this painting is believed by him to be an authentic work of the mid-11th century master Wu Tsung-yüan, and it undoubtedly is one of the most powerful of all early Chinese figural compositions.[26] Although one of the few figure paintings that C. C. Wang has collected, it nevertheless provides one of the names used for his studio, Pao-Wu T'ang, The Hall Where Wu is Preserved. Formerly in the collection of Yamamoto Teijirō, the Wu Tsung-yüan painting made its way from Japan to an American lawyer's collection after World War II. This lawyer's son later gave an American museum the opportunity to acquire it, but with another version of this scroll already in its collection (judged by C. C. Wang to be a poor imitation and generally recognized as such today), this offer was rejected. An experienced private collector, Walter Hochstadter, then purchased the scroll, and from him Wang was able to acquire it by trade, giving six paintings for two.

C. C. Wang gave up three Yüan paintings—*Dream of the Butterfly* by Liu Kuan-tao, Fang Ts'ung-i's *Cloudy Mountains*, and Wang Yüan's *Bamboo and Blossoming Gardenia Growing by a Rock* of 1347 (the last of these now in the Museum für Ostasiatische Kunst, Berlin)—in addition to three Ming paintings. In return, he acquired from Hochstadter the Wu Tsung-yüan masterpiece and a Ni Tsan landscape (*Woods and Valleys of Mount Yü,* dated 1372, now in the Metropolitan Museum). Their former owner, not liking the structure of some tree roots depicted in the Ni Tsan painting, had apparently had them altered to seem more natural; Wang, by his own hand and with the aid of an old photograph, subsequently restored them to their original form. Within a year, in 1956, Wang was sued by Hochstadter to have the Wu Tsung-yüan painting returned, ostensibly on the questionable authenticity of the Liu Kuan-tao painting. But Wang prevailed in court after a two-year battle, fought in the district and appellate courts of New York. The trial was marked by scholarly discussion and expert witness that observers must have found highly esoteric and hard to disentangle. The final verdict, by Manhattan State Supreme

Court Justice Louis Capazzoli, ruled essentially that given honest intentions, Chinese connoisseurial judgments are so subjective as to be unenforceable in a court of law: *caveat emptor.* Unsuccessful in court, Hochstadter sold off the disputed Liu Kuan-tao, and Wang subsequently reacquired it for his collection (it is now in the Metropolitan Museum of Art).

While the process of collecting might not always be so dramatic, detailing the growth of the C. C. Wang family collection—which includes not only paintings but ancient ceremonial bronzes, ceramic tomb figurines, miniature stone mountains, and other Chinese art forms—both requires and deserves a separate, lengthy essay. In building up his collection, C. C. Wang was sometimes able to obtain paintings that he had known or even owned in China. He was able to reacquire the T'ang Yin handscroll *Planting Bamboo in the Mountains,* which had been in his family since the time of Wang Ao but which was lost to him in his departure from China. Another example is the famous Tao-chi *Album for Taoist Yü* (figs. 11, 19), which he had purchased in Shanghai and to which both he and his fellow student Hsü Pang-ta added inscriptions; as a favor, he had exchanged it for lesser works with Victoria Contag, his friend and coauthor, shortly after the end of World War II, then reacquired it much later when her collection was dispersed. A third such work is his Chu Ta landscape scroll (fig. 17), which he had recommended that Contag purchase from a Shanghai dealer and then reacquired from her at the same time as the Tao-chi album. Still another is Tung Ch'i-ch'ang's *Painting Wang Wei's Poetic Feeling* (fig. 10), which he knew in Shanghai when it was in the collection of Sun Fang-jui, a friend of Wu Hu-fan, and which he obtained in the 1960s from his painter-friend Chang Ta-ch'ien.

Compared to his years in Shanghai, C. C. Wang's activities as a painter in the 1950s took place in relative solitude. But in addition to his time spent painting and teaching Chinese style art, he began to explore the realm of Western style painting. He joined the Art Students League in 1949 almost immediately upon his arrival, selecting it primarily because of the flexibility it allowed him in scheduling. He particularly appreciated its evening classes and the availability of studio space at practically any time. He never studied with any teacher for long, usually attending regular classes for only a month or two at a time and preferring to paint after hours when the teachers were gone and the studios were left to students.

In a group like the Art Students League, I could paint and nobody bothered me. I painted with all these young students—which is what I wanted, because to paint always with old teachers is no use. The students gave me lots of energy.

Nevertheless, over the years he took courses in a broad range of subjects, including numerous classes in life drawing and anatomy, painting in watercolor, oil, and casein, and fashion illustration. His instructors included, among others, George Grosz, Robert Beverly Hale, Julian Levi, Stephen Greene, and Harry Sternberg, all of whom taught life drawing and painting;

Robert Ward Johnson, who taught the innovative Nicolaides method of spontaneous drawing; Marshall Glasier, a student of Grosz who emphasized large brush drawings; and Dagmar Freuchen, an illustrator for *Vogue Magazine* who taught fashion drawing. Although by the 1950s, New York's place as the center of modern developments in Western art was unquestionable, the education offered at the Art Students League was essentially academic in nature and hardly avant-garde. The only truly avant-garde painter with whom C. C. Wang ever studied was Stephen Greene. His own interest in Western art was focused on painters of an earlier era, particularly the Post-Impressionists and early Cubists, and his paintings from that time may be typified by his still-life study in the manner of Georges Braque, done in dark, somber tones of blue-green and red-yellow casein (fig. 31). Except in a general way, he remained unaware of his fellow students and of such soon-to-be-famous contributors to New York's artistic scene as Robert Rauschenberg and James Rosenquist—"I knew what I liked," he says, "but I never remembered names."

As a deeply conservative Chinese artist, in the 1950s C. C. Wang did not seek to become a Western style painter and tried only to learn Western art "for reference, to find out what Chinese painting can do." By "modern Western art" he did not primarily mean contemporary, preferring turn-of-the century artists to those of mid-century. He was surrounded by gallery exhibitions and magazines that displayed the Abstract Expressionism of Jackson Pollock, Franz Kline, Robert Motherwell, and Willem de Kooning; yet while their artistic movement would ultimately have an important impact upon him, even today he admits to only partially having understood or appreciated them:

They didn't have too much for me to see, like singing a simple song with only a few words. They were good in many ways, they were modern but not artistically rich, and not worthwhile for me to look at all the time because it offered nothing for me to follow. My taste in modern art is old-fashioned. The early de Kooning was quite wonderful. I saw some early de Kooning, some figure painting, which was great, really great. But he threw it away and became purely abstract, and once he was abstract I could not see anything in it. What he was thinking, only he could know. Although there must be some reason why he went so far with it, I cannot understand it. Even Pollock and Motherwell—although some Motherwell is very beautiful—besides their historical importance, I don't see what they achieved in an artistic sense. I don't understand what these painters are doing now.

Vase and Brushes. 1966. Hanging scroll, ink on paper.
34 x 17¾ in (86.4 x 45.1 cm).
Collection of Mr. and Mrs. Frank Cho.

Inscribed
"Sketched by Chi-ch'ien at the north window of the
Bamboo Studio."

Seals
Chi-ch'ien lü Mei chih tso (right, above); *Hsing wan-li lu*
(right, below); *Ch'i neng chin ju jen i* ("How can I work
completely according to other people's conceptions?";
left, not illustrated)

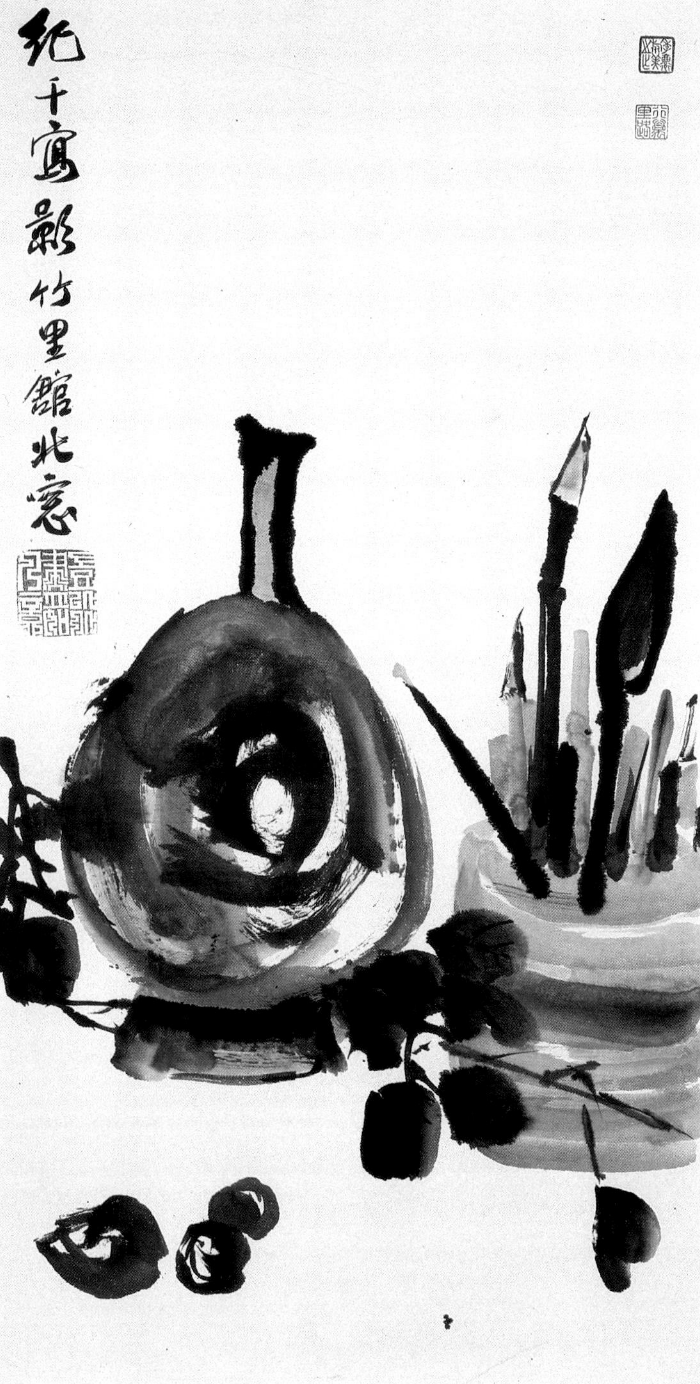

The only significant artist he actually spoke with was Mark Tobey, an artist deeply inspired by Oriental calligraphy whom he met at the Mi Chou Gallery's Chang Ta-ch'ien exhibition in 1957 but of whom C. C. Wang says, "I can't see why he is great. I never think that these people were as great as the Impressionists."

He realized—and friends reinforced his conclusion—that although his own Western style paintings were not bad by student standards, they were scarcely up-to-date in style and held little promise of future success. "This Western kind of painting I did with no confidence, but I could do it and Wang Yüan-ch'i at the same time." Throughout the 1950s, his Chinese landscape paintings remained conservative even by Chinese standards, virtually unaffected by his American experience except for an occasional flirtation with Western color schemes (as in fig. 32, from a slightly later date). "I had no idea I could really establish something of my own, and I hesitated for many years." Ironically, it was in his more decorative paintings of flowers and genre subjects (figs. 7, 24, 30)—all but abandoned after his landscape painting began to flourish in the mid-1960s —with their strong brush gestures and simple design qualities, that he came closest to his New York contemporaries; but this was less a matter of his consciously seeking to bring their qualities into his art than of his grudgingly trying to meet a market demand in which contemporary New York taste obliged him to work in the Chinese mode that happened to be most consonant with theirs.

C. C. Wang's circle of close artistic and personal contacts remained almost exclusively Chinese. In 1954, one of his more serious students of painting and connoisseurship, Cho Fu-lai or Frank Cho, a graduate of Yenching University (in Peking and Ch'eng-tu) and of Harvard University's Graduate School of Business Administration, approached Wang about the possibility of opening a Chinese art gallery. "In the early nineteen fifties," Cho recounts,

the morale of the Chinese in America was extremely low. Some of my contemporaries had lost contact with their families in China for months or even years due to the turmoil of the Civil War years. Tragic stories of broken homes were frequently heard.... While it was hard for any young artist to find a place to show his or her work, it was even harder for a Chinese artist. Very few Americans had ever been exposed to Chinese art. There being little interest or demand, no gallery wanted to exhibit works by Chinese artists. Because I had a MBA degree and therefore, thus the reasoning went, should have some idea about business, I was often thought to be the one among my friends to try to form a gallery to exhibit works by Chinese artists.[27]

Among those offering encouragement to Cho Fu-lai was Professor William Hung of Harvard. C. C. Wang responded to Cho's request by offering the rear ground floor of his own home on West 81st Street, which had a separate entrance, for a nominal rent. Cho recalls the simplicity of the gallery:

With some two-by-fours and wall boards, I built a wall at one corner of the main room to set aside—a small space barely enough for a bed. On the other side some additional wall space was gained for picture hanging. The next weekend I painted all the walls a neutral gray. The charcoal black linoleum tiles on the floor were quite appropriate for a gallery.... After the completion of the electrical work and decoration, we looked around with pride, and we were quite pleased. The interior compared favorably with the first rate galleries in town, except that our space was smaller.[28]

This gallery, which also served as Cho's cramped sleeping quarters, became America's first gallery of Chinese art and soon began to play a role that belied its unpretentious character. It was given the name Mi Chou, meaning "Mi's boat," after the pleasure boat which the Sung artist Mi Fu stocked with China's finest private collection of painting and calligraphy. The inaugural exhibition, opening on 29 April 1954, was a group show of modern style artists, followed in June by a group exhibition of traditional style painters that included Chang Ta-ch'ien and Fu Pao-shih. The first individual exhibition, held that November, featured Ch'i Pai-shih. By late 1956, it was clear that to survive the Mi Chou Gallery would have to be moved to a more desirable location than C. C. Wang's Upper West Side apartment, and a spot was selected on West 56th Street, three blocks from the Museum of Modern Art.

The Mi Chou Gallery continued to operate until 1971, and among the early exhibitions held at its new location were major ones by Chang Ta-ch'ien in September 1957, when Chang's style was still relatively traditional; by Ch'en Ch'i-k'uan, an American-trained architect who taught at M.I.T. and practiced with I.M. Pei, and whose remarkably imaginative and often witty compositions reflect both his skill as a draftsman and an exuberantly calligraphic flair, held in November 1957; and a commemorative show for the recently deceased Ch'i Pai-shih in January 1958.[29] In February and March 1959, an individual exhibition of C. C. Wang's paintings was held—including flowers (fig. 24) and landscapes—Wang's first major exhibition since 1950. The exhibition, he says, "was not a success at all. I saw there was nothing there. I had no confidence in myself." He says that his painting style remained stuck within the "circle of old-fashioned composition. Still, I didn't know what I could do at all with my painting." James Cahill, who wrote the exhibition notes, coupled his praise of C. C. Wang as "definitely the real thing" with a frank estimation of the artist's predicament: "I am afraid that the subtle stylistic allusions in his paintings, and others of their most admirable qualities, may escape some casual Occidental viewers." C. C. Wang was not alone in his frustration; at the time of Chang Ta-ch'ien's 1957 exhibition, Wang says, "He sold his works at very low prices and few people bought them. We began to discuss this, and Chang Ta-ch'ien wondered what we should do next. He had no confidence in himself, and I didn't know what to do either."

It was in the mid-1960s that C. C. Wang's landscape painting style first began to deeply reveal the effects of his artistic sojourn in the West (figs. 33-37). When this happened, it seemed to occur suddenly, and almost everything appeared to change at once, from execution to composition. Although the change was coupled with his return to painting primarily landscapes, only the beloved landscape subject remained the same. The past styles in which his landscape paintings had been grounded also remained, but now they were treated differently and forced to grow in new and challenging ways.

27. Frank Cho, "Reminiscences of Mi Chou, The First Chinese Gallery in America." *Chinese American Forum* 1 (May, 1985), p. 4.

28. Ibid., p. 4.

29. Ibid., p. 8. Cho's article includes a chronology of exhibitions not prepared by him and not free of a few errors (those cited here have been confirmed).

Brushwork had always been the most revered element of his art, exercised with scholarly aloofness and restraint in the conservative tradition of Wu Hu-fan, and however old-fashioned, brushwork was always his greatest strength. Suddenly, however, C. C. Wang changed his style and complemented his brushwork with impressed textures done without the use of the brush (figs. 34, 35, 39-42). Applied for the most part by crumpled paper, these impressed ink textures were marked by "accidental" effects which balanced the formal control of his brushwork. These effects, which James Cahill has accurately labeled "semi-random configurations" because of the significant degree of control the artist retains over them,[30] brought to C. C. Wang's paintings a kind of "artistic naturalism" that was deeply in accord with the artist's landscape subject matter.

Although aware of the Chinese precedents for such accidental effects—8th century and later artists were known to have poured their ink on the paper before applying the brush, to have blown it on with their mouths, to have spattered it on through a screen and wiped it on with rags, to have brushed it on with their own hair and applied it with their hands and fingernails—C. C. Wang says such examples were rare eccentricities. And while he can no longer remember exactly what, if anything, triggered his initial use of applied textures ("perhaps something I saw in a magazine"), he says his inspiration was probably Western. The use of various techniques for applying pigments characterized New York's Action Painters of the late 1940s and 1950s, whose media and methods of application ranged widely, from pigments floated in a water or oil bath, to house-painting brushes, to the artist's own hair. While C. C. Wang does not feel he was directly imitating others in this movement and admits to being baffled by their intentions, as a New York artist he was subjected to their pervasive influence throughout the fifties.

By the end of the 1950s, Abstract Expressionism had already suggested to several innovative Chinese painters a means to pursue new technical possibilities in response to purely Chinese needs. A few Chinese-born painters were notably successful at this experimentation with textural methods and developed distinct artistic personalities. Ch'en Ch'i-k'uan in America and Liu Kuo-sung in Taiwan were among the first and most distinguished and could have served as influential intermediaries. Hugh Moss has written that

each artist involved believes that he or she was a seminal force, but the most likely answer is that it was an idea whose time had come. Ch'en Ch'i-k'uan then working in the United States, Tseng Yu-ho [Betty Ecke, b. 1923, recently retired as professor of Chinese art history at the University of Hawaii], Wang Chi-ch'ien in New York and Liu Kuo-sung then in Taiwan were all deeply involved, each applying his or her particular method and ideas to the same end.[31]

But among various sources of inspiration for this change in C. C. Wang's technique, the most important may have come from his work at the Art Students League, which was more academic and less contemporary in nature: "I didn't have any hope of accomplishing something of my own, which is why I went to the Art Students League to learn. I wanted to know what modern art was all about and began to see its qualities, and then I began to change." More specifically, he says,

I think that this inspiration may have come from my learning to sketch, to do Western style sketching. I did some sketches on watercolor paper, a very rough paper which gives a natural feeling. Why is it rough? Because that makes it natural. If it was smooth, then the lines wouldn't be natural, there wouldn't be anything natural in it. I discovered that Western artists also want this natural roughness. Then I began to use this roughness. Accidental effects, which give this natural feeling, depend partly on the paper. This gave me the idea that if I could get some of that natural feeling by using wrinkled paper, I might come up with the same result. It's something similar, but not exactly the same.

In addition to changes in his painting technique, C. C. Wang's compositions took on a new quality. In traditional Chinese landscape painting of the 14th century and after, interest in composition bowed to the concern for fine brushwork, and if the brushwork was sufficiently good the composition need not matter at all. Linear surface abstractions dominated; objects, surface planes, and recessional space mattered little. But in C. C. Wang's new-found style, object integrity and spatial clarity suddenly mattered a great deal (see figs. 36, 37, 49). Linear surface abstractions gradually settled back into formal planar abstractions, achieved with a spatial illusion that allowed his landscapes to attain monumental proportions (e.g., figs. 45, 51). Once again, Chinese precedents could be adduced, and Sung painting—that rare item which few painters or collectors ever saw or acquired, but which since 1935 Wang had seen far more of than others had—influenced his style greatly. But here, too, the artist feels that Western influence was dominant:

Before I came to America, I still could not compose very well. Composing seemed very difficult. I thought that my teacher [Wu Hu-fan] was wonderful, since he could compose so easily while I could not. But since I came here [to America], after a few years suddenly I understood. I don't know why. I learned sketching here—Westen art. I tried and tried. Gradually I got it. I studied in the Art Students League for several years in New York, sketching in modern style, using casein, not oil paints, sketching from the model with charcoal or pen. This helped me to compose my pictures.

30.　James Cahill et al., *C. C. Wang: Landscape Paintings* (Hong Kong: Hsi An T'ang, 1987), p. 11.

31.　Moss, *Some Recent Developments*, p. 19.

The third element of his painting style to undergo radical alteration was his use of color, but this took more time to evolve. Only gradually did he forego the traditional use of color as a secondary (if sometimes wonderfully subtle) aspect of painting style, but eventually, his colors became more striking, particularly emphasizing strong juxtapositions of cool and warm hues (figs. 13, 22). His colors also began to reinforce the compositional structures of his paintings in a way that was uncommon in traditional Chinese painting (figs. 22-54). Like the other elements of change, C. C. Wang's newly emerging color sense was influenced by European and American artists: Gauguin, van Gogh, Modigliani, and Braque, as well as contemporary painters in the Art Students League whose names he usually did not even know.

In evaluating the factors that underlay C. C. Wang's sudden change of style, which undoubtedly came about as the result of complex and compounded causes, no one of which was sufficient and all of which, collectively, may be inadequate to explain so dramatically inspired an artistic event, two additional observations might be added: first, that his relative shift away from landscape painting during the 1950s coupled with his new attention to flowers and desk-top genre subjects (figs. 7, 24, 30) —the latter seemingly trivial but with remarkable hidden virtues that will be explored in the last chapter of this essay— helped greatly to set the stage for the artist's stylistic leap into modernity; and second, that this stylistic transformation occurred directly after he had spent two years as chairman of the Fine Arts Department at the Chinese University of Hong Kong, where he once again became immersed in a Chinese artistic environment, and then returned to New York to feel anew the impact of Western art.

In all of these changes, C. C. Wang did not substitute modern for old, Western for Chinese, but worked to synthesize the two. His paintings after the mid-1960s can no longer simply be viewed in terms of a visual performance on traditional themes, but neither can they be seen as a mere mix and match of borrowed styles, traditional and contemporary, appending parts and aspects of each. Sources of influence were increasingly masked by C. C. Wang's *own* emerging stylistic identity and increasingly difficult to perceive. Yet stylistic origins, both Chinese and Western, were by no means done away with and they show (to those who can still identify them) an unsuspected consonance, in the same way that children sometimes reveal unexpected similarities in their parents' features. Unless one knows something of the parent style as seen in C. C. Wang's painting before the 1960s, this expression of the new through the old is not recognizable. Writing on a theoretical level about this synthesis, Arnold Chang concludes,

Wang learned enough about modern art theories to realize that many of the current ideas about art were consistent with the principles of traditional Chinese painting, and by emphasizing these aspects in his work he was able to create an art that was both modern in concept and traditional in spirit. Wang discovered parallels between traditional Chinese painting and [modern Western] non-objective art, the most significant of these for him being the cultivation of the "controlled accident."[32]

Within a very short period of time, butterfly-like, the old-fashioned C. C. Wang emerged as a "modernist." But unlike the butterfly, he did not leave all traces of the past behind. Inked lines—whether applied with the traditional Chinese brush or impressed—were still the first focus of his efforts as a painter and the central criterion of his artistic self-evaluation. His forms were still drawn from a careful selection of his traditional predecessors' forms, albeit less obviously than in earlier years. C. C. Wang increasingly began to paint for himself, but not without consciously striving to contribute to the Chinese painting tradition. His contribution has been made to what Hugh Moss describes as the "common aim" of "contemporary [Chinese] *avant garde* painters," namely "to bring this ancient art form into consonance with its time."[33]

Although C. C. Wang cannot himself precisely date this great change in his painting style, let alone account for the specific timing of it, early examples are dated to late 1964 (figs. 34, 35). It is tempting to refer to this as *the* critical moment in his career, a change that was long anticipated but slow to arrive. The artist was fifty-seven years old in the year 1964 and he had been painting since 1921, a period of forty-three years. So, while long in gestation, C. C. Wang's stylistic transformation did not arrive as an infantile artistic experiment. Even if it was not yet fully mature at its inception, it nevertheless attracted immediate attention as being significant contemporary art, and as very significant Chinese painting. "After I changed my style," C. C. Wang says, "I seemed to see the light in front of me. Then I had the courage to do an exhibition. Otherwise, I fear I would have had nothing to offer, and I wouldn't even have tried."

32. Chang, *Landscape Painting*, p. 27.

33. Moss, *Some Recent Developments*, pp. 16-17.

C. C. Wang's first major exhibition was held when this style was still young, in October–November 1968, at San Francisco's M. H. deYoung Museum. The exhibition was organized by Professor James Cahill, formerly at the Freer Gallery and now at the University of California at Berkeley, and by now a long-time scholarly associate of C. C. Wang. The two had examined former Imperial Palace paintings together in the late 1950s and again in the early 1960s, and two years before this exhibition Cahill had written the introduction to the new English translation of Contag and Wang's book on collectors' seals. Cahill was one of the first to recognize the ultimate potential of C. C. Wang's painting, evaluating Wang's accomplishments historically—in the context of traditional Chinese painting and its modern revival—rather than as a contemporary painting critic. Cahill wrote in the exhibition notes at the time,

Partly because he is unconcerned with self-publicizing, partly because of his relatively small output (he has never been facile), Wang's painting is not yet so well known as it should be, and will be. He works with an integrity hard to match today: no flamboyant and empty gestures, no superficial splashing of ink, neither attractive Orientalisms nor stylish genuflections to the West.... Wang's understanding of traditional Chinese brushwork and technique (to which he by no means is bound), and his unwillingness to move outside his area of rigorous technical control, set him apart from most other Oriental artists working today, and allow him to create powerful landscapes that are visually exciting, dramatic, entirely original, and yet endowed with that quality of "rightness" that marks the best Chinese painting down through the ages. Whether Wang will take his place among the major figures of the Chinese literati painting lineage, it is too soon to say. But he is, I think, one of the leading candidates among those now working.[34]

The 1968 exhibition was a success, and although lacking a catalogue it led to the first book on C. C. Wang's painting, *Mountains of the Mind*, in 1970, edited by publisher Meredith Weatherby and largely written by Joan Stanley-Baker (Hsü Hsiao-hu, then a Princeton University graduate student). Stanley-Baker aptly described Wang's painting accomplishments as achieved "in bizarre obscurity" despite his international fame as a collector, scholar, and authenticator.[35] But even then, artistic success did not suddenly overtake C. C. Wang, and a stable market for his work was still lacking. The artist says that even at the end of the 1960s "I didn't feel like I could become a very good master. The way seemed to be blocked. There was no market here, and I could make a living only by teaching." Yet by 1968, the artist had still only presented an artistic proposition: his paintings, however expressive, were still undeveloped and would take the better part of a decade to mature.

C. C. Wang's permanent move to America in 1949 did not mark the end of his incessant travels, which had begun in the later 1930s. After he received his citizenship in 1956, he was able once again to begin spending time in Asia, although barred from the mainland. In the early 1960s, he served as the chairman of the Fine Arts Department at the Chinese

University of Hong Kong (in the University's New Asia College) for two years. He cites his continuing urge to travel as a reason for his unwillingness to hold a steady job and admits that it is, in good measure, rooted in the urge to collect: "I'm always looking for something to buy. All the time." Throughout the 1960s, foreign travel to Japan, Hong Kong, Taiwan, and even Switzerland enabled him to continue building his collection. The most important landscape still in his collection today was acquired at this time: a rare 10th-century painting thought by Wang to be an original work of Tung Yüan (fig. 9). It was acquired from the collection of Chang Ta-ch'ien, then in Taiwan, and is now known by a name that Chang wrote on it, *Thatched Hut by the Riverbank*, believing it to be the original title on the basis of textual study. While not convinced of this title, C. C. Wang is so convinced by the painting itself that he has taken this as one of the names of his painting studio, the Hsi-an T'ang or Riverbank Hall.

Increasingly, to avoid selling his older paintings and to keep acquiring ever better ones, C. C. Wang depended on brokering real estate for an income. Occasionally, financial need overcame the collector's retentive nature and a few paintings were sold. American museum holdings were greatly enriched as a result. The Cleveland Museum of Art was the first to benefit, due to the diplomatic skills of museum director Sherman E. Lee. By the end of the 1970s, Cleveland had acquired or been promised a broad range of paintings formerly in the C. C. Wang family collection, including, among others, five Southern Sung album leaves or fan paintings by Li An-chung, Wu Ping, Li Ti, and Ma Yüan (2); six Yüan paintings: *River Village—Fisherman's Joy*, an early work by Chao Meng-fu; *Lily and Butterflies*, the only surviving work of Liu Shan-shou; *The Nine Songs*, dated 1361, by Chang Wu; *Buddha's Conversion of the Five Bhiksu* by Li Sheng; Ni Tsan's *Bamboo, Rock, and Tall Tree;* and Hsü Pen's *Streams and Mountains*, dated 1372; as well as the Ming and Ch'ing paintings, *Nine Elders of Mt. Hsiang* by Hsieh Huan; Tu Chin's *The Poet Lin Pu Wandering in the Moonlight; Scholar-Hermits in the Autumn Mountains* by T'ang Yin; the Tung Ch'i-ch'ang masterpiece *River and Mountains on a Clear Autumn Day; Lady Hsüan-wen chün Giving Instruction on the Classics*, dated 1638, by Ch'en Hung-shou; Ts'ui Tzu-chung's *Hsü Cheng-yang Moving his Family;* Tao-chi's *Reminiscences of Ch'in-huai River;* and others by Wang Shih-min, Wang Chien, and Yün Shou-p'ing.[36] Kansas City's Nelson Gallery—Atkins Museum was able to acquire Wang's Liu Kuan-tao handscroll, *Whiling Away the Summer.*[37]

34. Reprinted in Meredith Weatherby, ed., Hsü Hsiao-hu [Joan Stanley-Baker] et al., *Mountains of the Mind: The Landscape Painting of Wang Chi-ch'ien* (New York: Walker/Weatherhill, 1970), p. 19.

35. Ibid., p. 18.

36. All of these works are illustrated in Wai-kam Ho et al., *Eight Dynasties of Chinese Painting: The Collections of the Nelson Gallery-Atkins Museum, Kansas City, and The Cleveland Museum of Art* (Cleveland: Cleveland Museum of Art and Indiana University Press, 1980), nos. 19, 32, 34, 52, 53, 80, 82, 96, 105, 110, 115, 133, 157, 162, 191, 208, 209, 238, 240, 241, and 242. A number of the early examples appear as well in Barnhart, *Along the Border of Heaven.*

37. Illustrated in Ho et. al., *Eight Dynasties*, no. 92.

But Professor Wen Fong of Princeton University and the Metropolitan Museum of Art was, in the long run, the one most able to turn to public benefit the accomplishments of C. C. Wang's private collecting. In 1969, Fong acquired for the Edward L. Elliott Family Collection at the Art Museum at Princeton a rare early work of Chao Meng-fu, the *Mind Landscape of Hsieh Yu-yü*.[38] In 1975, the Art Museum at Princeton acquired from C. C. Wang's collection a rare early handscroll, *The Classic of Filial Piety*, attributed to the pioneer literati-painter Li Kung-lin of the Northern Sung period and perhaps the only work by him in the West.[39] Fong also acquired a number of Ming and Ch'ing paintings for the private collection of Earl Morse, mostly destined for the Metropolitan Museum, including Ch'ien Ku's *Gathering at the Orchid Pavilion*, dated 1560; a number of works by Wang Shih-min, Wang Hui, and Wang Yüan-ch'i; and two early Ch'ing masterpieces, Wu Li's *Passing the Summer at the Thatched Hall of Inkwell* of 1679 and Wang Yüan-ch'i's *Wang River Villa*, dated 1711, perhaps the finest works by these two artists.[40] Wang Yüan-ch'i's handscroll (fig. 23) is one of the supreme accomplishments in all later Chinese painting history. It is also the one painting that C. C. Wang had known longest and studied most intensively throughout his painting career, having belonged to Wu Hu-fan before becoming his own.

The single most important transaction in C. C. Wang's career and one unmatched in the history of Chinese art collecting in the West was the purchase by the Metropolitan Museum in July 1973 of a group of twenty-five Sung and Yüan dynasty paintings. Ten of these works had formerly been in the Chinese imperial collection. The grandest among them was a profoundly conceived monumental landscape entitled *Summer Mountains* (fig. 8) and, at least since the 17th century, attributed to the 10th-century court painter, Yen Wen-kuei. Among the other works included in this transaction were attributions to the major Sung and Yüan artists Mi Yu-jen, Ma Ho-chih, Li T'ang, Ma Lin, Chao Meng-fu *(Twin Pines, Level Distance)*, Ch'ien Hsüan, Ni Tsan *(Woods and Valleys of Mount Yü)*, and Wang Meng, and what may well be the finest surviving works by the Yüan artists Lo Chih-ch'uan, Fang Ts'ung-i *(Cloudy Mountains)*, Chao Yüan *(Farewell by a Stream on a Clear Day)*, the great bamboo painter Li K'an, and the finest of all plum painters, Wang Mien.[41] Selected by Wen Fong, special consultant for Far Eastern affairs to the museum, these twenty-five paintings represented some, although only a fraction, of the finest early works that C. C. Wang had amassed. The total sale price was 2.5 million dollars.

The sale was extremely controversial. It resulted in considerable publicity for C. C. Wang, by no means all positive. This was the Metropolitan Museum's first significant Chinese painting acquisition since the unfortunate A. W. Bahr purchase of 1947, which had left a residue of cynicism, and it came on the heels of a controversial purchase in the classical department. Nobody acted quite normally as a result, and this was hardly an ordinary event. It raised issues that deserved serious consideration. One was that of bulk purchasing. Some saw this as "preempting" the market, as departing from the gentlemanly tradition of acquiring works one by one—slowly, patiently, "lovingly." Works acquired one at a time usually came from a variety of sources, and questions of selection (authenticity, providing overall balance to a collection, and so forth) were answered by the purchasing collector or curator rather than by relying on the taste and curatorial expertise of the seller. What was new in this case was perhaps brought about by an environmental change. The usual method of collecting in China and Japan depended on very private and usually well established connections, and American curators had generally followed that practice. But in the 1960s and 1970s, C. C. Wang's collection was not a hidden one, and his Manhattan apartment provided an open, modern environment in which Wen Fong and his students, as well as many other American scholars, were treated to long, invaluable study sessions. While it was C. C. Wang who insisted on not selling these works piecemeal, Wen Fong personally made the final selection for the Metropolitan Museum purchase, and he had known these works for many years. He did not snatch them quickly and quietly, he suggested to *The New York Times*, but had been gradually "stalking the collection for years."[42] Modernity and the virtual disappearance of large private collections of early Chinese painting, combined with the Metropolitan's belated determination to establish itself in this field, dictated this bow to the last major private collector of this caliber. As Thomas Lawton, director of the Freer Gallery, wrote to the Metropolitan's director, Thomas Hoving, at the time of the purchase:

It is no exaggeration, I think, to describe the Sung and Yüan dynasty scrolls owned by Mr. C. C. Wang as the last group of such paintings still available in a private collection. Given the conditions that now prevail, I cannot foresee any possibility whereby an individual or an institution could again bring together a comparable group of early Chinese paintings. Consequently, any museum having the chance to acquire so many important early Chinese paintings, is facing an extraordinary and unique opportunity.[43]

38. Painted around the year 1286, this work is the topic of a chapter by Shou-chien Shih in Wen Fong et al., *Images of the Mind: Selections from the Edward L. Elliott Family and John B. Elliott Collections of Chinese Calligraphy and Painting at The Art Museum, Princeton University* (Princeton: The Art Museum, 1984), pp. 238-54.

39. Three sections of this are illustrated in Barnhart, *Along the Border of Heaven*, figs. 10, 14, 15; see also idem, "Li Kung-lin's 'Hsiao-ching T'u'," Ph.D. diss., Princeton University, 1967.

40. See Roderick Whitfield et al., *In Pursuit of Antiquity: Chinese Paintings of the Ming and Ch'ing Dynasties from the Collection of Mr. and Mrs. Earl Morse* (Princeton: The Art Museum, 1969), nos. 4, 10, 13, 14, 21, 27, 31, and 32.

41. All twenty-five of these works are illustrated in Wen Fong and Marilyn Fu, *Sung and Yuan Paintings* (New York: Metropolitan Museum of Art, 1973); twenty of them are illustrated in Barnhart, *Along the Border of Heaven*.

42. In John Canaday, "25 Major Chinese Paintings Acquired by the Metropolitan," *New York Times*, 13 July 1973, p. 37.

43. In Malcolm N. Carter, "The Perils of Chinese Art Scholarship," *ARTnews* 75, no. 6 (Summer, 1976), p. 63.

Ch'ü Ting (active c. 1023-1056), attributed to. Summer Mountains (section). Late 10th-early 11th century. Handscroll, ink and color on silk. 17¾ x 45¼ in (45.1 x 114.9 cm). The Metropolitan Museum of Art, Gift of the Douglas Dillon Fund, 1973. (Formerly in the C. C. Wang Family Collection).

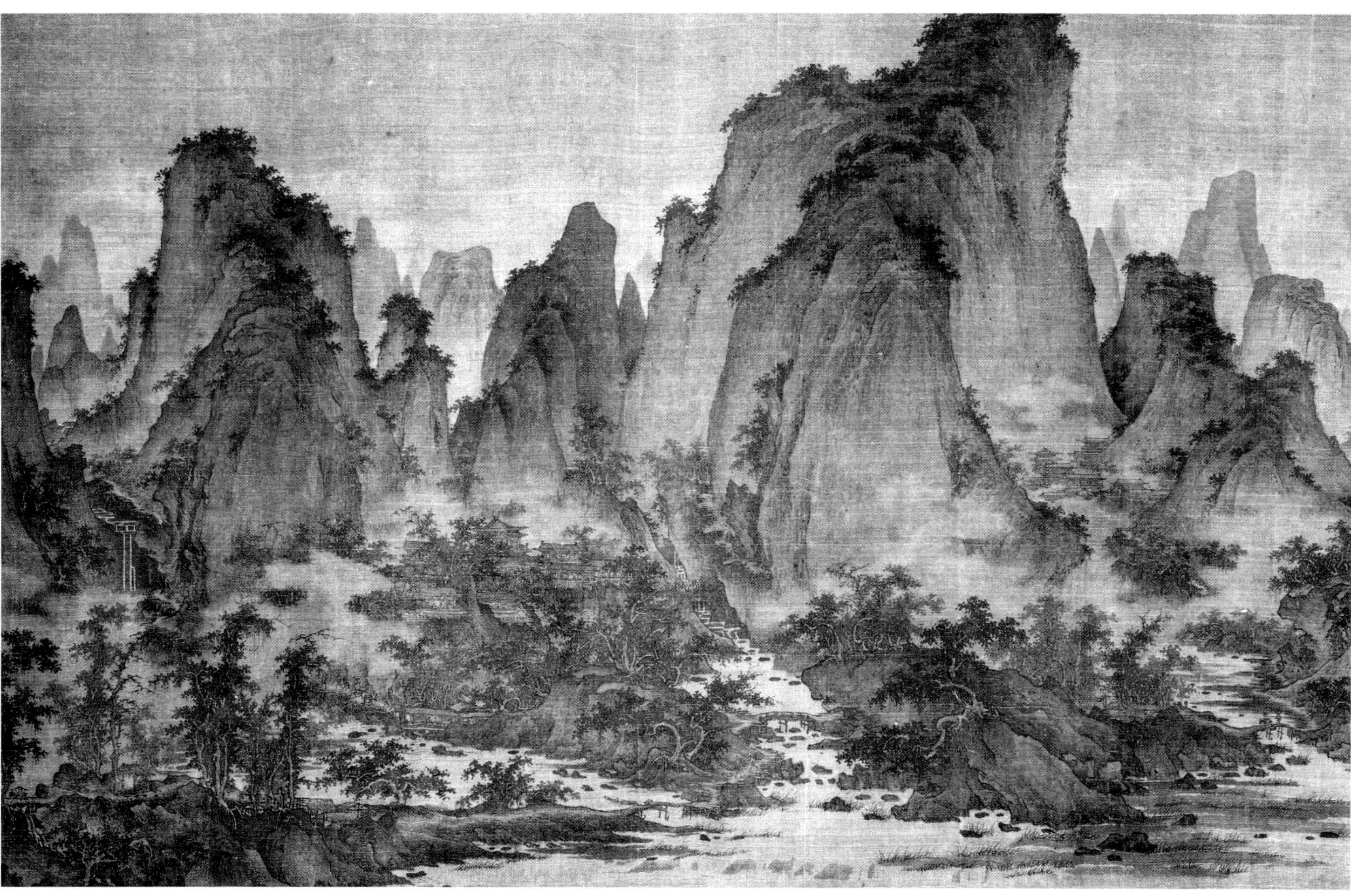

More significant, perhaps, were questions about the authenticity of these twenty-five paintings, which put C. C. Wang's reputation as a connoisseur and those of his Western counterparts to a rare public test. Sherman Lee, Thomas Lawton, Richard Barnhart (then at Princeton University), Laurence Sickman (then director of Kansas City's Nelson Gallery–Atkins Museum), and Jan Fontein (then acting director of the Museum of Fine Arts, Boston) were all consulted on the matter. Because of the Bahr purchase and other more recent controversies, the Metropolitan wanted to be cautious even while breaking all precedent. Professor Barnhart and directors Lee and Sickman were requested to "grade" each of the paintings individually (each of them, however, applied a different grading scale). When, to the surprise and dismay of these three scholars, the museum publicly disclosed the graded results, the diversity of connoisseurial opinion on Chinese painting was made available for all to see. While praising many of the paintings, Lee had judged one 12th-century attribution to be a 14th- or 15th-century copy and Sickman had given two paintings "B" grades; questions of price had been raised, and the public had the opportunity to speculate whether the museum had made another grievous Chinese painting purchase.[44] The *Summer Mountains* handscroll (fig. 8) proved to be most controversial of all: soon after the purchase, Wen Fong reattributed the work to a pupil of Yen Wen-kuei, Ch'ü Ting (active c. 1023-1056), even though no other work by Ch'ü exists for comparison, and Richard Barnhart subsequently concurred; a larger body of well-known scholars ultimately diverged still further from Wang's assertion of its Yen Wen-kuei authorship.[45] Other, less important paintings provoked as much disagreement, if less well-publicized controversy.[46] But the Metropolitan stood behind Fong's attributions of these twenty-five works, which were published in a catalogue, *Sung and Yuan Paintings,* by the end of the year, followed in 1975 by a second book in which Fong defended his reattribution of *Summer Mountains.*[47]

The subjectivity and uncertain state of the connoisseurship of Chinese painting, and the divergence between Chinese trained and Western trained scholars, were deeply exposed by this event. C. C. Wang's attributions, based primarily on brushwork, seals, and historical documentation, tended to be much more supportive of long-held traditional Chinese attributions; Western scholars' views were based primarily on a structural analysis of landscape composition—forms and space—and proved to be more skeptical of seals and documentation, and took a much "darker" view of traditional attributions than C. C. Wang did. This was a striking reversal from earlier years, when Wang's assessment of the Bahr purchase had helped to put Western museums on notice, yet it accurately reflected the much improved standards of scholarship and connoisseurship as well as a new and deeply-seated skepticism that had emerged in American studies of Chinese art since the 1940s.

By the same token, most leading scholars at the time (and much of the public, subsequently) realized that disagreement in judging any such group of paintings was unavoidable.

Sherman Lee wrote to Hoving, "On the whole I part company on only four to six out of the 24 [that Lee saw] . . . an exceedingly rare phenomenon among specialists in Oriental painting, who are always at opposite poles with each other."[48] Whether the best of these paintings, the *Summer Mountains* handscroll, was actually painted by Yen Wen-kuei of the late 10th century as Wang believes, or by his pupil Ch'ü Ting as Fong has proposed, or by a Southern Sung artist as others have suggested, is indeed an important art historical question. But it hardly alters the extraordinary artistic stature of the painting. Richard Barnhart asserted that the C. C. Wang purchase had put the Metropolitan's Chinese painting collection "on a par with, or above the Cleveland Museum and draws it close to the collections in Boston, Kansas City and Washington."[49] C. C. Wang himself saw this far more modestly: "Twenty-five paintings do not make a collection, though they are important paintings. The Met cannot rival the four great U. S. collections."[50] Yet with this single purchase, the Metropolitan Museum overcame years of neglect of Chinese painting and initiated the largest American acquisition program in this field in the 1970s and 1980s. The Metropolitan Museum has continued to acquire other major paintings from C. C. Wang, including (in 1982) Lu Kuang's late Yüan period *Spring Dawn at the Cinnabar Terrace.*[51]

That other equally fine paintings—including his personal favorites by Tung Yüan (fig. 9), Ni Tsan (fig. 5), Tao-chi (figs. 11, 19), and Chu Ta (fig. 17)—remained in C. C. Wang's family collection after the 1973 Metropolitan purchase, in addition to others added since then, is a testament to the depth of the collection. The particular depth of C. C. Wang's collection in the early periods of Chinese painting is illustrated in Richard Barnhart's *Along the Border of Heaven: Sung and Yüan Paintings from the C. C. Wang Family Collection.*[52] The greatest effect of the Metropolitan Museum sale on C. C. Wang was to enable to him to rebuild his collection on a still larger scale.

Buying paintings—that's my hobby. My living improved only after I sold twenty-five paintings to the Metropolitan. It didn't change my life, but then I had money to buy more paintings. For selling one painting, I could afford to get five more. Now I still have more than two hundred paintings.

His most recent major purchase is an album of ten landscapes attributed to the leading Southern Sung court painter, Ma Yüan, with matching poems by the empress Yang Mei-tzu, which if authentic would constitute the only complete album of its kind in the West.

44. Ibid.

45. Barnhart, *Along the Border of Heaven,* pp. 38-44; Professors James Cahill, Roderick Whitfield, Max Loehr, Richard Edwards, and Nelson Wu all joined Sherman Lee and Laurence Sickman in suggesting a date no earlier than the 12th or 13th century (James Cahill, *An Index of Early Chinese Painters and Paintings: T'ang, Sung, and Yüan* (Berkeley: University of California Press, 1980), p. 196; Roderick Whitfield, "Review of Wen Fong, *Summer Mountains: The Timeless Landscape,*" *Oriental Art* N.S. 22, no. 2 (Summer, 1976), pp. 194-95; Wu quoted in David Bershstein, "Museum Art Controversy Stirs China Scholars," *The Village Voice,* 3 May 1976, p. 16). For C. C. Wang's brief published defense of the original Yen Wen-kuei attribution, which dates back to Liang Ch'ing-piao, see Barnhart, *Along the Border of Heaven,* p. 185.

46. The public nature of this controversy is evident in several popular journal articles: Bershstein, "Museum Art Controversy," pp. 15-17; Carter, "The Perils of Chinese Art Scholarship," p. 61-66; and John L. Hess, "Can the Met Escape King Tut's Curse?" *New York Magazine,* 13 November 1978, pp. 79-85.

47. Fong and Fu, *Sung and Yuan Paintings;* Wen Fong, *Summer Mountains: The Timeless Landscape* (New York: Metropolitan Museum of Art, 1975). See also Wen Fong, "Asian Art for the Metropolitan Museum," in Thomas Hoving et al., *The Chase, the Capture: Collecting at the Metropolitan* (New York: Metropolitan Museum of Art, 1975), pp. 133-39.

48. In Carter, "Perils," p. 63.

49. In Canaday, "Chinese Paintings," p. 37.

50. In Bershstein, "Museum Art Controversy," p. 15.

51. Illustrated in Barnhart, *Along the Border of Heaven,* fig. 68.

52. See note 36, above.

53. Wang Chi-ch'ien, "*Ni Yün-lin ti sheng-p'ing chi shih-wen* (The Life and Writings of Ni Tsan)," *National Palace Museum Quarterly* 1, no. 2 (Winter, 1966), pp. 29-42; "*Ni Yün-lin chih hua* (The Paintings of Ni Tsan)," *National Palace Museum Quarterly* 1, no. 3 (Spring, 1967), pp. 15-46; Wang Chi-ch'ien and Li Lin-ts'an, "*Wang Meng ti 'Hua-hsi Yü-fu T'u'* (A Study of Wang Meng's Masterpiece, 'Hermit Fisherman on the Hua Stream')," *National Palace Museum Quarterly* 1, no. 1 (Autumn, 1966), pp. 63-68. (All in Chinese, with English summaries.)

54. C. C. Wang, *Album Leaves from the Sung and Yuan Dynasties* (New York: China Institute in America, 1970).

55. Hsü Hsiao-hu [Joan Stanley-Baker], "Hua-yü lu," *Ku-kung wen-wu yüeh-k'an* 13 (April, 1984) and 15-28 (June, 1984-July, 1985).

56. Max Loehr, brochure for "Mountains of the Mind: Rockscapes by C. C. Wang," Fogg Art Museum, Harvard University (Cambridge, 1973).

57. The relationship between C. C. Wang and Chang Ta-ch'ien will be explored in Carl Nagin's forthcoming biographical study of Chang, *Painter from the Great Wind Hall* (New York: Atheneum Press), which promises to examine issues of collecting, dealing, and forgery in considerable detail and with concern for the different values attached to them in China and the West.

Biographically, except for his 1968 exhibition and the 1973 Metropolitan Museum purchase, the late 1960s and 1970s seem comparatively uneventful, at least to C. C. Wang himself. Major events were few, and artistic interests rather than biographically notable events shaped the period. "This period was not very colorful for my life. But things weren't dull in my mind." The direction of his artistic development remained, as usual, independent of the details of his daily affairs and it was a time of increasing variety in C. C. Wang's artistic activities. He lectured at various universities—Columbia, Berkeley, and others. In 1967-68, he published articles in each of the first three issues of the new scholarly journal of the National Palace Museum in Taiwan, one of the few times that he has actually organized and published his research. Two of these articles concerned his favorite artist, Ni Tsan, while the third, coauthored with the Palace Museum curator of painting, Li Lin-ts'an, was on Ni's contemporary, Wang Meng.[53] In 1970 he served as curator of an exhibition of Sung album paintings for the China Institute in New York and wrote a brief accompanying catalogue, only the second time he had organized such an exhibition.[54] In the mid-1970s he provided Joan Stanley-Baker (Hsü Hsiao-hu), coauthor of the first book on his paintings) a series of interviews that explored his views on connoisseurship. Never published in English, these have recently been translated into Chinese and released in the (Taiwan) National Palace Museum's new journal, *Ku-kung wen-wu yüeh-k'an*, in a sequence of short selections relating his views on the appreciation of brush and ink, painting categories, the aesthetic term *ch'i-yün* ("spirit-consonance"), critical standards external to painting, texture methods, washes, the concepts of tastefulness and vulgarity, balanced and unbalanced brush technique, restraint, traditionalism, and the artists Hsia Kuei, Liang K'ai, Huang Kung-wang, Ni Tsan, Wang Meng, Shen Chou, and the Four Wangs.[55]

After 1970, solo exhibitions of his paintings became an increasingly common affair, held at the Los Angeles County Museum of Art (1971), the Indianapolis Museum of Art (1972), New York's China Institute (1972), the Honolulu Academy of Arts (1972), Harvard University's Fogg Art Museum (1973), Columbia University (1975), the Chinese Culture Foundation of San Francisco (1976), the North Carolina Museum of Art in Raleigh (1977), the Brooklyn Museum (1977), Pennsylvania State University's Museum of Art (1979), the Taipei Fine Arts Museum (1984), the Hong Kong Arts Centre (1983 and 1986), and the Birmingham Art Museum (1987), among others. Each successive exhibition—generally of his most recent works, pre-1949 paintings being included only in the Los Angeles County Museum exhibition—helped to consolidate his reputation. In his notes for Harvard's Fogg Art Museum exhibition, Professor Max Loehr wrote,

A glimpse of even a few of C. C. Wang's mountain images makes us feel that we are in the presence of a formidable artistic intelligence. That these images have deep roots in Chinese traditions, specifically those of the literati painters, is obvious. Yet it is difficult to single out any particular master, past or present, with whom he is closely affiliated. Rather it seems as if those traditions had coalesced into a more or less homogeneous, new, and fertile substance, a living force that is his inner possession. It is not sufficient to see his works only in relation to the past, however. As a painter, C. C. Wang is a twentieth-century, cosmopolitan figure, no less aware of contemporary Western art than of his native inheritance.... The high rank of C. C. Wang among the Chinese painters active today is not in dispute. The question is whether, perhaps, he ranks supreme.... In my opinion, there is no serious contestant in Wang's generation.[56]

During this period he took increasing advantage of the opportunity to see America's landscapes, putting in his proverbial ten thousand miles at the more dramatic sites such as Yellowstone, the Grand Tetons, the Grand Canyon, and Yosemite. He returned twice to Switzerland, one time with Chang Ta-ch'ien, whose friendship demonstrated the ability Chinese artists acquired after the war to overcome the factionalism that had been so great in Shanghai during an earlier era, when Chinese painters had little common perspective on their role in world art.[57] He also continued his Oriental travels. A year spent with his family in Japan in 1976 also varied his routine, but C. C. Wang feels it failed to provide him adequate contact with Japanese collectors and painters due to language difficulties and the attention to family that was required.

In August 1980, his son, Shou-k'un, was released at last from the People's Republic of China after three decades of separation from his family. C. C. Wang took this as a sign of the government "loosening up" its policies, and within two months he had joined a group of American historians of Chinese painting for a three-week museum tour hosted by the Chinese Ministry of Culture. This paved the way for a series of return visits—four so far—which provided him with the opportunity for reunions with old associates like Hsü Pang-ta and Liu Hai-su, for meaningful encounters with artists from different groups that in earlier days had held little interest for him, and for meeting younger painters such as Ch'eng Shih-fa (b. 1921) who had come of age as artists only after Wang's departure from China (for Ch'eng's figural contribution to one of C. C. Wang's landscape paintings, painted on one of these occasions, see fig. 53). But neither his residency in Japan nor his China travels had any great impact on his style, due to his lack of deep appreciation for most contemporary Japanese or mainland Chinese painting. Nor was his own current painting style particularly well received among old friends, Hsü Pang-ta finding it, he remembers, "wild" and "out of his circle" of classical taste. Only among a few younger mainland artists, intrigued by the impact of Western art on Chinese painting abroad, does Wang now appear to have made some initial impact.

Throughout this period, C. C. Wang continued to paint at the Art Students League, formally enrolling for the last time in 1974 (a sketching class with Marshall Glasier) but as a Life Member continuing to go occasionally, as recently as 1985, and paint independently after 5 o'clock "for stimulation." Of the League's offerings, he says, "Even now I regret I didn't study more."

More important to the artist himself than biographical events in this period was the gradual artistic evolution of his "modern" style, set forth in an initial phase that began as powerful but somewhat raw in the mid-1960s (cf. figs. 33-40), followed by a decade of gradual maturation which arrived at an artistic plateau by the mid-1970s (figs. 40, 41, 49-51). The latter half of the 1970s proved to be relatively dormant artistically: on the one hand, the artist felt "unsure what to do next"; on the other hand, financially secure for the first time since arriving in America as a result of the 1973 Metropolitan Museum purchase, he no longer had to maintain his artistic production out of economic necessity. In addition, more time was required to manage his increasingly important financial investments in real estate. C. C. Wang now had greater time and financial means to turn his art collecting energies in new directions, beginning to acquire—in addition to more paintings— important examples of early Chinese ceramic vessels, Bronze Age ritual vessels, and ceramic tomb figurines. His new pattern of collecting was accompanied by intensive and time-consuming studies of artistic media that had previously been of only secondary interest to him.

Not until 1980 did C. C. Wang return to his painting with renewed vigor, no longer constrained by considerations of commercial success and audience response. Within a year, a more mature artistic style than ever before had clearly begun to emerge (e.g., figs. 22, 53, 55-59), marked by a striking clarity of compositional design and a distinctive coloristic flair. His integration of Chinese and Western qualities was never more successful. Perhaps the most fruitful moment of his entire career occurred in the first five months of 1983. At that time, not simply refining older modes, C. C. Wang began to experiment anew with a number of different possibilities, one of which resulted in a series of paintings (beginning with fig. 61) that used a single dominant color which was applied not only to the front side of the paper but also to the back side. The landscapes of this series were also usually more abstract in form, flat and simple in appearance, and in some ways seeming to revert back to the early years of his "modern" style. This second "new" style was as distinctive and inventive as his earlier "modern" paintings from the mid-1960s through the early 1970s had seemed. At one point, during fourteen weeks in early 1983, the artist painted well over a dozen such paintings of surpassingly high quality (including figs. 21, 52, 61-66), along with others representing the best of the artist's more typical style (fig. 13).

Surely it is not just coincidental that during this period C. C. Wang was recovering from two successive surgeries that almost cost him his life. In August 1982, it was discovered that a persistent back pain was in fact the result of an aneurism of the abdominal aorta. Surgery conducted at that time in New York, designed to repair the vessel, accidentally resulted in its rupture; the availability at that moment of a specialist who was rushed in from a neighboring operating room is thought to have saved his life. The procedure was left uncompleted until late November, when a second operation was successfully undertaken in Houston. All of this left the artist physically weakened for the next several months. Unable to travel and obliged to leave financial matters in the hands of his son, there was little he could do other than to sleep and paint. His daughter, Yien-koo, who took over the management of his artistic activities at that time, describes him during the months of this extraordinary artistic activity as being

in a dreamy state, not alert to the outside world. Yet all the debris was cleared away and his whole being was completely true to itself. He was totally open, totally elusive, like the clouds in the sky.

Both father and daughter are agreed that the artistic freedom of the moment and the heightened degree of abstraction that emerged in his painting style were the result of his physical— and mental—condition.

By the middle of 1983 this abstraction had disappeared. But the artist, in renewed health, proceeded to complete still more of his finest works, experimental and ranging broadly in stylistic character from works of monumental power (fig. 68) or daring tonal complexity (fig. 70) to others of remarkable softness (fig. 75) and simplicity (fig. 18). In 1986, James Cahill wrote that C. C. Wang "represents, perhaps more than any other living Chinese painter, the achievements of 'traditional' Chinese painting today," apparently feeling that in the 1980s the painter has at last fulfilled his artistic potential.[58]

An increasingly youthful attitude has become evident in recent years, in the artist's personality as well as in his innovative artistry. With good humor, he imagines himself getting mentally younger, more imaginative, and at the age of seventy-nine he said,

I never think I'm old. I'm old now, but in my mind I still feel I'm twenty, or fifteen. If I have more time, I would even like to be in kindergarten.

58.   Cahill et al., *C. C. Wang*, p. 9.

One of the artist's seals reads, *Chi-ch'ien ch'ang-shou* or "Long life to Chi-ch'ien." Unable to account for his unceasing creativity, C. C. Wang says, "Really, I don't know how I change, myself. I can't explain it. I just experiment." But he is well aware that he differs from the norm, from the majority of elderly Chinese painters whose desire was to maintain their well-established artistic personalities at the risk of self-imitation, and even more from others who suffered a creative decline:

My attitude toward Chinese painting is different from the old masters'. For instance, all the old masters after seventy were already settled into their styles, and they didn't change any more. They played around all the time with their "maturity," but within limits. Wang Yüan-ch'i, for example, didn't want to create something "new." I want *to develop new ideas. That's where I'm different. My attitude is different. I'm still young in mind. It's odd, but I've never rested, not in my mind.*

It was an auspicious discovery for him when, after he had changed the Chinese characters for his name, Chi-ch'ien 己千 , for the last time (in 1970), he realized that this rendition coincided with an old Chinese aphorism about hard work, *jen shih chih, chi ch'ien chih* 人十之 己千之 , which means "what others do ten times, I will do a thousand." Explaining this, he concludes:

Everything that I want to know about, I want to know about completely. When I appreciate art, I want to appreciate the highest level of art. Every artist starts at a low level. Some just stop at a middle level, while some can go further to a higher level. It's like climbing a mountain, and I want to climb to the peak, not just stop in the middle. Even now, I think I have achieved something, and maybe I'm already ahead of some artists, but I have still further to go. Yet I aim for the highest level. I want to know the reason for everything, and if you say my work is good —even if you always *say it's good—or if someone else says its bad, I want to know why you like it or not. I don't want an empty name, or just to show off. I want to satisfy myself and achieve what I'm thinking.*

No conclusion can be written to the biography of an eighty-year-old artist whose art increasingly dwarfs in significance the reportable events of his life and whose best works may not yet have been painted. It is in his artistic thought and practice that the artist endures, and these are the topics of the next two chapters of this essay.

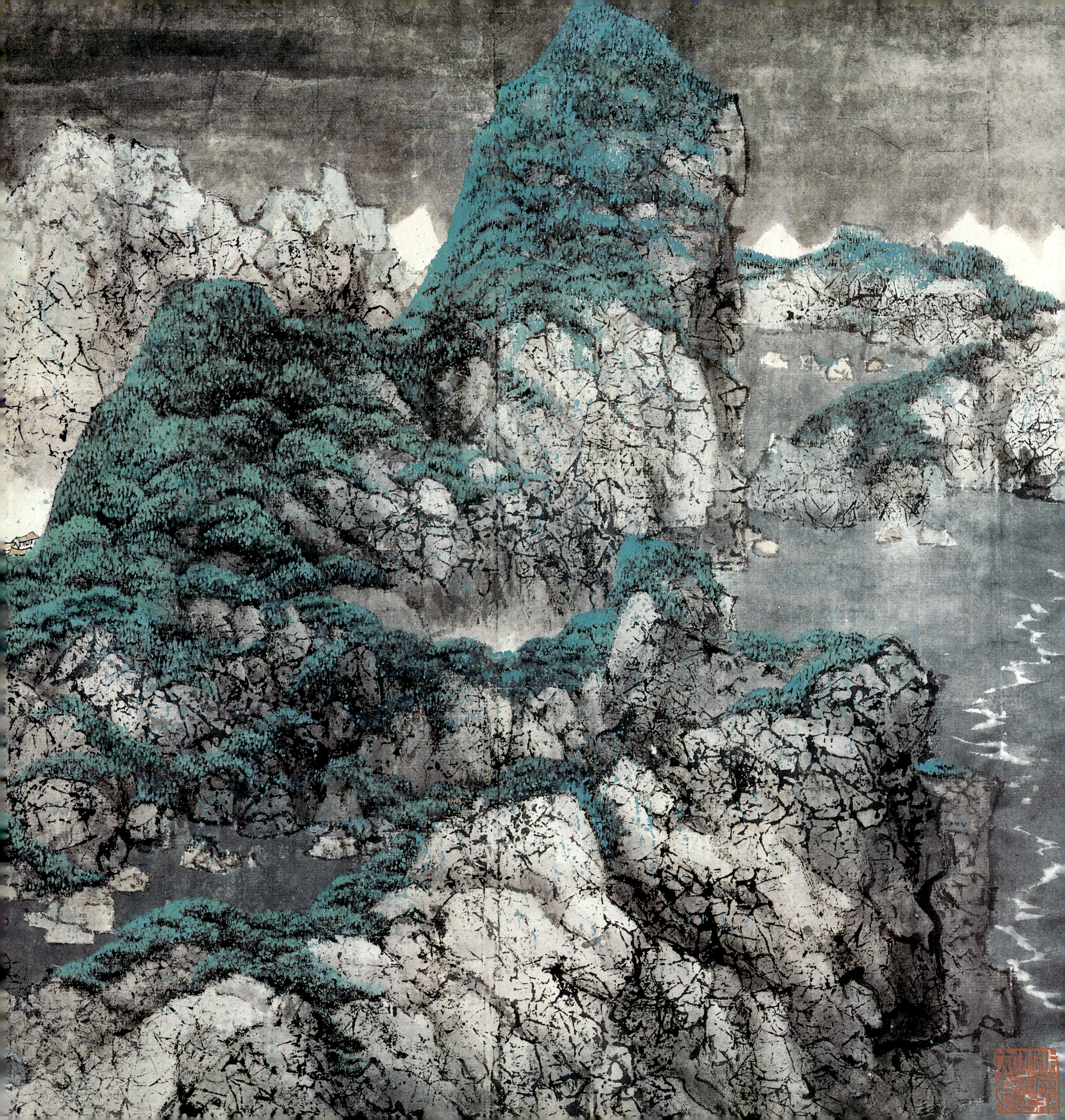

2

Detail of *Landscape No. 419*. Reproduced in full in fig. 56, page 99.

What makes "traditional" Chinese painting traditional, rather than merely conservative, is its self-conscious basis in the art of the less-than-immediate past. Since the 14th century, in the hands of amateur artists from China's ruling scholar class, the real subject of Chinese landscape painting has often been past styles, or what Max Loehr has dubbed "art-historical art." This art-historical art did not merely perpetuate what was handed down from the immediate past, from master to pupil, but was based on the painters' ranging over the entire corpus of past traditions, selecting what was personally most valued from them. The more creative artists transformed this stimulus into new and personal statements which in time might join the corpus of past traditions. But, verbal or visual, artistic comments were coded in terms of the past, referring to past art and to previous comments on past art. Such an art form presumed of its artists that they master art history, that they become connoisseurs and, if possible, collectors. Among contemporary painters, C. C. Wang epitomizes the artist who knows his historical base, who has gathered it up for close personal scrutiny:

Being a collector has definitely influenced my work. There is always some painting in my collection that's on my mind. When I paint, a work like Tung Yüan's will give me some idea, so sometimes if I'm working out a composition, a large composition, I'm influenced by him. It's not direct—I don't want to copy him—but the idea, the feeling is influential.

In his study of art, C. C. Wang does not think of himself as a theoretician, and his only published writings are historical studies. He says:

1. James Cahill et al., *C. C. Wang: Landscape Paintings* (Hong Kong: Hsi An T'ang, 1987), p. 9.

I have no need to think about aesthetics. In China, nobody ever wrote theoretically about the exact meaning of "good" or "bad" painting. They never said what it really is. All the art critics miss the point. Their writing is mostly a merry-go-round. Even Tao-chi and Tung Ch'i-ch'ang didn't write very well about aesthetics. What they wrote theoretically is not consistent with their art. They were not like Western scholars, for whom everything should be systematic.

The Artistic Values of a Connoisseur-Collector-Painter

To be sure, C. C. Wang's success as a painter and his solutions to painters' problems are a painter's solutions, achieved visually. Nevertheless, his artistic efforts have been directed by values that are conscious and well articulated. Like all major contemporary Chinese painters, throughout his career he has faced a highly visible central artistic problem, that of revitalizing the aged and weakened tradition of Chinese painting at a time when tradition itself holds little sway in the face of iconoclastic modernism. James Cahill has written,

To write an essay on Wang Chi-ch'ien is to write about Chinese painting in the second half of the twentieth century. Saying that is not saying only that he is one of its central figures, as of course he is. It is also recognizing that he represents, perhaps more than any other living Chinese painter, the achievements of "traditional" Chinese painting today, and also the problems it must face and resolve in its relationship to its past and to the contemporary world. We can begin by observing that no Chinese artist now active has dealt with those problems more consciously or more effectively than Wang Chi-ch'ien.[1]

For all of these painters, the solution at its simplest is to produce good art, but for each of them the question of *how best* to preserve traditional Chinese painting has become a question of *what* to preserve, *what* is good? The larger question is resolved in terms of smaller answers. "What is good?" is answered in terms of "What is good brushwork? What is good color?" For C. C. Wang, painting discussions are structured according to a matrix of topics, values, and referential models, just as literati discussions were in earlier times. The leading topics that he raises—the old traditional categories, really—are brushwork, texture, composition, color, and content. To each of these topics are attached values, constellations of aesthetic preferences that are cross-topical and yet find unique expression in each topical category. In this, C. C. Wang speaks with a new voice: brushwork is associated with "musicality" and, ideally, is "naïve"; texture is appreciated for "natural" effects that appear through "accident" or the partial relinquishing of artistic control, through a kind of selflessness; color is valued for its abstract, expressive potential and its abstractly patterned relationship to composition; composition is valued for natural beauty and naturalistic structure, but also for abstract beauty and naïveté; and content is strictly limited to landscape, always emphasizing naturalness and naturalism. The values most appreciated in brushwork, texture, color, composition, and content—naturalness, abstraction, musicality, naïveté—are presented in C. C. Wang's discussions with frequent reference to exemplary models, taking the place of much verbiage but also relieving discussions of some of their precision. This also follows traditional form and presumes a visual acquaintance with major painters and paintings from the past, particularly those positive models who most deeply influenced his art and who form the backbone of his collection: Tung Yüan of the 10th century (fig. 9); Ni Tsan of the 14th century (fig. 5); Tung Ch'i-ch'ang (fig. 10), Wang Yüan-ch'i (fig. 23), Tao-chi (figs. 11, 19), and Chu Ta (fig. 17) of the 17th century.

Tung Yüan (active c. 975), attributed to. The Riverbank. Late 10th century. Hanging scroll, ink and color on silk. 87¼ x 43¼ in (221.6 x 109.9 cm). C. C. Wang Family Collection.

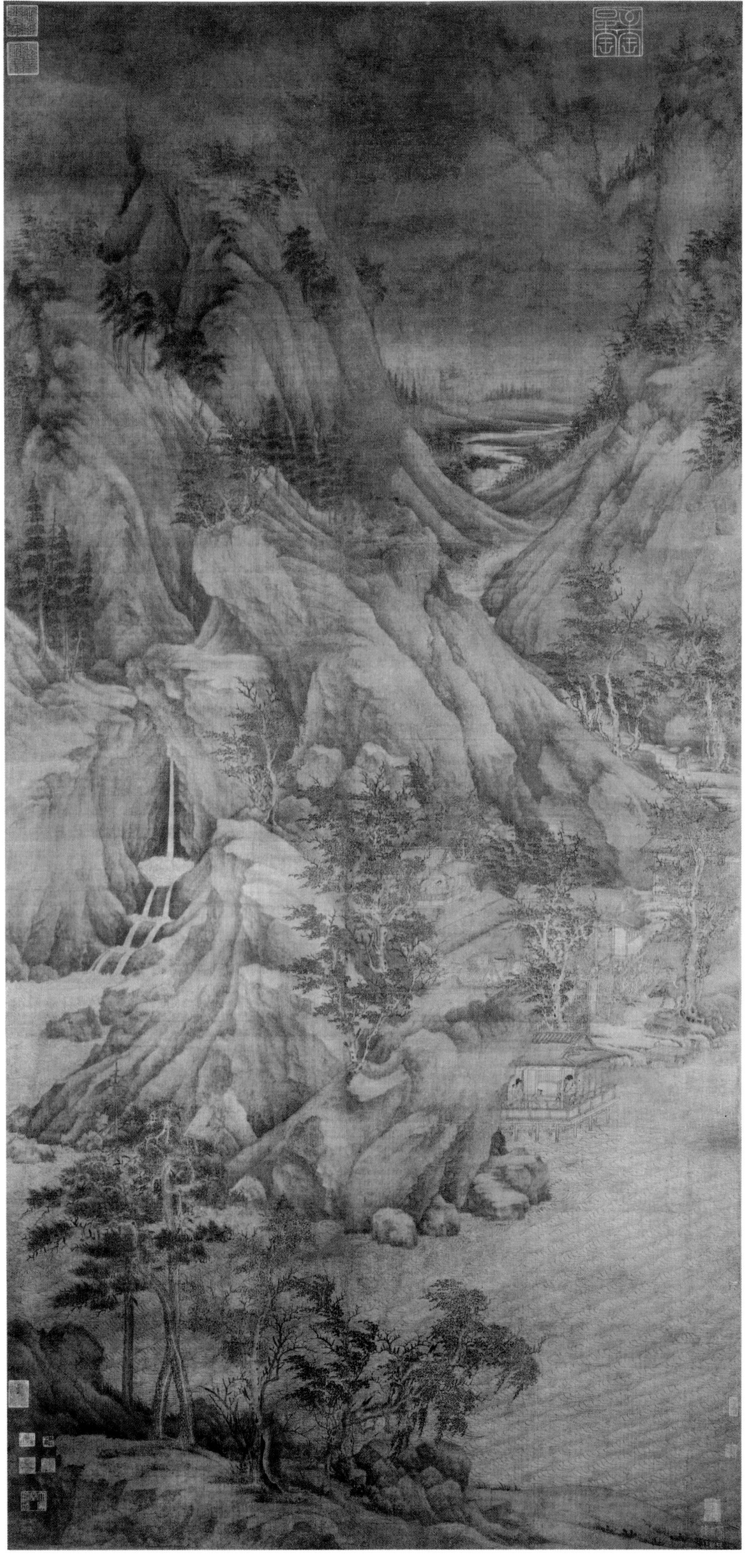

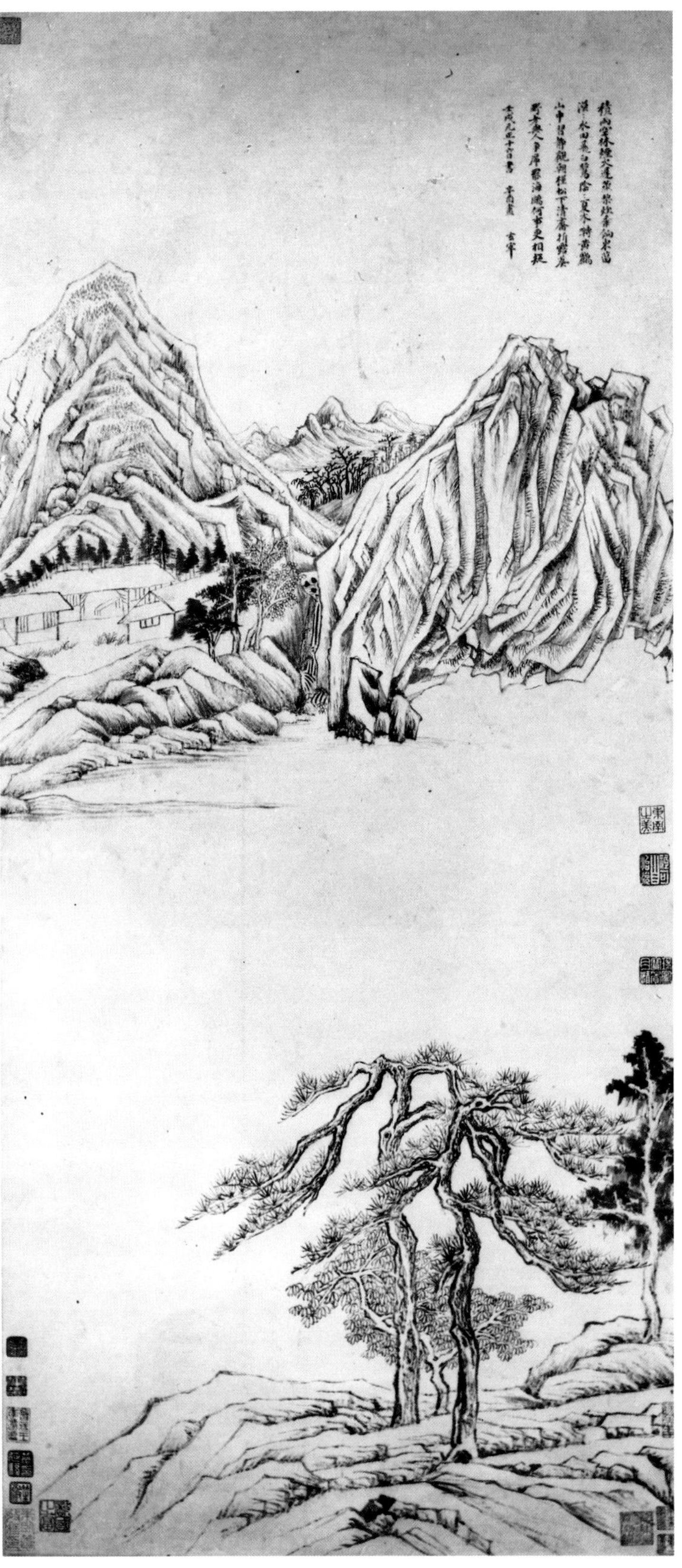

Tung Ch'i-ch'ang (1556-1636), Painting Wang Wei's Poetic Feeling. 1621. Hanging scroll, ink on paper. 42⅞ x 19⁵⁄₁₆ in (109 x 49 cm). C. C. Wang Family Collection.

In organizing these constituent elements in relation to the larger question of the Chinese painting tradition and its historical decline, C. C. Wang's solutions (both conceptual and visual) have taken the form of a selective synthesis, or what the Chinese traditionally called *ta-ch'eng:* the Grand Synthesis. His solution is in many regards highly conservative and presumes that what worked in the 17th century for Tung Ch'i-ch'ang in a similar predicament can work again: namely, that the past holds a sufficient store of artistic stimulus to engender new life. New life can still be based on old art, by identifying the best and transforming it (what Tung Ch'i-ch'ang referred to as *fang,* or creative imitation). But for C. C. Wang, "the best" must be chosen from a larger set of options—it must include a greater appreciation of the goals of early Chinese art than Tung Ch'i-ch'ang had, and it includes a Euro-American art historical base as well. Like Tung Ch'i-ch'ang, C. C. Wang chooses to pursue a broad "middle path," working from the given strengths of the tradition with the hope of adding to them. This contrasts with many modern innovators of the Chinese tradition, whose artistic trajectory has taken them down much narrower, less centrally based pathways in their pursuit of new solutions, and which has often led them to artistic isolation.

The pitfalls of a synthetic approach—which, after all, has held sway in Chinese painting for the past several hundred years without guaranteeing the continued health of that tradition—are that the selectivity will be too restrictive (as it was with most of Tung Ch'i-ch'ang's followers), or else be too indiscriminate (a more common problem in C. C. Wang's generation), or perhaps most importantly, that the past styles selectively introduced into the artist's own work will be insufficiently transformed by the artist's own creative input. Mere electicism, a patchwork of disparate elements that neither fit together nor form a uniquely creative product, is no stranger to modern Chinese painting. C. C. Wang is intensely aware of the lack of transforming creativity in most Chinese painting since the early 18th century, which he feels was abetted by the increasingly traditional standards of Ming and Ch'ing patrons, including the Manchu court. He is conscious of the need to match borrowed virtues with his own and proclaims this in a seal frequently impressed on his paintings: *Chi-ch'ien ch'uang-kao,* "Invented by Chi-ch'ien." Another of his seals reads *Chiao yüeh ch'ing po tu wang-lai,* "Beneath the bright moon, on clear waves, traveling alone"; more than mere poetry, it serves as a metaphor for artistic independence.

A synthesis, while not going to extremes, draws the extremes to it. While in theory it supplants competing antitheses, in a thoughtful and open-minded individual its constituent elements remain part of an organic system of values that are never truly resolved—they may attain temporary states of balance, but they remain in constant dynamic tension. C. C. Wang's values and paintings are synthesized from a broad range of elements, from earlier and later Chinese traditions, Chinese and Western alternatives, historically acquired traits, and his own unique contributions. All through his thought and art run value tensions acquired from this mixture of sources: tension between the attainment of skill through disciplined practice and the rejection of skill as superficial; between the love of strong brushwork and the appreciation of reserve and self-restraint; between appreciating the naturalness of impressed textures and recognizing the potential gimmickery of texturing techniques; between admiring technically competent naturalism and preferring intentionally naïve naturalism; between his pursuit of individual creativity and his esteem for artistic selflessness; and so forth. Artistically and intellectually, C. C. Wang seems always to have been intrigued by such alternatives, to have gathered them about him and thrived in their midst, to have relied on them to prick his creativity.

Many of C. C. Wang's views on Chinese art are best understood in light of such alternatives or value tensions—for example, his views on the relative importance of brushwork, in comparison to other constituents such as composition. Brushwork has been the foremost element of Chinese painting since the 14th century. C. C. Wang, on the one hand, feels that this primacy has done much damage to later Chinese painting. On the other hand, in his traditional way, he remains a foremost advocate of the preeminence of brushwork in both judging and producing Chinese paintings.

Brushwork

"My taste," says C. C. Wang, "is focused more on brushwork, less on composition. This is not the same as American taste. When I came here, nobody understood what I preferred. But gradually, more and more, my taste has become popular." Explaining this preference, he says,

Chinese brushwork is really individual, like Western color. Good brushwork is so beautiful. It can make you look at it many times. I don't have to see all of Ni Tsan's paintings, because they're all the same [in terms of composition]. But still I want to see them all. What makes me want to see them? It's just like with voice—when I hear one song, if the voice is good I want to hear another song. It's the same voice, but each time it's a little bit different: that attracts me so much. Good brushwork is just like that. Other artists who do compositions as simple as Ni Tsan's aren't worth looking at.

Other artists in addition to Ni Tsan (fig. 5) whose brushwork C. C. Wang most admires include Tung Yüan of the Five Dynasties period (fig. 9)—whom he regards as Ni Tsan's model, although artists of Tung Yüan's day did not yet paint on paper and Tung's brushwork was limited by the technical constraints of painting on silk—as well as Tung Yüan's later followers, Tung Ch'i-ch'ang (fig. 10), whose brushwork is characterized by an exquisite simplicity or naïveté, and Wang Yüan-ch'i (fig. 23), of whom he says, "If Tung Ch'i-ch'ang's brushwork is like a musical solo, Wang Yüan-ch'i's may be like a quintet. The beauty of Wang Yüan-ch'i's brushwork makes me crazy. When I see a *very* good work, it *really* makes me crazy." What Wang finds most remarkable about the brushwork of all these masters is that they are all "so soft but also so strong."

At the same time, C. C. Wang laments that many later painters gave such exclusive attention to brushwork that little else, even composition, mattered or proved successful in their art—one important cause of the eventual decline of the Chinese painting tradition:

Kung Hsien's brushwork is not as good as Wang Yüan-ch'i's, but Wang Yüan-ch'i's composition is not as good as Kung Hsien's. Comparing the two, I would definitely take Wang Yüan-ch'i over Kung Hsien. If Kung Hsien is worth looking at for two hours, Wang Yüan-ch'i is worth twenty hours. That's the difference [in value between brushwork and composition]. But this is a shortcoming of Wang Yüan-ch'i. Once Wang Yüan-ch'i became a great painter, he did pretty much the same thing all of the time. Of course he was great, but if he could have done more in terms of composition he would have been even greater.

The remedy which C. C. Wang proposes is a synthesis of selected qualities: "I think that great art should bring the qualities of Kung Hsien [fig. 6] and Wang Yüan-ch'i [fig. 23] together, that in the future Chinese painting should try to combine new compositional ideas with first-class brushwork."

A synthesis is but one possible solution, a resolution of the antitheses. But the antithetical alternatives do not disappear from the artist's historical consciousness, and they each

11

Tao-chi (1642-c. 1707), "Rainstorm," from *Album for Taoist Yü.* c. 1695. Album leaf, ink on paper. 9½ x 11 in (24.1 x 27.9 cm). C. C. Wang Family Collection.

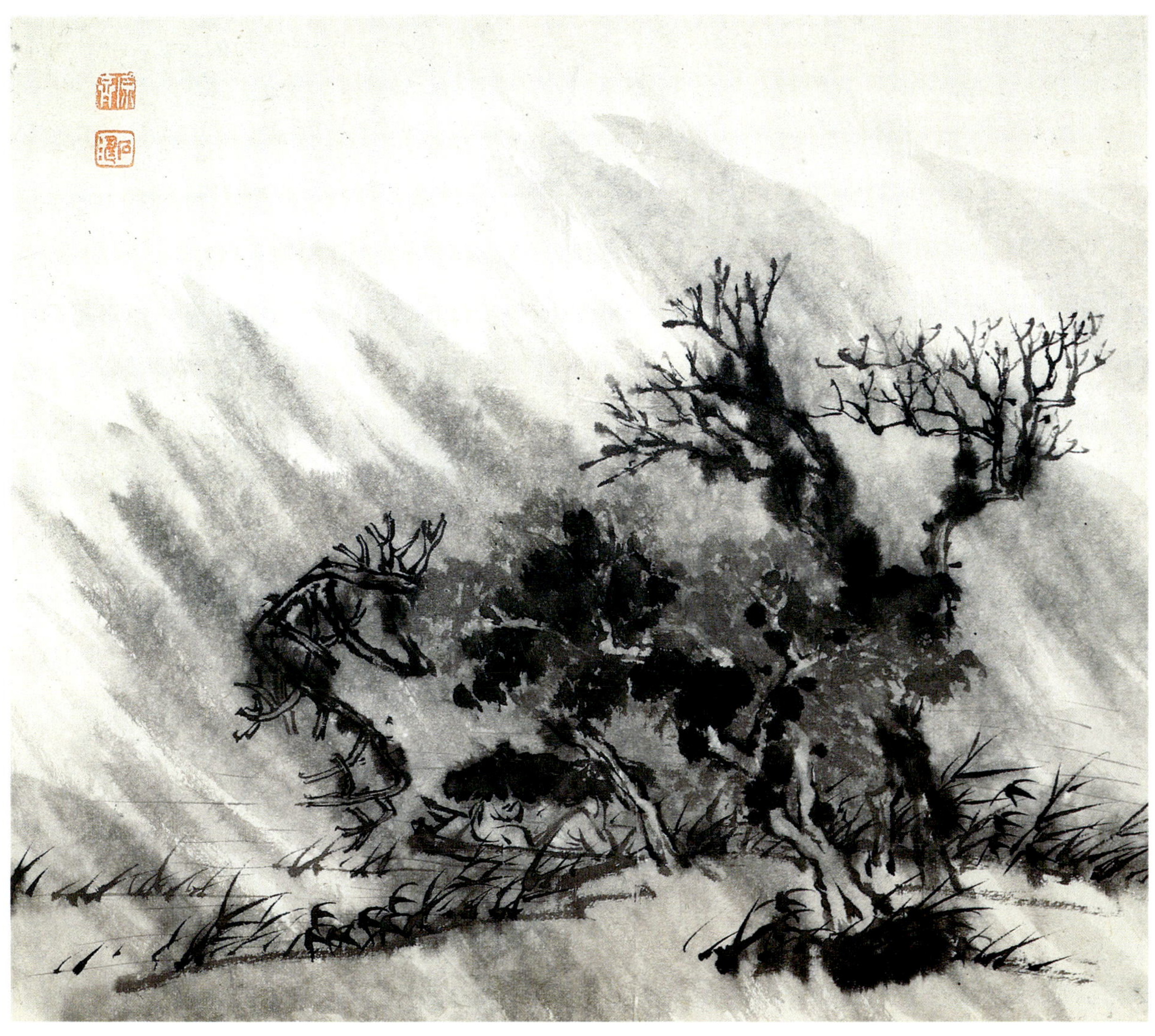

continue to offer their particular virtues as models. At a different time, his approach might be to dismiss the need for a solution, to make a virtue of "shortcomings" like the weakness of Wang Yüan-ch'i's, or Ni Tsan's, or Tung Ch'i-ch'ang's compositions. In the case of Tung Ch'i-ch'ang, C. C. Wang says,

When I look at Tung Ch'i-ch'ang's paintings, I feel much more free. When I see other paintings by other masters, I feel tight, because I don't have as much skill as they do, but when I see Tung Ch'i-ch'ang, I think I can play in any way, do anything to achieve what I want. This is the important quality of Tung Ch'i-ch'ang. Actually, Tung Ch'i-ch'ang's brushwork was the same as the Yüan masters'; he can really tell you what brushwork means. Tung Ch'i-ch'ang is a repeat of the Yüan masters, but he wasn't as logical. Tung Ch'i-ch'ang frees my mind to play with the brush, that's all. Tung Ch'i-ch'ang, just like America, gives you freedom to experiment. He doesn't want to give you any definite rules or theory. He hopes you can understand art directly, intuitively, not through any steps. The main thing is for an artist to have naïveté. Being naïve doesn't mean being ignorant, and it doesn't mean being incapable. Naïve means natural. If you have the quality of being natural, that's literati painting. Once I saw Tung Ch'i-ch'ang's painting, I felt I could do anything. Tung Ch'i-ch'ang really is so naïve. With Tung Ch'i-ch'ang I always ask whether he's incapable or whether he intentionally doesn't care. That I don't know. Maybe he's just incapable and he knows that it's not important to be capable.

That is to say, with brushwork as fine and natural as Tung's, the painter is liberated from other concerns. Good composition really does *not* matter after all. Tung's compositions may be spatially illogical or internally inconsistent, as in his *Painting Wang Wei's Poetic Feeling* (fig. 10), where the three sections of foreground, upper right, and upper left are scarcely integrated in style or structure—something which Wang can point out but then conclude, "I don't even pay attention to it." Rather than imposing a standard of logic, C. C. Wang suggests that any internal contradictions or inconsistencies be accepted with forebearance, provided the brushwork merits attention.

   Brushwork, despite its centrality to traditional Chinese painting, is the most difficult aspect of the art to understand by those who have never practiced Chinese calligraphy. It is the great divide that separates Chinese historians and connoisseurs from their Western counterparts. While recognizing that brushwork has sometimes been overemphasized by Chinese traditionalists, C. C. Wang never teaches connoisseurship independently from lessons in brushwork and has made it one of his prime tasks to educate Western viewers to its critical importance. (He laments that it is not only Westerners who lack this understanding: "The Japanese don't understand, Westerners don't understand, even most Chinese don't understand; only the Chinese artists in *my line* of thought understand"). Unlike most Western viewers who are struck first by the composition, color, or the narrative details of a painting, Wang views a painting largely in terms of the brush, reconstructively following the brushwork as if it were once again being executed before his eyes. Wang describes brush quality in terms of brush balance: regardless of whether the brush is held upright or at a slant, it must retain a center of balance based on its trajectory, much as ballet dancers must keep well balanced as they move about the stage. The tip of the brush must remain in the center of the line or the dot. This can only be achieved if the artist anticipates the direction of the brush while moving forward spontaneously and without hesitation.

At the same time, he has increasingly come to accept that the techniques and effects of brushwork as seen in painting cannot adequately be put into words—"It is impossible to write about brushwork"—and that one must actually pick up the brush and practice its use in order to understand. Often, he resorts to analogies that his Western audience might more readily understand, particularly that of music. Brushwork, he says, is like voice, distinctive to the point that it can scarcely be imitated, and for this reason it is the most reliable basis for connoisseurial authentication. Composition, he suggests, is like the lyric or verbal element to a song. To explain what he means by skill and naïveté, he has recently begun to employ analogies to different forms of Western music:

Sung brushwork [which is adjusted to compositional or descriptive ends] is like opera singing. Yüan brushwork [which is far more abstract] is like jazz. When you come to jazz, you can't accept it at the beginning. Opera has more skill, but jazz has naïveté. Naïveté has to be original. Now my painting has become just like jazz music.

A major conflict of values associated with brushwork is that between skill and naïveté, the latter epitomized by Ni Tsan, Tung Ch'i-ch'ang, and Wang Yüan-ch'i. One naturally expects that as an artist practices, his skills will mature. Yet to C. C. Wang, as to many Chinese literati painters, skill stands in the way of Chinese artists' deepest motive, which is self-expression, an encounter with one's real self and not a facade. The *real* self, in this sense, is the *nature within*, pure "landscapes of the mind"—and it is selfless. Seen from this vantage, manually developed skills are but an artifice, an unnatural facade, the resort of misdirected artists. The artist's ultimate challenge should not be the development of skill but the overcoming of it. He must develop his skills and techniques to the point that they no longer show, where they appear easy and the artist creates as effortlessly as nature itself. His brushwork must avoid being too articulate, too attractive, too obvious:

I have skill. Although I try to stay naïve, my brushwork isn't entirely naïve. Having already trained not to be naïve, it is hard for me to be artificially naïve. I try not to show my skill. I have skill but I don't want to show it too much. It's very ugly when you appear to be too skillful. You should hold something in reserve. If you understand taste, you will have some reserve, meaning you don't show your skill, you hide it.

C. C. Wang's "naïve brushwork" is associated with notions of natural brushwork that have their origins in early Chinese legend, expressive of a society in which the ability to read and write was a rare blessing—the key to social and cultural achievement, but acquired by only a few and only with painstaking slowness. Accordingly, writing itself was said not to be man's invention but Heaven's, and its original state was characterized as "natural," extreme in its simplicity and abstractness. Early calligraphers sought to imitate in their writing various kinds of natural markings, such as the pattern of holes left in a worm-eaten book or the footprints of birds, in order to seem "Heavenly," and some of these were standardized into rarely used calligraphic types. One of the seals that C. C. Wang impresses on his paintings reads *Ch'ung-shu niao-chi*, "Wormy books and bird-tracks." He explains, "This doesn't simply mean archaic, but natural—no talent. Worms and birds don't *need* talent, they don't *need* skill." Other seals of his also emphasize being natural: *Wu lou hen*, meaning the pattern of water spots left on a ceiling beneath a leaky roof, an expression used from an early time in calligraphic criticism to describe beautifully natural brushwork; *Ou-jan shih-te*, "Gotten by accident," selflessly natural; and *Wu jen wu wo, fei ku fei chin*, "Not [derived] from others, not from myself, not from the past, not from the present," which means not associated with any school or tradition, nor even with the artist himself, but simply, in his words, "dropped from Heaven."

Great brushwork must be strong yet soft, its skill must be held in reserve. Yet what is meant by strength and softness, skill and reserve can hardly be put into words, and C. C. Wang would prefer to point to models instead. The primary exemplars of "brush naïveté" are Ni Tsan (fig. 12), Tung Ch'i-ch'ang (fig. 10), and Wang Yüan-ch'i (fig. 23):

Tung Ch'i-ch'ang's art is purely a matter of brushwork. He's not a good composer. At first, I didn't appreciate Tung Ch'i-ch'ang. It took me five years. I didn't understand naïveté and only appreciated skill. That's why I started with Wang Hui. Wang Hui had more skill than naïveté. Then, even before I understood Tung Ch'i-ch'ang, I understood Ni Tsan. Ni Tsan is easier. His naïveté is on the inside; superficially his painting is not that naïve. Tung Ch'i-ch'ang was a second step after Ni Tsan, and Wang Yüan-ch'i was a third step.

It is not at all easy to avoid being too skillful or too attractive. Of his teacher, Wu Hu-fan (fig. 1), much respected by C. C. Wang and whom he is most reluctant to criticize in any fashion (a propriety maintained by Chinese students), he says,

He's really a born Yüan master, but he's not as great as the Yüan masters. Why? Because he's too sophisticated. He put too much emphasis on beauty. I know from talking to my teacher that he somewhat wanted to please people. But I believe Yüan masters, the great masters, didn't want to please people. If my teacher had realized he didn't need to please people, he could have been one of the Yüan masters, too.

12

Detail of Ni Tsan, Pine Pavilion, Mountain Scenery, 1372, showing the brushwork. Reproduced in full in fig. 5, p. 22.

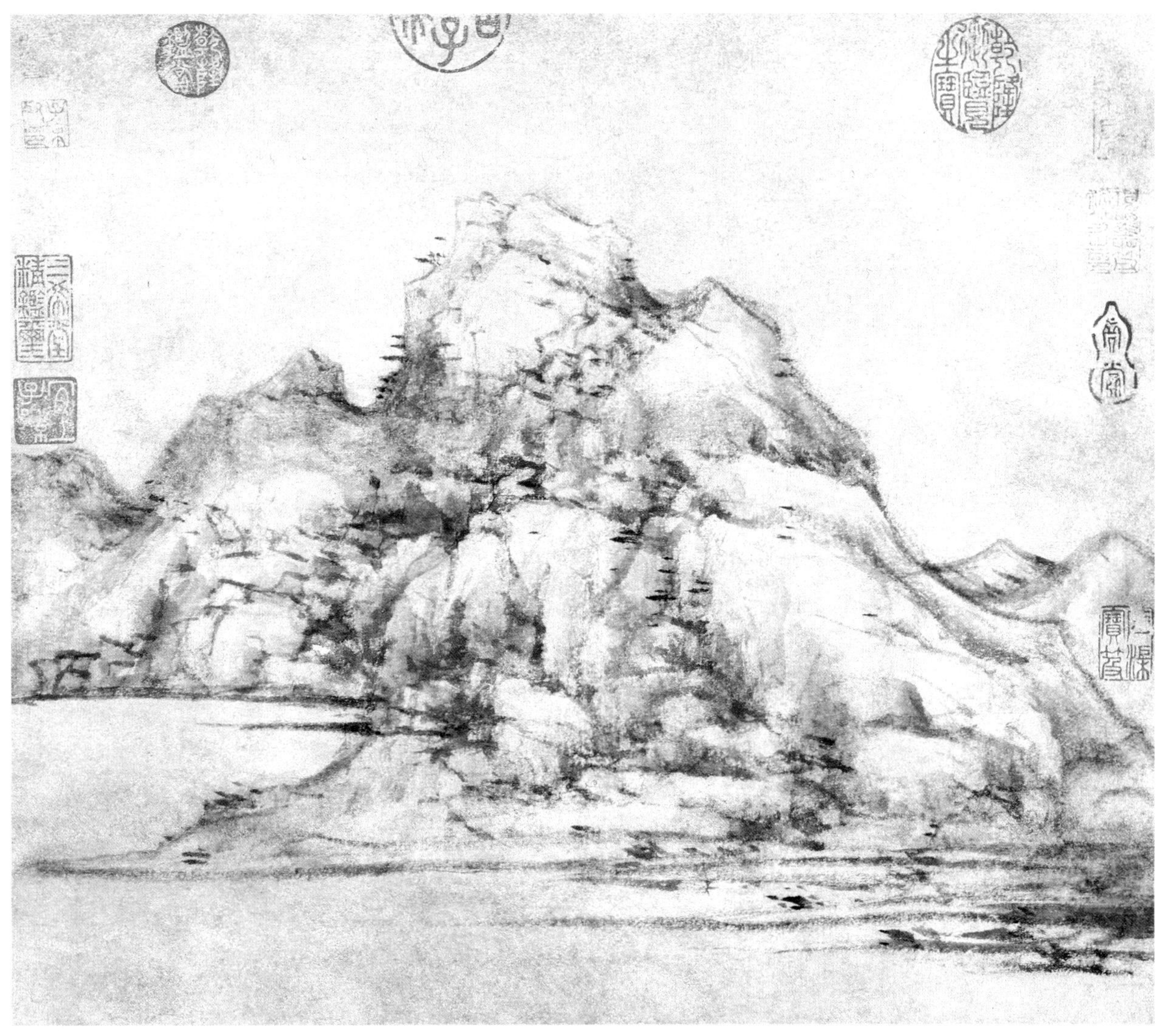

Wang saves his serious criticism for Chinese "popular" painters like Wu Wei or Chang Wu of the Ming dynasty, for contemporary Chinese painters whom he feels pursue skill in order to attain popularity, and for Japanese painting in general, which has generally reflected the Japanese appreciation of the perfection of one's skill. A Japanese painter once told him, "Your skill has some naïveté. Our skill has more skill." "This is true," he agrees.

C. C. Wang's own brushwork is derived particularly from that of Ni Tsan, or Ni Yün-lin, so that one of the names for his painting studio is the Huai-Yün Lou, The Hall Where [Ni] Yün[-lin] is Treasured—a phrase also inscribed on several of his seals. Like Ni Tsan, C. C. Wang frequently uses the side of a slanting brush but always keeps its tip in balance (as in figs. 53, 13). Despite all the changes that have taken place in the past two decades in his own painting, his brushwork has remained a stable fixture, deeply rooted in his early traditional training, and already quite mature by the time he left China. By his own standards, he has acquired too much skill. To get rid of skill once it is developed, to be strong and yet appear soft, he says "is very difficult. . . . I try not to pay too much attention to skill, but I myself am still too skillful, not too naïve. But I have some naïve quality." Judging his brushwork in an historical context, he concludes, "I think my brushwork, in personality, is not as strong as Ni Tsan's, or Huang Kung-wang's, or Wang Yüan-ch'i's. But my brushwork *could* be as strong as that of Tao-chi." Of one of his works, *Landscape No. 910* (fig. 18), where all other elements are so simplified as to not compete with the brushwork—which itself is as reserved, as dignified and antique as could be—he states with unaffected pride, "Every line is beautiful."

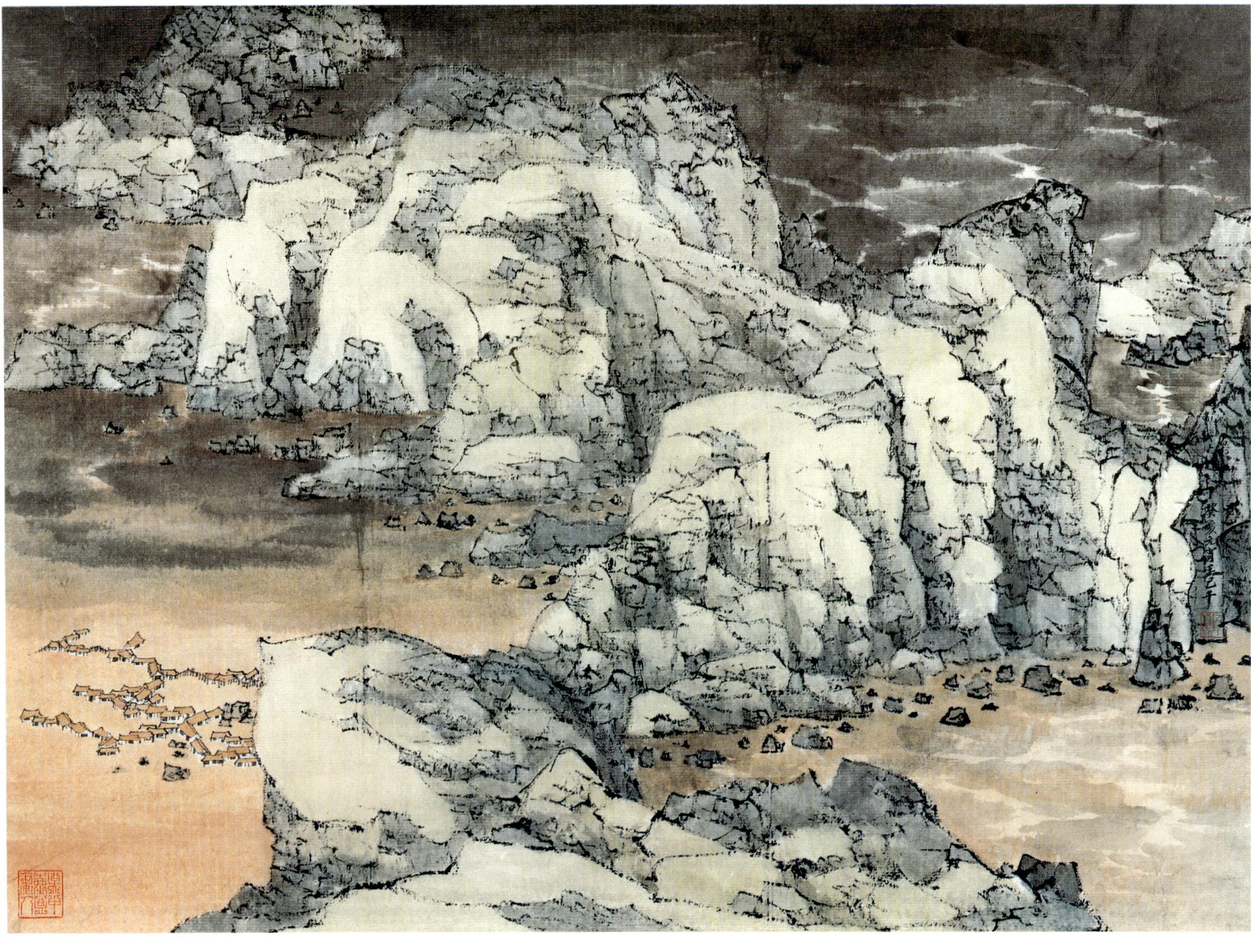

13

Landscape No. 450. 25 February 1983. Hanging scroll, ink and color on paper. 23¼ x 32 in (59.1 x 81.3 cm).
C. C. Wang Family Collection.

Inscribed
"*Kuei-hai* [1983], *yüan-hsiao* [February 25]. Wang Chi-ch'ien."

Artist's Seals
Chi-ch'ien ch'uang-kao (lower left); *Wu-chung i-hua-jen* (no. 24, lower left)

Exhibited
National Museum of History, Taipei, 1983; Hong Kong City Hall, 1986; Hong Kong Arts Centre, 1986; Birmingham Museum of Art, 1987

Published
Contemporary Chinese Painting (Hong Kong: Chinese University of Hong Kong, 1986), p. 20; Cahill et al., no. 26

Texture

Perhaps it is his appreciation of the naturalness of brush*work*, more than of the brush itself, that led C. C. Wang to go beyond an exclusive emphasis on brush techniques in his paintings to introduce a strikingly untraditional component into his painting style in the mid-1960s: that of applied textures (e.g., figs. 34, 35, 36, 37). The thinking which led him in this direction is lodged in his description of the very finest brushwork, which he finds, ironically, transcends the brush itself, and which even seems to transcend the artist's control and become selfless, natural, and "accidental":

You know, brushwork is brushwork, but the Chinese say of Ni Tsan, "no mark" of the brush. What do they mean, "no mark"? If there is brushwork then the mark of the brush must be there, but you have to paint like there is "no mark." *It signifies good brushwork when you have brushwork but don't see the brushmarks. Then your brush avoids exposing your skill, and you have such naturalness that it looks like it comes from Heaven. Ni Tsan's* Pine Pavilion, Mountain Colors *[fig. 5] is marvelous. But why is it so good, so beautiful!? It's such a good voice, and it's all full of accidental effects. Brushstroke is placed on brushstroke, so they melt together. The accident is that the brushwork doesn't reveal the marks of the brush. You cannot trace his brushstrokes. I cannot get the same kind of accidents that he got. He had talent to do that. Even when I get something similar, it's not the same. The upper portion of this painting, there is so much accident there. This accident is no accident. My accident just comes by accident.*

The value in C. C. Wang's painting of applied textures—sometimes achieved by impressing crumpled, inked paper to the painting surface and sometimes by a technique of folding the painting paper—is as much conceptual as visual. In the painting process, these impressed textures precede the application of brushwork and produce a highly abstract pattern. Before the artist begins to paint, in the traditional sense of applying ink with the brush, he is already faced with a schematic design which serves as a matrix for the painting process that follows. This must then be transformed into a landscape composition by means of traditional brushwork. The Chinese have always thought of the universe, of nature, as emerging from primordial abstraction rather than from the design of a thoughtful Creator. In using applied textures that are only partially controlled compared to drawing with the brush, C. C. Wang manages to make his landscapes more abstract and more "thoughtless." Thus, they more closely reflect a natural process of creation. The unexpected texture patterns, coming at the beginning of the painting process, give the artist what he calls "ideas that I would never think about." He says, "I like to have something there, for that gives me a way of thinking and guides me to a certain picture." Returning to a musical analogy, he suggests, "My brush has a musical voice, and my texture has a kind of voice, too, but one that's composed by nature, not by man. It's like the noise of a bird singing, or an insect singing, some kind of accidental noises to inspire music. I use *nature's* voice to go together with *my* voice."

James Cahill has recognized the inherent tension between the value systems of brushwork and texture in C. C. Wang's paintings. In the traditional school of painting that he was trained in, brushwork was all important, and one of the criteria of beauty in this tradition is that each brushstroke be highly controlled and calligraphically proper. "In what sense," Cahill asks, "can the crumpled-paper textures and other forms of this new style be considered brushwork at all, least of all *good* brushwork?"[2] Wang is aware of the problem, admitting that some of his favorite artists, like Wang Yüan-ch'i (whose own brush-produced textures are particularly rich), would have thought his accidental effects "tricky." Among the literati painters, he says, "Nobody painted using accidental effects, only Tao-chi and Chu Ta." But Cahill provides an insightful answer to his own question:

If we were to try to isolate the quality most treasured by connoisseurs of Wang's group in the paintings they most admire—the landscapes of the great Yüan masters such as Huang Kung-wang, Ni Tsan, and others, of Tung Ch'i-ch'ang, of Wang Yüan-ch'i—we would find it not so much in the strength or beauty or interest of individual strokes, or even of assemblages of individual strokes, although these qualities can also be admired, as in an all-over richness and randomness of texture, achieved in a fabric of varied brushstrokes which can be described as variety in consistency, order in the seemingly uncontrolled. The brushwork of these artists at their best appears to follow no simple system or set of rules.... The effect they pursue in this seemingly unsystematic way is a quality of naturalness; *the forms of their landscapes escape the artificiality of lesser artists' efforts by looking unplanned, innocent of human intent, like a passage of unspoiled natural scenery. It is an effect beyond skill .... The semi-random configurations and textures achieved in this way can be recognized as representing an equivalent to good brushwork.*[3]

Such textures are an equivalent to good brushwork to the degree that they achieve the fundamental goals of traditional brushwork—an answer that C. C. Wang would agree with. "It's the same *principle* as brushwork," Wang says, and he adds ironically, "It was just by accident that I discovered this."

2. Ibid., p. 11.

3. Ibid., p. 11-12.

A scholar of Chinese painting history, C. C. Wang is aware of
the historical precedents for working with accidental textured
effects, sometimes accomplished with the brush, sometimes
not. He now collects paintings by two of the most important
such masters, Tao-chi and Chu Ta, whose "accidents" were
achieved with brush and ink on wet, often rough paper, and he
owns some of the very finest paintings by each (figs. 17, 19). (He
says, that while living in China, "I thought that there was not so
much for me to admire in them—I was prejudiced," although
he had already first acquired his Tao-chi album at that time.)
He also knows of earlier precedents from literature for the use
of unusually applied textures, the most memorable of which
come from the 8th to 9th centuries. Although no works survive
to provide a visual record, Chu Ching-hsüan of the mid-9th
century described how Wang Hsia (or Wang Mo), would get
"sufficiently" drunk and then "spatter the ink onto the painting
surface…stamp on it with his feet and smear it with his
hands."[4] Wang Hsia's near contemporary, Master Ku (possibly
Ku K'uang), used to pour his ink onto the surface, cover it with
a cloth and have someone sit on the cloth while he pulled it
around and around, before adding descriptive brushwork to
the pools of ink. Others would spit the ink on from their
mouths or apply it with their hair, but these were eccentrics
whose influence extended no farther than to other eccentrics.
Kuo Hsi, a famous court painter of the 11th century, used to
draw inspiration from the irregular surfaces of plastered walls
he painted, urging that the plaster be made rougher still, but
this too was exceptional, if not eccentric.

Regardless of these few notable precedents, they were not
direct sources of inspiration for C. C. Wang. Nor, according to
the artist, were some of the other contemporary sources that
have been suggested: not the Action Painters of the 1950s and
early 1960s, who were part of C. C. Wang's environment in
New York but whom he says had no direct impact on him, nor
some other "expatriate" Chinese painters who embarked on a
course similar to Wang's own and of whom he was well aware.
Rather, he locates his inspiration in chance discoveries and
experiments, particularly in his own works using Western
watercolor paper. But watercolor paper itself has no intrinsic
value, and without their having some signfcance in his value
system Wang would never have pursued these chance effects
through two decades of his work. The role of applied texture in
his value system has nothing to do with paper *per se,* the
immediate trigger, but with C. C. Wang's basic concepts of
brushwork and naturalness, which are as essentially Chinese as
they are original to C. C. Wang.

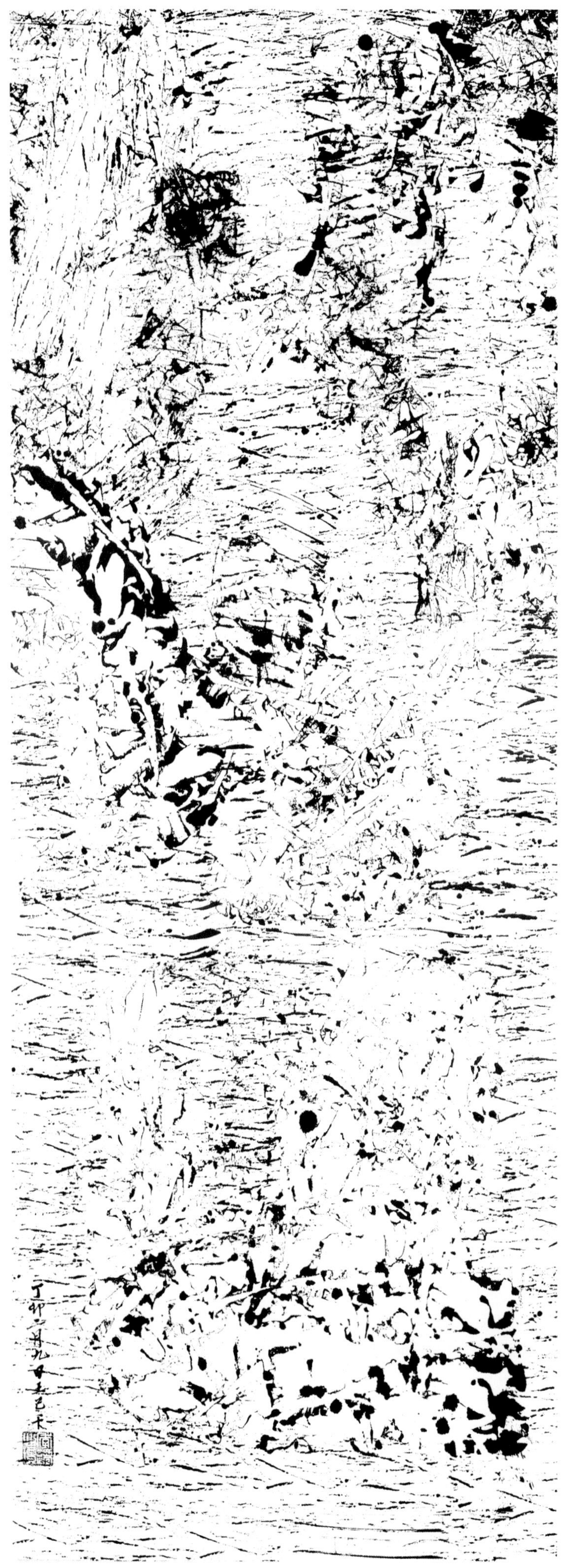

14

Landscape No. 970. 9 February 1987. Hanging scroll,
ink on paper. 48⅜ x 18⅛ in (122 x 46 cm).
Collection of Jean and Sun-chang Lo.

Inscribed
"*Ting-mao* [1987], 2nd month, 9th day. Wang Chi-ch'ien."

Artist's Seals
Chi-ch'ien hsin-ching (lower left)

4. In Shujiro Shimada, "Concerning the *I-p'in* Style
of Painting part 1," J. Cahill, trans., *Oriental Art* N.S. 7,
no. 2 (Summer, 1961), p. 68.

15

Landscape No. 170. April 1972. Hanging scroll, ink and color on paper. 22¹⁄₁₆ x 28⅛ in (56.1 x 71.5 cm). Collection of Mr. James Stark.

Inscribed
"*Jen-tzu* [1972], 4th month. Wang Chi-ch'ien."

Artist's Seals
Wang Chi-ch'ien hsi (right); *Ch'ung-shu niao-chi* (no. 31, lower left)

Exhibited
Fogg Art Museum, 1973; Brooklyn Museum, 1977

Published
Katz and Wang, no. 26

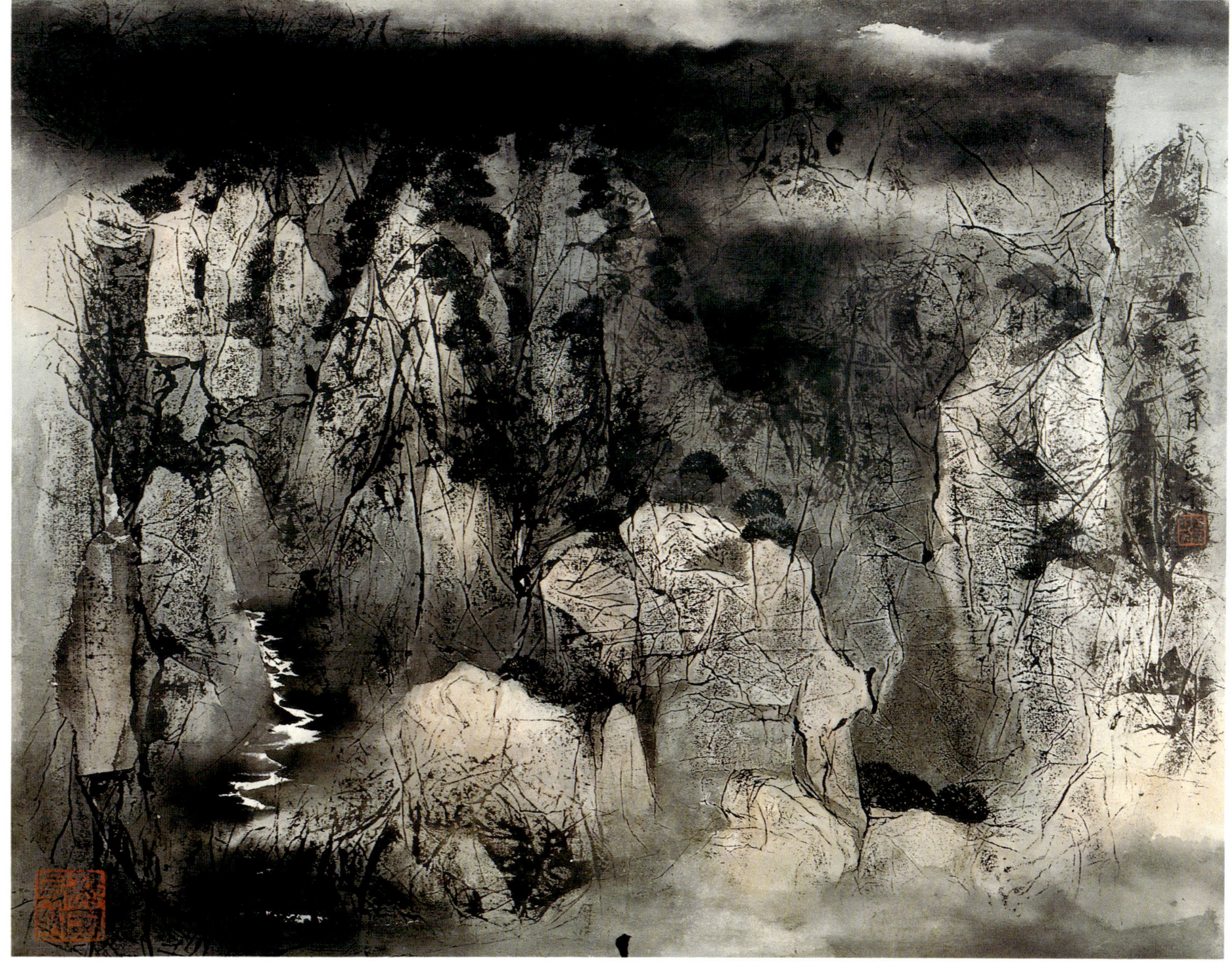

C. C. Wang does not use impressed textures in all of his
paintings, but by his own estimation only about half of the time
(figs. 13, 18, 33, 38, 53, 55, 75, for example, do not have it).
Moreover, textures played a *dominant* role in his paintings only
in the first few years of their use (e.g., figs. 38, 40, 41, 42),
and by the early 1970s they had become considerably toned
down and better integrated into his system of brushwork
(e.g., figs. 44, 45, 46). The reason for this, of which the artist is
quite conscious, derives from a tension within his values, an
ambivalent feeling toward texturing as a technique. On the one
hand, he regards it as more natural than brushwork, while on
the other he is wary of its potential to become a mere gimmick,
a substitute for the basic skills and techniques of the painter (as
it did for so many Action Painters seeking recognizable and
readily marketable "signatures"). Alert to this potential danger,
C. C. Wang avoids becoming dependent on his applied
textures:

*I try not to use texture, artificial texture and nothing more, because
I want to put more of my personal emotion, my personal feelings into
my paintings. I rely only partly on accident, because if I have nothing
but accident, of course, this is sometimes too easy—too shallow and
not deep enough. So I go back and forth.*

The chronology of his paintings reveals his rapid withdrawal
from the use of impressed and folded textures in a manner that
dominated his paintings (as in figs. 40-43) and his movement
toward an increasingly skillful integration of applied texture
with traditional brushwork, making his texture seem ever more
like the brushwork while altering his brushwork to blend with
applied textures (e.g., figs. 46, 50, 58). In many of his later
paintings (e.g., figs. 21, 52, 68), the artist himself can scarcely
distinguish lines of applied texture from brush-produced
textures. C. C. Wang is quite right, in recent times, in referring
to his accidental textures as "*controlled* accidents." Of no painting
is this more true than his recent, heavily textured *Landscape No.
970* (fig. 14).

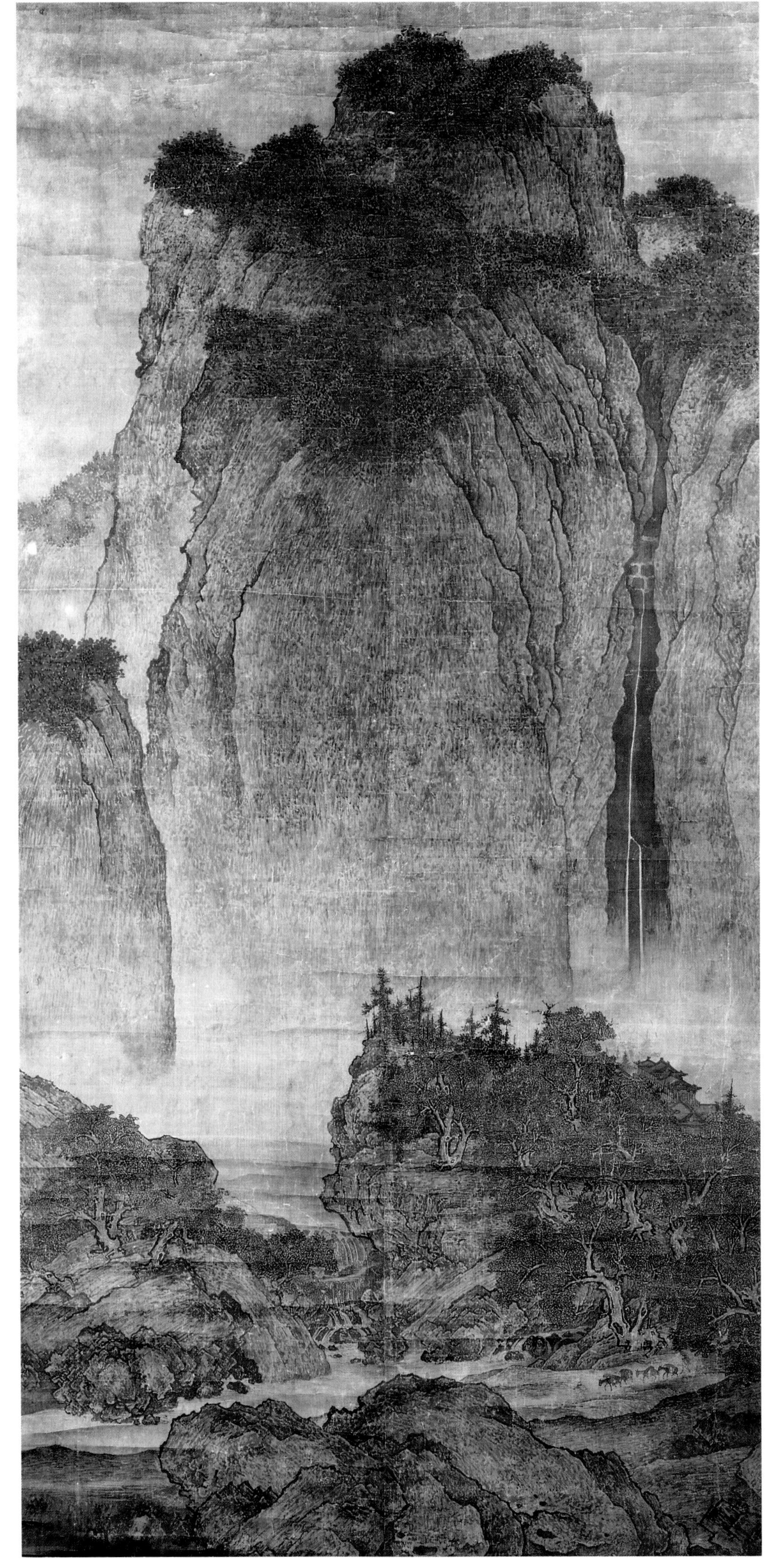

16

Composition

Whatever else they may have contributed to his painting style, C. C. Wang's visually suggestive textures, applied before the use of brushwork, broke his dependence on the limited vocabulary of compositional structures that had dominated his paintings from his earliest years of training. At the same time, after years of working with this technique, he has come to develop significant artistic control over the placement of these textures and regulate their influence on his compositions, so while some writers have simply referred to C. C. Wang's texture as "accidental patterns," James Cahill has perceptively chosen to designate them as "semi-random configurations."

The theme of synthesis and unresolved tensions may easily be followed into the area of composition, with a shift in balance now to the importance of composition rather than to its unimportance. In one of his musical analogies, C. C. Wang says,

In jazz music, you don't have to know what the singer is singing about. Good brushwork is so beautiful it can make you look at it many times, like a good voice. When you hear singing, do you expect the singing to have a good story? It doesn't have to. But I do both—I try to have good brushwork and good texture, but I also try to put some meaning into my composition. I could leave out composition, but then my paintings would seem a little empty.

Wang appreciates why the finest brush painters, like jazz singers, need no lyrics (a parallel between Ni Tsan and Ella Fitzgerald readily comes to mind); but his comments on Ni Tsan reveal why he feels that his own art cannot be so liberated, though he perhaps would like it to be otherwise:

I think Ni Tsan is superb. He's first rate. His brushwork and his simplicity are so sensible. Even if I imitate his simplicity, my brush doesn't sing with as good a voice as Ni Tsan's had. I can't focus on all aspects of painting equally, so since I don't have a voice like Ni Tsan, since my talent is not equal to his, I emphasize something else, which is composition. It's just like when you sing a song that's good but not superb, you have to depend on something else, on the composition, on the story, on the acting, everything, to make it into fine music.

Whether or not this self-effacing evaluation of his brushwork accounts adequately for C. C. Wang's emphasis on composition, it is the strength of his landscape compositions that Western audiences find most compelling about his painting. The brush-oriented literati painters of the Yüan like Ni Tsan, whom he appreciates most of all, were not the ones to provide a model for such compositions. Instead, his grandest compositions owe much of their inspiration to painters of the Northern Sung period, when a sense of vast space and attention to structural coherence still prevailed, not yet swept away by the literati preference for abstraction.

Late Chinese art is not skillful enough. Things went bad after Tung Ch'i-ch'ang, because so many of those who called themselves literati painters only played with the brush. I feel that the old masters' compositions were really not very well constructed, except for those by Sung artists. After Sung, their paintings placed too much emphasis on the brush-voice, and they didn't care for the story, the narrative, the composition. They thought that if the voice is so good—like Caruso's voice was so good—they didn't even have to pay attention to the song itself. I have tried to develop Yüan-type brushwork and combine it with the Northern Sung concept of composition, although I put less emphasis on Northern Sung. I think Ni Tsan is too simple, so I make him more complicated to give people something more to see. Ni Tsan's quality is good, but still I can play with him. His brushwork is better than mine, of course, but his compositions aren't so attractive.

C. C. Wang's paintings, then, offer a synthesis of Yüan brushwork and composition from the Five Dynasties–Northern Sung period. Among the Five Dynasties–Sung artists who most inspired his compositions are Tung Yüan (fig. 9) and Fan K'uan. Wang was first able to view Fan K'uan's famous *Travelers Among Streams and Mountains* (fig. 16), from the old Imperial Palace collection, in 1935-36. But Fan's only surviving work, one of the grandest of all Chinese landscape compositions, had little apparent influence on his style until the early 1960s when he began to change his style (by which time he had seen the Fan K'uan painting several times more). "The modern sense," he says, "came together with a feeling for monumentality." In using Fan K'uan, it was necessary to extract Fan's feeling for space from his brushwork (which "shows off too much") in order to achieve a viable model.

Fan K'uan had the best of Sung composition and the most skilled brushwork in the Sung. But Fan K'uan's brushwork was still descriptive, and every time he added a dot, it was still intended to create a landscape. When Ni Tsan drew a line, of course he wanted it to make a rock, but to him the rock was less important and the line itself was more important. Combining Ni Tsan with Fan K'uan—that is my purpose.

Of later Chinese landscape painters, only Chu Ta strikes
C. C. Wang as compositionally "logical" or as offering him a
logical basis on which to model his own compositions
(compare fig. 17 by Chu Ta and figs. 18, 33, 51, 53, and 75 by
C. C. Wang), while only Kung Hsien's compositions offered
something of the Sung masters' monumental scale and
dramatic spatial conception (compare fig. 6 by Kung Hsien
with Wang's figs. 58 and 68.)

   C. C. Wang also emphasizes the significance of Western
influence with regard to logical perspective and grand scale in
his compositions, and its role in turning his attention to the
naturalism of earlier Chinese (Sung) painting models:

*Later painters weren't knowledgeable; they didn't know that large trees
will make a mountain look small. They just piled up what they learned
from the Four Masters. They tried to make the viewer look here, and
then look there, and make them feel like flying over the mountains. This
is because they didn't know perspective. My scale is modern scale.
I look from one point of view. I have the feeling that in the logic of
landscape composition, I'm sometimes better than the old masters. Maybe
this is due to influence from Western art—maybe, I don't know. Even
now my paintings don't have Western perspective, but I have a sense like
Cézanne had, and even with no true perspective I still have a sense of
proportion, some logical basis on which to build form.*

Yet even without his use of a truly "Western" perspective, by
which he means the one-point perspective that few European
or American painters actually used, Wang is often likely to
stress that his years of study at the Art Students League were
essential to the development of his compositional skills.

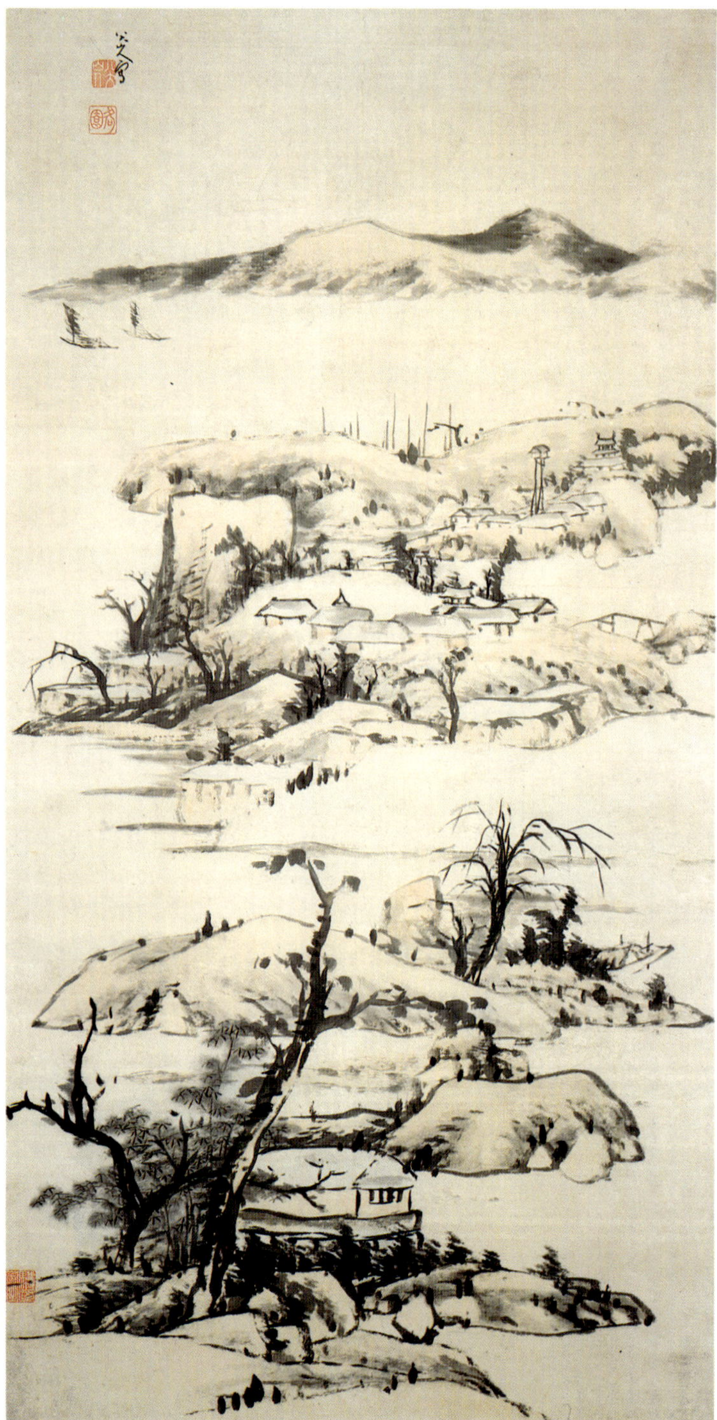

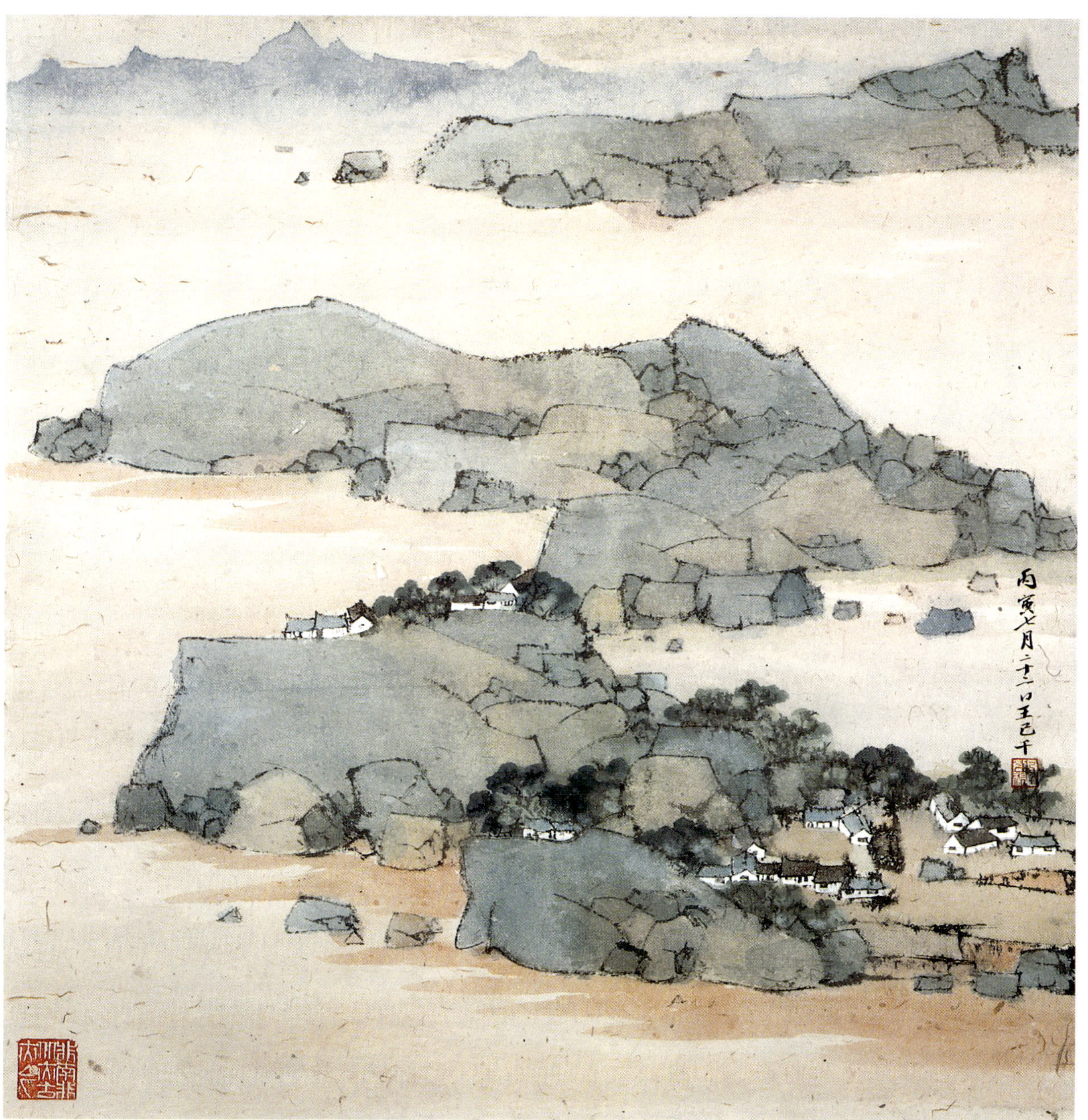

Despite the naturalistic aspects of his compositional style, they are not what C. C. Wang considers central to his compositions, basic to his notion of "modern," or even the primary benefit of his study of Western painting. What he finds compellingly *natural* about Western painting is not its visual *naturalism,* which so many 20th-century painters have already relinquished, but relates instead to *human nature,* self-expression, and the free expression of one's *artistic* nature—as expressed in his seal, "Obtained from beyond the realm of appearances." Wang sees himself as a formalist, like his favorite Western painters, concerned not with accurate narration but with abstract pattern and the pursuit of subjective ideals of beauty.

When I paint, it's just like a ceramicist making a vase. In my painting, I don't make a vase for flowers, I make a vase for its own shape. If I were to design a table, I'd want to create a table like you never have seen before, a new kind of table; the point is, whether you use this as a table or not, my purpose is to give the table a feeling of beauty. Beauty is my main theme. I think you should eliminate as much as you can of the likeness, but you should use the painting to represent the beauty.

The Chinese paintings that C. C. Wang collects and studies have influenced the formal aspects of his paintings in a variety of ways. What Tung Yüan offered was a sense of "emphasis" and "gesture"—creating major areas of focus, setting these against minor areas, and generating a sense of compositional movement within a painting. It was from the Tung Yüan masterpiece *Thatched Hut by a Riverbank* (fig. 9), acquired shortly before the "modernization" of his style, that C. C. Wang claims to have "learned that Northern Sung paintings are so well constructed." Later artists such as Ni Tsan (fig. 5) and Tao-chi (figs. 11, 19), he says, lacked this idea of focus and gesture, particularly in their large paintings, and Tung Ch'i-ch'ang (fig. 10) had it only in isolated elements. Wang Yüan-ch'i alone (fig. 23) was able to instill an entire painting with the sense of gesture and movement. From Wang Yüan-ch'i, he also discovered ways in which to achieve variety of form: "In Wang Yüan-ch'i, in one picture you never find the same rock repeated. In any one picture, each one is a little longer, a little shorter, than the others, always with changes."

Although acknowledging that his landscapes occasionally reflect something of his world travels to places as far apart as Switzerland (figs. 49, 69), Yellowstone Park (fig. 50), or Yosemite (fig. 68), he says,

I will never do a painting like a real landscape, because it's too close to being a photograph. I don't care for that. I don't want that. I can paint a painting like a photograph, with clouds and beautiful scenery, but I think that's not my purpose. My purpose is more to build form rather than just depict pretty scenery. Form is more important. Scenery is telling stories; I don't tell stories. I think beauty is the form itself, it's the shape. I want to build mountains. If I wanted to tell you a story, the mountain would really show the clouds or show the sunshine. But instead I want it to show my feelings, and you can only see the feeling in my heart through my paintings. I never use subject matter to describe things, because I'm not an illustrative painter. I paint for myself, definitely for myself. You can share it with me if you can understand what I am feeling.

Accordingly, as a connoisseur and collector, he now looks with disinterest on Wang Hui, the first painter he studied in depth, because of Wang Hui's strongly narrative approach, which he contrasts with the purely formalistic art of Wang Yüan-ch'i.

Yet natural subject matter is of deep value to C. C. Wang as a vehicle for the expression of beauty—the ideal vehicle, he feels, because nature itself is so beautiful: "I paint landscapes with my own ideas, borrowing something from the real landscape, combining my ideas with nature. But we got our idea of beauty from nature, and how can we surpass it with our own beauty?" By beauty, C. C. Wang does not mean decorative beauty, which he finds unnatural and which lies at the heart of his rejection of some of the basic tenets of the Japanese visual aesthetic. Instead, he has in mind what might be described as a more subtle "inner beauty" or the manifestation of an "inner essence," best pursued through careful selection and reduction.

Good painting, like a novel, should be very plain, subtle, and very deep. Not exciting—like Hung-lou meng *[China's most famous novel, Dream of the Red Chamber]. The highest Chinese art is just the same, with no movement. Ni Tsan's painting has no movement, just like a carved piece of sculpture with no movement. I prefer meditation more than action. A painting is most beautiful when it is quiet.*

As such, he finds it necessary to simplify or limit his landscape subject matter, lest nature's variety distract from the formal pursuit of his art. "In my paintings it is the rock which is the main feature, that is, the monumentality of the rock, the movement of the underlying structure, the formation of the rock and the color of the rock. It is the rock which creates the movement and the mood."[5] He elaborates on this, saying:

I'm always limited to rocky mountains, to the natural texture of mountains. I don't want to paint dogs or other animals, horses or cats, nor to be purely abstract. I think these would all waste too much of my time. I just want to show you mountains only. If I wanted trees, I'd have trees all over. I want one subject matter. I don't want to have everything. Figures walking and so forth—I don't need that.

Landscapes, he feels, more than figures or any other subject, offer him the freedom to express himself artistically.

I love exaggeration. The figure has so much variety in its movement, which is why in the West they use the human figure and twist it around. Picasso uses heads like I use rocks. He wants to turn the face, but then he makes the face so that it doesn't really look like a face, which seems irritating to me. But because I use landscapes, I can twist things around any way and nobody bothers me, because originally the objects really could be this way. Matisse and Picasso chose figures just as I choose mountains. The beauty in my painting could be borrowed from anywhere, but some subjects give me a greater sense of beauty, some give me less. I can see furniture and be inspired to paint a landscape

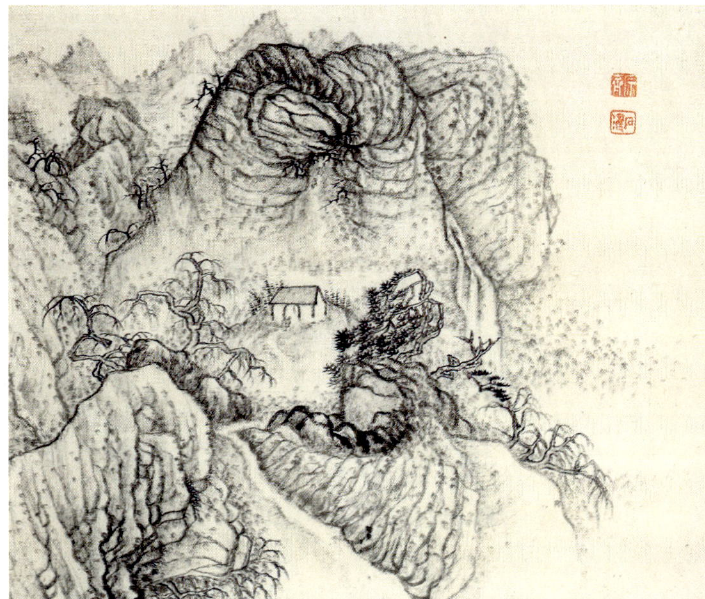

19

Tao-chi (1642-c. 1707), "Hut at the Foot of Mountains," from *Album for Taoist Yü.* c. 1695. 9½ x 11 in (24.1 x 27.9 cm). C. C. Wang Family Collection.

20

Landscape No. 888. 14 December 1985. Hanging scroll, ink on paper. 38¼ x 25 in (97.2 x 63.5 cm). C. C. Wang Family Collection.

Inscribed
I-ch'ou [1985], 12th month, 14th day. Written by Wang Chi-ch'ien in San Francisco.

Artist's Seal
Chi-ch'ien ch'uang-kao (lower left)

Exhibited
Hong Kong Arts Centre, 1986; Birmingham Museum of Art, 1987

5. Lois Katz and C. C. Wang, *The Landscapes of C. C. Wang: Mountains of the Mind* (New York: AMS Foundation, 1977), pp. 10-11.

6. Ibid., p. 10.

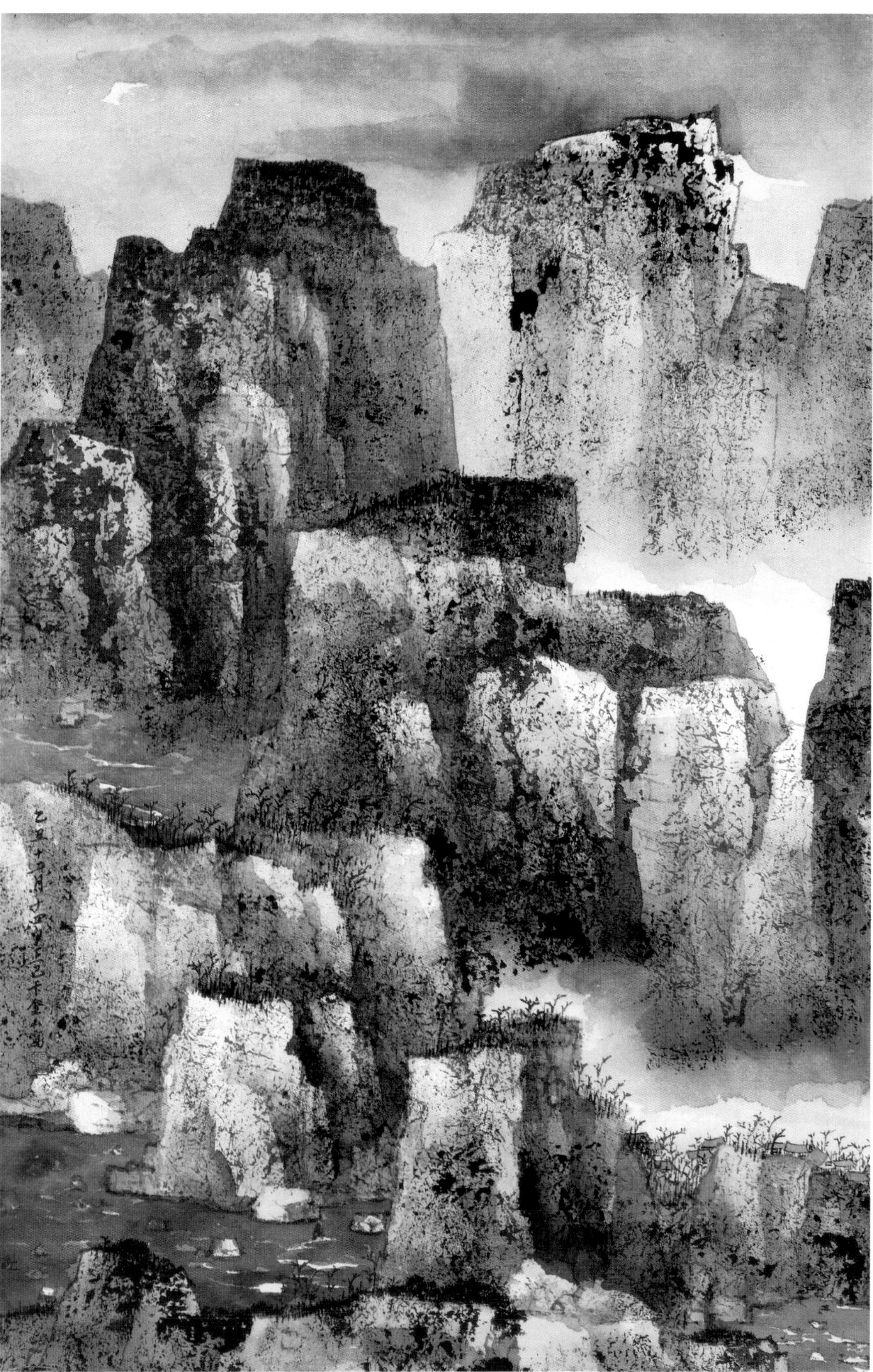

painting. Whenever I feel beauty, it stimulates me. But I am far from figure painting, because figure painting to me is a limitation. Yet if I wanted to paint figures, I would prefer to be like Matisse, to exaggerate and make things simple. Or like Modigliani. I don't want to be realistic.

Placing this more in a Chinese context, he comments,

Chinese love strange forms, but not too many people can make strange forms. After the Yüan masters, they became so tight they didn't know how to exaggerate. Tao-chi knew and Chu Ta knew, which is why people appreciate them so much. But of the Four Wangs, only Wang Yüan-ch'i knew, and he exaggerated only the component parts so that you almost can't recognize it. Tao-chi and Wang Yüan-ch'i were both great at this, but Wang Yüan-ch'i just played inside, with the details, while Tao-chi played inside and outside too.

As a landscape "purist," C. C. Wang has eliminated from his paintings the scholarly inscriptions that were traditional in literati landscape paintings and common in his own early works, lest they distract from the abstract virtues of his composition. Usually, only a date and a signature are included. "I don't mix calligraphy with painting…. I never put any poems on my paintings. I don't leave any space for writing. I just see the painted image as a picture, like the painters of the Northern Sung period did."[6] Also eliminated are titles, with a few exceptions such as *Landscape No. 240: The Spring of the Immortals* (fig. 44), *No. 510: Heavenly Lake* (fig. 69), and *No. 881: Clearing After Snow on the Nine Peaks* (fig. 73). Normally, only when obliged to has he given titles to his paintings, after the fact, as for the first book on his painting in 1970: "For instance, if some painting looked a little dark, I might name it *Yü-lai*, which means 'The rain will come soon from the mountains.' It might have really looked true to this title, but when I painted it I had no idea what the mountains were going to do."

Color

In color, as in brushwork and composition, it is naïveté that the artist values most. Although when he first transformed his style in the mid-1960s his use of color was not drastically affected (figs. 39, 40), bold colors or color combinations have become an increasingly prominent aspect of his style in the past fifteen years (figs. 13, 21, 22, 49, 53, 56, 57, 67). This, he says, was primarily influenced by European and American artists, by Gauguin and van Gogh, Modigliani and Klee, and by contemporary artists as well, including fellow painters in the Art Students League whose names he never knew. The use of colors in Chinese literati landscape painting might also, in most cases, be regarded as "naïve." But Chinese paintings on paper relied on pale applications of water-based natural pigments, which played a relatively minor role in painting, however sensitively they may sometimes have been selected and applied (see some of Wang's own more traditionally colored works, figs. 4, 18, 60, 75); only the colors of Wang Yüan-ch'i (fig. 23), rich and woven into complex color layers, were an adequate model for study.

Today, in order to obtain stronger effects, C. C. Wang often uses Western gouache or casein pigments interchangeably with Chinese pigments—the latter usually limited to indigo or *hua-ch'ing,* which he always mixes with ink; rattan yellow or *t'eng-huang;* cochineal or *yen-chih;* carmine or *yang-hung;* green, mixed from indigo and rattan yellow; shell white; and yellow ochre or *che-shih.* Following Western predilections, he more strongly integrates his color patterns with his compositions than traditional literati artists did, but—like both his traditional Chinese and his favorite Western sources—he rarely models his forms naturalistically through the use of graded shades of color.

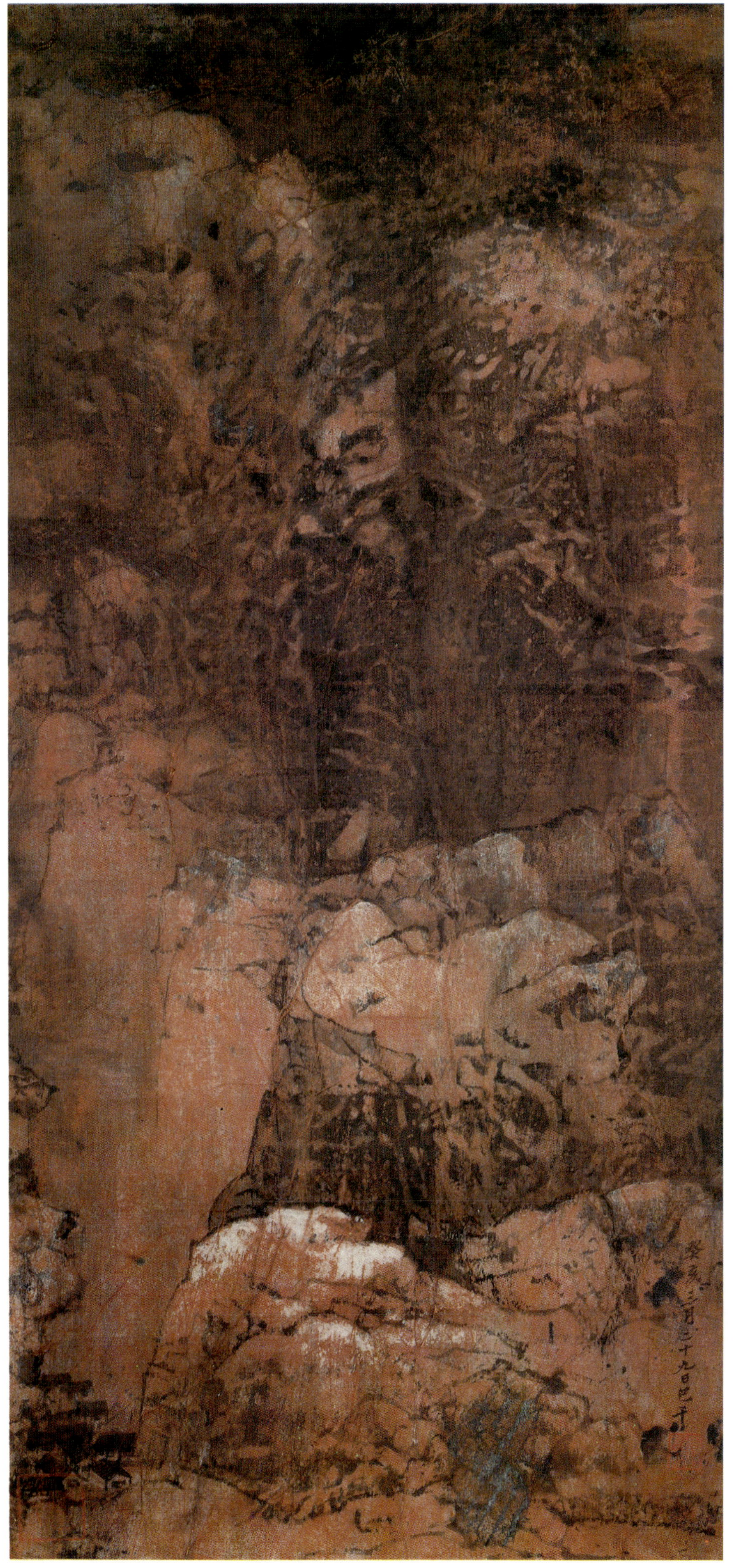

21

Landscape No. 466. 29 March 1983. Hanging scroll,
ink and color on paper. 27 x 13⅛ in (68.6 x 33.3 cm).
Collection of Joan Stanley-Baker.

Inscribed
"*Kuei-hai* [1983], 3rd month, 29th day. Chi-ch'ien."

Artist's Seals
Chi-ch'ien ch'uang-kao (lower right); *Wen-ko Kung hou-jen*
(lower left)

Exhibited
Hong Kong Arts Centre, 1986

Published
Stanley-Baker, "Closed Cycle," p. 26; Cahill et al., no. 14

22

Landscape No. 397. August 1981. Hanging scroll, ink
and color on paper. 24 x 34 in (61.0 x 86.4 cm).
Private Collection.

Inscribed
"*Hsin-yu* [1981], 8th month. Chi-ch'ien."

Artist's Seal
Wang Chi-ch'ien hsi (lower center)

Exhibited
Taipei Fine Arts Museum, 1984; Hong Kong Arts
Centre, 1985; Hong Kong Arts Centre, 1986;
Birmingham Museum of Art, 1987

Published
Cahill et al., no. 9

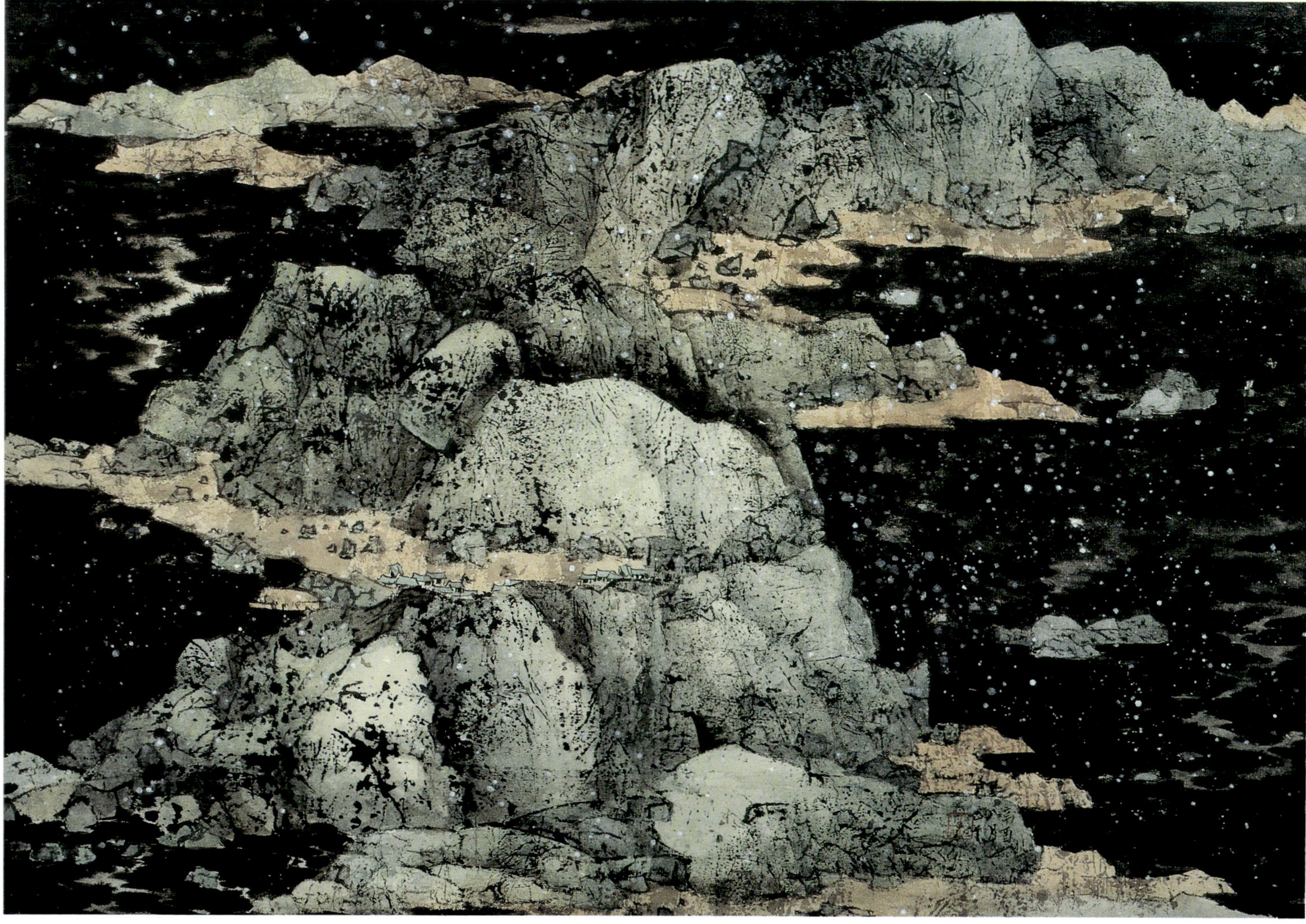

Values, East and West

The naïve quality that he seeks in his paintings, both in his colors and his compositions, he regards as the highest expression of artistic creativity:

The quality of naïveté gives you more than nature does, more than what you can see. Actually, there is naïveté in nature, too, but the naïve quality is inside of nature. I learn from children. When I draw a house, even if this doesn't represent an actual house, still it is a house. When children draw a house, or when Grandma Moses draws a house, it doesn't look like a house but it is a house, and I think that at that stage it's even better than nature. This creates nature. It's scenery that differs from nature but that has it's own nature. It doesn't borrow too much, and with a very little bit drawn from nature it creates another piece of nature but of a kind you cannot find in nature—this, I think, has reached the limit of beauty. I cannot be this primitive because I've already learned too much. But I prefer this type as the highest in art. I cannot [go back to the primitive], but if I could I would be even better.... This uses a piece of nature to build an alternative nature.

C. C. Wang's appreciation of youthful naturalness is expressed in a seal that reads, "Heart of a child, unobscured." It is this naïveté that he regards as the most important common ground between Chinese art and modern Western painting (and other arts as well, such as African and Pre-Columbian sculpture, of which he is very fond.)

Wang Yüan-ch'i is an educated Grandma Moses. I think Grandma Moses is greater than Dali and all those people. Dali is so artificial. Grandma Moses is entirely natural, so much higher than him. This kind of naturalness cannot be done except by instinct. Dali is conceptual only. I can copy Dali exactly, but not Grandma Moses. She is like Tung Ch'i-ch'ang and Wang Yüan-ch'i in Chinese painting. Wang Yüan-ch'i is an educated Grandma Moses. He trained himself to achieve a very skillful period and then to go back to naturalness. That's why he's great, I think. He's really great. Like Gauguin, and van Gogh also.

In his own highly personal, unorthodox view, he feels that the aesthetic relationship between artists like Wang Yüan-ch'i (fig. 23) or Tung Ch'i-ch'ang (fig. 10) and Western painters is more than merely coincidental and has a significant historical basis. It is a relationship which may best explain his own affinity for modern Western art.

The modern sense comes from Chinese art—through Japanese art, because Japanese art comes from China. "Modern" is an improvement of the Chinese sense. Braque, Gauguin—I think they were very Oriental. They developed from the Chinese root of things. They got it from Japan, but Japan's root is in China. They got the idea of geting rid of shadows and not concentrating very much on emotional expression. They liked pattern, design, and color. Actually, Chinese pattern and brushwork are like a river, one of the rivers of modern art, that comes from China. I think we Chinese can now use what they achieved with this.

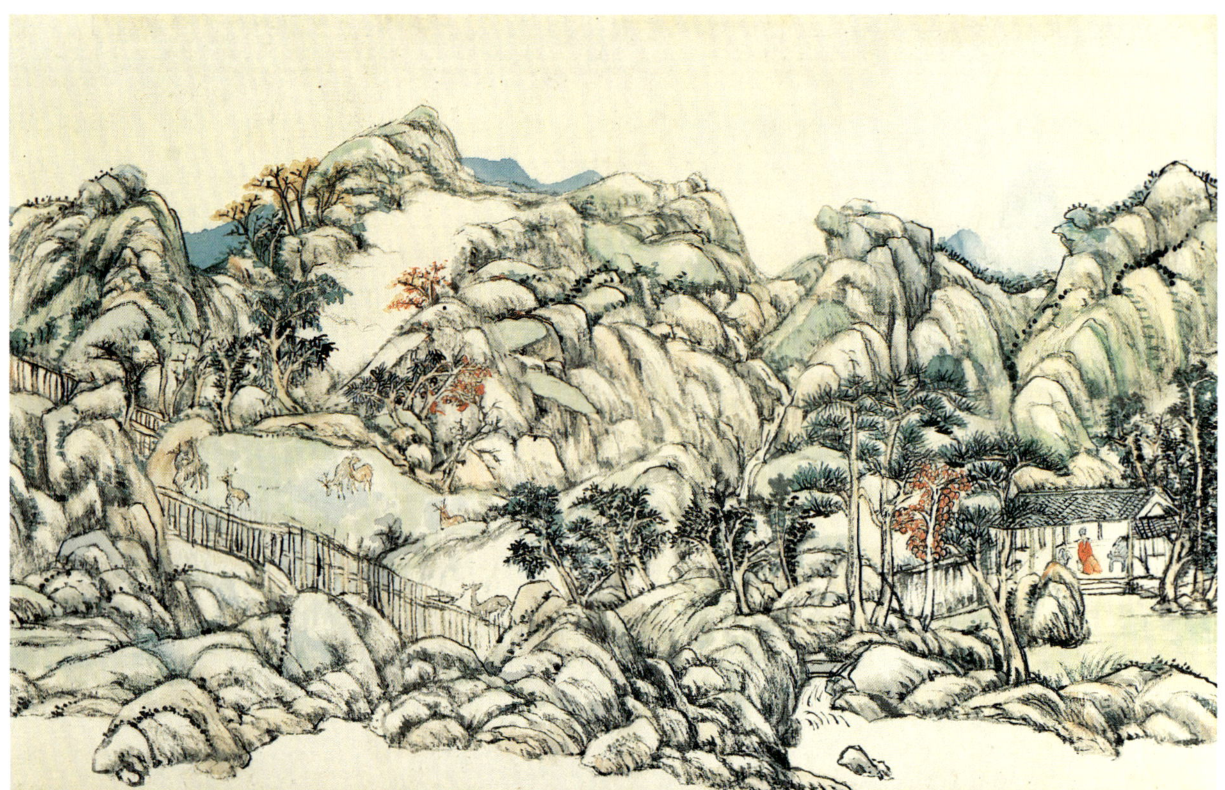

23

Wang Yüan-ch'i (1642-1715), The Wang River Villa (section). 1711. Handscroll, ink and colors on paper. 14¹⁄₁₆ x 214⅝ in (35.7 x 545.1 cm). The Metropolitan Museum of Art, Gift of Douglas Dillon Fund, 1977. (Formerly in the C. C. Wang Family Collection).

If he is correct, then C. C. Wang's own painting represents the closing of an historical circle of interrelatedness between Oriental and Western art.

But the Orient and the West are not equal in C. C. Wang. He is not a Western painter who came from China, nor simply a "Chinese-American painter." He remains not only Chinese but particularly traditional in his values. His statement that while "the painting I do now doesn't look like modern Western painting, it doesn't look like traditional Chinese painting either"[7] proclaims an equal degree of independence from Chinese and Western traditions; but he also admits, "While I tried to get something from Western art, from modern art, it's only from my imagination, since I really didn't go into it too much"—not something he could assert with regard to his Chinese heritage. C. C. Wang does not stand equally far from Chinese and Western sources, nor are his goals as much Western as they are Chinese. All the modern innovations of C. C. Wang's painting have served to strengthen the Chineseness of his art, helping to preserve what he sees as the best of it: "I examine Chinese tradition to find out what is worthwhile in it to continue and what is not." Restoring the vitality of traditional Chinese painting, not rebelling against it, is his broader artistic goal, and Western art is but a means. Nor does he imagine that it could be the other way around, that he could change Western art with his Chinese art. "I don't want to be *radically* new," he says. "Americans artists want to create a place for themselves in art history. But I think that Chinese art is a local art."

His ability to make historically meaningful innovation within the smaller sphere of Chinese painting lies in large part in his traditional skills, acquired through training with teachers like Wu Hu-fan, in contrast to many of China's innovative painters who pursued Western art from the outset. Arnold Chang has pointed out that "whereas artists like Lin [Feng-mien], Liu [Hai-su], Kao [Chien-fu] and Hsü [Pei-hung] were trained primarily in Western painting and generally turned seriously to Chinese painting only relatively late in their careers, Wang was thoroughly trained and highly accomplished as a traditional painter before he absorbed any Western influences."[8] On the other hand, despite the breadth of C. C. Wang's training, whether Chinese or Western, versatility *per se* is not his greatest strength. "His strength," writes Chang, "lies in his overall development, in his progression from one style or technique to another, and in his ability to merge disparate ideas into a single, cohesive whole."[9] His success at blending East and West is but an historically fortunate by-product of his broad-ranging curiosity, of his desire to get outside of himself and learn from other artists' views of the universe. And in the last analysis, even his breadth of training and experience cannot account for the most important quality of all, without which C. C. Wang's art would remain but a dilettante's experiment, namely the profound originality of his artistic vision, of those landscapes within his mind which Tung Ch'i-ch'ang described as "a gift of nature."

The last chapter of this essay will explore those mental landscapes, C. C. Wang's own natural gifts.

7. Ibid., p. 8.

8. Arnold Chang, *Painting in the People's Republic of China: The Politics of Style* (Boulder: Westview Press, 1980), p. 39.

9. Ibid.

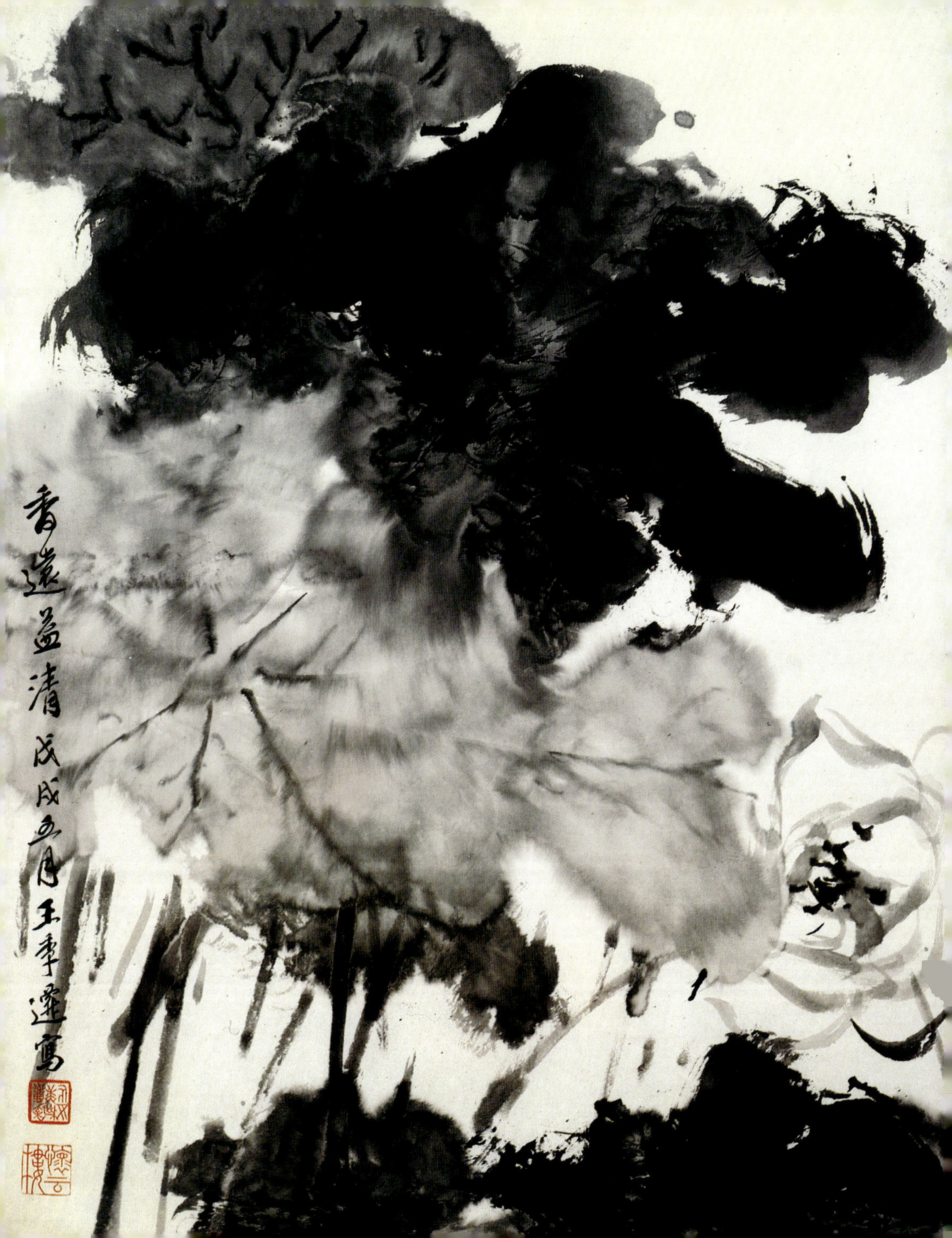

3

24

Lotus. May 1958. Hanging scroll, ink on paper. 24½ x 19½ in (62.2 x 49.5 cm).
Collection of Mr. and Mrs. Frank Cho.

Inscribed
"Distant fragrance is even more pure. *Mou-hsü* [1958], 5th month. Inscribed by Wang Chi-ch'ien."

Artist's Seals
Chi-ch'ien lü Mei chih tso (lower left, impressed upside down); *Huai-Yün Lou* (no. 9, bottom left)

Exhibited
Mi Chou Gallery, New York, 1959

Only through art can we get outside of ourselves and know another's view of the universe which is not the same as ours and see landscapes which would otherwise have remained unknown to us like the landscapes of the moon. Thanks to art, instead of seeing a single world, our own, we see it multiply until we have before us as many worlds as there are original artists.

Marcel Proust

As this passage from Proust's *Maxims* suggests, the notion of mental landscapes representing imaginative inner worlds, most effectively given form by the creative artist, is hardly confined to the Chinese. For Proust, perhaps, the image is more figurative than for C. C. Wang. But for C. C. Wang, to whom landscapes literally provided the imagery through which to express himself, as for Proust, the measure of artistry lay in the originality of these images, in their distinct difference from other people's mental landscapes. The effort to create original landscapes, as unknown and compelling as the landscapes of the moon, required of C. C. Wang an entire lifetime dedicated to the art of painting.

Phase One, Earliest Works from 1932 to 1964: Chinese Traditionalism

In 1932, C. C. Wang's new teacher, Wu Hu-fan, executed for him a pair of study scrolls, prescribing some of the models and methods that the young student might follow; each scroll incorporated four Yüan styles, arranged in a four-seasons format (fig. 1 illustrates a detail of one, with the styles of Huang Kung-wang, Wu Chen, Wang Meng, and Ni Tsan, shown in the standard sequence of spring, summer, autumn, and winter from right to left). By Chinese standards, the didactic purpose of such scrolls in no way diminished their value as works of art —no more than do Bach's compositions for Anna Magdalena or Wilhelm Friedemann seem diminished to us today. Indeed, except for their inscribed dedications to the student, they might be taken as part of the normal practice of a well-established artist and even regarded as something of a tour de force. C. C. Wang's earliest surviving work, an album also painted in 1932 (figs. 2, 25) when he was twenty-five, is, like most of his early works, a study-piece couched in a variety of earlier masters' styles, including Mi Fu of the Sung, Lu Kuang of the Yüan, and Yün Shou-p'ing, Hua Yen, Wang Ch'en, and Huang Ting of the Ch'ing. The album is a more natural format for such an exercise, not requiring the skillful knitting together of different styles and seasons found in Wu Hu-fan's scrolls, and the young student's paintings are clearly less mature than his teacher's work. Some of these leaves document the kinds of paintings then available to C. C. Wang for study through the auspices of Wu Hu-fan, although a master like Mi Fu (whose authentic works no longer survive) could only have been known to him through a historical sequence of copies after copies. Not only the Mi Fu album leaf (fig. 2) but also its inscription was copied; its text suggests that the original was probably by Wang Hui, painted from his memory of a "Mi Fu" painting (itself not likely to have been authentic) in the collection of one of his teachers, Wang Shih-min or Wang Chien of T'ai-ts'ang.

Mi Fu was perhaps the first great exemplar of the painter-collector-connoisseur and a pioneer in the development of China's literati painting style, pursuing an aesthetic of simplicity and understatement and rejecting the dramatic accomplishments of recent predecessors such as Fan K'uan and Kuo Hsi. His brushwork was reduced to a system of dots and lines that closely reflected calligraphic principles, as restrained in technique and stingy as his critical judgments; but this was off-balanced by a generous use of ink that was needed to enrich the mist and clouds of his landscapes, for which he was famous. The inscription on the Mi Fu leaf of this album (fig. 2) reads: "Mi Hai-yüeh worshipped clouds and mist. This is a copy from memory of part of a painting now in the collection of Mr. Wang of T'ai-ts'ang. But I haven't captured one ten-thousandth of the original." What C. C. Wang, like his immediate predecessor, *has* captured are a number of the essentials of Mi Fu's standardized image: the reductionist brushwork, limited to a lattice of primarily horizontal and secondarily vertical hatching strokes laid over areas of pale wash; the use of sleek, moist black ink; the standardized Mi Fu compositional format—rounded spits of land leading backward from a triangular apex over a

low ground plane to a vertical screen of conical mountains
at the rear, with a dark grove of trees toward the front and a
sprinkling of domestic buildings providing visual accents; and
of course the spared out areas representing clouds and mist,
contrasted with the richness of ink, breaking up the landscape
design into a series of horizontal bands. What Wu Hu-fan
would have found promising in such a painting would less
likely be found in compositional aspects than in the individual
brushstrokes: well-rounded, weighty, firmly placed, and
executed with obvious artistic self-assurance.

The other leaf in this album which is done after an "early"
(pre-Ming) master imitates Lu Kuang of the late Yüan period
(fig. 25), and its basis in Lu Kuang's style can be measured by
Lu's *Spring Dawn at the Cinnabar Terrace,* formerly in C. C.
Wang's collection.[1] As these album leaves show, the young
artist's selection of study models provided him an opportunity
to achieve and demonstrate versatility. In contrast to Mi Fu's
repetitively arched forms, Lu's forms alternate between
irregularly rounded earthen slopes and flat-topped plateaus;
Mi Fu's forms are set on a stable ground plane, while Lu's shift
and tilt, first one way then the other; Mi's landscape elements
are clearly separated into middle ground and background
distances, while the recession of Lu's mountains link these
distances in a more dynamic visual pattern. Lu's brushwork
also contrasts sharply with that of Mi Fu: whereas Mi Fu's
brushwork was well rounded, his brush held upright, his
strokes distinct, and his ink moist, Lu Kuang shared the late
Yüan preference for dry, scratchy brushwork done with
sweeping strokes on the side of a slanted brush, masking the
individuality of brushstrokes—a technique closely related to
that of his contemporary Ni Tsan (fig. 5), who ultimately
became C. C. Wang's favorite model.

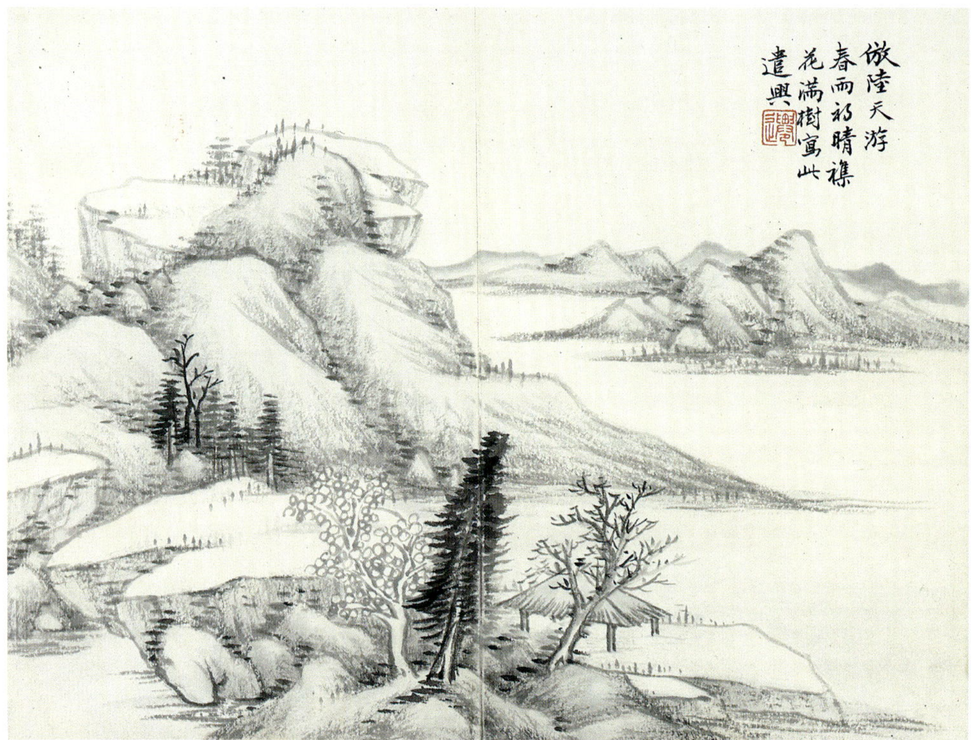

25

Landscape After Lu Kuang, from *Ink-play by Shuang-wu.* 1932. Album leaf, ink on paper. 6⅛ x 9¹⁄₁₆ in (15.5 x 23 cm).
Collection of Mr. Chen-hua Lee.

Inscribed
"Imitating Lu T'ien-yu [Lu Kuang]. Clearing after a fine spring rain; trees filled with heaps of flowers. Drawn at leisure."

Artist's Seal
Ch'ien (upper right; not illustrated)

26

Landscape after Wang Shih-min. mid-1930s. Hanging scroll, ink on paper. 37⅜ x 17⅞ in (95 x 45.4 cm).
Collection of Brad Davis and Janis Provisor.

Inscribed
"This is a copy of Yen-k'o's [Wang Shih-min's] imitation of the brush-manner of Ta-ch'ih [Huang Kung-wang]. For my colleague [in art, Hsü] Pang-ta, to correct. Written by Wang Chi-ch'ien of Mo-li."

Artist's Seal
Hsüan-ch'ing ("Selected Youth," not illustrated, upper right)

Additional Inscription
"Nan-ch'uan [unidentified] asked for a painting by [Wang] Chi-ch'ien but didn't get one, so I got this scroll to give him, which should satisfy his appreciation [of Wang's paintings]. Recorded by [Hsü] Pang-ta at the Distant Heart Thatched Hall, in the summer of the year *K'uei-wei* [1943]."

Additional Seals
Fou-yin (right, above); *Hsü Pang-ta* (right, below)

1.   This work is illustrated in Richard Barnhart, *Along the Border of Heaven: Sung and Yüan Paintings from the C. C. Wang Family Collection* (New York: Metropolitan Museum of Art, 1983), fig. 68.

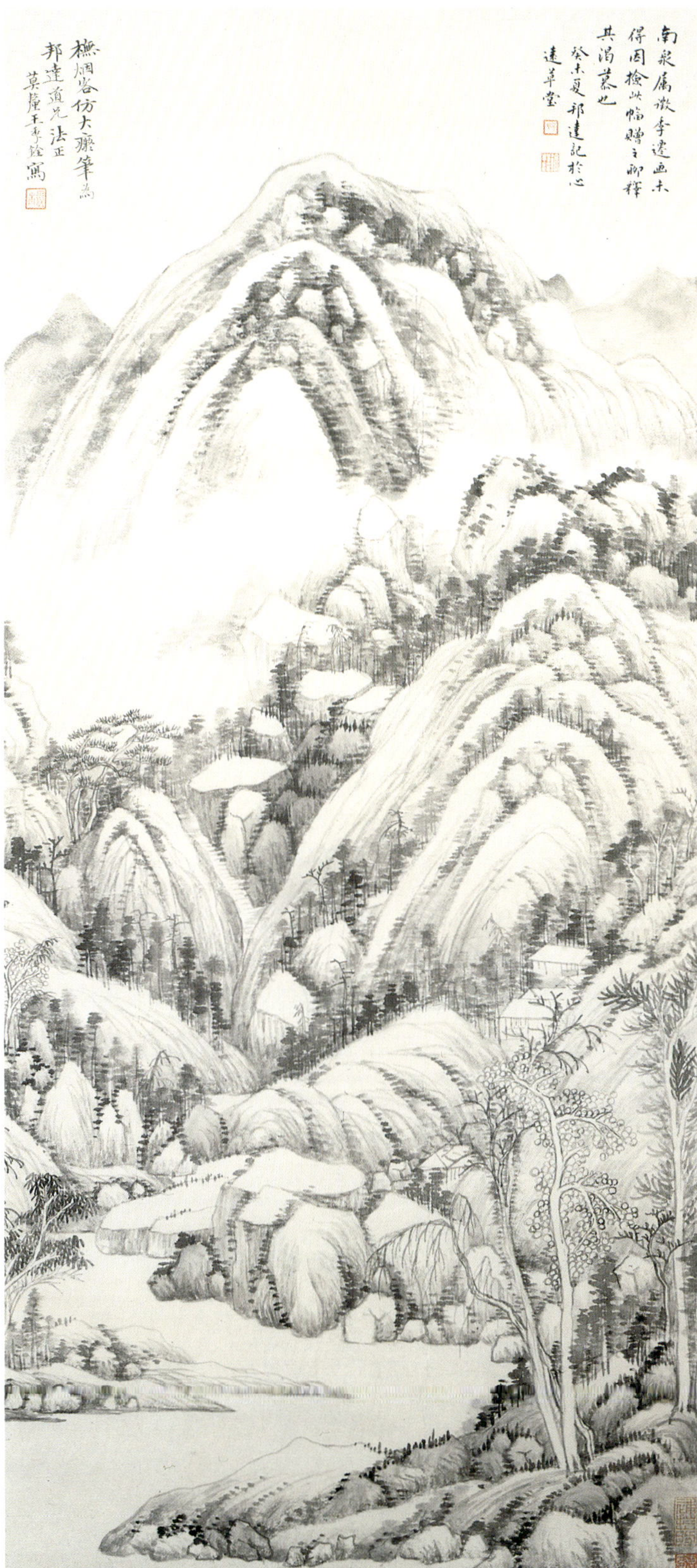

C. C. Wang, like most Chinese artists, did not always place the highest premium on originality, as his early works show. To "create one's own school," as Chinese critics put it, was certainly not expected of the young artist, not in a traditional, gerontocratic society, where the role of the young was to model themselves obediently on the patterns set down by elders. Even the mature artist, if not much of an original composer, might establish a reputation as an outstanding performer, as a practitioner of standardized traditional styles. Such was the case with Wang Shih-min, whose works were mostly based on earlier paintings and who relied on the formulaic methods of his immediate master, Tung Ch'i-ch'ang, in his reduction of past masters' styles to conventionalized brush and compositional routines. It is a formulaic Wang Shih-min painting done in imitation of the manner of Huang Kung-wang that C. C. Wang himself has copied in figure 26. Wang's own modern copy is so close and effective that when recently shown a poor reproduction of it, he replied, "This looks like Wang Shih-min," not realizing at first that it might be his own work. And then with a touch of recognition, "Is *that* Wang Shih-min?" The painting is undated, but it was painted and dedicated in the 1930s to his fellow student, Hsü Pang-ta, who himself inscribed it in 1943. C. C. Wang's painting presents all the major elements of Huang Kung-wang's art as standardized by Tung Ch'i-ch'ang and Wang Shih-min (elements related to both Mi Fu's and Lu Kuang's work): the long contours of conical earthen forms, the clusters of smaller, so-called "alum" rocks paralleling these contours, the occasional flat-topped plateaus, and especially the short hatching strokes, both horizontal and vertical.

Nothing new has been contributed by the painter. But then, nothing new would have been expected by Wang's viewers in the 1930s—judgment would have been rendered on the quality of brushwork alone. Brushwork is what the painting is all about, a surface full of beautifully rounded brushstrokes that keep the viewer close to the painting, unable to see (and uninterested in seeing) whether or not the overall composition offers anything original. The composition is uninspired (a Chinese viewer would probably have already seen this composition in hundreds of other paintings), but that need not matter as long as the performer is capable of producing beautifully calligraphic lines, like a musician filling a hall with the repetitive but lovely sound of arpeggios and trills. Done in the early to mid-1930s, the painting is somewhat more mature than the album leaves of 1932 and shows considerable accomplishment at the level of brushwork. A Chinese critic might have remarked on its "softness," perhaps claiming that there "is not one harsh brushline in the painting." The tonal structure of the painting is also "soft," the lightly sketched earthen contours and the dark accents of vegetation being distributed evenly over the surface of the whole painting—again, in an undramatic but harmonious fashion.

Each of these paintings (figs. 2, 25, 26) may be said to well represent the first phase of artistic development in the career of C. C. Wang, one of four phases that will be referred to here: the first phase lasting from the artist's youth until about 1964, when he first began to change his style dramatically; the second from 1964 until about 1972, representing that striking first step; the third, lasting through the remainder of the 1970s, which first saw the maturation of his new style, was followed by a period of dormancy; and the fourth, from about 1981 until the present, which has included subsequent stages of maturation and some significant new developments. The notion of stylistic phases, so frequently employed by historians of art and literature, always threatens to be trite and, worse, to condition viewers to see an artist's career and creations as compartmentalized into separate, easily recognized niches. But, at the same time, if the admittedly artificial device will be tolerated, it highlights the different problems that an artist consciously or unconsciously faces at various times in his career. If the turning points in an artist's career are not always as time-specific as the device suggests, it is nevertheless true that an artist's focus of attention does change, that problems are solved and new ones emerge. Indeed, it is the artist's ability to recognize new problems, to take upon himself new challenges, that is indispensable to creative development. But before leaving China, C. C. Wang's artistic challenges were all of one kind: to master the brush manners and compositional types of a variety of great masters of the past.

Other paintings from this earliest phase (which continues for a full decade and a half after his immigration to America) vary primarily by the particular historical model being followed rather than by any strikingly individual departure or development on the part of the artist. Four such paintings illustrate variations of this original pursuit, done in the styles of Wang Meng (fig. 4), Wu Chen (fig. 27), Wang Fu (fig. 28), and Hsia Kuei (fig. 29). The painting after Wang Meng, an undated work from the 1940s, is as unoriginal in its composition as his copy of Wang Shih-min's imitation of Huang Kung-wang. It is indeed a literal copy of portions of two separate works by Wang Meng that were owned at the time by his friend Chang Ts'ung-yü, seaming together the bottom of one painting and the top of another, as the artist's inscription unabashedly, even proudly, acknowledges. The lower portion of the scroll is copied after a work entitled *A Quiet Life in a Wooded Glen*, dated 1361 and now in the Chicago Art Institute (fig. 5), while the upper portion comes from Wang Meng's undated *Thatched Hut in the Western Suburbs*, now in the Palace Museum in Peking.[2] (Literary inscriptions of this type, often a marvelous aid to the historian, will later disappear from C. C. Wang's "modernized" paintings.)

The inscribed poem, like the composition, is a copy rather than the artist's own.) The only significant compositional variation occurs in the elimination of all but one human figure and in the simplification of the architecture.

Wang Meng is a considerably more difficult model to follow than Wang Shih-min: his tense, twisting brushwork and his convoluted, tightly packed forms represent a challenge that many hardy artists shied away from. The harmonies that appear here are no longer simple, and the analogous musical arpeggios are dense and highly coloristic like those of Chopin or Rachmaninoff rather than Haydn or Mozart. Yet the painting is composed of only two colors, a pale ochre and a delicate indigo blue mixed with ink, which are intertwined below in a frame surrounding the seated figure. The painting is rich in both color and movement, yet it is not truly dramatic. The brushwork is not as rugged, the texture not as woolly, nor the forms as tense as Wang Meng's own. The painting appears dramatic only in contrast to C. C. Wang's earlier landscapes and others from this period, such as his lyrical *Fisherman's Boat on Evening Waves* after Wu Chen (fig. 27).

C. C. Wang's landscape after Wu Chen is gentle, even delicate, with its fluid, curvilinear brushlines and its tiny, precisely located ink-dots. This painting is much less accurate in rendering the qualities of its model, Wu Chen, than the landscapes after Wang Shih-min and Wang Meng; particularly missing is the bluntness of Wu's brushwork, done with a worn and stubby brush and his generous use of ink. Today, C. C. Wang does not particularly like the painting and finds the curves "uninteresting," the brushwork "so-so," the rocks "repetitive" in shape, the forms lacking proper linkage. But it is nevertheless a lovely and delicate landscape, and it further delineates the range of the artist's abilities at that time. Like many of his traditional paintings, the historical layers are piled one upon another, and in this case the Wu Chen style was filtered through another of the Four Wangs, Wang Chien, whose painting provided the specific model for this work and which in good part accounts for its divergence from the original qualities of Wu Chen.[3]

C. C. Wang's stylistic range and his sophisticated understanding of the historical layers through which past styles reached the present era is further illustrated by a 1943 painting (fig. 28) which in its details—particularly the rocks and earthen forms—effectively captures something of the style of Wang Fu, an early follower of the so-called Four Masters of the late Yüan, while suggesting in the trees something of the early Yüan artist Chao Meng-fu, who in turn derived his technique for painting bark and branches from the early Sung manner of Li Ch'eng and Kuo Hsi. Again, the artist completes the traditional exercise with an inscribed poem not his own but drawn from a T'ang anthology.

The artist's range is extended beyond expectation by his 1946 fan painting in the manner of Hsia Kuei (fig. 29), done as a fiftieth birthday gift for Ch'en Ting-shan, a writer who is now ninety years old and resides in Taiwan. It is surprising that C. C. Wang would have chosen to work in the style of Hsia Kuei,

2. The Peking painting is reproduced in Osvald Siren, *Chinese Painting: Leading Masters and Principles* (London: Lund Humphries, 1958), vol. 3, pl. 110a.

3. Wu Chen, Wang Meng, and Huang Kung-wang were grouped together by later critics as three of the Four Masters of the Late Yüan, along with Ni Tsan, who in time came to be be C. C. Wang's favorite model. These four formed the stylistic basis for the art of Tung Ch'i-ch'ang and the Four Wangs, including Wang Shih-min, who in turn were the most important of C. C. Wang's early models.

27

Fisherman's Boat on Evening Waves, After Wu Chen. Early 1940s. Album leaf, ink on paper. 17⁹⁄₁₆ x 13¼ in (43.7 x 33.6 cm). Shuisongshi Shanfang Collection.

Inscribed
"Fisherman's boat on evening waves. In the brush-manner of the Plum Priest [Wu Chen, 1280-1354]. Written by Wang Chi-ch'ien."

Artist's Seal
Wang Chi-ch'ien yin (no. 2, upper right)

Published
Moss, *Experience*, p. 79

28

Landscape. Summer 1943. Hanging scroll, ink and light color on paper. 30 x 11⅝ in (76.2 x 29.5 cm). Private Collection.

Inscribed
" 'Who rests in the flat boat, in Confucian seclusion on the waves? / In autumn, duckweed grows along the level sands and shallows. / The fishing rod was used to hook a reputation / In ancient times, by men of the Wei and T'ung Rivers.' Summer, *kuei-wei* [1943]. For Po-keng [not identified]. Wang Chi-ch'ien."

Artist's Seal
Wang Chi-ch'ien yin ("Seal of Wang Chi-ch'ien"; not illustrated)

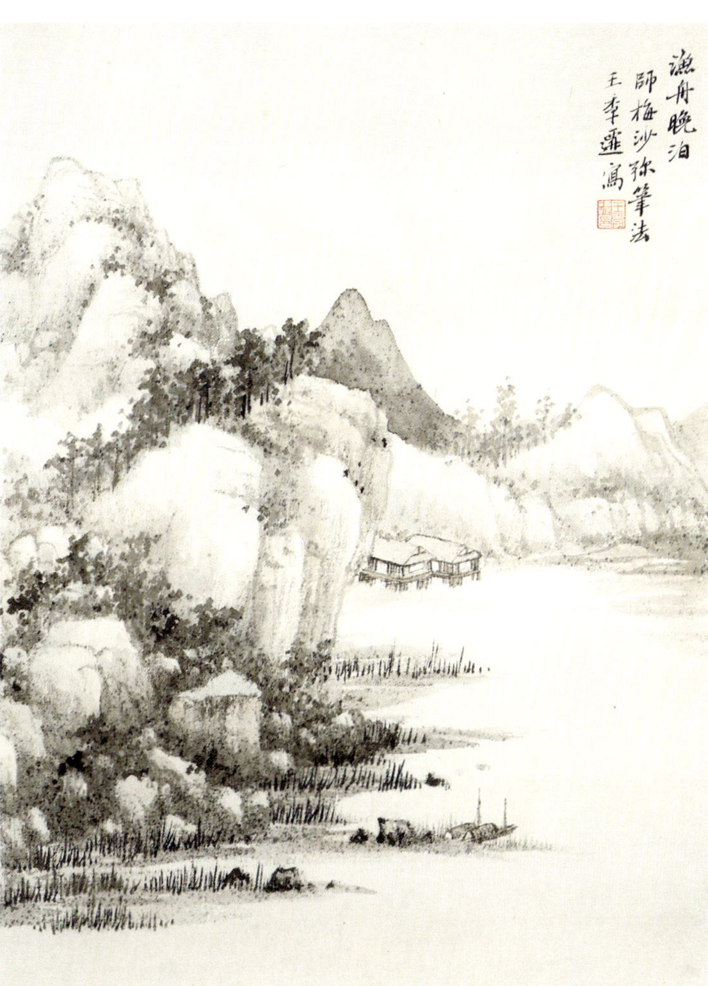

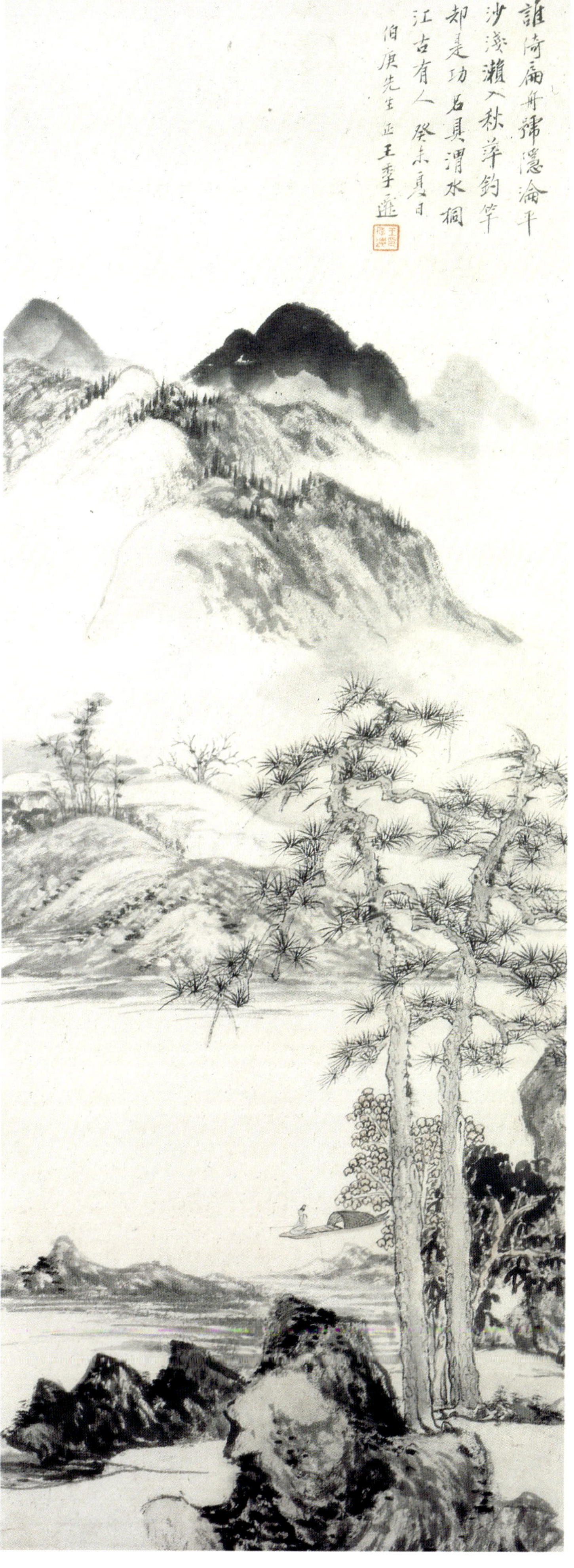

a Southern Sung court artist outside the circle of models
normally considered acceptable by traditional literati painters
but a style which he used chiefly for commercial purposes
in Shanghai. The broad, wet, smooth brushwork and the
compressed, tightly focused composition (well adjusted for the
arched shape of a folding fan, which poses unique difficulties)
demonstrate the artist's grasp of this style. Both the relaxed
yet firm brushstrokes and the rich yet well-controlled use of
ink wash reflect C. C. Wang's strength and self-assurance in
practicing the Hsia Kuei style. Particularly effective is his
handling of the 13th-century manner of contrasting near and
far in a so-called "one-corner" composition. The darkest tones
are placed in the foreground, primarily focused along the
central axis of the fan; they are balanced there along a nearby
spit of land on the left and an embankment on the right that
presses to the surface of the painting. Both a bridge on the
right of the central promontory and a thatched hut on the far
left side enclose these tonally dominant features, leading into
the scene but offering no physical means of departure. Yet the
bridge and hut establish a diagonal axis that points toward the
distant left, across a body of water where a remote shoreline,
pale and lacking detail, balances all the dominant features of
the foreground by means of effective understatement and
careful placement.

None of these works (figs. 4, 26-29) was designed to show
originality. Rather, fluency was their goal. The language of art
was thought of as fairly well set; one could learn to express
himself most effectively by working within the rules of artistic
grammar. Almost twenty years would pass before C. C. Wang
began to change those rules, not just to depart from the styles
of individual earlier artists but to alter the language of Chinese
landscape painting.

The decade and a half after C. C. Wang's departure from
China saw no abandonment of his traditional mode of
painting, but economic realities soon dictated that different
subjects and other styles be added to those he brought with
him. Painting wallpaper or ceramic lamps for a living and
teaching young students—all relying for the most part on
floral-vegetal subjects done in decorative styles—extended his
range beyond landscapes. This coincided with his decision
(at the advice of his friend, New York art dealer Alice Boney)
to pursue Ch'i Pai-shih-type genre paintings for a gallery
audience that had too little understanding or appreciation of
his traditional, esoteric landscape scrolls. Throughout the
1950s, his landscape painting did not cease, but it was eclipsed
by this new subject matter in which he was quick to develop
his skills. It cannot be overlooked that such works enabled the
artist to operate more closely to the aesthetic sphere of New
York's Abstract Expressionism, particularly its Action Painters
who themselves were occasionally tinged with Oriental
calligraphic influence.

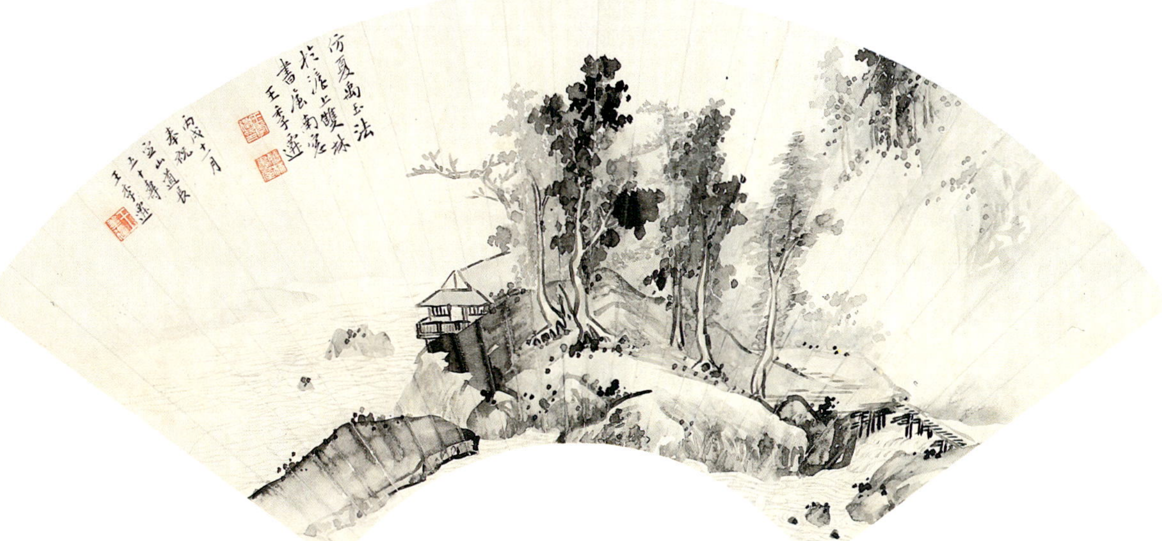

29

Landscape in the manner of Hsia Kuei. November/
December 1946. Folding fan, ink on paper. 9½ x
19⅞ in (24 x 50.5 cm).
C. C. Wang Family Collection.

Inscribed
First inscription: "Imitating the manner of Hsia Yü-yü
[Hsia Kuei]. Done at the south window of the Shuang-
lin Studio in Wu-shang."
Second inscription: "On the 11th month of the year
ping-hsü [November/December, 1946], respectfully
presented to my colleague, Ting-shan [Ch'en Ting-
shan, b. 1896] on his fiftieth birthday. Wang Chi-
ch'ien."

Artist's Seals
Wang Chi-ch'ien yin (following first inscription, above);
Shuang-lin shu-wu (following first inscription, not
illustrated, below); *Wang Chi-ch'ien* (following second
inscription)

30

Apples. Autumn 1960. Hanging scroll, ink on paper.
36⅞ x 17⅞ in (96.2 x 45.3 cm).
Ching Yüan Chai Collection, On Extended Loan to
the University Art Museum, University of California,
Berkeley.

Inscribed
"*Keng-tzu* [1960], Autumn. Inscribed by Chi-ch'ien at
the north window of the Bamboo Studio."

Artist's Seals
I wen pu chih, wan kuan pu mai ("Even if not worth a
penny, I would not sell it for ten thousand strings of
cash"; lower right, not illustrated); *Chi-ch'ien lü-mei chih-
tso* (left)

Exhibited
de Young Museum, San Francisco, 1968

One such painting, masterful in its handling of wet ink
washes, is his 1958 *Lotus* (fig. 24). With such small scale subjects
shown large, even more than in large landscapes made small,
the artist's brushwork is put on clear display, and here,
decorative appeal is fully matched by artistic discipline. Even
the casual viewer will appreciate the skill required to retain
formal control of the fluid medium, as well as the power of
brushwork that transcends mere "messing around" and
manages to turn converging tones of liquid ink into curling,
leafy forms. Behind this image stands the tradition of two great
lotus painters from the past, Hsü Wei of the Ming and Chu Ta
of the Ch'ing, both masters at achieving accidental effects while
maintaining control of the results.

Typical of C. C. Wang's Ch'i Pai-shih-type paintings is *Vase
and Brushes* (fig. 7), done in 1966, slightly later than most of his
works in this genre. This example playfully combines the
depiction of a traditional subject—fruits and branches—with a
less traditional one—the painter's materials: a vase, perhaps for
holding water, and Chinese brushes in a jar. In the best Ch'i
Pai-shih fashion, objects are rendered in broad, rather free yet
well-rounded brushstrokes, with the artist's skill displayed both
in the quality of these strokes as well as in his reduction of such
objects to the smallest number of well-adapted strokes possible.
Also typical of Wang's work of this type (a genre which,
arguably, can be traced back through Chu Ta, Shen Chou of
the Ming, and Ch'an Buddhist painting of the late Sung) is the
yin-yang-like interplay of complementary forces: dark ink on an
unpainted, white background; solid objects set against the void;
organic leaves and fruits set beside the inorganic vase and jar;
two leafy branches (round forms paired with straight lines)
opposed to three fruits (uniform shapes rather than paired); a
vase in which vertical and circular forms are united in one body
(base, belly and neck), as contrasted with the duality of jar and
brushes; the juxtaposition of two basic ink tones; the interplay
of calligraphic painting with calligraphy in the inscription;
and so forth. A good painting of this kind manages to tuck
numerous complementary pairs into a seemingly simple design
and does it as naturally as possible, revealing less of a schematic
intention on the part of the artist than of his intuitive grasp of
the artistic possibilities inherent in a dualistic worldview.

In a third example of non-landscape subject matter, his
Apples of 1960 (fig. 30), C. C. Wang comes still closer to
matching the virtues of Ch'i Pai-shih in both the seeming
effortlessness of his design and the simple strength of his
brushwork. The best of Ch'i Pai-shih's works seem so totally
unaffected that often, except by comparison with other
paintings, they may not seem to be great at all. But an
undefinable "rightness" of form and a comparative surety of
brushwork—simple but beautifully rounded, undramatic but
somehow possessing remarkable weight—distinguishes such
works. Similarly, this unpretentious painting of apples and
bowls, which might easily be passed off as trivial compared with
C. C. Wang's landscapes—viewed in terms of the unfortunate
but temporary, economically necessary disruption of an
otherwise significant career—displays brushwork of an order

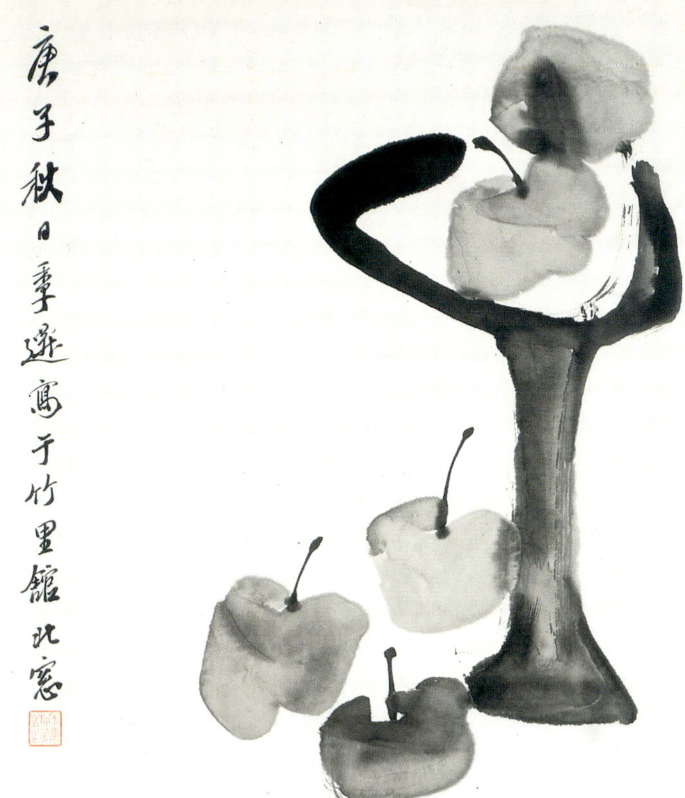

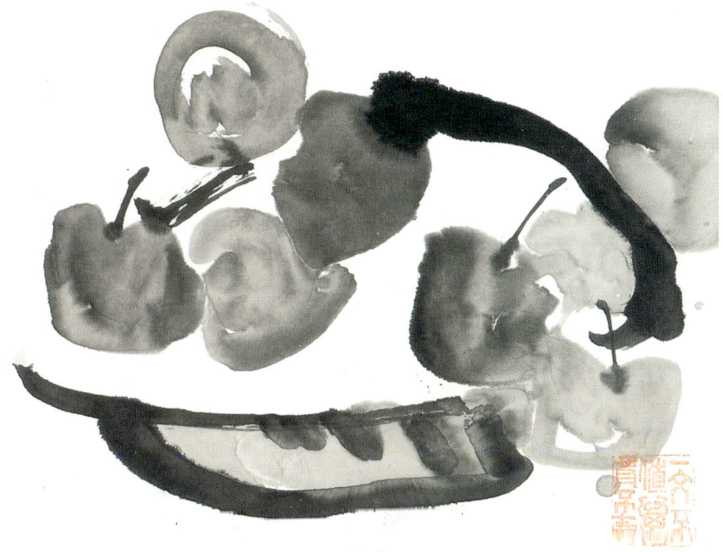

that the artist himself feels he has rarely matched. The brushwork of his *Vase and Brushes* is by comparison rougher, more nervous, and less fully controlled (although closer in spirit to contemporary New York artists such as Franz Kline). While the relation of such paintings to the development of Wang's landscape style may not be immediately obvious, the long-term benefit of painting these works of a "lesser" genre was in fact considerable, found in their focus on simpler, more "readable" compositions and their reliance on looser, broader, more spontaneous brushwork than he had practiced before. One needs only to look slightly ahead in time, to some of his landscapes in the mid-1960s (such as figs. 33, 36, 37), to see the results. That these flower and genre paintings came at a time of relative inattention to his landscapes only helped promote their ultimate effect once his attention to landscape was renewed.

Of equal or greater significance for the future direction of his landscape painting—while not holding a future of their own—were C. C. Wang's experiments in Western style painting, done at the Art Students League. Outside of his classes, he worked primarily in casein rather than in oil, and a 1956 still life done on wood (fig. 31), represents both the best of this work and the seriousness of his commitment to understanding the Western tradition. From subject matter (a lute, half a melon, paired fruits, a basket, a striped tapestry) to style (broken tonal planes, strong linear rhythms, somber hues limited to combinations of blue with green and dark red with yellow), the origins of this formal study can easily be traced back to Georges Braque, with roots still further back in Cézanne and Matisse. (In the black linear pattern of this work, the artist admits as well to a bit of influence from Franz Kline's work in the 1950s). Although in 1956, such work could only be regarded as academic, even *retarditaire*, compared to the pulse of contemporary of New York art, it was typical of what many serious art students were practicing; and while the historian may judge it fortunate that C. C. Wang, with the persuasion of friends, was convinced not to pursue this path seriously, this painting compares favorably with the work of most such students. Built up in no consistent manner—no complete paint base or underdrawing, broad black lines of paint laid down first in some areas and then covered over or filled in, in other areas just the opposite—the original shapes of every object are subjected to repeated changes and the resulting forms are complex and entirely broken up. The painting surface presents a rich play of hues and shades set to a rhythmic motion. And yet, because of the subtle hues, the action is stilled to the point that the artist can refer to it as "silent movement."

It is just as interesting to note in this painting the presence of features that are as much Chinese as Western, more consistent with C. C. Wang's traditional training than might be initially recognized. A lesser aspect of this is his retention of subject matter (at a time when non-representational art held sway among New York's progressive styles)—a reminder that traditional Chinese painting, however abstracted, always retained a basis in recognizable subject matter. Also Chinese, despite its correspondence with Western style, is his handling of

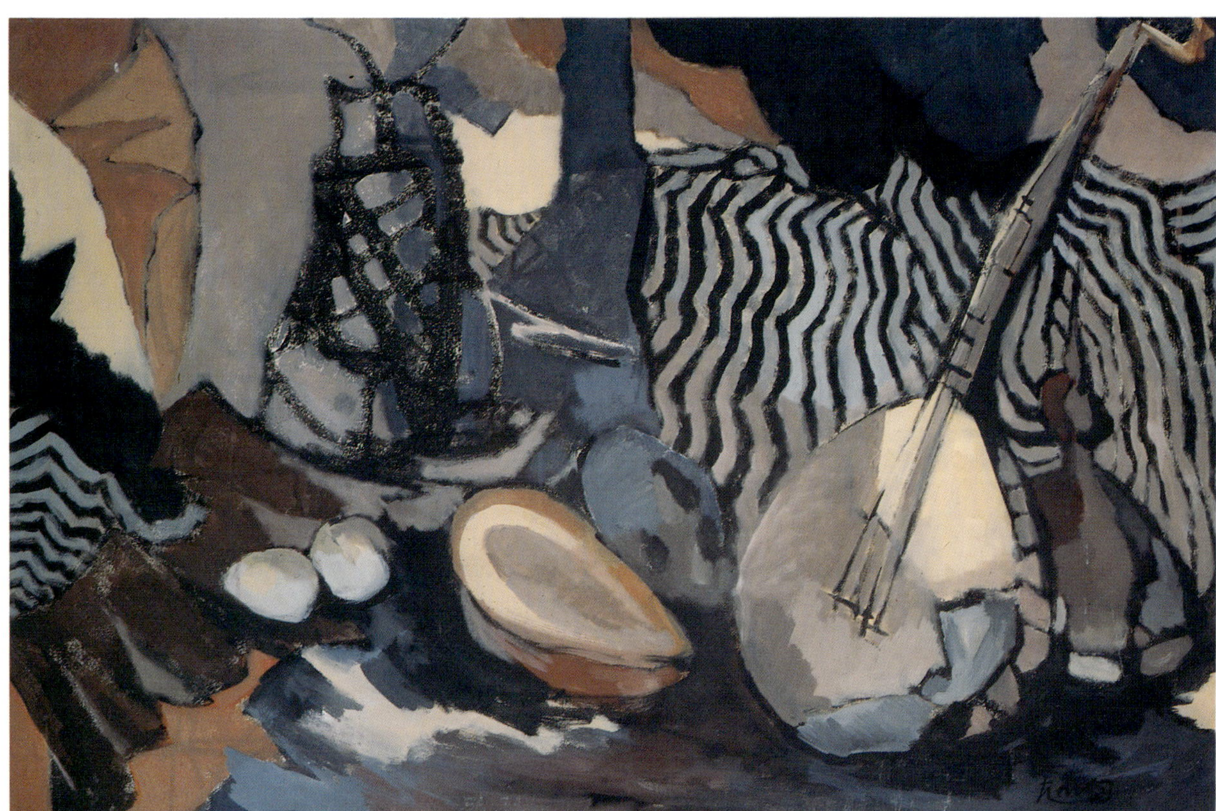

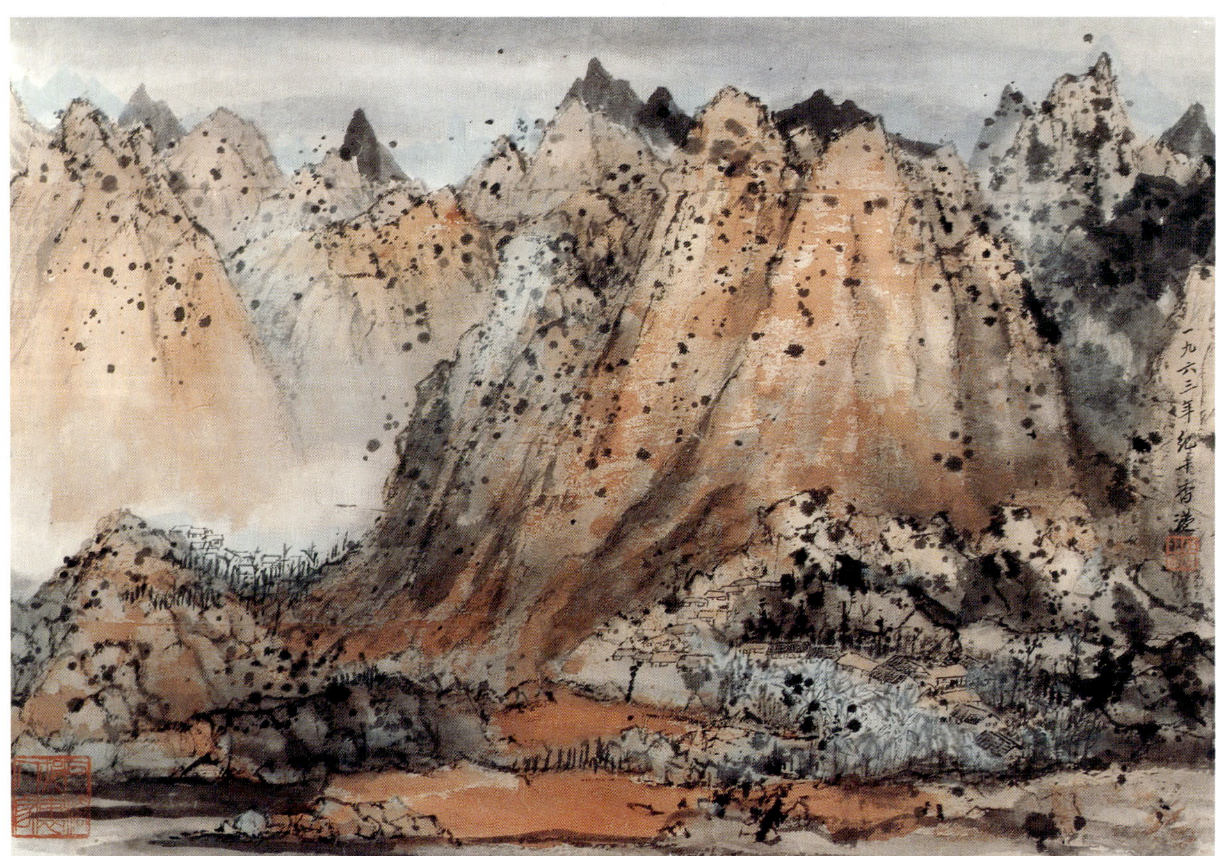

31

Still Life. 1956. Casein on wood panel. 26 x 40 in (66.0 x 101.6 cm).
Private Collection.

Inscribed
"Wu yen" ("Silent")

32

Landscape No. 284. 1963-69. Hanging scroll, ink and color on paper. 17³⁄₁₆ x 26 in (44.5 x 66.1 cm).
Private Collection.

Inscribed
"1963. Chi-ch'ien, in Hong Kong."

Artist's Seals
Wang Chi-ch'ien hsi (right); *Shih-ch'iao-ts'un-li jen- chia* (lower left)

Exhibited
Brooklyn Museum, 1977

Published
Katz and Wang, no. 49

4. Lois Katz and C. C. Wang, *The Landscapes of C. C. Wang: Mountains of the Mind* (New York: AMS Foundation, 1977), no. 49.

5. Huang Kung-wang's scroll is illustrated in James Cahill, *Hills Beyond a River: Chinese Painting of the Yüan Dynasty* (New York: Weatherhill, 1976), pls. 5, 41-43.

the subject in terms of positive and negative areas locked in dynamic interaction. A comparison with his 1966 painting *Vase and Brushes* (fig. 7) reveals certain significant similarities. Perhaps most striking is the strong linear element retained from C. C. Wang's Chinese training, visible in the rhythmic lines of the tapestry and the basket; while Braque and later Kline presented similar linear rhythms, this is in part because they, too, were influenced by Asia's calligraphy and its strength in two-dimensional design.

A decade of work in Western styles, classes in painting and drawing, anatomy and composition, ultimately made their mark on C. C. Wang's landscape style, yet it is striking that this impact was not felt significantly until the middle of the 1960s. A 1959 exhibition of his Chinese paintings—including flowers, genre paintings, and traditional landscape scrolls—held in the small Mi Chou Gallery of his friend, Frank Cho, was by his own admission unsuccessful, even depressing. *Landscape No. 284* (fig. 32), done a few years later in 1963, while he was chairman of the Fine Arts Department at the Chinese University of Hong Kong, shows C. C. Wang's landscape style at the end of this earliest painting phase. (In 1969, the artist came back to this work, adding as final touches some of the dark ink dots and washes that give it something of the appearance of his later, more dramatic works.) Perhaps the most striking aspect of the painting for its time is the use of a rich ochre pigment, in addition to areas of black ink and blue wash. Throughout the 1950s and early 1960s, unable as yet to effect a marriage of his conservative training with his Western experience—except perhaps for a few landscapes done in a more vigorous, wetter brush manner, possibly affected by the notion of Action Painting but hardly successful by Chinese splashed ink standards—Wang's one area of occasional experimentation lay in his use of color, where the mutual influence of Wang Yüan-ch'i (fig. 23) and the Western palette could be observed; a painting colored somewhat like this one was one of the more successful landscapes displayed in the Mi Chou Gallery exhibition, although it failed at that time to find a buyer. However, the painter himself later explained the color of *No. 284* in more anecdotal terms:

There was a place where men were working on some kind of a project. I don't remember exactly where it was. I think it was in Hong Kong. All around where they were working the red clay was coming out of the mountains. When I painted this painting, I didn't paint it in front of the area where I saw this red clay, but somehow I remembered it and that is why I made the painting in this color. It is not a real place.[4]

It is typical of the traditional Chinese artist that while a real place might make some impression upon him and stimulate him to paint, he virtually never painted on the spot and seldom recorded an actual scene. This landscape, too, despite its specific inspiration, remains a traditional literati vision: a level staging area in the foreground, dotted with clusters of small huts set at the base of mountains which rise up like a landscape screen behind them. Other traditional elements may be found throughout the painting. The compositional structure is strongly reminiscent of early monumental landscape handscrolls like *Summer Mountains* (fig. 8), owned in the 1960s by C. C. Wang, or even more like Huang Kung-wang's famous *Dwelling in the Fu-ch'un Mountains* (1347-50), which by 1963 he had viewed repeatedly in the Palace Museum collection.[5] The shapes of the mountains and their component parts are specifically related to Huang Kung-wang, as are the representation of trees by vertical striations, sometimes forked (best seen along the left margin of the painting), and the spare, dry texture strokes used for the mountain folds.

Landscape No. 284 (a designation not given until the institution of a cataloging system in 1972) is the most mature of C. C. Wang's early landscape paintings included here and can be judged quite favorably by modern Chinese painting standards. More effectively than most contemporary Chinese painters—and many distinguished earlier artists as well—C. C. Wang has achieved a delicate balance between the depiction of real space, grand yet inhabitable, and pure art: dry ink brushlines, abstract forms, and a striking color combination of ochre and blue. It is only by the artist's own later standard that the painting seems too traditional and stylistically tame, with no great drama, no significant spatial disjunctures, no interplay between areas of major and minor focus or of nearby and far away, no strong contrast between light and dark ink tones or between wet and dry textures (at least not until the painting was retouched in 1969). Color and texture are used as a unifying screen over the entire painting surface rather than coordinating with the landscape forms to create compositional momentum. Coming as it does a year before the artist began to thoroughly modernize his painting style, this painting provides a point from which to gauge what C. C. Wang might have looked like in later years had he not changed his style so drastically, so intentionally. What distinguishes his later works from this one is not improved technique, for the artist's brush skills are already well developed here, but a reevaluation of the goals his artistic skills were to serve.

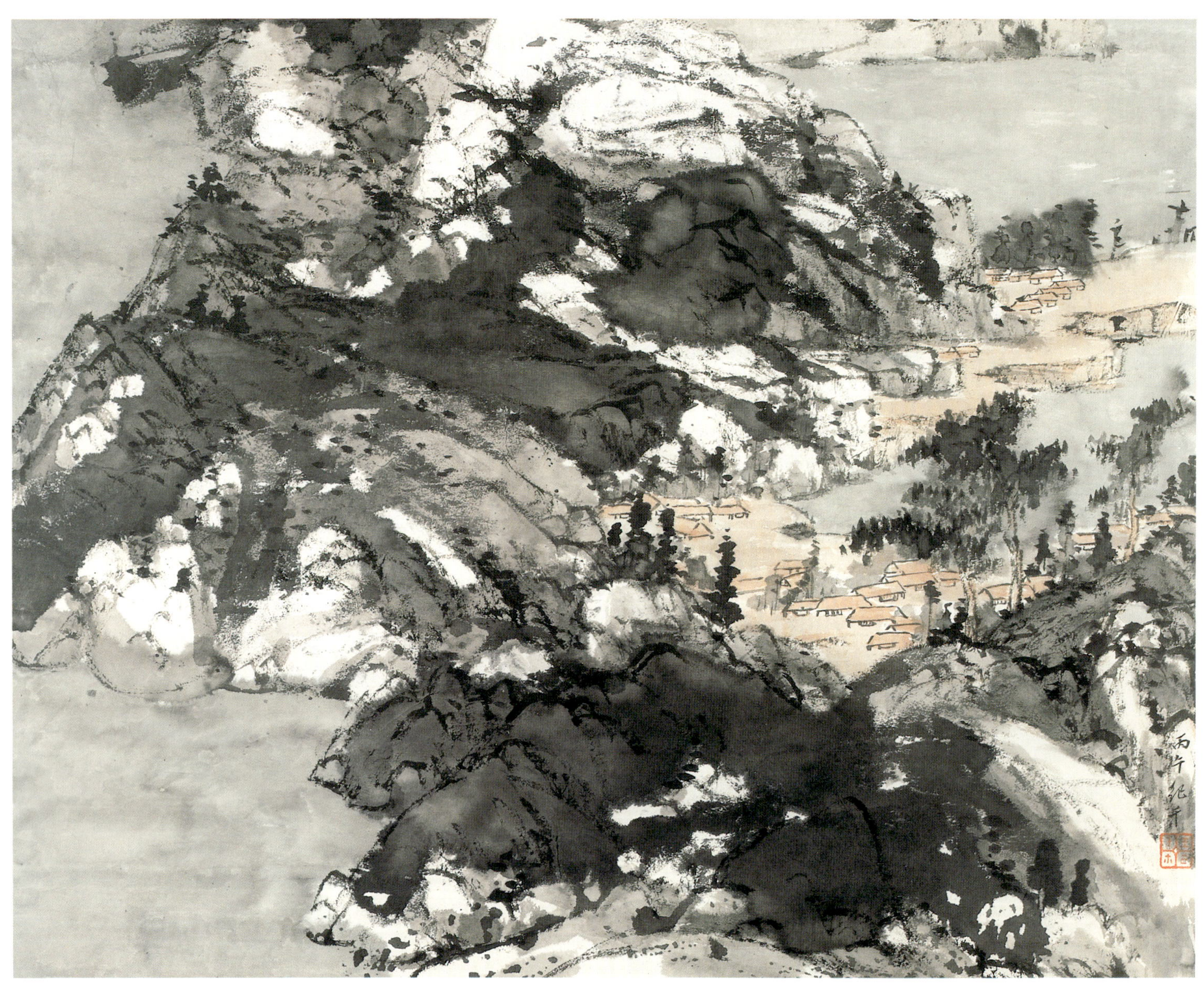

River Village in a Rainy Dawn. 1966. Hanging scroll, ink and color on paper. 18⅞ x 25³⁄₁₆ in (48 x 64 cm). Ching Yüan Chai Collection, On Extended Loan to the University Art Museum, University of California, Berkeley.

Inscribed
"Ping-wu [1966]. Chi-ch'ien."

Artist's Seal
Wang Chi-ch'ien hsi (lower right)

Exhibited
de Young Museum, 1968

Published
Weatherby, pl. 10; Chang, "Landscape," fig. 3

6.   James Cahill et al., *C. C. Wang: Landscape Paintings* (Hong Kong: Hsi An T'ang, 1987), p. 11.

7.   For Kung Hsien precedents, see the Nelson Gallery-Atkins Museum album leaves of 1671, illustrated in Wai-kam Ho et al., *Eight Dynasties of Chinese Painting: The Collections of the Nelson Gallery-Atkins Museum, Kansas City, and The Cleveland Museum of Art* (Cleveland: Cleveland Museum of Art and Indiana University Press, 1980), nos. 214B and 214D. For Tao-chi, several such precedents are illustrated in Richard Edwards et al., *The Painting of Tao-chi* (Ann Arbor: Museum of Art, University of Michigan, 1967), such as no. VII from the Los Angeles County Museum of Art; suggestions of this are also found in leaves from two albums that were then in the C. C. Wang collection, illustrated in Edwards et al., *Tao-chi,* nos. XIV and XIV.H (now in the Cleveland Museum of Art), and nos. XIX.D and XIX.J, from the *Album for Taoist Yü.* Various other late artists also used this convention.

8.   Chu-tsing Li, *Trends in Modern Chinese Painting: (The C. A. Drenowatz Collection)* (Ascona: Artibus Asiae, 1979), p. 180. For illustration of Chao's *Water Village,* see James Cahill, *Hills Beyond a River,* pls. 12, 41.

9.   Li, *Trends,* p. 181.

10.   For Kung Hsien and Tao-chi, see note 7, above; Fang's painting is illustrated in Barnhart, *Along the Border of Heaven,* frontispiece and fig. 81.

Phase Two, 1964-1972: Beyond Traditionalism

Although change seems late in coming to C. C. Wang's painting style, throughout his early years in the United States his exposure to Western art offered new ideas and led him to question deeply the nature of his work and of Chinese painting traditions in general. After a long period of gestation, a new style was born, and born in a manner that seemed almost precipitous to his observers. James Cahill, who watched this change in progress, writes that "for some of Wang's admirers, who had thought of him as the very guardian of orthodox brushwork in our time, the shock was like that felt by Stravinsky's followers when, late in life, he abandoned the diatonic scale."[6] But C. C. Wang's new style was not born fully developed. A period of infancy may be observed in the mid-1960s, followed by a period of initial maturation lasting through the mid-1970s.

Two works now in the Rietberg Museum (Charles A. Drenowatz Collection), Zürich, dated to July and August of 1964, are the earliest published examples of C. C. Wang's "new style" as defined by the inclusion of impressed texture strokes (figs. 34, 35). In his *Sailing Boats and Misty Mountains* (fig. 34), the artist has for the first time supplemented his usual brushwork with a distinctively untraditional technique, using a deeply ridged paper to apply his ink to the mountains toward the right of the painting and a waxed or unabsorbent paper for applying the dotted texture seen on peaks toward the left. These two patterned areas do not dictate the shape of the mountains as clearly as they often will in the next few years: on the right, the impressed texture suggests mountainous form only in the most general way and tends to flatten out the complex pattern of projecting and receding earthen folds which the artist has otherwise effectively shaped with patterns of light and dark ink; in the foreground, on the lower right, they are scarcely noticeable at all. But one can see how the area of impressed texture suggests the twisting central contours of the main mountain on the left, which the artist isolated simply and effectively between dark structural washes. On both peaks, left and right, one can see how the artist has returned with brush and ink to pick out and transform the textural pattern into foliage, using more horizontal strokes on the right and looser, more rounded dots on the left.

The pattern of dark mountainous bands rippling across the upper part of this painting, separated by a ribbon of mist from a diminutive foreground ridge, will soon mature into one of the compositional configurations most frequently found in C. C. Wang's painting (for example, figs. 38, 48, 68). Compared to many of these, the dynamics of this composition still seem tame, the artist working delicately over the rise and fall of numerous lesser peaks in the middle ground, as well as lingering over minor details of foliage and architecture in the foreground. Still, the physical liberation of the middle ground mountains from the ground plane, their transformation into a dark ribbon of form, tonally separated from and dominant over the nearby land mass, represents a major step by the artist toward greater clarity and power of design, more vigorous than his previous works although not without traditional precedent

in late 17th-century paintings by masters such as Kung Hsien and Tao-chi.[7]

In the second work of this pair, *Flowing Water in Spring River* (fig. 35; like the previous work, not named by the artist himself), an initial impressed textural pattern of stretched webbing and concentrated focal points has been turned into a broad plain of fields and rivers (the webbing) and a succession of mountains (the focal points) that establish a broken diagonal leading across the plain from foreground to back. Zigzag rows of rustic houses, many of them tucked deeply into their surroundings, reinforce the pattern of diagonal recession. The mountains are linked with each other by touches of light blue wash, while the fields are tinged primarily with brown and gray. Upon the broad, open ground plane, the sequential movement of rising mountainous forms establishes a certain compositional impetus, but these forms have yet to be knit together in an uninterrupted and more powerful compositional unit, as they soon will be (fig. 37). The use of impressed ink texture visually enhances the painting's surface texture, and the artist has used this as a point of departure not only for the compositional arrangement but also for additional ink, applied with the brush, which is loose and abstract, free and playfully rendered, sometimes seeming to represent long lines of trees following unpainted waterways and including a group of calligraphically rendered waterfowl in the lower right corner.

Both of these paintings open the way for dramatic compositional statements and textural effects unseen in C. C. Wang's earlier work. Yet in comparison with later examples, they do not yet seem wholly "new": their energy still seems potential, their forms and rendering remain rather gentle, and their compositions have yet to take on dynamic form (particularly so in the pastoral landscape of *Flowing Water*). Nor are these compositions any freer of traditional predecessors than C. C. Wang's earlier paintings. Professor Chu-tsing Li has insightfully compared the composition of *Flowing Water* (fig. 35) to the painting *Water Village,* done in 1302 by Chao Meng-fu.[8] Li also writes that *Sailing Boats* (fig. 34) "captures the spirit of Northern Sung monumental landscape" with its "airplane window" view;[9] but it is probably from the art of later, literati painters such as Kung Hsien or Tao-chi of the early Ch'ing that this composition derives, as previously mentioned, or even from Fang Ts'ung-i of the late Yüan (e.g., Fang's *Cloudy Mountains,* sold by C. C. Wang to the Metropolitan Museum in 1973).[10] It can hardly be overlooked that Kung Hsien, Tao-chi, and Fang Ts'ung-i were themselves a great deal less traditional than the stylistic sources for earlier C. C. Wang paintings already discussed, and that while C. C. Wang never abandoned a base in traditional compositions (the impact of models like Ni Tsan and Wang Yüan-ch'i would never be erased), he began at this time to significantly broaden that base to include both Sung monumental and Ch'ing "individualist" models.

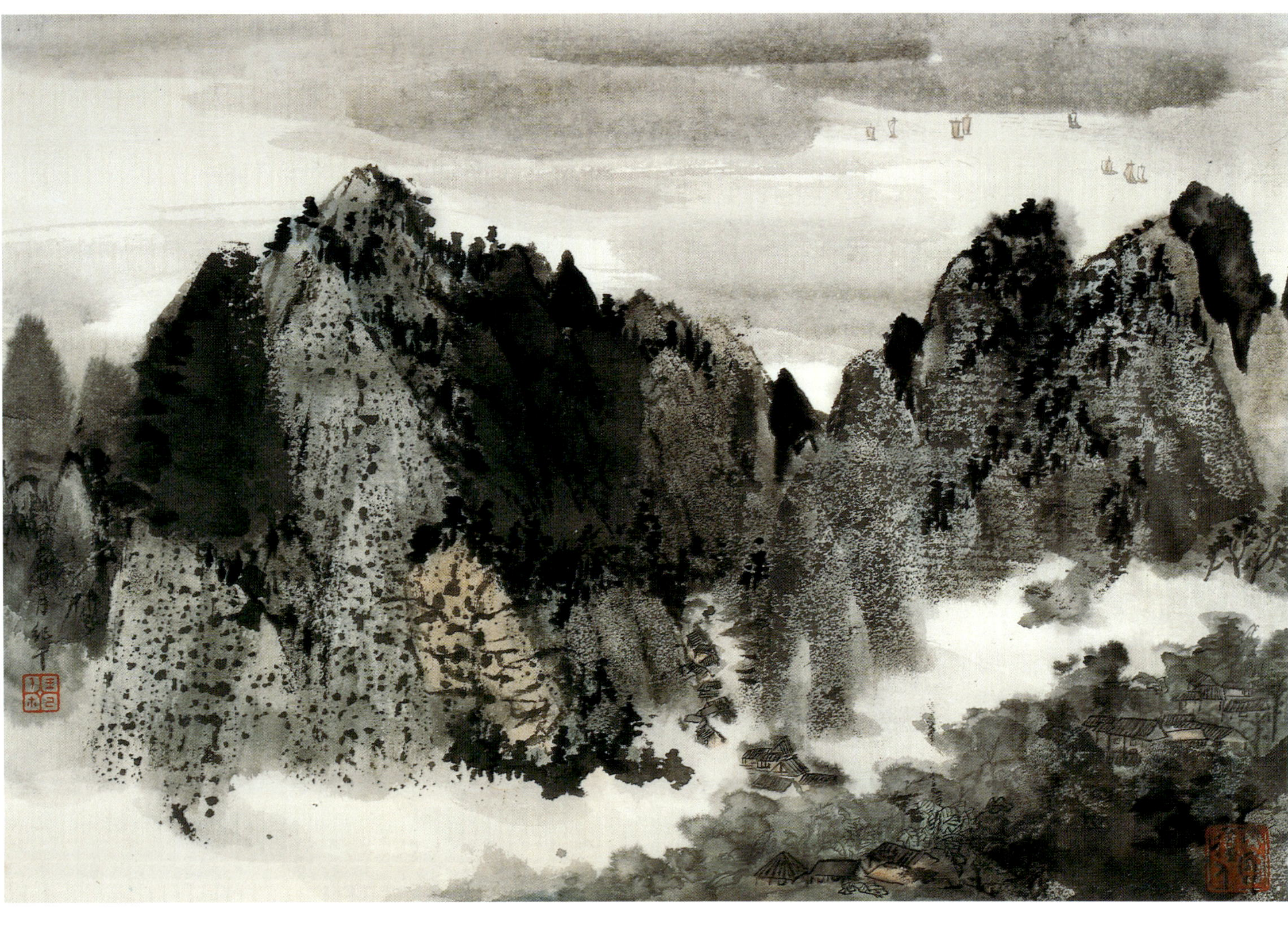

Sailing Boats and Misty Mountains. July 1964.
Hanging scroll, ink and color on paper. 15¾ x 23⅝ in
(40 x 60 cm).
Rietberg Museum, Zürich, Charles A. Drenowatz
Collection.

Inscribed
"Chia-ch'en [1964], 7th month. Chi-ch'ien."

Artist's Seals
Wang Chi-ch'ien hsi (lower left); *Wen-ko hou-jen* (lower
right)

Published
Li, pl. 63

35

Flowing Water in Spring River. August 1964.
Hanging scroll, ink and color on paper. 15⅜ x 22¹³⁄₁₆
in (39 x 58 cm).
Rietberg Museum, Zürich, Charles A. Drenowatz
Collection.

Inscribed
"Springtime River, Warm Waters. Chia-ch'en [1964], 8th
month. Chi-ch'ien."

Artist's Seals
Wang Chi-ch'ien hsi (lower right); *Wen-ko hou-jen* (lower
left)

Published
Li, pl. 64

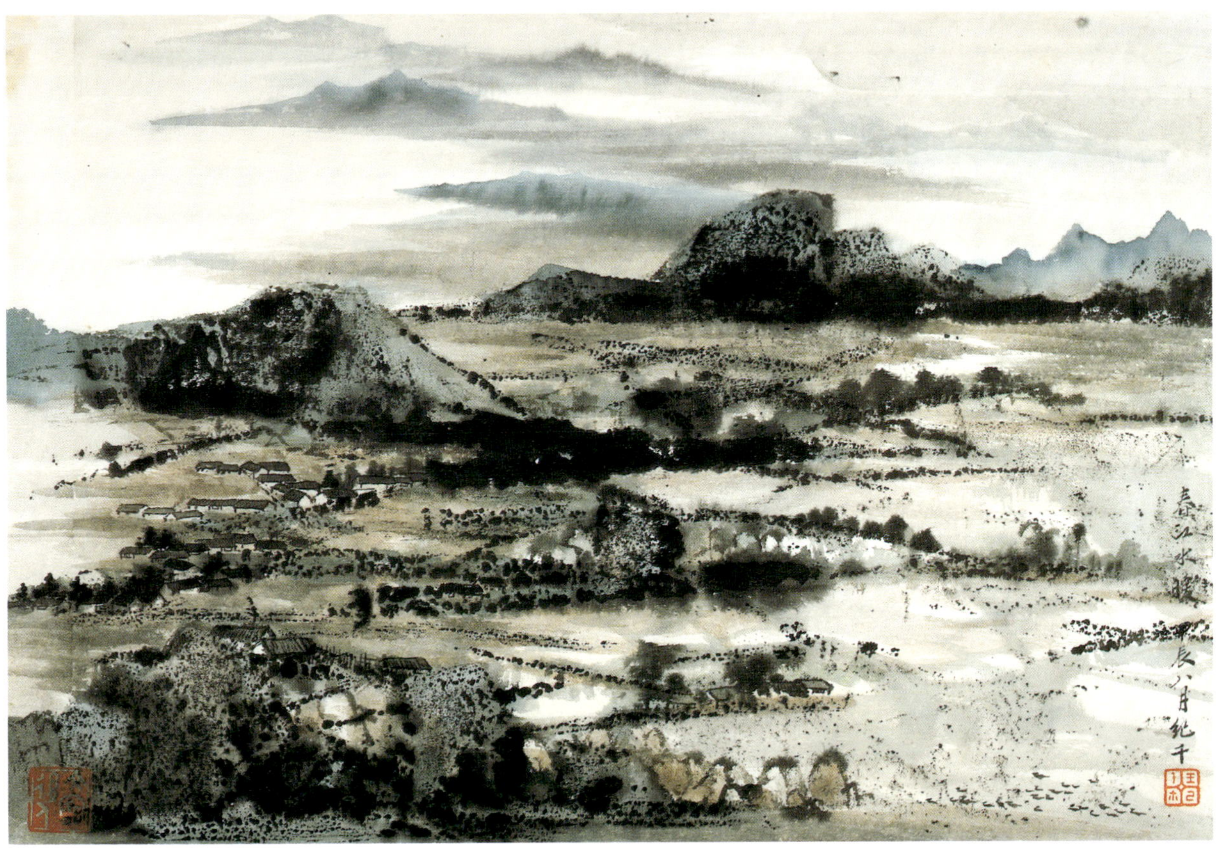

Sailing Boats and *Flowing Water* clearly deserve to be thought of as "transitional" (a term the artist himself reserves for them), only one step removed from the landscapes before them. There are other paintings of this period which are as "new" as these, only some of which use impressed ink textures. All share in the artist's new departure by virtue of compositionally more unified and increasingly dynamic forms as well as by their more liberated, energetic brushwork. If transitional, they are nevertheless much less tentative as statements about the artist's new sense of direction. Two such works, both unnamed, are dated 1965 and March 1966 (figs. 36, 37). Both include the use of impressed textures, and the former also introduces the first hesitant use of folded paper texture, in which creases in the painting paper made prior to the application of impressed textures and brushwork create an additional type of textural variation—best seen running vertically down the center of the uppermost mountain ridge, with a series of folded texture lines laid crosswise upon it. More striking in this painting, however, are the artist's brushwork, far more vigorously applied than in any landscape previously seen here, and the powerful, unified landscape design—both aspects, as suggested earlier, which may have benefited from C. C. Wang's concentration on flower and genre paintings during his first decade in America. In the design of this landscape, the mountains fit into a simple, unified, oval frame stretched horizontally across the paper: the familiar "space-cell" of Six Dynasties–T'ang landscape painting (cf. fig. 23). Set within this frame is an open space, transformed into depth by clusters of huts that line its base. The design is further enhanced by an ochre wash placed in this space and along the base of the painting, which establishes a visual relationship between these areas, and which is softened along the edges to look like colored clouds. The cloudy lower perimeter also suggests that these peaks are but the upper reaches of a lofty range which rises from a ground plane far beneath the lower border of the picture. This particular design, like that of *Sailing Boats,* is one that will become a recurrent part of the artist's later compositional vocabulary (as in figs. 39 and 68).

The design of *Flowing Water* (fig. 35) will similarly provide a compositional standard for C. C. Wang once its structure has been more clearly unified, as it first is in an unnamed painting from March 1966 (fig. 37; for later examples of this design, see figs. 13, 22, 51, 52, 53, 64, 71, 72, 73). In this work, one can readily imagine the artist consolidating into a single design unit the once-isolated mountain forms of his *Flowing Water:* the pattern of the mountain chain now snakes over a flat earthen plane in a well connected back-and-forth diagonal pattern, clearly leading the eye along the mountain ridges from foreground to rear—from the lower left toward the right, back towards the left, and then right again (with a distant, secondary mountain chain branching off toward the upper left of the painting in pale shades of blue and gray, somewhat reminiscent of the *Flowing Water* landscape). Only a small amount of impressed texture has been used in this painting, and it is hard to distinguish this from the artist's use of dry brushwork.

Dominating the brushwork here are broad washes that help
unify each separate link of this mountain chain, softer, more
rounded, and less vigorously applied than in the previous
painting (fig. 36)—a contrast parallel to that already seen in
C. C. Wang's flower and genre paintings, *Vase and Brushes*
and *Apples* (figs. 7, 30). A pleasant feature of this painting,
somewhat conservative by later standards, is the attention paid
to what the artist might call a "narrative" aspect, plowed fields
depicted by parallel green and brown brush stripes, alternately
vertical and horizontal.

The structural linkage of mountain formations seen in
this painting is referred to by the Chinese as "dragon veins"
(lung-mo). It is associated geomantically with the system through
which *ch'i*—spiritual energy, life breath, manifested in the form
of mist and vapor—circulates through the mountains of the
earth. This compositional principle is linked to a significant
system of thought and values in China, with historical
dimensions that range from philosophy and religion to
geography and cartography. "Dragon vein" is but a principle
and can appear in many physical configurations, as it has in the
work of diverse masters. As used here, there is a historical
relationship to masters like Ni Tsan (fig. 5), who used it most
subtly, and Tung Ch'i-ch'ang (fig. 10), in whose works the
relationship of cubic mountains to planar water became well
established, and to two of Tung's followers in landscape
painting: Chu Ta, who intuitively understood its compositional
logic (fig. 17), and Wang Yüan-ch'i, to whom the principle
"dragon veins" was of major interest and an ever-present force
(fig. 23).[11]

Another work of this period that uses this "dragon vein"
principle but which does so more subtly and with greater
artistic effect is dated 1966 and belatedly acquired the title *River
Village in a Rainy Dawn* (fig. 33). Painted without any impressed
texture, it marks a clear departure from C. C. Wang's earlier
paintings in a number of important ways. The landscape forms
relate to those found in his *Landscape After Wang Shih-min*
(fig. 26) of the 1930s—long, rounded major contours; smaller
lumps called "alum rocks"; flat plateaus and equally flat water—
yet these forms seem less stereotypic and more subtle in their
geometry and structural integration. The alum rocks are
detectable but only barely so, no longer emerging clearly from
their larger matrix, no longer so insistently repetitive. The
mechanically repetitive hatching strokes used for vegetation
(trees and "moss dots") in the earlier painting are also almost
gone, with reference to them found only in the few foreground
trees and a small number of dotted accents. These are now
so wet and so freely executed that they speak of an entirely
different aesthetic than the tasteful and cautious landscapes
executed when the artist was in his twenties and thirties.

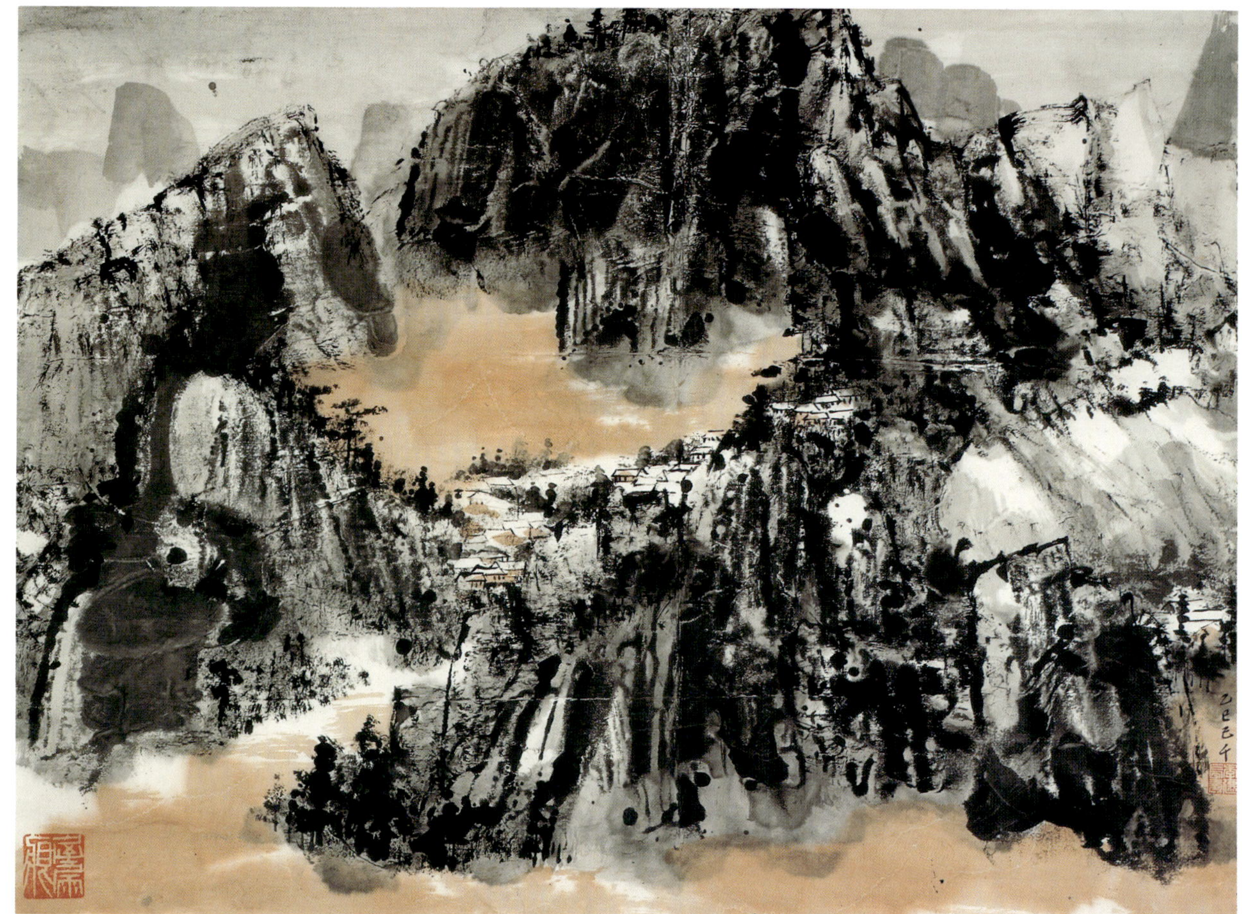

36

Landscape. 1965. Hanging scroll, ink and color on paper. Dimensions unknown.
Collection unknown.

Inscribed
"*I-ssu* [1965]. Chi-ch'ien."

Artist's Seals
Chi-ch'ien ch'ang-shou (lower right); *Wu lou hen* (no. 23, lower left)

37

Landscape. March 1966. Hanging scroll, ink and color on paper. Dimensions unknown.
Collection unknown.

Inscribed
"*Ping-wu* [1966], 3rd month. Chi-ch'ien."

Artist's Seals
Wang Chi-ch'ien hsi (right)

11.   See Susan Bush, "*Lung-mo, K'ai-ho,* and *Ch'i-fu:* Some Implications of Wang Yüan-ch'i's Three Compositional Terms," *Oriental Art,* N.S. 8, no. 3 (Autumn, 1962), pp. 120-27.

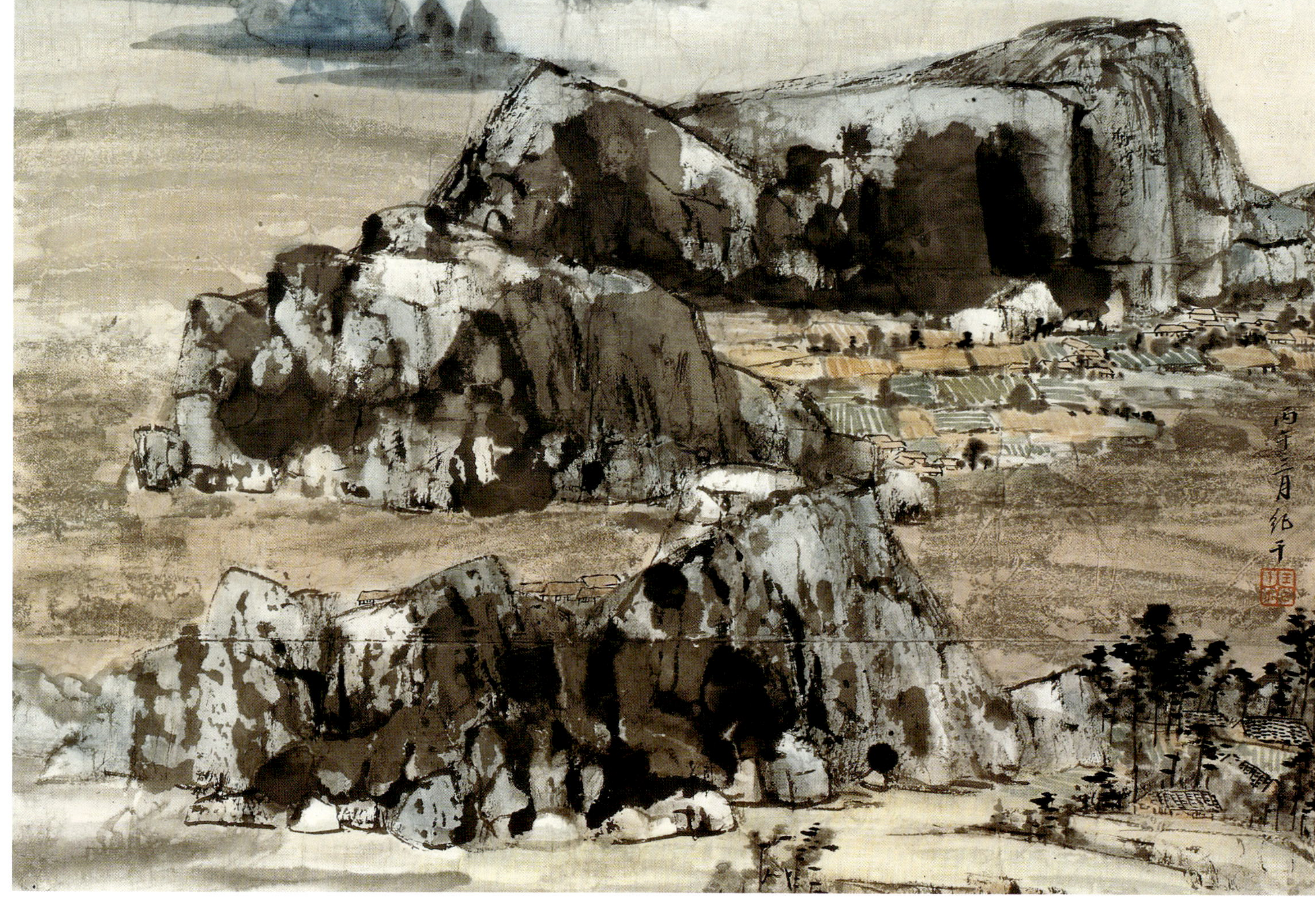

Freely executed, too, and most striking of all the components of the painting are the broad, wet washes of dark ink spread boldly across much of the painting surface, reminiscent of the explosive brushwork in the artist's earlier painting, *Lotus* (fig. 24); although the painting lacks any impressed "accidental textures," these washes display their own sense of accident, demonstrating a particular affinity with the art of Tao-chi (fig. 11). Like visual bursts of energy, they complement the basic disposition of the land forms without strictly adhering to them, vying with them for compositional dominance and surging more powerfully through the painting than does the landscape itself. They supplant the artist's earlier mellow brush harmonies and give to this composition unprecedented momentum and new artistic significance. The water is also painted with broad, wet movements of the brush, something not typical of Chinese literati painting but common in C. C. Wang's later work. On the other hand, the artist's forceful wet brushwork and ink washes are contrasted throughout the painting with pale, dry drawing in the manner of Huang Kung-wang or Ni Tsan (fig. 5) and are highly literary in flavor, creating within the work a balance between extremes of dark and pale, wet and dry, explosive and restrained. The brushwork in the painting, as Joan Stanley-Baker has suggested, represents C. C. Wang at his best, at least at this juncture in his career.[12]

In this painting, the land mass forms an arc across the surface of the painting. Entered in traditional Chinese fashion from the lower right, it leads upward toward the left and finally swings back toward the right. The elevated portions of the landscape enclose a series of low plateaus on the right which serve as a simple complement to them—flat, free of any bold effects of brush and ink, pale in tone, and colored with light orange or ochre pigment, and populated by peasant homes. These houses are miniaturized to create a sense of the landscape's monumentality, which is reinforced by the aerial point of view. The land mass is largely surrounded by water, not completely indicated within the borders of the painting but sufficiently so as to accentuate the earthen forms and their continuous movement in depth. The "logic" of Chu Ta's landscape style (fig. 17) is very much in evidence here, but it is not slavishly imitated: the composition is now tightly cropped at the top and compressed along the sides, so that despite its monumentality and implied distance from the viewer, the image remains immediate and compelling, in contrast to the artist's earlier paintings such as *Landscape No. 284* (fig. 32), whose setting within a spatial envelope suggests the *idea* of a landscape, remote and detached, like that of a Sung dynasty painting. This painting may also be somewhat immature ("transitional") by the standards of Wang's later work. But in the context of his painting career, it signals a bold and powerful departure from his earlier art and is a remarkable success in its own right.

Typical of the majority of his paintings from this time on, the landscape is horizontal in form and two-to-three in proportion, although mounted as a vertical hanging scroll. (C. C. Wang typically uses a half sheet of painting paper for his horizontal landscapes, a full sheet for his vertical paintings, giving a three-to-one proportion to the latter.) As in most of his later works, the artist includes here only the briefest inscription, four characters giving the year and his first name, so as not to detract from the visual impact of the painted image.

Yet another painting that the artist himself refers to as "transitional" is *Landscape No. 40* (fig. 38), painted in December 1968. It presents a configuration—bands of mountains, ribbons of clouds—related to that of *Sailing Boats* (fig. 34) and numerous later works. One can see that this design concept is more clearly developed here as a frontal presentation of two forms in tension, the background mass becoming darker and more dominant and beginning to loom ominously forward from the upper portion of the painting. By traditional standards, the composition seems unorthodox, top-heavy and unbalanced, but its powerful effect cannot be denied. Some of the elements of the previous painting, *River Village*, can also be seen here: the contrast of rising earthen forms, dark and wet, with a flat plateau, left unpainted and dotted with naively painted houses; the aerial view and monumental scale; the horizontal format; and the absence of a lengthy inscription. This painting may not be as compelling as the previous one, but the handling of the wet grey-to-black washes is masterfully controlled and particularly beautiful.

The artist's impressed ink textures, introduced in four of these paintings, constitute C. C. Wang's most obvious departure from the literati painting heritage and from his own previous style. In these paintings (figs. 34, 35, 36, 37), the applied texture is still light and exploratory. The heavily textured works that follow immediately seem to leave this "transitional" moment behind and more fully characterize the stylistic qualities of the artist's second phase. These works remain, in the minds of many, the most characteristic of C. C. Wang's "modern" work; despite the considerable refinement of his style since that time, this is still the best known and most widely published period of his career. During this period the artist employed a wide variety of texturing techniques, some of which were exploratory and are no longer used or even preserved. "The very first time," he says, "I used melted wax on the brush," and then proceeded to draw with it. But after trying this several times, "I began to use wax directly on the paper, like batik." Of course, unlike batik, the wax could not be removed after the painting was done and the experiment was hardly successful. The technique which he came to rely on most frequently, however, was that of applying dense black ink to a separate piece of crumpled paper and then impressing that on the painting paper, leaving a rough and unpredictable pattern of dark patches—patches which then served as the matrix for his brushwork.

12.   In Meredith Weatherby, ed., Hsü Hsiao-hu [Joan Stanley-Baker] et al., *Mountains of the Mind: The Landscape Painting of Wang Chi-ch'ien* (New York: Walker/Weatherhill, 1970), p. 74.

Landscape No. 40. 21 December 1968. Hanging scroll, ink on paper. 17¼ x 22⁷⁄₁₆ in (43.75 x 57 cm). C. C. Wang Family Collection.

Inscribed
"*Hsü-shen, tung-chih* [21 December 1968]. Written by Wang Chi-ch'ien."

Artist's Seals
Wang Chi-ch'ien hsi (right center); *Wu-chung i-hua-jen* (no. 18, lower left)

Exhibited
de Young Museum, San Francisco, 1968; Honolulu Academy of Arts, 1972; Brooklyn Museum, 1977

Published
Weatherby, pl. 4; Katz and Wang, no. 1

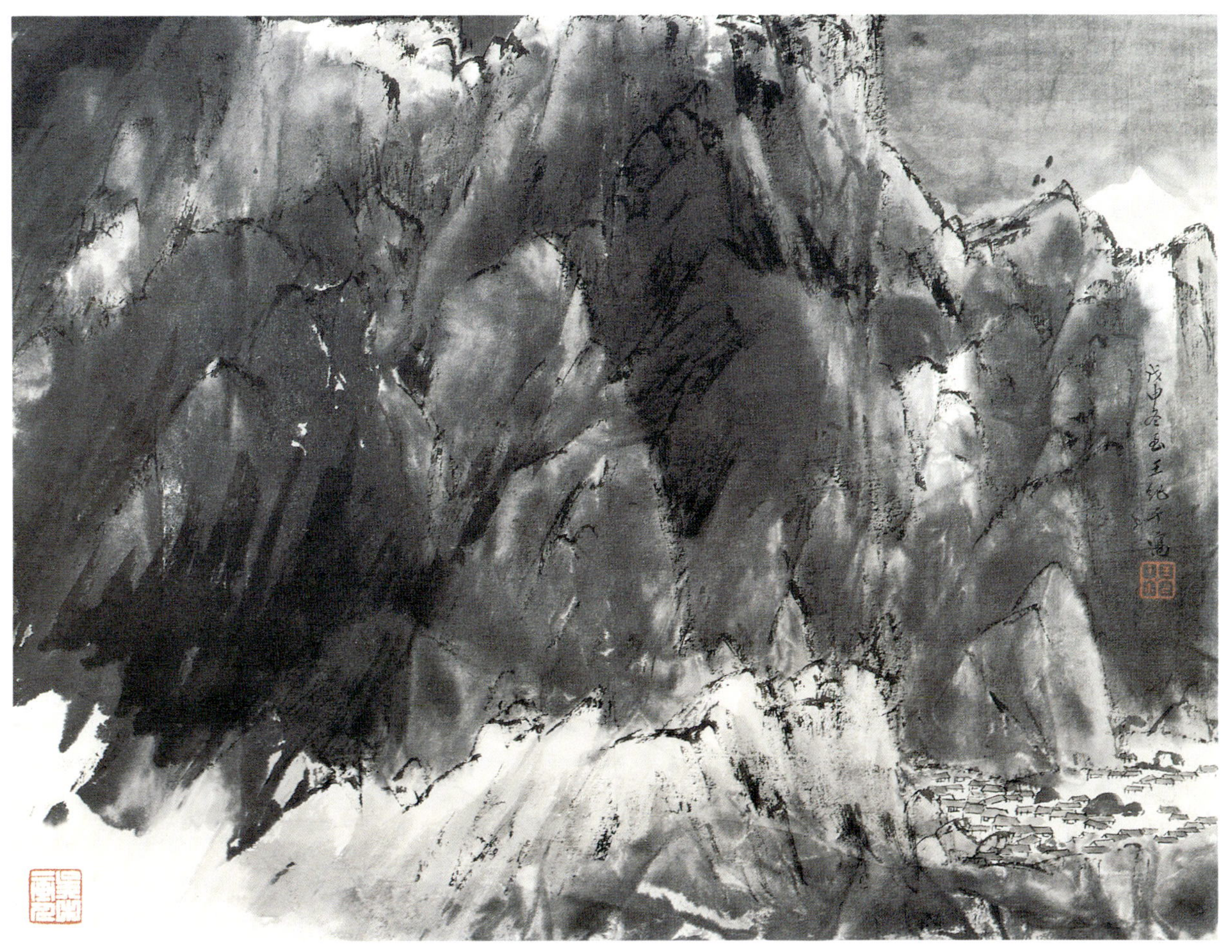

Soon, C. C. Wang also found himself experimenting with different papers for the crumpled paper, since roughly textured papers leave a more distinctive imprint. For his painting paper, he also explored a variety of types and settled on Japanese mulberry paper because it enabled him to manage the "accidental" spread of ink more effectively than did the highly absorbent Chinese painting paper, *hsüan-chih*, which he had used in previous years. Later on, he would also use mulberry papers from mainland China, Hong Kong, and Taiwan as well, always selecting handmade papers that varied from lot to lot and generated an increased variety of textural effects. Sometimes, he would melt wax on the crumpled paper before inking it so that it failed to absorb the ink and left a distinctive dotting pattern on the painting paper, or else he simply used a very unabsorbent paper—as seen in *Sailing Boats, Spring River*, and *Landscape Nos. 239, 240, 241, 334* (figs. 34, 35, 50, 44, 48, 45).

Frequently, before beginning to paint, the artist would fold or crease the painting paper so that the areas within the folds would remain protected from the application of impressed textures and washes, leaving long white streaks in reserve on the painting surface, as seen in *Landscape No. 112, Landscape No. 1: Clearing Skies After Snow on the Nine Peaks, Clouds in the Mountains of the Immortals*, and *No. 104* (figs. 40-43). However this effect was often made still more complicated by going over the folded areas with broad, powerful brushwork, as is evident in *Landscape Nos. 112* and *104* (figs. 40, 43). On still other occasions, by not placing any protective felt beneath the painting paper, the artist would capture the texture of his wooden painting table, as seen in the streaked texture of the large central mountain in *Landscape No. 76* (fig. 39), onto which the ink was poured and washed with a brush rather than impressed with another piece of paper. (All of these works were done in 1968-1969.) Altogether, what has been referred to as the artist's "crumpled-paper texture" or his "impressed-texture technique" is actually a complex set of techniques, developed through considerable experimentation, and not an easily-gotten gimmick designed to win attention. But if the techniques themselves are unorthodox by Chinese literati standards, at least the media are not—the artist has used only ink and paper, refusing to try cloth, hair, flesh or other materials, although he says that at some point he would like to try painting landscapes directly onto textured cloth. "I can use all kinds of texture," he says, "but really I don't use too many different textures because there are so many possibilities it makes me dizzy. I only do a few. I have lots of them in my mind, but I never try them."

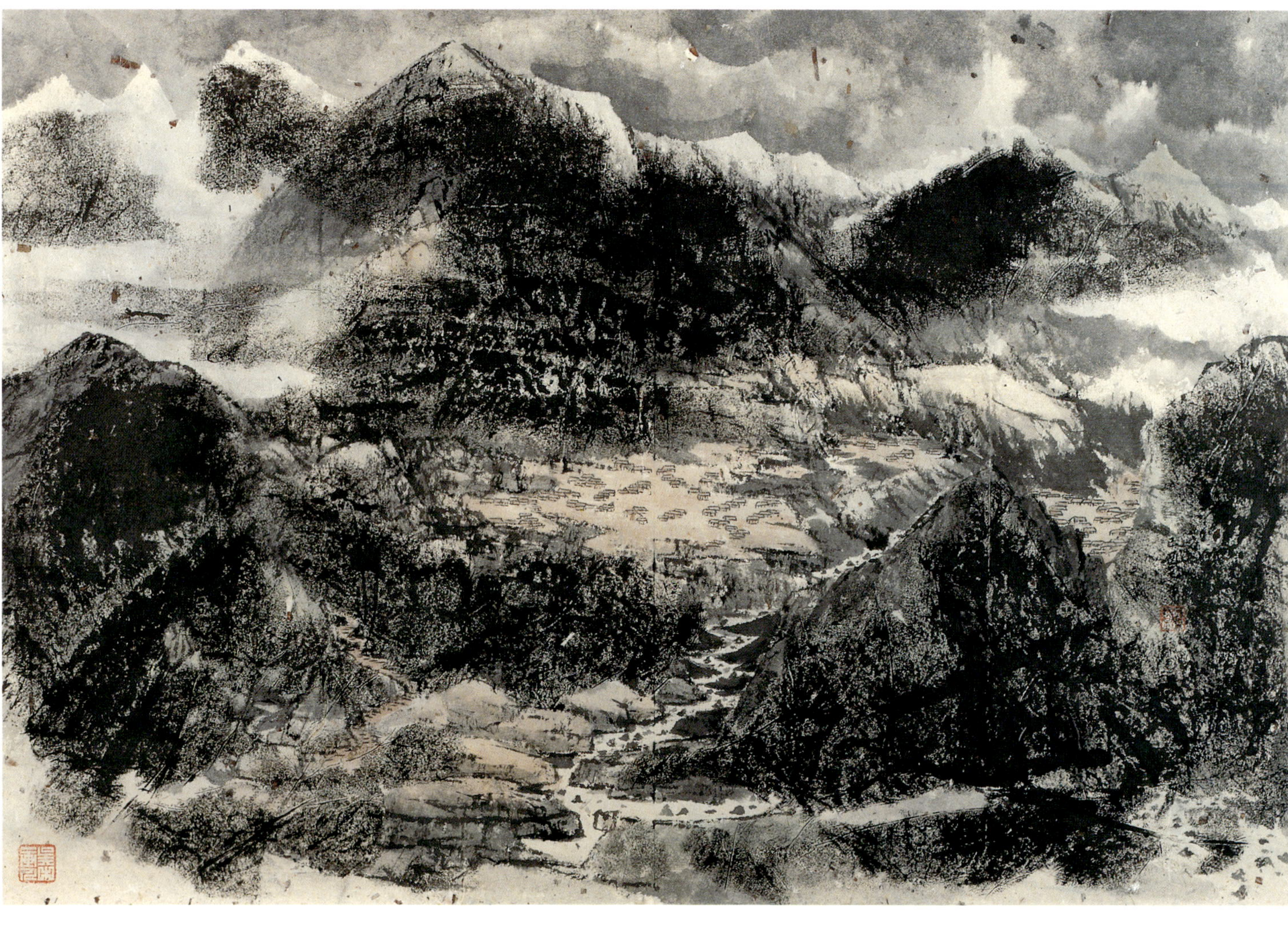

39

Landscape No. 76. 1969. Hanging scroll, ink and color on paper. 21³⁄₁₆ x 36³⁄₁₆ in (61.4 x 91.9 cm). C. C. Wang Family Collection.

Inscribed
"*Chi-yu* [1970]. Chi-ch'ien."

Artist's Seals
Wang Chi-ch'ien hsi (right); *Wu-chung i-hua-jen* (no. 18, lower left)

Exhibited
Honolulu Academy of Arts, 1972; Brooklyn Museum, 1977; Taipei Fine Arts Museum, 1984; Hong Kong Arts Centre, 1985; Birmingham Museum of Art, 1987

Published
Katz and Wang, no. 4

40

Landscape No. 112. March 1969. Hanging scroll, ink and color on paper. 24½ x 36 in (62.2 x 91.5 cm). C. C. Wang Family Collection.

Inscribed
"*Chi-yu* [1969], the beginning of spring. Wang Chi-ch'ien."

Artist's Seals
Wang Chi-ch'ien hsi (lower right); *Wu lou hen* (no. 23, lower left)

Exhibited
de Young Museum, 1968; Brooklyn Museum, 1977; Taipei Fine Arts Museum, 1984; Hong Kong Arts Centre, 1985

Published
Weatherby, pl. 17; Katz and Wang, no. 18; Byrd, fig. 1

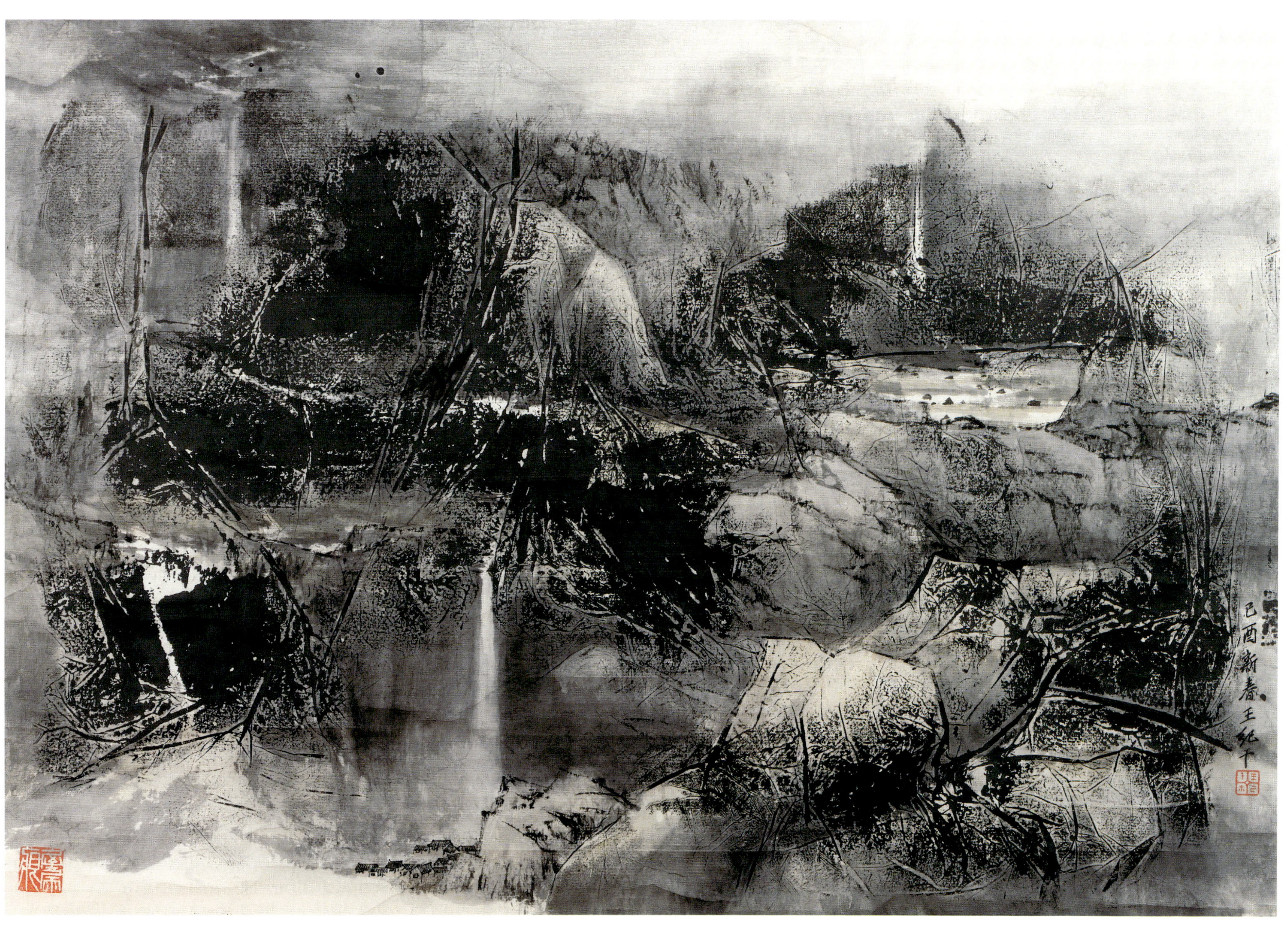

Two of the finest examples of the artist's work from this second phase are *Landscape Nos. 76* and *112* (figs. 39, 40), both from 1969. Like many of the paintings done at about that time, their texture consists of broad, bold, dark patches of ink, the former painting capturing the rough wood grain of the artist's painting table, the latter using crumpled, impressed-paper and folded-paper techniques. In both cases, the flat, frontal textured patterns pose a compositional challenge to the artist: how to create a sense of depth perpendicular to the heavily inked painting surface so as to establish a feeling of monumentality in the landscape. In *Landscape No. 76*, the individual areas of texture remain separate vertical mountain forms parallel to the picture plane, but the space between them is turned into flat plateaus and rendered recessional by means of houses placed on them, or converted into a river that winds forward from the middle distance, between two larger mountains and past a series of smaller overlapping rocks that help define the water's twisting course. The primary design (like that of fig. 36) is an oval arrangement of mountains surrounding a village. *Landscape No. 112* (fig. 40), by contrast, remains dominantly frontal. Recession is achieved only in isolated areas: by a diagonal contour that runs from the lower center to middle right, creating overlapping frontal planes between which a spared-out waterfall spills into unseen space just above a cluster of tiny houses; and by a small riverbed, perpendicular to the picture plane, which the artist has managed to insinuate into a spatial pocket toward the upper right with the aid of some smaller rocks that mark its passage left and right.

The success of these two paintings, however, lies not in spatial subtlety—indeed, not in subtlety at all—but in their blunt suggestion of primordial earthen forms. *Landscape No. 76* seems to depict a high mountain terrain, the center of which has been scooped out by some earlier glacial action, reminiscent of a scene such as the artist might have seen in Switzerland. *Landscape No. 112* seems less refined spatially and yet it is more powerful still, as if revealing the earth still raw, half-formed and steaming, in the grip of powerful geological forces at some early period of creation. The small houses at the lower center of the picture, while helping to define a monumental scale, are not really necessary for this effect and do not convincingly suggest that this primal landscape is yet habitable.

Two works related to *No. 112, Landscapes No. 104* and *No. 240* (figs. 43, 44), while ultimately neither as powerful nor as artistically significant, illustrate further artistic dimensions of this mode, more aesthetically oriented in the former case, more playful in the latter. Like *No. 112, Landscape No. 104* is dominated by pure landscape form, by an almost solid facade of rock. Yet despite its receding crevasses, left and right, and strikingly creased boulders, this work lacks the uncompromising harshness of the previous two examples; through a tasteful combination of blue and red hues and an elegant display of surface patterns—brushwork, textures, folds, and fissures—that seem to be its primary concern, it proclaims a more gentle, artistically pleasing intention.

Landscape No. 240 is a playful variant on the structural model of *Landscape No. 112*. Here, an increased number of local spatial pockets appear and all are filled by separate landscape scenes, two with human habitations. Somewhat like an enlarged Chinese garden rock—deeply eroded, full of grotesquely-shaped cave-like hollows, and associated with Taoistic notions of paradise scenery (in Chinese, the paradise of the immortals is referred to as *tung-t'ien* or "Heaven within a cave")—the openings into this earthen form represent just such grottoes, and the artist has entitled the work *The Spring of the Immortals*. Although C. C. Wang's painting is typically concerned with more purely formal effects than this and usually more sober in mood, both the playful form and the fanciful narrative aspect of this work reflect something of the artist's gentle sense of humor, ever-present in his daily life yet rarely revealed in his paintings. Done in the springtime of 1973, this work remains characteristic of the second phase of the artist's development even as in most other paintings of that time he was moving into a subsequent stylistic phase.

13. Ibid., p. 77.

41

Landscape No. 1: Clearing Skies After Snow on the Nine Peaks. 1968. Hanging scroll, ink on paper. 47⁷⁄₁₆ x 22¼ in (120.5 x 56.5 cm).
Collection unknown. (Copied from Weatherby).

Inscribed
"*Hsü-shen* [1968]. Chi-ch'ien."

Artist's Seal
Wang Chi-ch'ien hsi (lower right); *Wu lou hen* (no. 23, lower left)

Published
Weatherby and Hsü, pl. 21

42

Clouds in the Mountains of the Immortals. 1968. Hanging scroll, ink on paper. 38⅜ x 24¹³⁄₁₆ in (97.5 x 63 cm).
Collection unknown. (Copied from Weatherby).

Inscribed
"*Hsü-shen* [1968]. Chi-ch'ien."

Artist's Seal
Wang Chi-ch'ien hsi (lower right)

Published
Weatherby, pl. 13

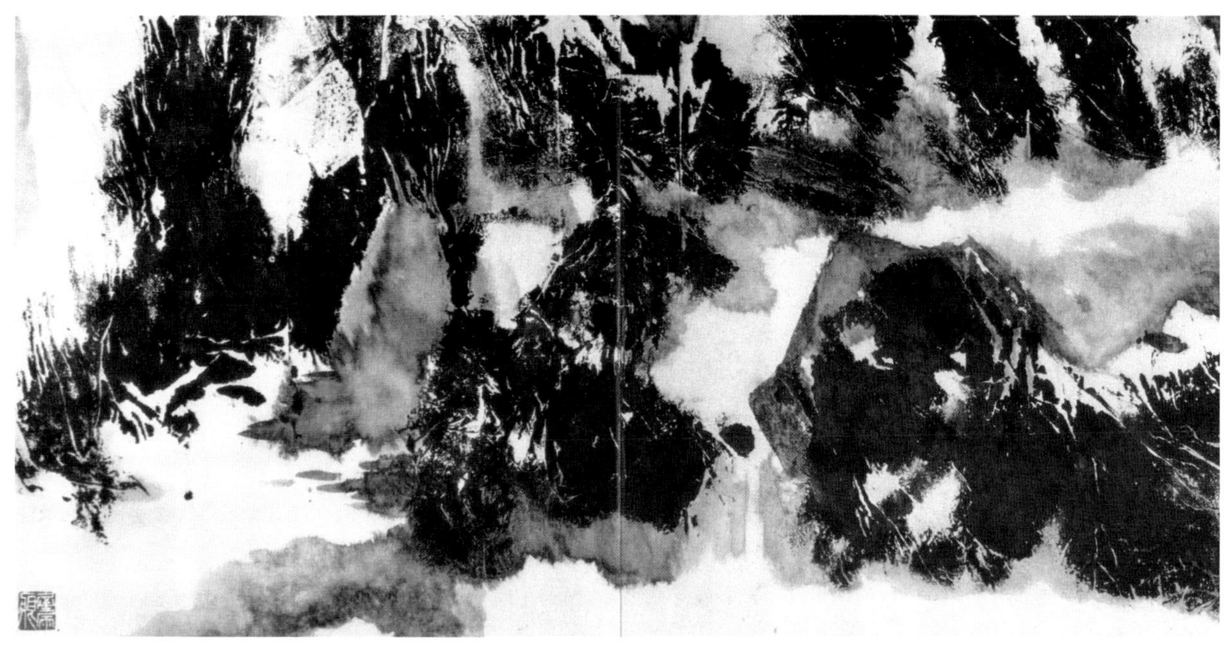

Two more significant representatives of the second phase of C. C. Wang's stylistic development, which lasted until the early 1970s, are *Landscape No. 1: Clearing Skies After Snow on the Nine Peaks* and *Clouds in the Mountains of the Immortals* (figs. 41, 42), both painted in 1968. *Clearing Skies After Snow* is distinctive in being almost wholly abstract, with no narrative elements whatsoever. Large geometric forms direct a restless scanning of the painting, but the shapes are so completely indeterminate that no consistent reading of scale or distance is possible. This work comes closer to Abstract Expressionist painting than any other mentioned so far, particularly through the textural effects achieved by folding the painting paper. Yet the artist's uncanny ability to suggest landscape—a grand, snow-covered view—purely through the broad patterns of ink on paper make this abstraction a worthy heir to the monumental tradition of Sung artists like Fan K'uan (fig. 16) and Li T'ang. It is also notably close to the contemporary style of Liu Kuo-sung. Joan Stanley-Baker has described this as a "stunning" landscape, and indeed it is.[13]

Even more stunning is *Clouds in the Mountains of the Immortals* (fig. 42), where dynamic textured effects are achieved by a more thorough, smaller scale wrinkling of paper of a more absorbent type, *hsüan-chih.* This material creates a more profound fusion of paper and ink, of voids and solid forms than found in most of C. C. Wang's painting. The ink looks as if it were poured onto the paper, while the spared out folded areas seem deeply etched into the painted forms. A few clustered huts and an occasional waterfall help to shift one's view around this wall of snow-encrusted, deeply fissured rock, while heavy moisture-laden clouds complement the rich surface texture of solid forms. This is one of C. C. Wang's grandest landscape visions, perhaps his earliest genuine masterpiece.

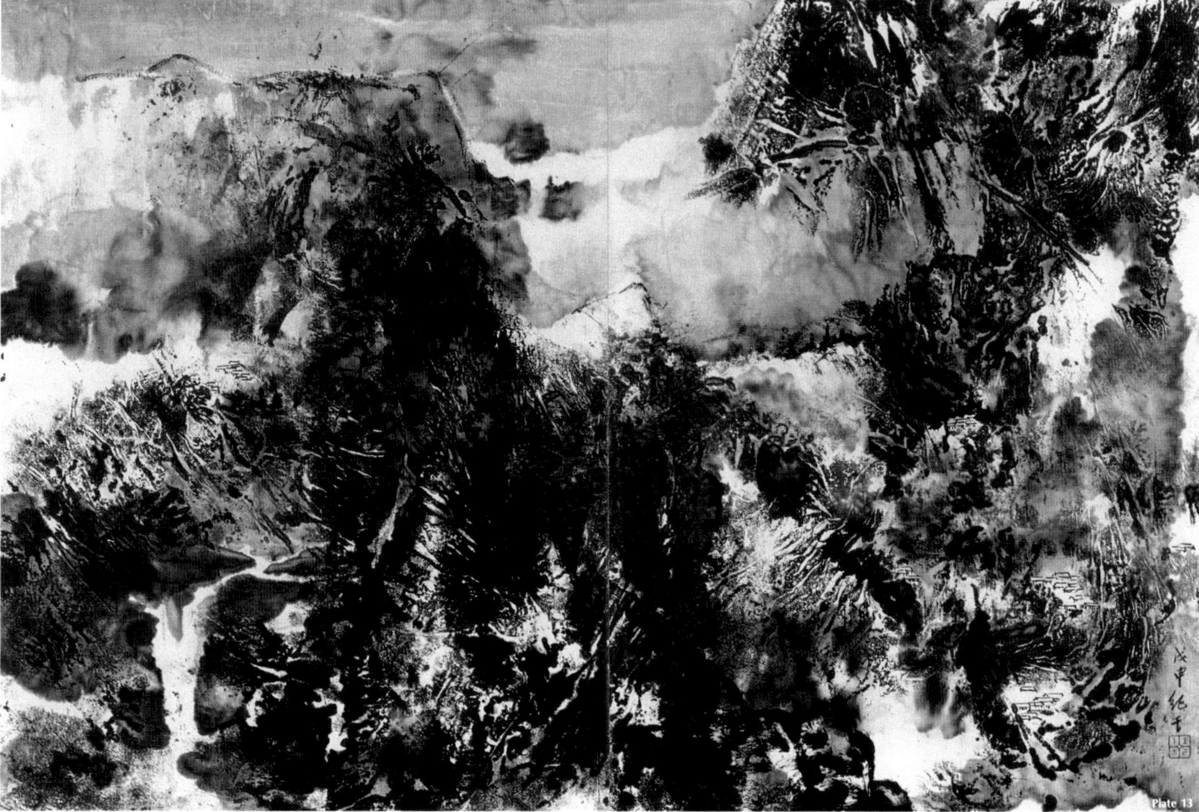

Joan Stanley-Baker has written perceptively of C. C. Wang's early textured paintings (specifying the years 1967-69, but appropriate, I think, to a slightly longer time span), that

Wang was more or less controlled by the natural marks. They *determined the configuration of the landscape. Working from the conditions provided by gravity, absorbency of the paper, disposition of fibers in the paper, its characteristics in wrinkling, Wang proceeds like a mountaineer, cautiously going over the "traces" to find a foothold here, a plateau there and is literally* led *to the final product.*[14]

Because this characterization of the artist as circumscribed by the very techniques that had "liberated" him rings true, his ability in *Landscapes No. 76* and *No. 112, Landscape No. 1: Clearing Skies After Snow on the Nine Peaks,* and *Clouds on the Mountains of the Immortals* to rise above such technical constraints makes these works of art all the more impressive.

Implicit in this characterization of C. C. Wang as "controlled by the natural marks" or textures, somehow constricted by the very technique that helped to free him from the shortcomings of his earlier, traditional style, is the inevitability that at some point further development would have to be predicated on overcoming this external constraint and reestablishing fuller control of his own artistic means. It was exactly this artistic accomplishment which marks what I have designated, not altogether arbitrarily, as the transition from the second phase to the third phase of C. C. Wang's stylistic development.

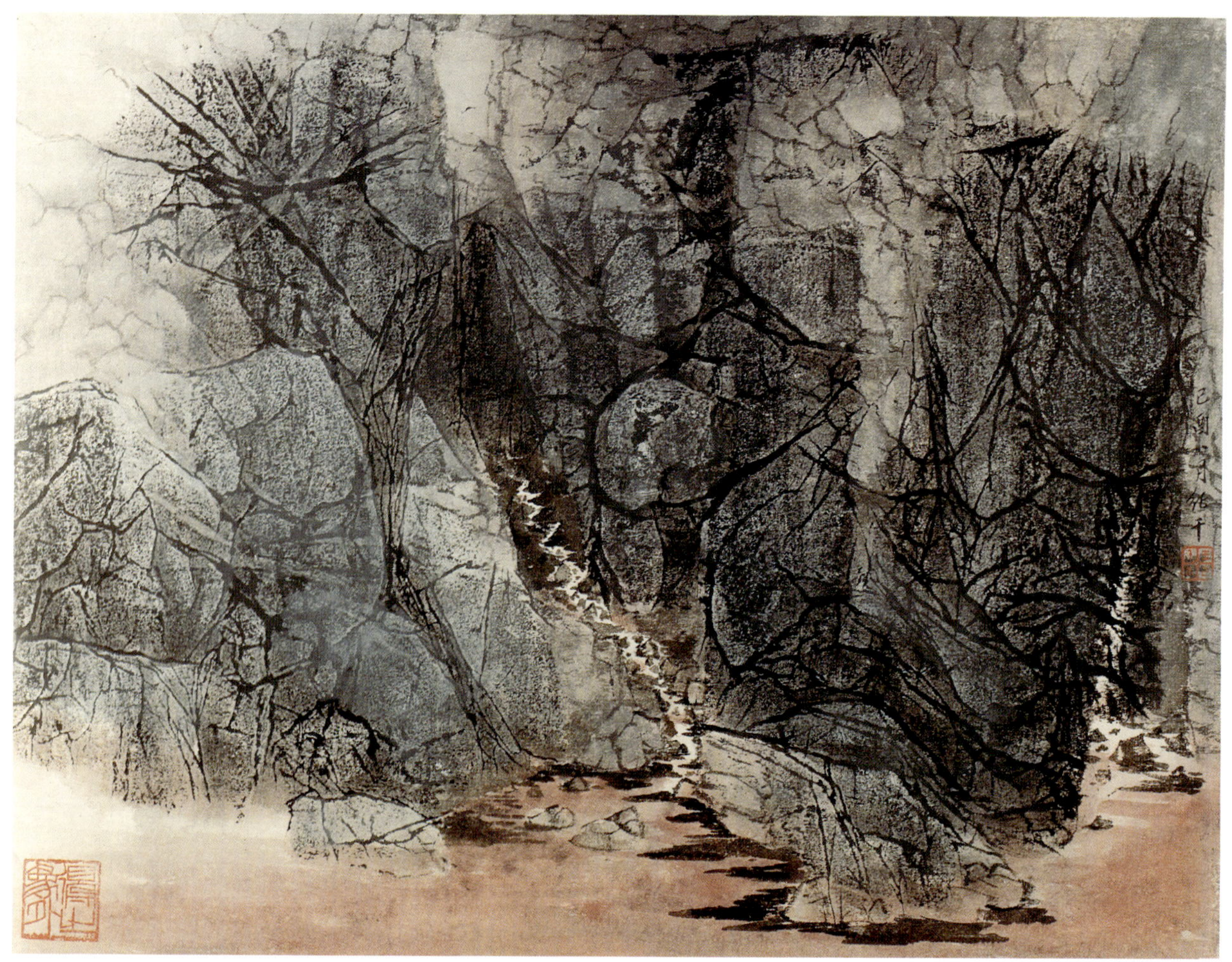

Landscape No. 104. August 1969. Hanging scroll, ink and color on paper. 18⅜ x 24¾ in (47.3 x 62.9 cm). Private Collection.

Inscribed
"*Chi-yu* [1969], 7th month. Chi-ch'ien."

Artist's Seals
Wang Chi-ch'ien hsi (right); *Te chih hsiang-wai* (lower left)

Exhibited
Honolulu Academy of Arts, 1972; Brooklyn Museum, 1977

Published
Katz and Wang, no. 16

44

Landscape No. 240: The Spring of the Immortals. Spring 1973. Hanging scroll, ink and color on paper. 24¾ x 35 in (62.9 x 88.9 cm). Herbert F. Johnson Museum of Art, Cornell University, Ithaca, New York

Inscribed
"*Kuei-ch'ou* [1973], Spring. A painting of the spring of the immortals."

Artist's Seals
Wang Chi-ch'ien hsi (right); *Shih-ch'iao-ts'un li jen-chia* (lower left)

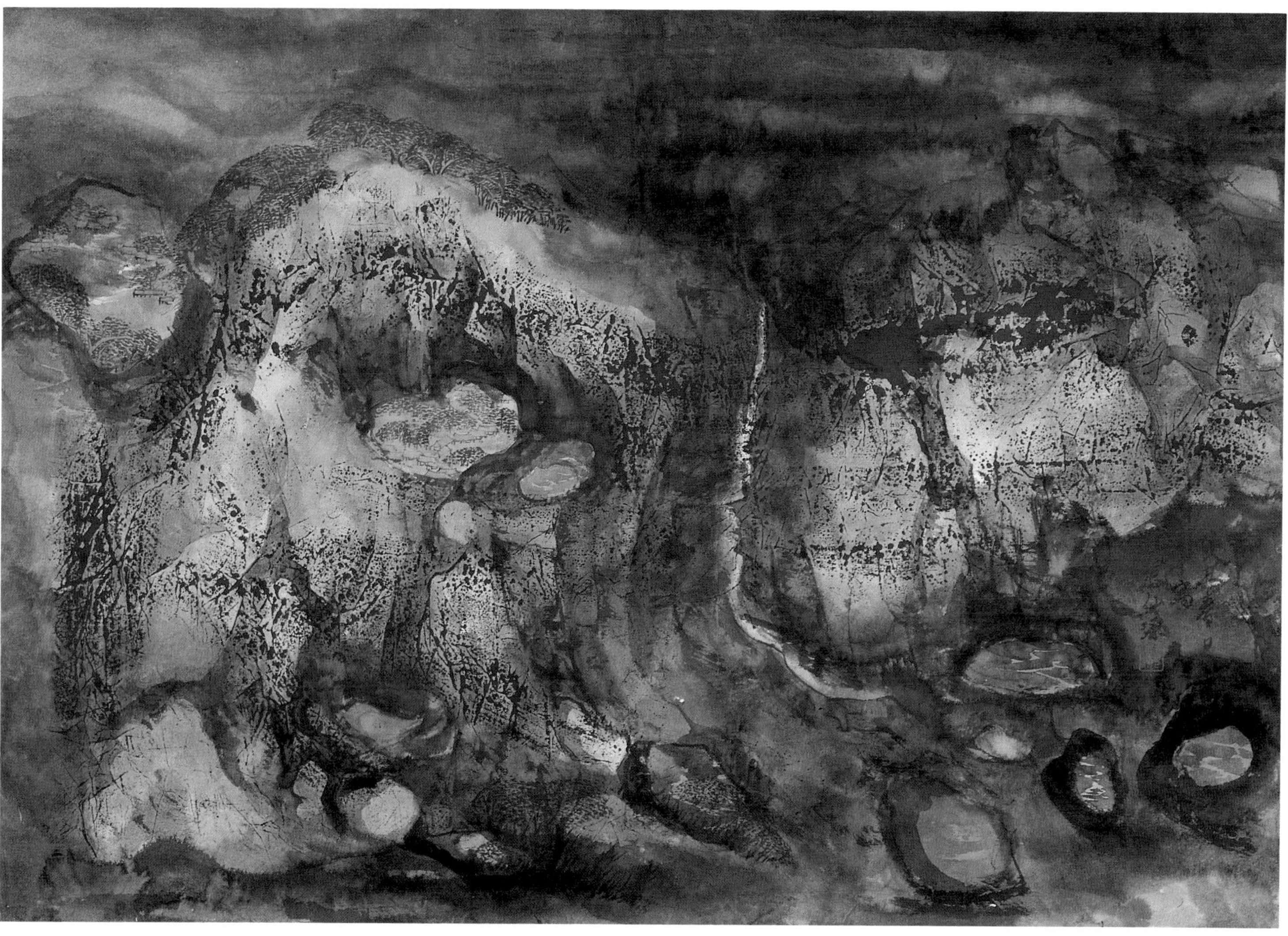

14.   Jennifer S. Byrd [Joan Stanley-Baker], "C. C. Wang, The Last Literatus," *Asian Pacific Quarterly* 7, no. 1 (Summer, 1974), p. 10.

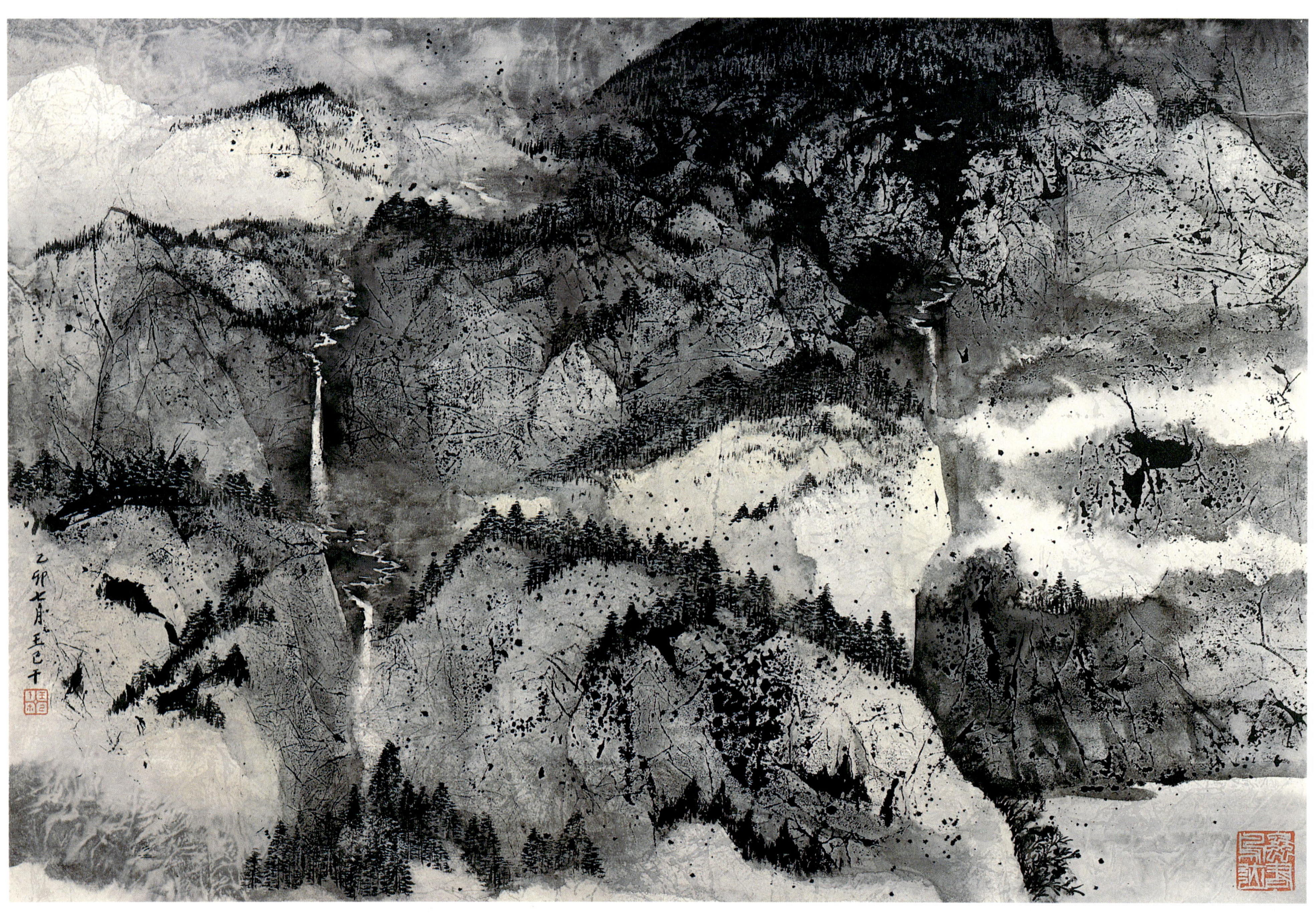

Landscape No. 334. July 1975. Hanging scroll, ink and light color on paper. 23⅝ x 35⅟₁₆ in (60 x 89.1 cm).
C. C. Wang Family Collection.

Inscribed
"I-mao [1975], 7th month. Wang Chi-ch'ien."

Artist's Seals
Wang Chi-ch'ien hsi (left); *Ch'ung-shu niao-chi* (no. 31, lower right)

Exhibited
Brooklyn Museum, 1977; Taipei Fine Arts Museum, 1984; Hong Kong Arts Centre, 1985; Aspen Art Museum, 1985; Emily Lowe Gallery, Hofstra University, 1986; Hong Kong Arts Centre, 1986; Birmingham Museum of Art, 1987

Published
Katz and Wang, no. 64; Chang and Davis, no. 37; Cahill et al., no. 10

15.   Richard Barnhart, "Recent Paintings by C. C. Wang," *Oriental Art* N.S. 19, no. 4 (Winter, 1973), p. 460.

16.   Byrd, "C. C. Wang," p. 13.

17.   Katz and Wang, *Landscapes*, no. 26.

Phase Three, 1972-1980: Maturity

There is no means of precisely dating the transition between what are here referred to as the second and third phases of C. C. Wang's painting. Unlike the passage from his first to second phase, in this transition no technical invention or other departure from his previous style marks the change. Indeed, the third represents the maturation of new stylistic features that originated in phase two rather than constituting an abandonment of them. Aspects of this transition can first be observed in three works, *Landscape Nos. 170, 188,* and *205* (figs. 15, 46, 47) from April, June, and December 1972. Facilitating this maturation was a restriction of the role of Wang's impressed and folded textures and the establishment of a more even balance between these textures and his highly developed brushwork, thus allowing the artist to regain greater control over his compositional designs. While this change is perhaps the most obvious, other changes were necessary to help sustain this new balance. Relying more on traditional, careful shading by means of ink and color washes applied with the brush, the local forms begin to take on greater bulk, generating more complex surfaces in the painting and engendering a more profound sense of monumentality in the landscapes. Greater clarity of painted form and landscape design express what seems to be a clearer sense of artistic intention. While these changes appear in some regards to be a step backward, shedding the experimental exaggerations of his new style and restoring certain more traditional practices, their effect was to consolidate the virtues of his stylistic innovations so as to assure their artistic survival and further development.

The few close observers of C. C. Wang's painting development in those years did not take long to note the significant change taking place. In a published review of the exhibition of Wang's works held early in 1973 at Harvard's Fogg Art Museum, Professor Richard Barnhart was generally critical of his work up to about 1968—finding it "vague and formless." But of Wang's latest paintings, meaning those from 1971 and 1972, he concluded that many "so powerfully and richly join the experience of the 20th century to the enduring truths of Ni Tsan and Tao-chi that one can no longer hesitate to join the name of C. C. Wang to those of his most distinguished predecessors.... Mr. Wang is already creating the most important Chinese landscape paintings of this century."[15] Writing a year later and in greater detail, Joan Stanley-Baker carefully observed that a major change had occurred in C. C. Wang's style by late 1972, concluding that after that time, "multiplicity gives way to a new monolithic grandeur," that "the traditional frontal view yields to an unprecedented volumetric presence," that his "rocks have become monolithic boulders with compelling mass and weight," and that "we are brought into the air-age and look down from thousands of feet above ground where peaks beyond peaks, oceans beyond mountains, are all visible, all beneath us."[16]

A comparison of *Landscape No. 170* (fig. 15), done in April 1972, with *No. 104* (fig. 43), done three years earlier, illustrates the initial aspects of this artistic maturation. These two works are related in their basic design: each has a central mass separated from flanking forms by receding spatial corridors, this recession marked by watery channels in three of four cases. But the forms remain largely superficial in the earlier painting, a mere surface for the play of striking textures, both impressed and folded, that are themselves the primary visual subject of the painting, while in the later work, mountains are the subject, —mountains and space—and the role of texture, together with well-matched brush lines, is to help shape the firmly rounded, sharply-faceted, crystalline rocks of this painting. Far from seeming to rest on the painting surface, these lines seem etched in deeply fissured rock, reminiscent of monumental landscape painting in its earliest phase of development, in the 6th through 8th centuries. Similarly reminiscent of this early period are the rounded, schematic trees which crown the hard-edged mountain ridges, emphasizing contour lines and recessional passages. The reduced vertical rise of the watercourse in this painting gives it an increased sense of projection into depth, as does its eventual disappearance behind a distant rocky cliff. The wet ink wash that cradles the course of this stream and elsewhere darkens the spatial corridors or covers the upper reaches of the mountains with a dense haze further contributes to the feeling of monumental space and palpable form. Of the mist which hangs like a pall over this rocky valley, C. C. Wang has written:

The sense here is of a mountain valley in the midst of a storm. I didn't set out to paint that kind of scene. The dark clouds on the top where the ink was heavily absorbed into the paper give it this feeling. Also the wrinkles in the shapes of the rocks add that jagged, nervous energy which gives a greater sense of storminess.[17]

The direction of this artistic maturation is pursued still farther in *Landscape No. 188* (fig. 46), dated June 1972. Impressed and folded textures play a nearly equal role here with traditional brushwork. One can perceive the artist adjusting his brushwork to match his impressed texture—modeling his brushwork on textural "accidents" so that it is not entirely evident which marks are applied texture and which are done with the brush. Impressed textures are reduced in quantity, and just as important as either impressed textures or brushwork in determining the rocky forms of the landscape are fracture lines produced by light, linear texture folds in the painting paper which the artist subsequently followed or in some places merely imitated with long strokes of the brush, restrained in tone and modulation. As a result, the larger mountain shapes are built up in a more logical manner than before, from smaller conglomerate units first molded by lines and supporting tonal washes and then folded together into larger masses. This composite structure—the larger masses taking their form from smaller yet already volumetric ones—establishes a sense of monumental scale that in earlier paintings was achieved only through the use of other, secondary structures. Very subtle in this painting is the restrained, rhythmic play of large landscape clusters spread in horizontal bands across the painting, accented by rows of low trees that line their upper contours. Softly mottled washes, executed with a minimum of pale wet ink, suggest clouds emerging from unseen valleys and rising to cloak some of the mountain ridges. Waterfalls—unpainted forms, spared out and framed by dark, wet washes—appear between large openings in the rocks to provide a sense of movement in depth along ground planes that recede from the painting surface.

The overall effect of this painting is one of blended elements, of conceptual unity, with no one of the painter's elements clamoring for attention. Altogether, the painting lacks the raw power of *Landscape Nos. 76* and *112* (figs. 39, 40), but it is ultimately more grand and dignified. The swelling of local forms gives the mountains greater mass; rhythmic curves leading from rock to rock, from ridge to ridge, make these mountains more visually animated. The composition is a variety of that type last seen in *Landscape No. 40* (fig. 38), with lower mountains that transmit the viewer's attention to those above—in part (here) by receding somewhat in their direction —and the higher mountains, pressed down from above by thick clouds and the tight border of the painting, looming forward over those below. But the more sophisticated handling of composition here gives this landscape greater presence. The merging of component forms into a common visual rhythm and their occasional, dramatic separation, their subtle curves and undulating surfaces that ripple like curtains across some geological stage, create an effect that is at once awesomely powerful and gently ethereal. Complemented by soft colors—blue interspersed with pale ochre, occasionally accented by green dots—the landscape takes on a shimmering, ghostly effect, like a display of northern lights given terrestrial form.

This painting offers a first sense of the innovative role that color will come to play in the artist's mature style.

Three paintings represent the artist's continuing maturation over the next three years: *Landscape No. 205*, done in December 1972 (fig. 47); *No. 241*, from November 1973 (fig. 48); and *No. 334*, from July 1975 (fig. 45). All are done within the general compositional type seen in *Landscape No. 40* and *No. 188* (figs. 38, 46): in each, horizontally-layered forms step progressively backwards into the painting, the closest major contour leading in from the lower left corner of the composition while taller, distant mountains fill the remainder of the paper and dominate the painting. In each, the mountain forms are generated from conglomerate units, with shaded washes used more than lines or impressed textures to shape each unit. Beyond this, the landscapes differ in numerous ways and establish individual identities. In *Landscape No. 205* (fig. 47), the tension between the abstract and representational qualities of the painting is well-balanced, miniaturized buildings stimulating imagination of what it would be like to dwell in such a place, while at the same time the mountain surfaces urge a tactile exploration of almost purely abstract, geometrically fascinating shapes. The artist's impressed textures are now even better integrated into the depiction of landscape substance, representing the surface of cold, hard, chiseled rock. The forms of the landscape are set forth in large scale: the central mass that looms discomfortingly over a cluster of dwellings, below, its bulging form recalling a number of paintings by Tung Ch'i-ch'ang (cf. fig. 10, upper right) although the artist might well have had an earlier source, Kuo Hsi, in mind; the handsome, well-rounded domical peak to the right; the peculiar horizontal motif extending inwards from the left edge of the painting, that is best read as a natural bridge like that found just left of center in *No. 188* (fig. 46).

Landscape No. 188. June 1972. Hanging scroll, ink and color on paper. 24 x 29¹⁵⁄₁₆ in (61 x 76 cm). Collection of Mr. and Mrs. Frank Cho.

Inscribed
"*Jen-tzu* [1972], 6th month. Wang Chi-ch'ien."

Artist's Seals
Wang Chi-ch'ien hsi (left); *Ch'ung-shu niao-chi* (no. 31, lower left)

Exhibited
Brooklyn Museum, 1977

Published
Katz and Wang, no. 29

Landscape No. 205. December 1972. Hanging scroll, ink and color on paper. 23¹¹⁄₁₆ x 29¾ in (60.2 x 75.6 cm). Private Collection.

Inscribed
"*Jen-tzu* [1972], 12th month. Chi-ch'ien."

Artist's Seals
Wang Chi-ch'ien hsi (left center); *Shih-ch'iao-ts'un li jen-chia* (lower right)

Exhibited
Brooklyn Museum, 1977

Published
Katz and Wang, no. 36; Byrd, fig. 13

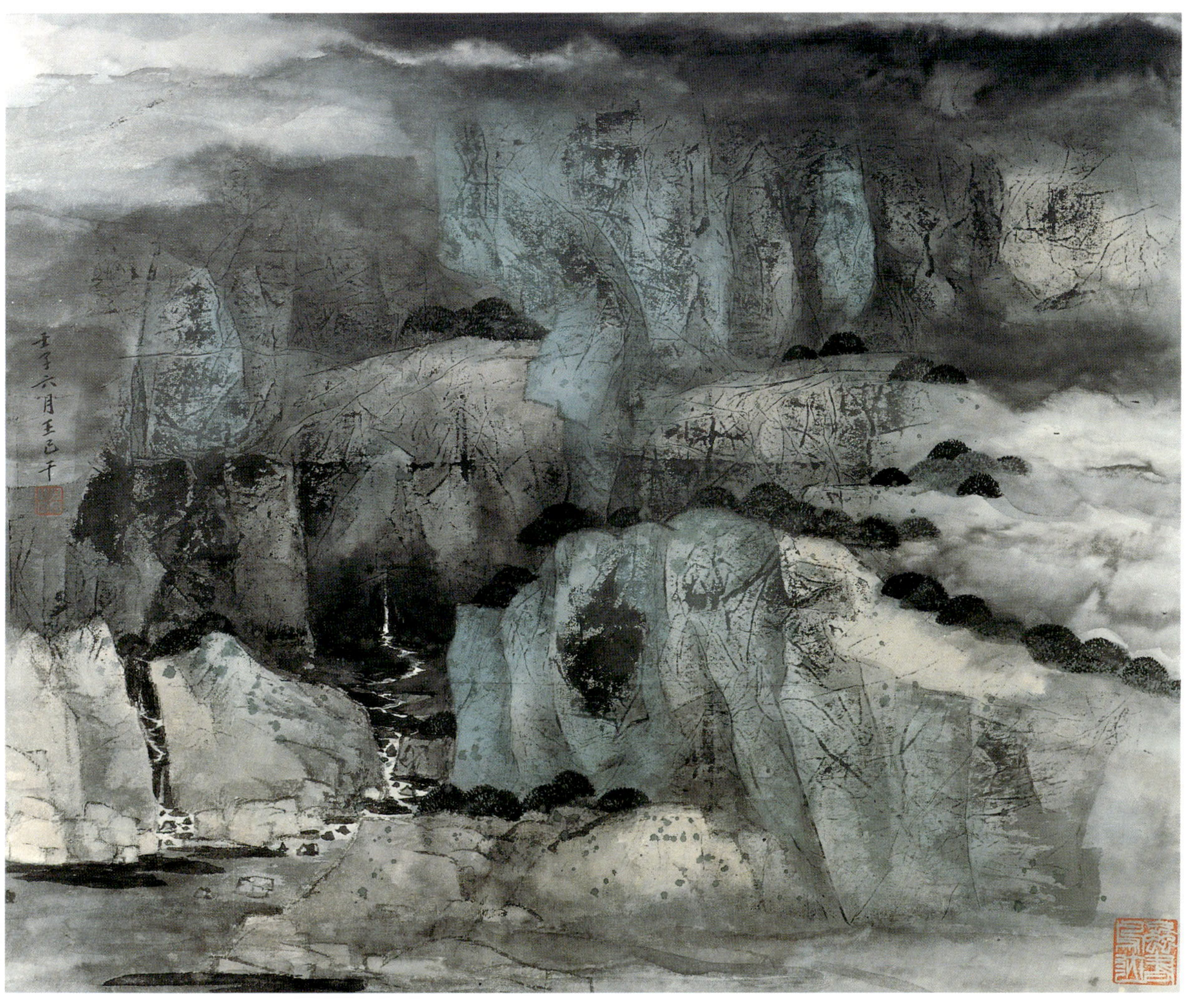

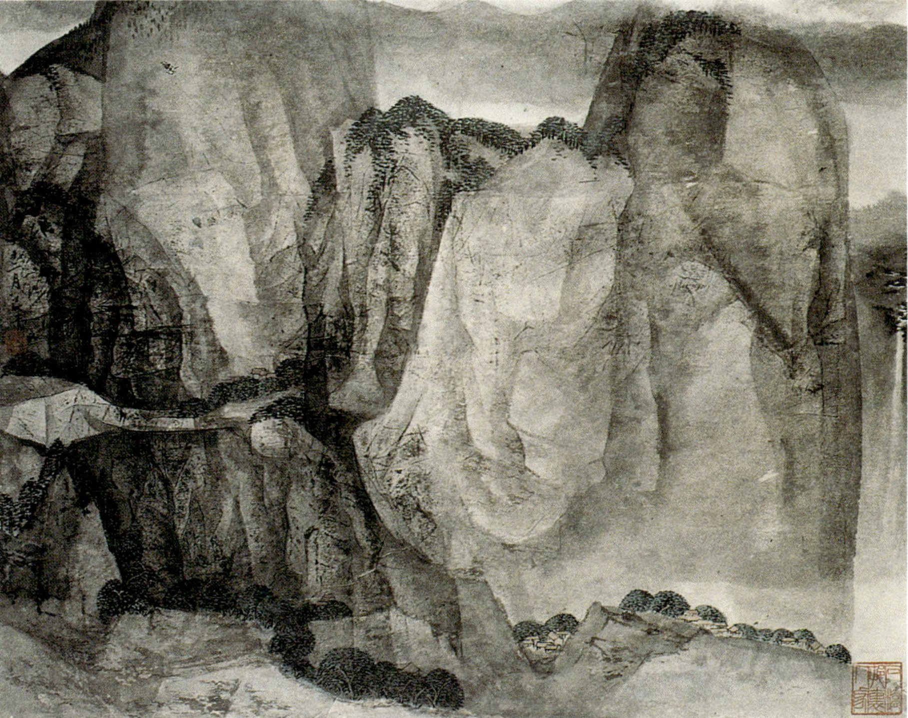

In *Landscape No. 241* (fig. 48), the scale is a bit larger, the mountains and buildings removed to a slightly greater distance. The foreground is more clearly separated from the distant mountain wall, a granite wall that is more unified into a single, vertical mass. This carved granite surface somehow manages to seem both hard and soft at the same time, its rocky forms veiled behind a pale mist and almost disappearing into thicker clouds at the top and upper left. Compared with *No. 205*, these landscape forms seem more subtle in their geometry and more intriguing in their tactile appeal, in a Cézanne-like manner almost ceasing to represent subject matter and to revel in a purely painterly exploration of abstract planar surfaces.

In *Landscape No. 334* (fig. 45), while the vertical fall of water at three different points is somewhat repetitious, the watery pathway including the two falls on the left provides a more open and continuous passage into depth than found in the two previous landscapes. So too does the carefully graded, diminishing scale of the trees, which are strikingly subtle in execution and perhaps the finest of any in the artist's landscapes. Among these three paintings—even among most of C. C. Wang's works—this landscape is unusually impressive in its naturalistic spatial scale and openness, its integration and continuous recession of form. In few of his works are the elements of his painting technique and the forms of his landscape so effectively blended into a coherently unified landscape vision. Like certain real landscapes such as that of Yosemite Valley, it seems balanced between the geologically exquisite and a landscape that could come only from the mind.

Occasionally, real landscapes *did* have their effect on the works of C. C. Wang, although indirectly, as noted with regard to *Landscape No. 284* (fig. 32). The encircling web of forms in *Landscape No. 162* (fig. 49), from April 1972, places equal emphasis on the chain of mountains and on the azure lakes which they surround. These lakes, like those of several other paintings at that time, drew their inspiration from the artist's repeated visits in the late 1950s and early 1960s to the Swiss alpine lakes near St. Moritz. The Chinese often called such lakes "heavenly lakes"—held up by the mountains to the heavens above. Similarly, *Landscape No. 239* (fig. 50), dated September 1974, was painted shortly after a tour of Yellowstone Park, and the artist acknowledges that his use of color and the forms of his trees were inspired by that visit. Yet both paintings remain balanced between site depiction and abstract study.

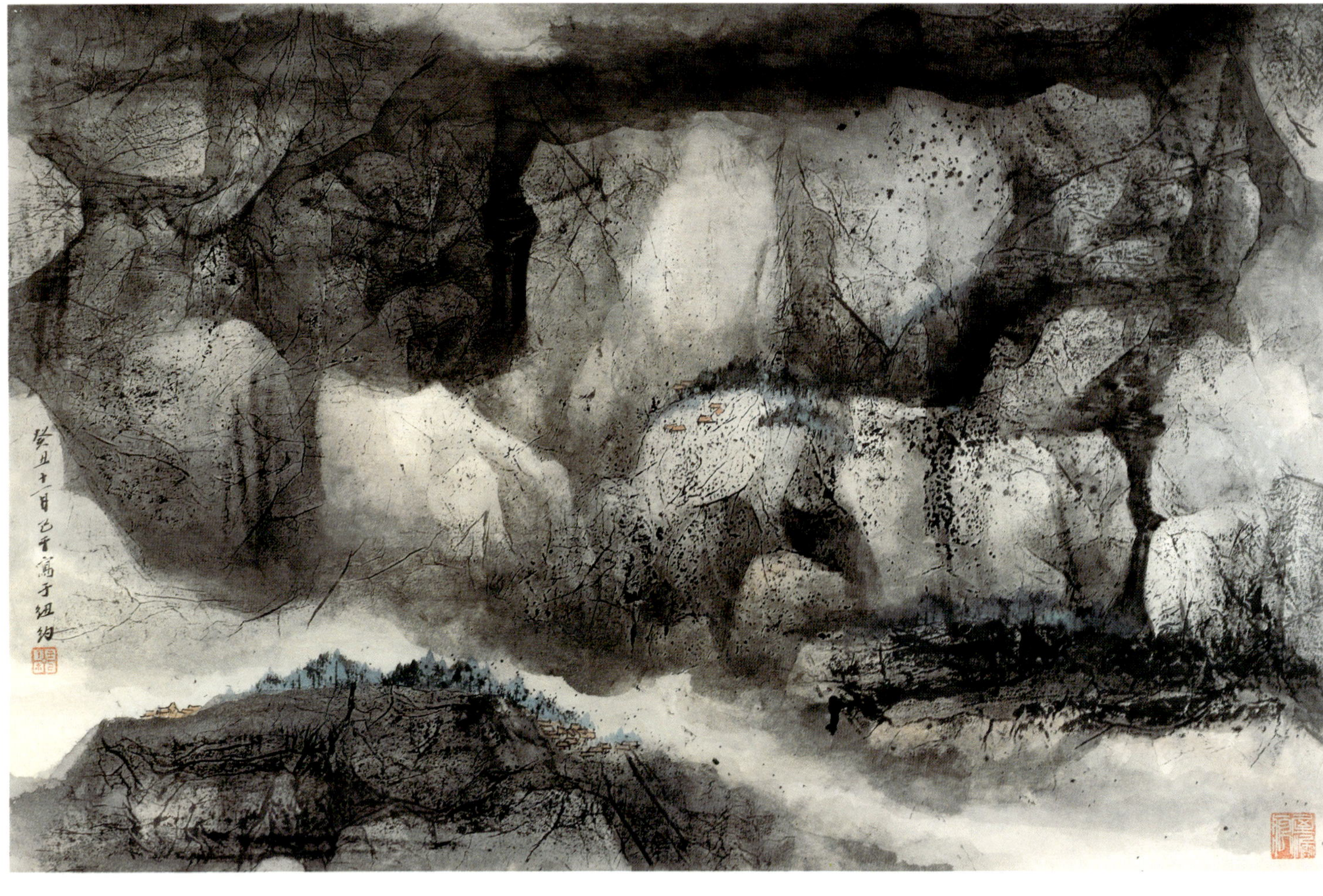

Landscape No. 241. November 1973. Hanging scroll, ink and color on paper. 22¹³⁄₁₆ x 35⅝ in (58 x 90.4 cm). Private Collection.

Inscribed
"*Kuei-ch'ou* [1973], 11th month, written by Chi-ch'ien in New York."

Artist's Seals
Wang Chi-ch'ien hsi (left); *Wu lou hen* (no. 22, lower right)

Exhibited
Chinese Culture Center of San Francisco, 1976; Brooklyn Museum, 1977

Published
Katz and Wang, no. 43

49

Landscape No. 162: Heavenly Pond and Stone Cliff. April 1972. Hanging scroll, ink and color on paper. 34¼ x 23 in (87 x 58.4 cm). Phoenix Art Museum, Gift of Jeanette Shambaugh Elliott.

Inscribed
"*Jen-tzu* [1972], 4th month. Wang Chi-ch'ien."

Artist's Seals
Wang Chi-ch'ien hsi (lower right); *Ch'ung-shu niao-chi* (no. 31, lower right)

Exhibited
Phoenix Art Museum, 1985

Published
Siu, p. 77; Cahill et al., no. 8

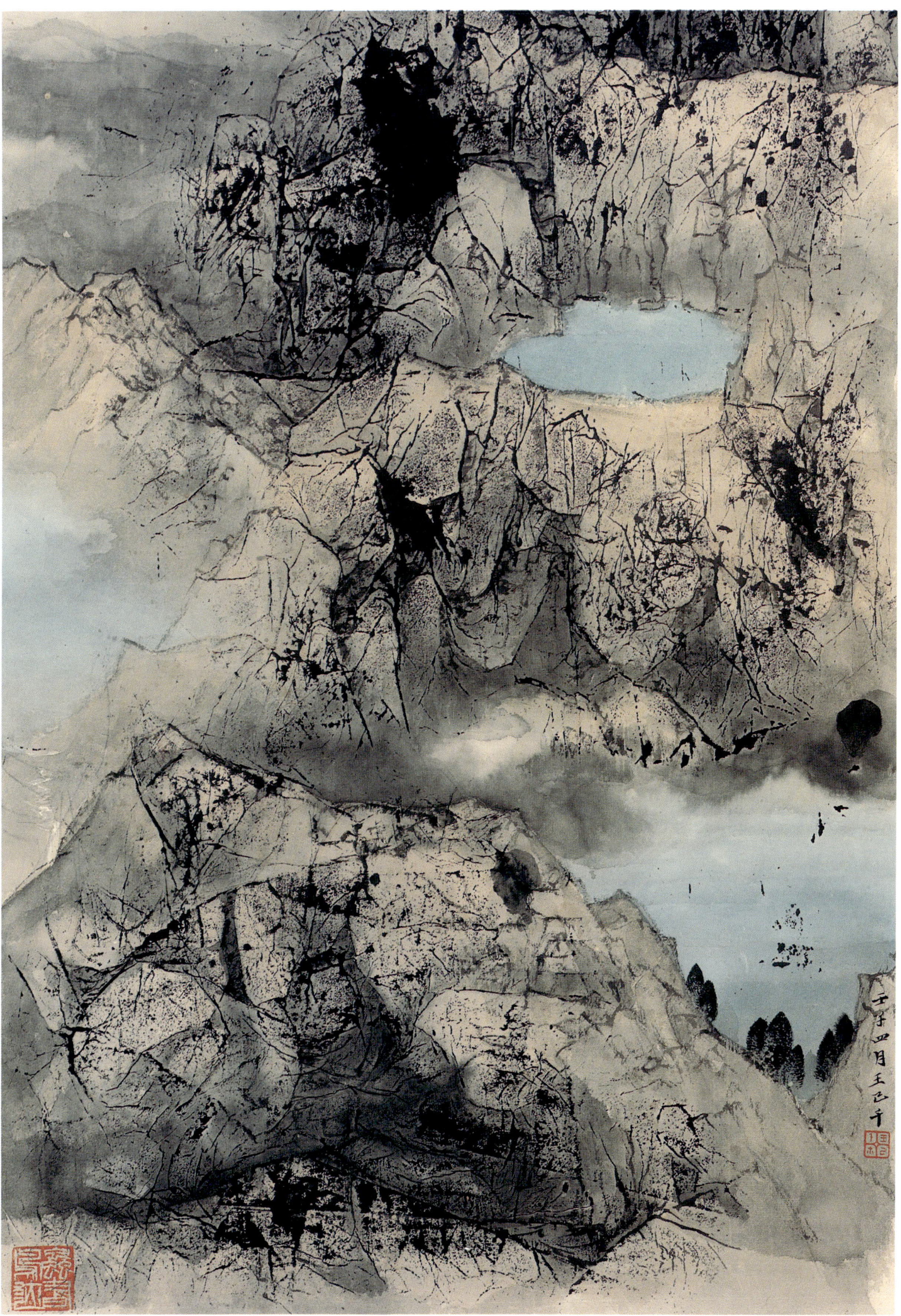

Landscape No. 162 (fig. 49), highly schematic in its structure, is particularly impressive for the unbroken linear movement of its mountains around stable pockets of watery color. The pale ochre-colored network of rock also assumes the function of an abstractly shaped ground for the display of impressed and folded textures and brushwork, while the blue water serves as a plain foil. Brushwork, applied textures, and folded textures play roughly equal roles; they are sleek, elegant, and calligraphic in character and impressive in quality. This handsome bit of landscape resembles a fine Chinese garden rock (named T'ai-hu rockery for the lake near Suchou where they are "harvested" off the bottom): deeply pocked and pitted, sometimes completely penetrated, yet structurally unbroken, and taken by the Chinese as miniatures or crystallizations of nature's grandest mountains. One might wonder whether C. C. Wang, who has collected more than sixty fine "miniature mountains" in rock, actually had such a visual pun in mind; if so, he would hardly be the first to paint such garden rocks (*Landscape No. 240*, fig. 44, has overtones of this), but he might be unprecedented in obliterating the distinction between such miniatures and real landscape. Nine small leaf-shaped trees (two in very pale ink), silhouetted against the lowermost lake, and a short watercourse that flows forward from the lake on the left are the only details which suggest a larger natural scale. This work extracts the basic structural principles of earlier examples such as *Landscape No. 112* (fig. 40) and *No. 240* and renders them with heightened abstractness. The simplicity of its design all but disguises the boldness of its conception and its skillful elegance in execution.

Landscape No. 239 (fig. 50) is remarkable for its layers of softly rounded and equally softly colored hills, piled up like blue and rosy sunset clouds. These are complemented by a delicacy of shading and line, whether done with the brush or applied texture, and a subtlety of detailed form, including stippling brushwork for distant vegetation and scarcely visible cottages tucked behind two of the mountain ridges. In its constituent forms and somewhat in its general openness of space, it is closely related to *No. 334* (fig. 45); its contribution to *No. 334* (which it precedes by ten months) becomes quite clear if one looks at the central, vertical third of the later painting. Although *Nos. 239* and *162* are related compositionally to other works, both are distinctive examples within the artist's *oeuvre* and demonstrate that C. C. Wang could continue to develop his mastery of spatial recession at this time even as he continued to work within frontal compositional modes.

The design in *Landscape No. 305* (fig. 51), painted in July 1974 and perhaps the most outstanding painting of this phase, illustrates the further progress of C. C. Wang's recessional "dragon vein" compositions. The configuration of mountains here is simple but forceful, forming a more powerful "dragon vein" than either of its predecessors, the untitled landscape of March 1966 and *River Village in a Rainy Dawn* (figs. 37, 33); in unbroken sequence, these mountains twist back and forth over a flat, watery plane, like the back of some undulating creature rising from the waves. The entire landscape is shown from above, clustered villages half-hidden beneath its mountain ridges. This painting is as monumental in artistic conception as it is in scale. Powerful bursts of ink—partly applied texture, partly brushwork—line the rugged mountain sides with landscape-calligraphy of the highest order. Smoky washes cast the mountains' base into shadows; at their feet, serrated spits of land plunge into blackened waters (such darkened waters being found in C. C. Wang's landscapes as early as 1969 but never before seen with such effect). The bit of brown color used locally throughout the painting and the faint traces of green add to its somber and subdued tone rather than detracting from the feeling of monochrome. This is a painting which eschews all suggestion of the decorative (something not quite avoided in other landscapes like *No. 188, No. 162,* or *No. 239,* figs. 46, 49, 50) and achieves instead the heroic. It is related to particular aspects of several previously discussed paintings— to *Nos. 239* and *334* (fig. 45) in its constituent landscape forms, to *No. 162* in the unity of its compositional structure—but it surpasses these and all other previous examples in its integrity as a work of art. Various elements of the painting also give hints of origins in the distant past: the arched earthen forms derive from Tung Yüan (fig. 9), while both the structural clarity of bare-sided hills and their coiled serpentine movement are highly reminiscent of Kuo Hsi of the 11th century. Yet it is in the quality of the work as a whole, rather than in such bits and pieces, that a link is forged between this painting and the noblest early works of China's ancient art.

The latter half of the 1970s was a period of relative dormancy in C. C. Wang's painting career. Uncertainty about what to do next, after a decade of constant innovation, and the turning of his energies to collecting after his sale of twenty-five major early paintings to the Metropolitan Museum were two reasons cited for this in the biographical section of this essay. Along with the period from 1949 through the early 1960s, this period forms the second major hiatus in the development of the artist's landscape painting style; as with the first period, few paintings are available for study and those that are document primarily the lack of artistic progress on the part of an artist who says, "I don't want to stand still."

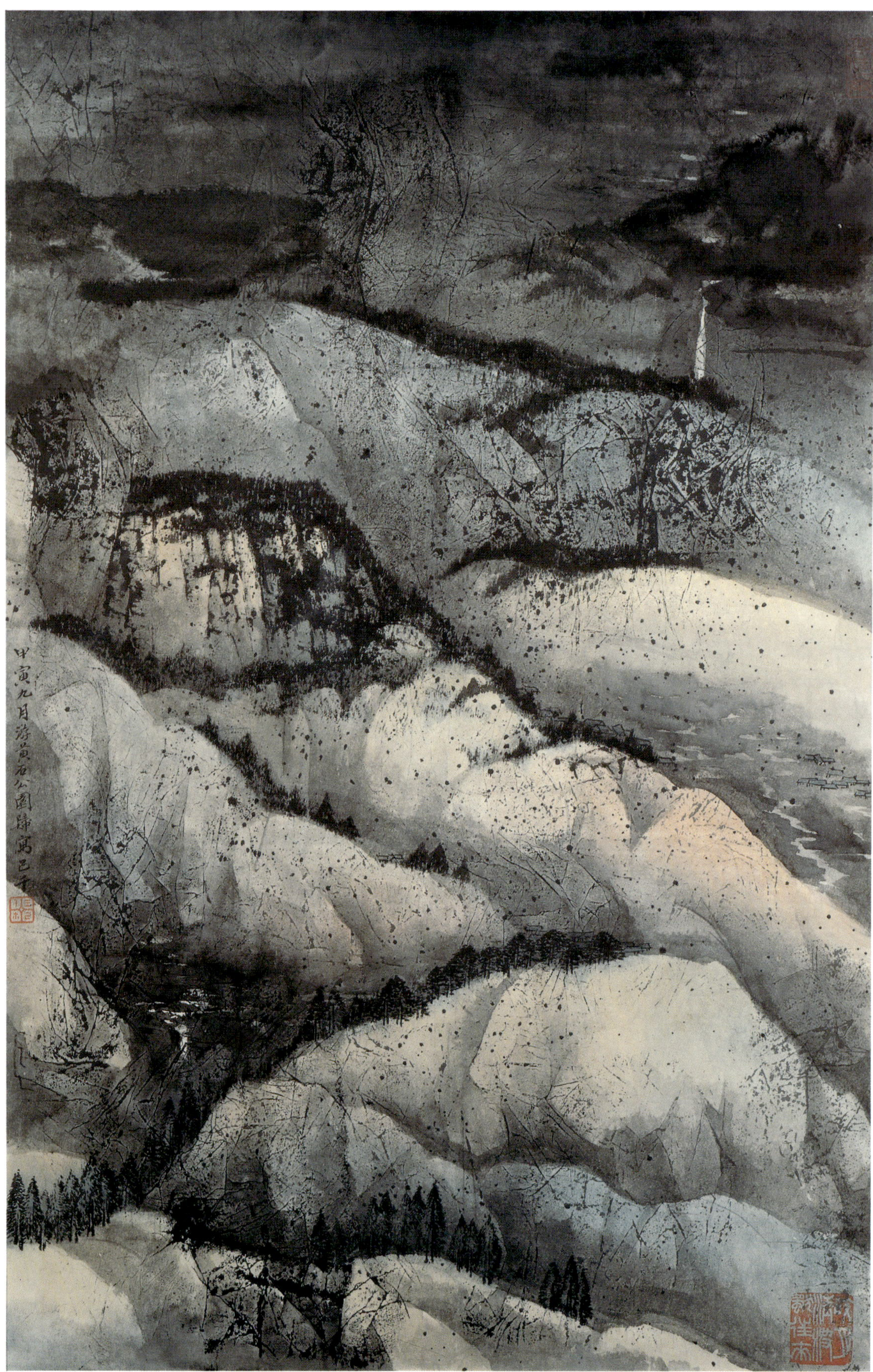

50

Landscape No. 239. September 1974. Hanging scroll, ink and color on paper. 31¹³⁄₁₆ x 23⅝ in (80.8 x 60 cm). Private Collection.

Inscribed
"*Chia-yin* [1974], 9th month. Written after returning from Yellowstone National Park. Chi-ch'ien."

Artist's Seals
Wang Chi-ch'ien hsi (left); *Chiao yüeh ch'ing po tu wang-lai* (lower right)

Exhibited
Chinese Culture Center of San Francisco, 1976; Brooklyn Museum, 1977; Hong Kong Arts Centre, 1986; Birmingham Museum of Art, 1987

Published
Katz and Wang, no. 42

51

Landscape No. 305. July 1974. Hanging scroll, ink and color on paper. 35½ x 24 in (90.1 x 61 cm). C. C. Wang Family Collection.

Inscribed
"*Chia-yin* [1974], 7th month. Wang Chi-ch'ien."

Artist's Seals
Wang Chi-ch'ien hsi (lower left); *Chiao yüeh ch'ing po tu wang-lai* (lower right)

Exhibited
Brooklyn Museum, 1977; Oriental Gallery, New York, 1983; Hong Kong Arts Centre, 1986; Birmingham Museum of Art, 1987

Published
Katz and Wang, no. 53; *Exhibition of Works by Chinese Artists in New York* (New York: Oriental Gallery, 1983), pl. 1; Chang, "Landscape," fig. 7 and cover; Cahill et al., no. 11

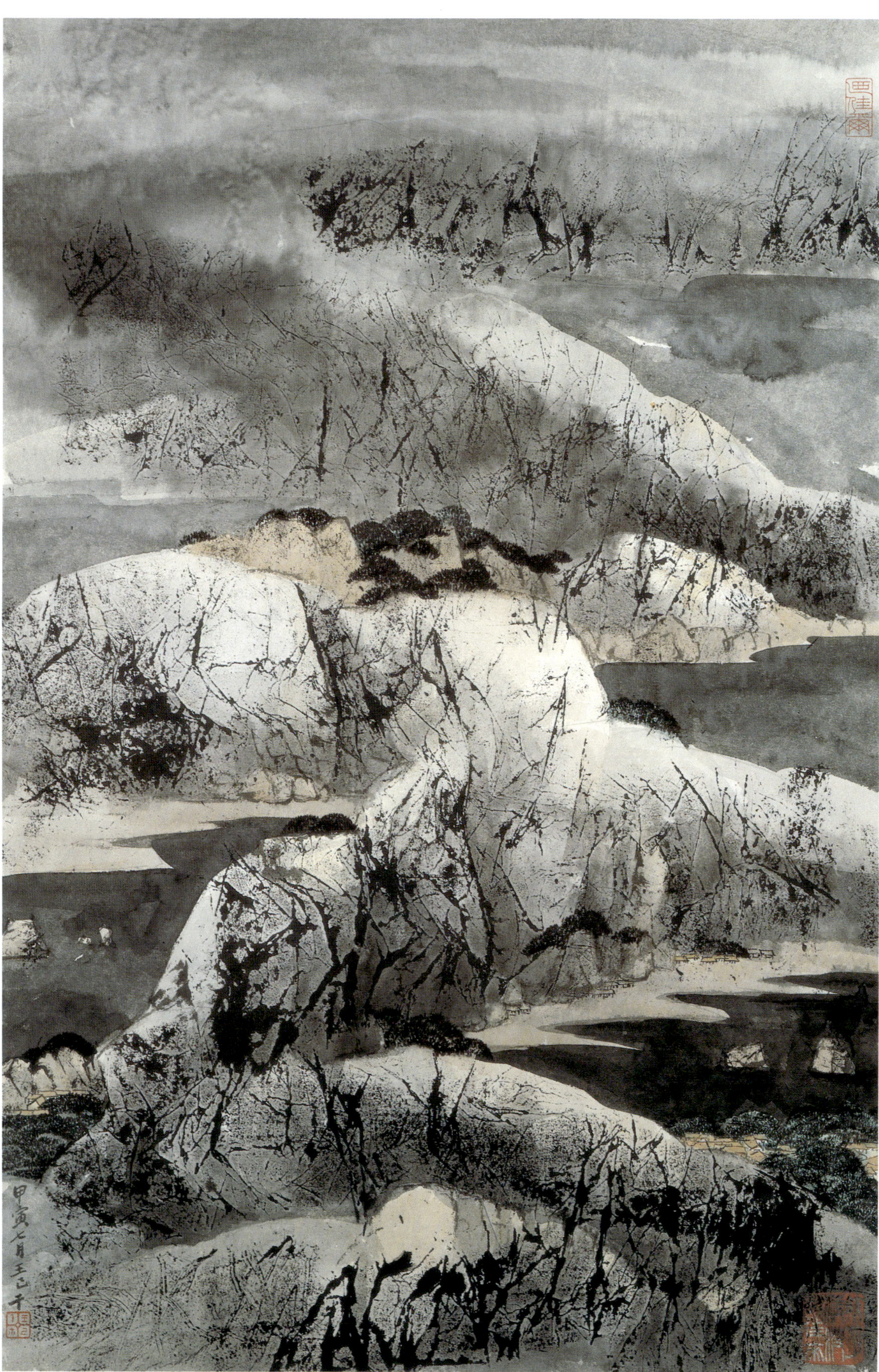

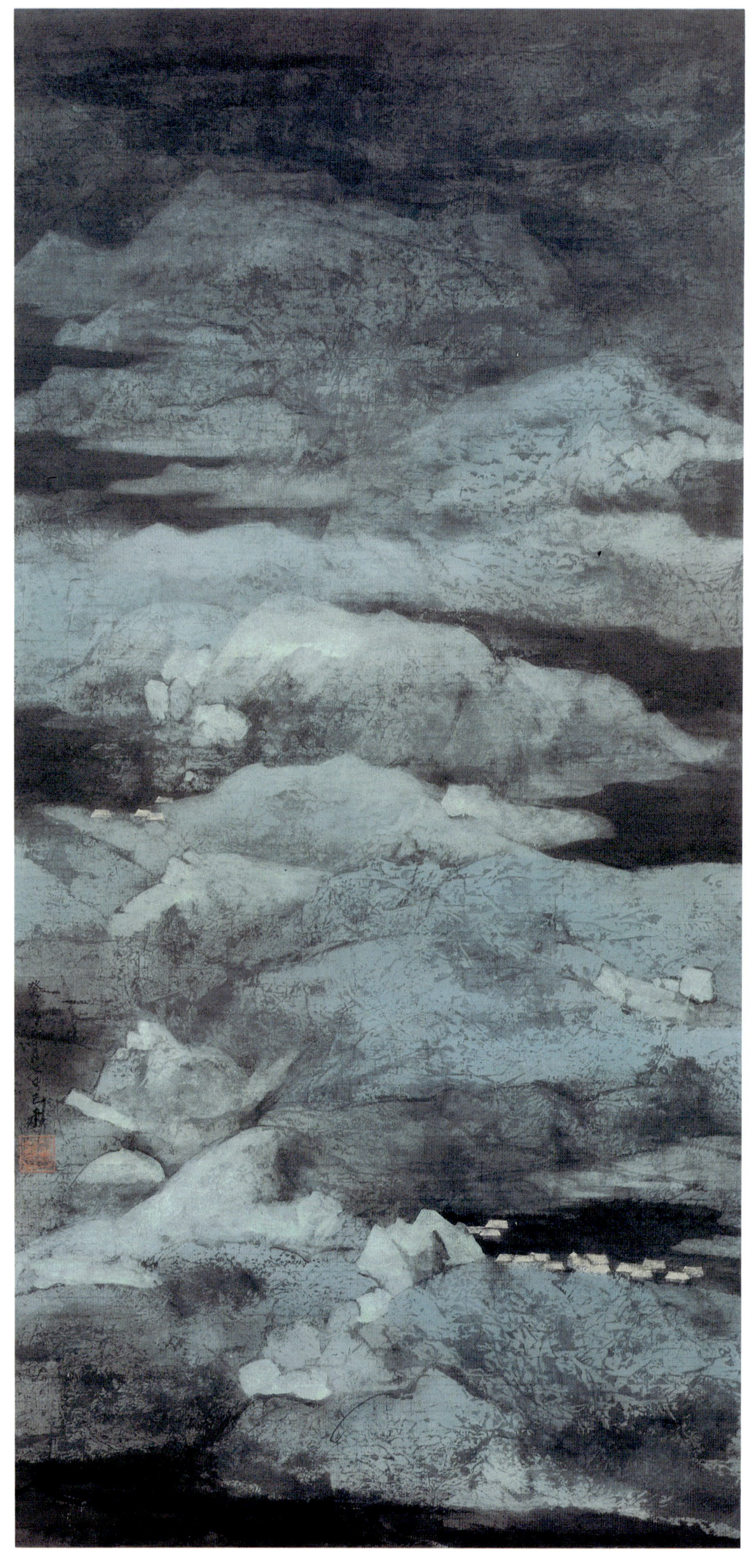

18.   Arnold Chang, *Painting in the People's Republic of China: The Politics of Style* (Boulder: Westview Press, 1980), p. 33.

Phase Four, 1980 to the Present: Beyond Maturity

This period of dormancy came to an end by 1980 or 1981 with a resurgence of activity and renewed creativity. *Landscape No. 305* marks one of the pinnacles in C. C. Wang's career, a crystallization of those features which characterize his third stylistic phase; it also forms a link with some of the finest paintings that helped initiate a fourth artistic phase. Two such paintings are *Landscape No. 398* (originally numbered *379;* fig. 53,), done in February 1981, and *No. 397* (fig. 22), painted in August 1981, which share with *No. 305* the compositional design of a land mass stretching backwards along the central vertical axis of the painting, swinging back and forth to either side of the center and silhouetted against a flat, watery plane—his "dragon vein" configuration. The first painting of this pair, *No. 398*, is distinguished by its complete lack of impressed texture, relying on brushwork alone. This feature is found in enough of C. C. Wang's work from this period for one of his closest observers, Arnold Chang, to have suggested that beginning in about 1980, the artist might be regarded as having embarked upon "yet another phase" of his career.[18] This suggestion is supported by still other hallmarks of Wang's work in this period of renewed activity, visible in both of these paintings, such as the more dramatic and increasingly easy handling of compositional problems that were first mastered in the mid-1970s in works such as *Landscape No. 305*. Both paintings also illustrate the increasingly prominent role of color in the 1980s, which often is just as striking as the compositions themselves and greatly enhances their dramatic effect.

The cumulative effect of these characteristics is to establish a new phase in which the artist's landscapes are often both ruggedly powerful and at the same time more readily pleasing than anything previously produced. For the first time, C. C. Wang's art faces the risk of becoming too skillful, decorative, and too pleasing. At the same time, the finest examples of this period, which avoid these aesthetic shortcomings, achieve at last a qualitative standard whose historical significance can scarcely be minimized even by the casual observer. As his own most severe critic and well aware of the new artistic problems he faces, C. C. Wang has continued to pursue new directions in painting and has become more inventive than ever, avoiding the stagnation that constantly threatens the successful artist.

The most important of the innovations occurring during this period involves a technique for staining his paintings with color from the back side of the paper, which is coupled with a severe simplification of form reminiscent of the two-dimensional frontality of paintings in the second phase of his career. This has yielded a group of more than twenty works distinctive enough to be placed into a separate stylistic group (including figs. 21, 52, 61-65, 74), all but a few of which were produced between January and May 1983. But despite the distinctiveness of these paintings, they belong together with other works of the period as recognizably responding to the same set of artistic problems—problems which he has met with a consistently high level of inventiveness and solved within an ever increasing range of stylistic variation. The new prominence of color, for example, is one of the most distinctive features of paintings throughout this fourth phase, and coloring his works from the back side is only one of various ways this has been expressed. Rather than merely continuing to do what he does well, C. C. Wang has continued to extend the range of his art, further exploring the nature of Chinese painting and its possibilities. With every year that passes, he seems to do this with greater ease and mastery of his art. If phase one might be called "traditional," phase two called "beyond traditionalism," and phase three thought of in terms of the artist's maturing mastery of his modernized style, then phase four may be thought of as going "beyond maturity."

To return to the pair of landscapes already mentioned as having helped to usher in this latest phase, it is *Landscape No. 398* (fig. 53) that best illustrates a number of differences from paintings of the 1970s, including its complete absence of impressed and folded textures. In this painting, the artist has employed a number of features from the stylistic mode of Ni Tsan (fig. 5): flat, thinly faceted earthen forms, often as much suggested as literally depicted (compare, especially, the more distant hills of this work with those of Ni Tsan); the dry, angular brushwork; and, with considerable dramatization, the composition. C. C. Wang here exercises his independence from the semi-accidental textures that helped liberate his compositions from the conventionality of his earliest years. The compositional principles learned with the aid of applied textures are now firmly established in the artist's mind and set forth without technical assistance. The design of this painting is reminiscent of that in *No. 305*, but this landscape offers a rich variety of local forms that invite close inspection, whereas the structural units of the earlier work are much more uniform and meant to be seen as a whole. The artist here applies a lesson which he says was learned from Wang Yüan-ch'i making each rock somewhat different in shape and scale, while structurally differentiating forms of smaller and larger scale: smaller rocks are scattered about the muddy flats at the foot of tall peaks, while piles of medium sized boulders establish contour lines along the sides of larger forms that constitute the primary mountain chain. This mountain chain is itself more radically varied as it moves from foreground to rear, curved peaks leading to pointed ones, then to flat-topped ones, and so on.

This sequence of mountain forms, like music, sets forth major and minor themes, alternately builds crescendos or trails off into near silence, sometimes issues forth in unison, sometimes divides into separate strains. An echo of this is found in the chain of houses in the foreground, set in a rhythmic arrangement that is capable for the first time of sustaining an independent focus of attention and is highlighted for the first time with white casein.

The use of color in this landscape is also more striking than ever before: warm reddish ochre and cool gray played off against each other like the strings and horns of an orchestra, the former providing the dominant mode for earthen forms, the latter used for the minor theme of chilly, forbidding looking waters. Yet the two are also interchanged, gray tones flickering along the side of the mountains, ochre colored mud flats rising in the foreground, just above the water level. Never before had the artist's use of color been so integrated with the formal structure of the composition, another lesson learned at least in part from Wang Yüan-ch'i but also influenced by his study of Western art. As varied as the shapes of rocks, the colors are constantly changing tone, and the textures of color washes are boldly contrasted—thin washes of pale gray ink for the middleground water played off against the dense, inky black washes of the far distance. Irregular streaks of spared out white paper, like piercing lightning, line the flat surfaces of mud and water. The dominant reddish ochre hue of this painting departs radically from traditional Chinese norms and calls more attention to the use of color than do any of C. C. Wang's previous paintings—although *Landscape No. 284* (fig. 32) and a few works from the 1950s may provide some precedent. From this time on, the artist began to express himself more strongly and freely through his use of colors, incorporating the lessons learned from the Post-Impressionist painters who first attracted him to the West.

The artist's brushwork here, free from competition with impressed texture strokes, is primarily pale, dry, and sketchy, yet it extends beyond that to include dark, wet, thick outlines and matches in variety the painting's range of form and color. Derived from Ni Tsan, it consists especially of hooked strokes that move horizontally to the right and then down, much of it done on the side of the brush and executed very quickly, with light, fillip-like movements of the brush. It is also characteristic of C. C. Wang's painting technique that he moves rapidly back and forth between different sections of the painting, working a little bit on one area here, then there, according to an inner feeling rather than building up each area thoroughly and methodically. Despite the lack of accidental texture in this painting, the brushwork itself is full of accident, irregularity, and visual surprise. One surprise detail in this

landscape did not take form until C. C. Wang carried the painting to Shanghai during a recent trip, displaying it at an exhibition of works by pupils of Wu Hu-fan. There, for the first time, he met Ch'eng Shih-fa, China's best known living figure painter, whose occasional landscape paintings still better justify his reputation. As a mark of their new friendship, Ch'eng placed two figures on the foreground promontory, overlooking the tiny world of human houses far below. While oversized and rather out of place in this perch, they create a triad of narrative elements in the painting, together with the houses below and the sailing vessels beyond.

Landscape No. 397 (fig. 22), done a half year later, in August 1981, shows parallel differences from works in the artist's earlier phase, although in this painting C. C. Wang again uses his impressed texture technique. The shapes and carefully shaded surfaces of his rocks seem close to his paintings of the early to middle 1970s (such as *Landscape No. 241,* fig. 48), yet a comparison with a range of works from *Landscapes No. 188* through *305* reveals a greater coherence of shaded form than was typically produced at that time. The greatest difference between this painting and earlier ones lies in its unusual color scheme: shadowy gray-green land forms set against strikingly jet black water, the two separated by thin bands of tan beaches and the entire surface covered by a sprinkling of snow-white casein mixed with an occasional touch of blue. The contrast between the darkened landscape and bright snowfall creates an unusual tension between recessional forms and surface pattern. In all of C. C. Wang's work, there is nowhere a more dramatic or original color scheme.

53

Landscape No. 398, with figures by Ch'eng Shih-fa.
February 1981. Hanging scroll, ink and color on
paper. 23½ x 33¼ in (59.7 x 84.5 cm).
Private Collection.

Inscribed
"*Hsin-yu* [1981], 2nd month. Chi-ch'ien."

Artist's Seals
Wang Chi-ch'ien hsi (lower right); *Shih-ch'iao-ts'un li
jen-chia* (lower left)

Additional Inscription
"Figures added by [Ch'eng] Shih-fa."

Additional Seal
Ch'eng [Ch'eng Shih-fa]

Published
Stanley-Baker, "Significant," p. 57

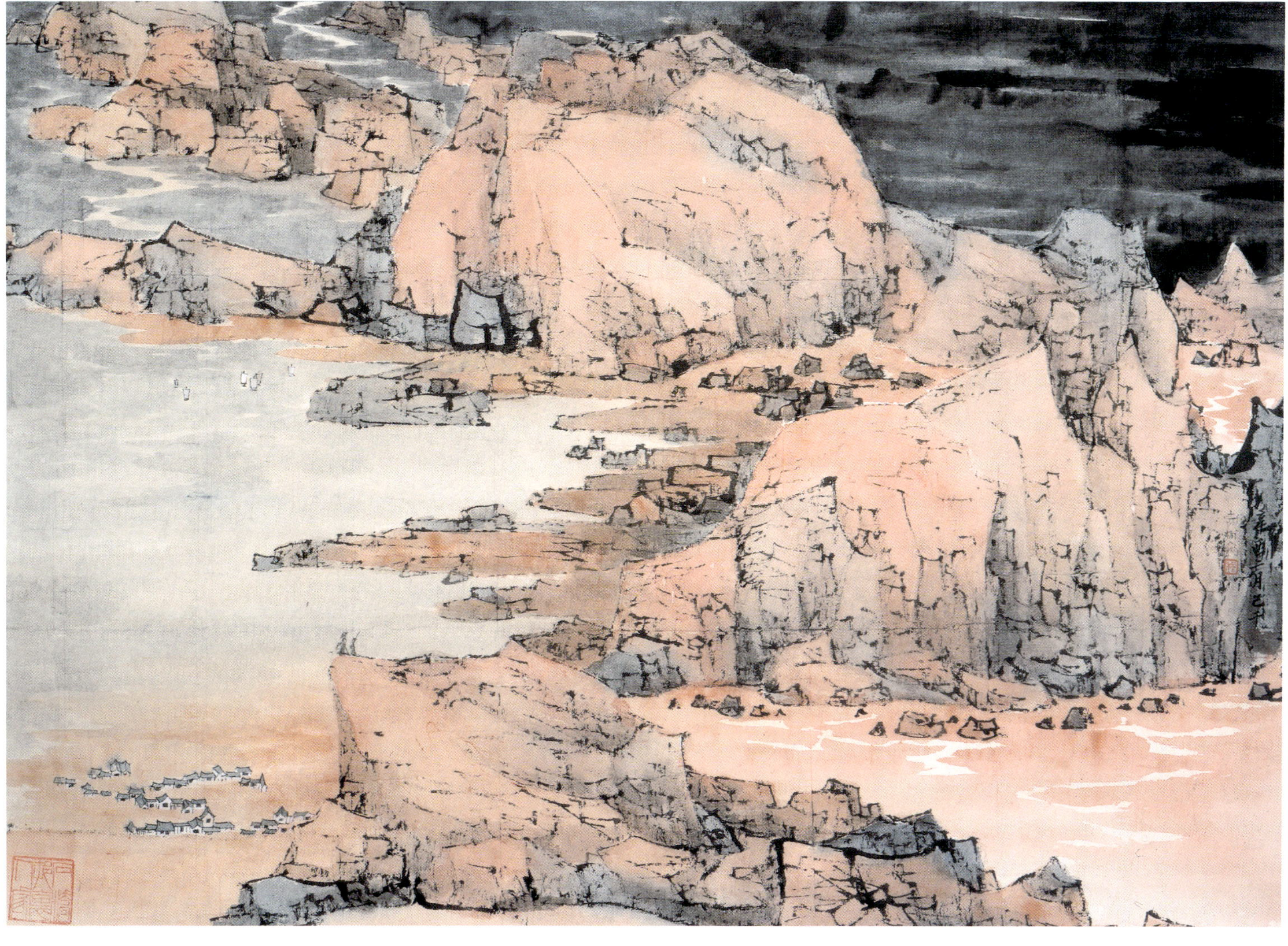

The juxtaposition of these two works, *Landscape Nos. 398* and
397 illustrates an important characteristic both of C. C. Wang's
work and that of most traditional Chinese painters, namely
the tendency to work for periods of time within a single
compositional mode, or no more than a few such modes, and
thereby to render composition a lesser factor in painting style
while focusing on ("playing with") the other elements of
painting: brush modes, the structural types of rocks and
earthen forms, color schemes. Throughout this last phase,
most of the artist's compositions are drawn from—albeit
frequently improving upon—a basic compositional vocabulary
established in his second and third stylistic phases. Numerous
variations on this particular compositional scheme were
produced in his fourth phase, perhaps a dozen of them nearly
identical to *No. 398*, for example *Landscape No. 450* (fig. 13),
done a year-and-a-half later, in February 1983. This painting
reveals the artist's continuing maturation. The composition of
its earthen forms is much like that of *No. 398*, as is its brush
type; but here the faceting is more rounded, considerably more
complicated, more substantial, and visually more engaging,
while the brushwork is less restless and more poised in
character, some of the finest brushwork in all of C. C. Wang's
paintings. Even the tracery-like pattern of his houses reveals
greater sophistication. This painting offers a reversal of the
earlier work, *No. 398,* in its color scheme, the earthen forms
now a cool blue-green, the surrounding flats warm brown.
If not a fresher artistic vision, it is nevertheless a more fully
developed work of art.

Yet another work which expresses the variety possible within
this compositional mode is *Landscape No. 369* (fig. 54), done in
July 1980, earlier than the others just mentioned. It differs by
virtue of its rapid brushwork, a type that the artist associates
with less orthodox, sometimes "flashy" professional painters
like Tai Chin and Wu Wei of the Ming period or the Yangchou
"eccentrics" of the 18th century. Although not generally
acceptable to him, the artist undertook this mode "to show that
I can do movement like theirs." The result, he says, is "like
singing too fast," yet he is pleased with this excursion into new
territory. More favorable precedents for such brushwork might
be cited, such as Hsü Wei of the Ming or Tao-chi of the Ch'ing;
but whatever the historical overtones of this style, the artist's
execution of such a rapidly moving brush style is done with
admirable strength and control and does not reach beyond the
bounds of the rhythmically undulating mountains of his
painting.

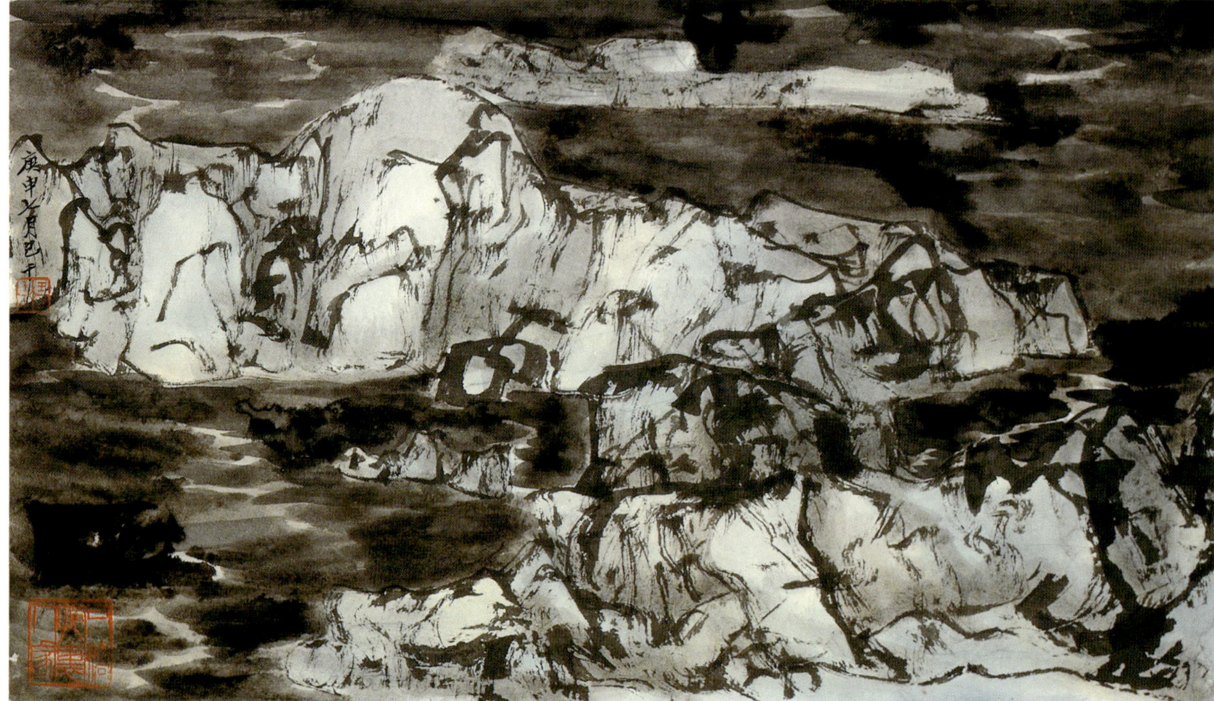

Landscape No. 369. July 1980. Hanging scroll, ink and color on paper. 13¼ x 23⅝ in (33.7 x 60.0 cm). Qing Xing Zhai Collection.

Inscribed
"*Keng-shen* [1980], 7th month. Wang Chi-ch'ien."

Artist's Seals
Wang Chi-ch'ien hsi (left); *Shih-ch'iao-ts'un li jen-chia* (lower left)

19.   See Katz and Wang, *Landscapes,* nos. 19 (*Landscape No. 139* from 1971) and 27 (*Landscape No. 173* from 1972).

Two landscapes, done in June and August 1982, *Nos. 418* and *419* (figs. 55, 56), represent the artist working perilously close to the limits of what he himself considers too skillful or too decorative. *Landscape No. 418* is generally subdued and anything but decorative except in use of color, but color tends to dominate the other aspects of the painting. Compositionally, although it shares the "dragon vein" principle of the four previous paintings, the mountains toward the left form a denser group than in the other examples and restrain the compositional flow, the linear extension mountain forms being noticeable only in movements toward the lower and the upper right. The brushwork on the hills, executed on paper that is unusually rough in texture, is particularly dry and done in a manner which the artist says is quite close to that of his master, Wu Hu-fan. Although it is an excellent example of the scholarly mode of brushwork, C. C. Wang describes the result as "monotonous" and lacking sufficient tonal variation. Attempting to make it "a little more exciting," he began to crown the mountain ridges with thickly clustered black trees—burying all but the roofs of his houses—then added blue-green tempera on top of that. (The use of such brightly colored trees, while occasional, can be traced back to the early 1970s.[19]) This was followed by the addition of blue water and white seagulls. The result is a tour de force of color, both by Chinese standards and C. C. Wang's own, and calls to mind Japanese painted screens of the late Muromachi and Momoyama periods, decorative works in age of decorative splendor. It is only the dryness of ink texture and his softly vanishing brush line, increasingly less visible as one steps away from the painting, that keep this work—perched on the edge of such splendor—within the artist's self-imposed aesthetic bounds.

Much the same could be said of *Landscape No. 419* (fig. 56), a lovely painting with considerable decorative appeal, yet also with no lack of scholarly qualities and subtle artistry. The impressed ink textures and much of the linear brushwork have a moist, sleek elegance like that already seen in *Landscape No. 162* (fig. 49), but there are also present here additional layers of fine, dry brushwork that tone down its beauty with a display of aesthetic subtlety. The rockery is handsome, like that of *No. 162*, but here it is also ephemeral, softly suggested rather than sharply defined, and largely without outer contours. The color scheme is bright and cool, blue-green tempera set against the blacks, grays, and white of Chinese ink and paper. But subtle areas of pale green and hints of rose are also present to soften the effect of brighter hues.

The composition of this painting, like that of *Landscape No. 162*, is notable for the integrity of a continuous, looping structure, but the design in *No. 419* is distinctly more complicated, working well whether read in two dimensions or in three. Indeed, the design is most unusual, one of C. C. Wang's most striking variations on the "dragon vein" principle and a compositional masterpiece if nothing else. At first, the foreground, middleground, and distant mountain ridges seem disconnected—dominated by the central range which rises toward a high pitch at the upper right border—especially if one lets the presence or absence of vegetation along the contours lead the eye and dictate the reading of their form. But on closer inspection, as one reads one's way around the painting, short arms, arcs, and twists take on added visual significance and connections emerge throughout the landscape, beginning with one along the left side of the scroll that links the distant and foreground contours into one semicircular movement embracing the central ridge. Lesser ridges connect the central range with the foreground and, in a curvilinear movement (physical or visual) in the upper right, with the distant range, the entire mass forming an astonishing visual loop. Linked together, the design is like a well coiled dragon. This is a painting which may seem merely decorative at first glance, at least by Chinese literati standards, but it ultimately draws the viewer into a landscape marked by genuine artistic accomplishment.

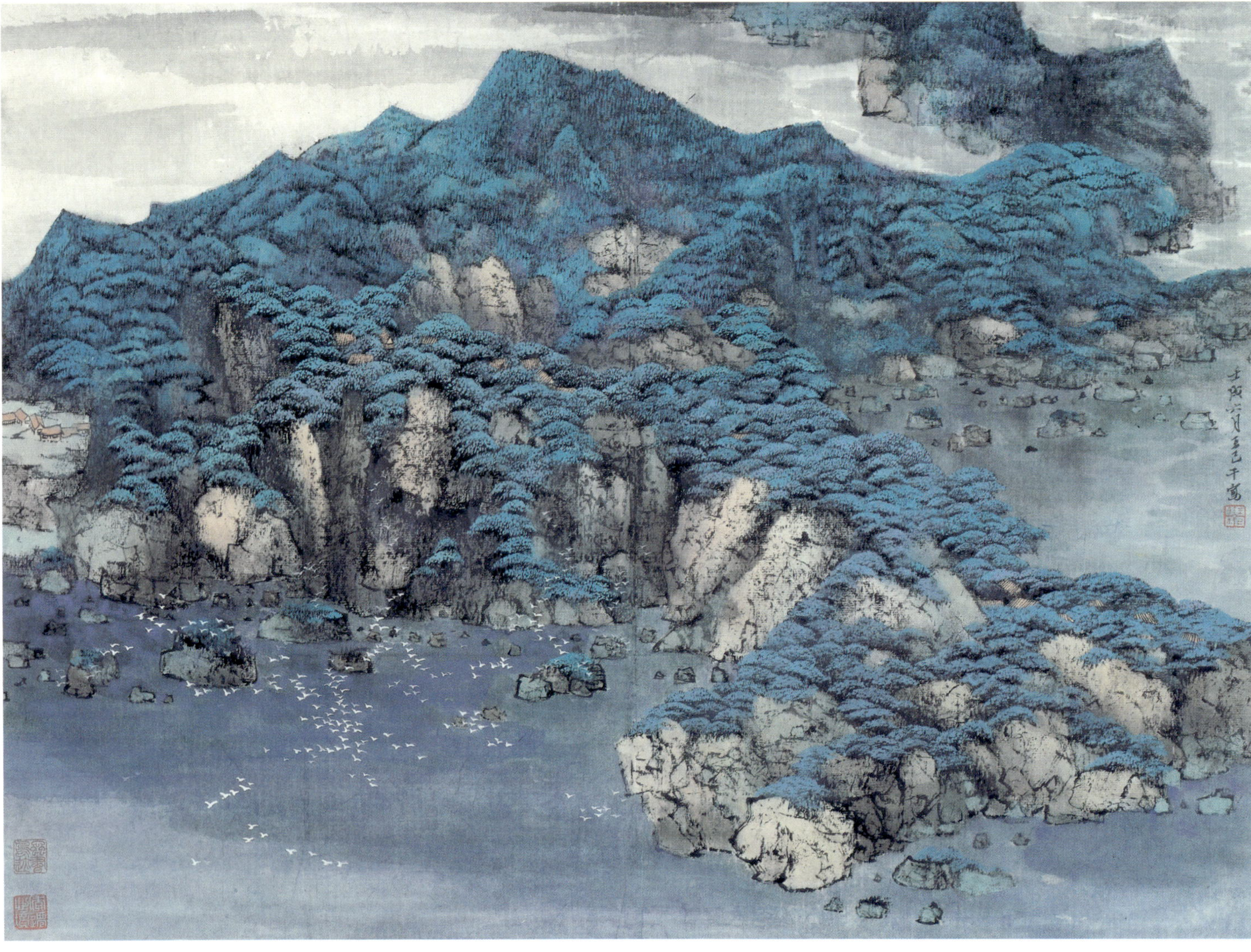

Landscape No. 418. June 1982. Hanging scroll, ink and color on paper. 29 x 39¼ in (73.7 x 99.7 cm). Private Collection.

Inscribed
"*Jen-hsü* [1982], 6th month. Written by Wang Chi-ch'ien."

Artist's Seals
Wang Chi-ch'ien hsi (right center); *Ch'ung-shu niao-chi* (no. 12, lower left); *Chi-ch'ien hsin-ching* (bottom left)

Exhibited
Hong Kong Arts Centre, 1986

Published
Stanley-Baker, "Significant," p. 58; Cahill et al., no. 20

56

Landscape No. 419. 12 August 1982. Hanging scroll,
ink and color on paper. 23 x 32 in (58.4 x 81.3 cm).
Private Collection.

Inscribed
"*Jen-hsü* [1982], 8th month, 12th day. Wang
Chi-ch'ien."

Artist's Seals
Chi-ch'ien ch'uang-kao (lower left); *Fei Nan fei Pei, i ku i
chin* (lower right)

Exhibited
Taipei Fine Arts Museum, 1984; Hong Kong Arts
Centre, 1985; Hong Kong Arts Centre, 1986;
Birmingham Museum of Art, 1987

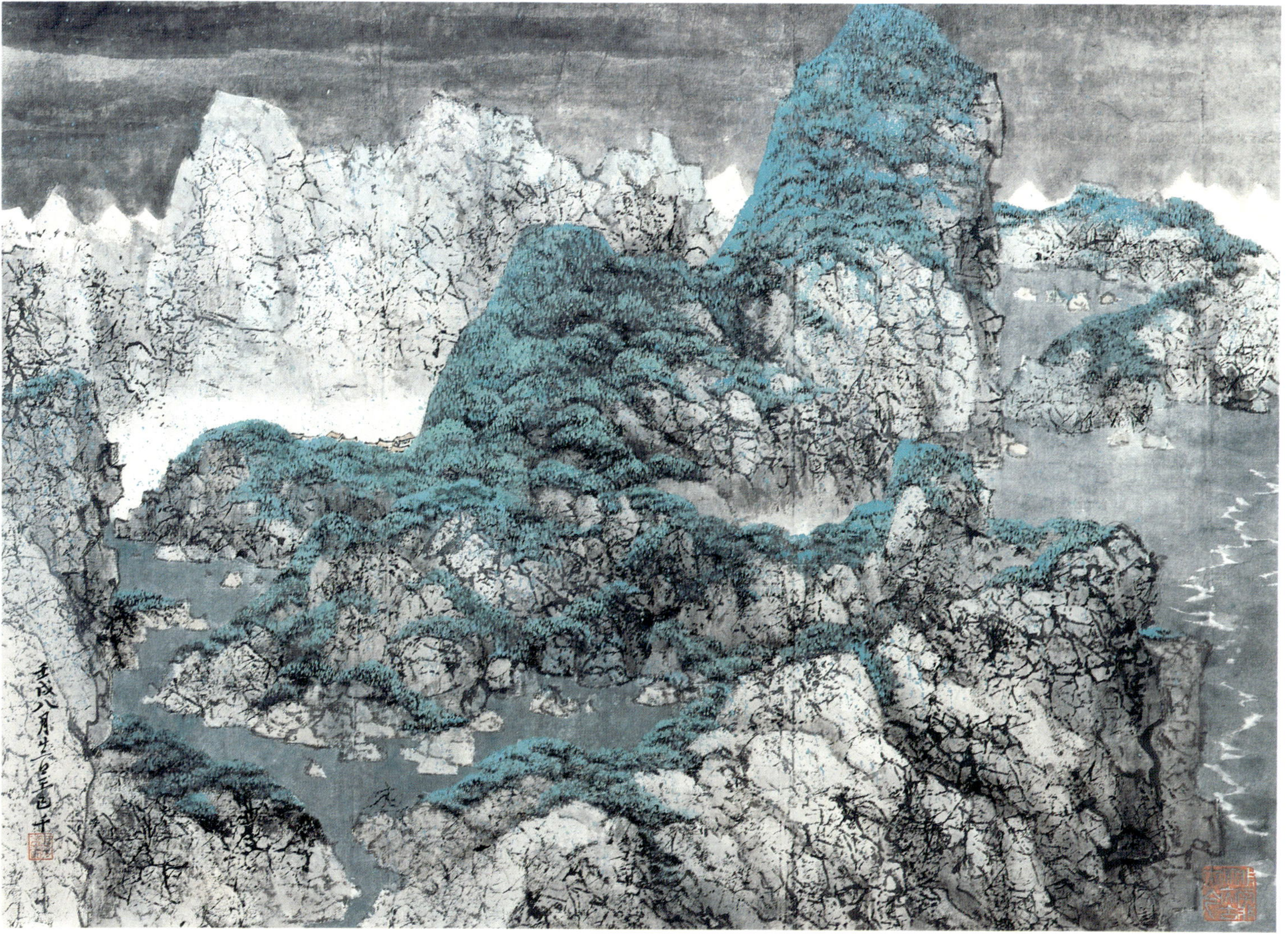

It is C. C. Wang's self-imposed aesthetic restraint, derived
from traditional scholarly values, that causes him to shun his
own most decorative works of art. One like *Landscape No. 420*
(fig. 57), done in July 1982, is simply "too decorative" for him,
although there are not many Chinese painters today who would
disassociate themselves from a painting of this quality. The
vertical composition here appears to be different from that of
the previous examples, but it can readily be obtained by
eliminating the right half of works like *Landscape Nos. 398* or
397 (figs. 53, 22). There is only a slight amount of texture and
much of the brushwork looks like fine, flat textural pattern.
With loosely organized brush lines and not much tonal wash,
the rocks have little integrity and the mountains insufficient
volume. Yet the aerial vantage point is impressive, the rooftop
view of whitewashed houses and the rising flight of white
birds combining to draw the viewer down from on high. The
strongest aspect of the painting is its bold use of color, and the
boldest touch is the unexpected reversal of the normal colors
used for mountains and water: the mountains painted blue,
the water (transformed into mudflats) a rich ochre. Yellow
pigment, sometimes mixed with blue to create a pale green,
also appears sporadically throughout the painting, while sharp,
elegant accents of white casein are used for clustered houses
and a flock of birds. The color scheme, while related to that in
No. 450, is markedly richer in hue. Of course intense colors can
be found in traditional Chinese painting, particularly in wall
paintings of the Six Dynasties and T'ang periods, when azurite,
malachite, and cinnabar were frequently used for painting
mountains, and in later works done in Six Dynasties or T'ang
style (like Wang Yüan-ch'i's handscroll, fig. 23). But it is for his
favorite Post-Impressionist painters that C. C. Wang declares an
affinity in this landscape, most importantly the sensuous
brown-blue colors of Modigliani. The painter's flirtation with
beauty and charm extends right down to the tiled roofs and
bar windows of the houses, seen in very few of his works (such
as the nearly contemporaneous landscapes, *Nos. 418* and *425,*
figs. 55, 58).

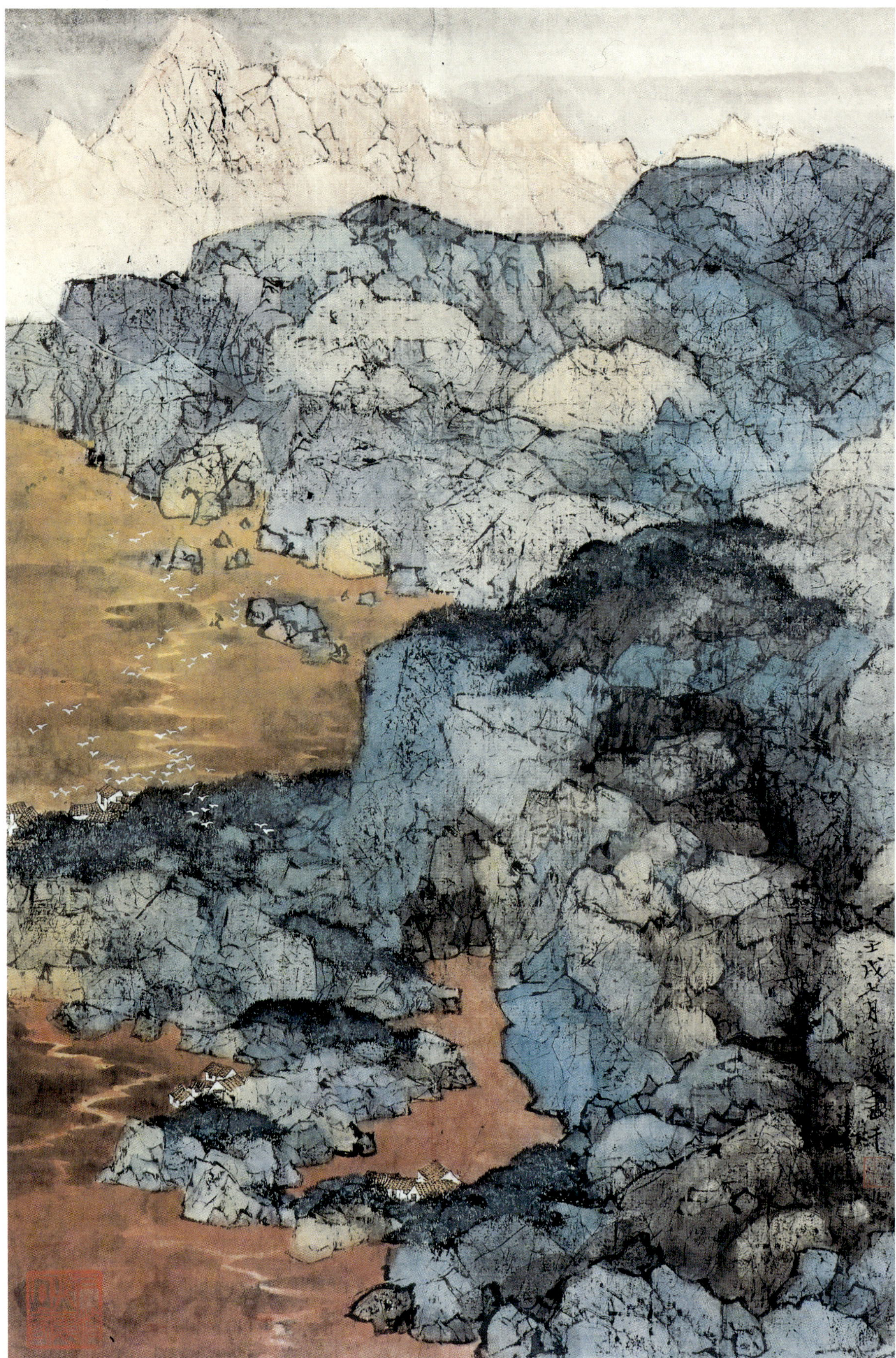

57

Landscape No. 420. 24 July 1982. Hanging scroll, ink
and color on paper. 28¾ x 19¾ in (73.0 x 50.2 cm).
Private Collection.

Inscribed
"*Jen-hsü* [1982], 7th month, 24th day. Wang
Chi-ch'ien."

Artist's Seals
Chi-ch'ien ch'uang-kao (lower right); *Shih-ch'iao-ts'un li
jen-chia* (lower left)

58

Landscape No. 425. May 1982. Hanging scroll, ink
and color on paper. 28⅝ x 40¾ in (72.7 x 103.5 cm).
Ching Yüan Chai Collection, On Extended Loan to
the University Art Museum, University of California,
Berkeley.

Inscribed
"*Jen-hsü* [1982], 5th month. Wang Chi-ch'ien."

Artist's Seals
Wang chi-ch'ien hsi (lower right); *Fei Nan fei Pei, i ku i chin*
(lower left)

Exhibited
Taipei Fine Arts Museum, 1984; Hong Kong Arts
Centre, 1985; Hong Kong Arts Centre, 1986

Published
Cahill et al., cover and no. 6

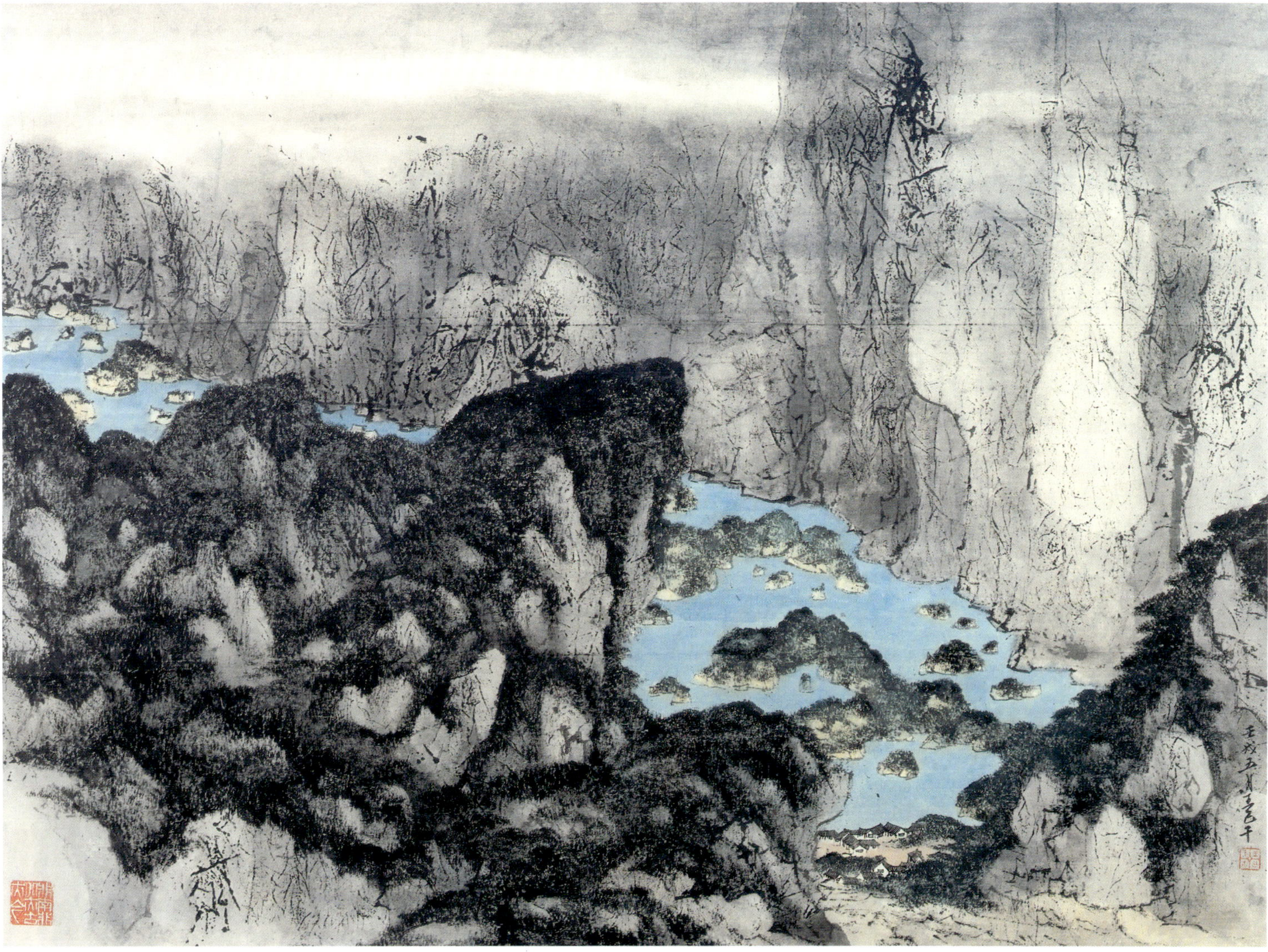

The decorative aspects of these last three works, *Landscape Nos. 418, 419,* and *420,* do not represent the general direction of his work at this time but rather illustrate the increasing diversity in his total artistic activity. Other paintings of this time were considerably more reserved, even consciously conservative by nature, using color only in the most restrained manner if at all and focusing on the most traditional aspect of Chinese compositional style: the interplay of solid mass and open form. One such work is *Landscape No. 425* (fig. 58), from May 1982, within the same three-month time span as the previous three examples. Impressed on this painting is a seal which reads, "Neither Southern nor Northern School, both ancient and modern." The Northern School refers to spiritual descendants of Sung artists who took form and space as their main concern, the Southern School to followers of the Yüan literati who focused instead on brushwork. This painting is particularly reminiscent of Kung Hsien's *Thousand Peaks and Myriad Ravines* (fig. 6), especially the lower right quarter of that work, once in C. C. Wang's own collection and noteworthy for its combination of the so-called Northern and Southern styles into one—much as C. C. Wang's own painting does. The building up of massive form through complex patterns of light and dark; the use of dark, stippling, brush-applied texture strokes to make these forms more palpable; the portrayal of solid forms as if caught in moments of dramatic gesture, seen at strange angles and silhouetted against pockets of open space, backed by tilted ground planes and impenetrable walls; the shapes of some of the more dramatically silhouetted ridges and the settling into these spatial pockets of trailing wisps of vapors; the earthen bridges stretched out upon the water: all these are Kung Hsien characteristics, though C. C. Wang's landscape lacks the mysterious and foreboding qualities of Kung Hsien's work.

The solidity of form and attention to dense, natural texture, the openness of space and atmospheric effects were all thought of as Northern School qualities; the formal gestures and distorted space could only be considered Southern. In Kung Hsien's hands, in the early Ch'ing period, the blend of Northern and Southern represented ancient and modern combined. In C. C. Wang's hands, Northern, Southern, and Kung Hsien are *all* ancient—to be modern is to go beyond Northern and Southern distinctions, to go beyond Kung Hsien, and to bring them all into the 20th century. That is his accomplishment in this painting, which pays homage to the past but could never be mistaken for a pre-20th century painting, nor for anything but a C. C. Wang original. Kung Hsien's turbulent spatial arrangements, unnatural lighting effects, and insistent tonal rhythms are nowhere to be found in the modern work. Instead, the brushwork, the crumpled-paper texture, the modes of constructing and linking solid forms, the treatment of architecture, and even the use of color in *No. 425* are unmistakably the product of the same artist and period of time that yielded *Landscape Nos. 418, 419,* and *420.*

Landscape No. 429 (fig. 59), done a month earlier in April 1982, is another rather conservative work that forms an interesting complement to *No. 425.* If, despite its combination of sources, *No. 425* still retains a dominantly Northern School character, *No. 429* must be seen as essentially Southern School or more scholarly in style, its model to be found in Wang Yüan-ch'i (fig. 23). Not only does the strong vertical and lateral movement of solid forms set upon a flat ground plane—the "dragon vein"—suggest a direct relation to the 17th-century master who used this principle more consciously and effectively than any other, but still more precise references may be found in the split ground plane divided by a middleground screen of mountains, in the radical upward tilt of the ground plane, ascending to a very high horizon line in the upper division, and particularly in the row of distant mountains (left in reserve, unpainted) that appears to be set beyond and *below* the horizon line. The more conservative use of color, too, the artist acknowledges, comes close to Wang Yüan-ch'i. The dry brushwork and flattened faceting of the landscape forms may go back to Ni Tsan, but only as filtered through Wang Yüan-ch'i. One may appreciate this painting, like *No. 425,* on two quite different levels: as a purely visual and particularly effective study in forms, lines, planes, and colors; or as a traditional study in artistic forms that makes a particularly knowledgeable set of references to the art of the past, while translating those referents into something quite modern.

A third landscape can be introduced into this group, *No. 514* (fig. 60), which recalls Tao-chi or his 18th-century followers among the so-called Yangchou Eccentrics. The emphasis on a nearby scholar's rustic cottage, the trees beside it, and the bridge that connects it to the landscape, but perhaps also leading back to the "real" world—all these partake in a narrative quality that seems alien to most of C. C. Wang's work except in its earliest phase, such as his *Landscape After Wang Meng* (fig. 4). Indeed, this is a work which seems much less like C. C. Wang's own than the previous two examples, even as a translation of past styles into a modern idiom, and represents the type of painting that the artist normally executes only for the benefit of his students and scarcely regards as his own. Yet it *is* the artist's own work, not a copy of any specific Tao-chi or Yangchou example and not readily confused with them. Not only does it suggest the artist's continuing ability to work strictly within traditional norms despite his individual departure into a modern style, it also represents what the mature art of C. C. Wang might have been like had he held more closely to tradition rather than choosing to go so far beyond it.

These last three examples reflect C. C. Wang at play within a more traditional vein, like a child dressing up in parent's clothing. A more significant series of works was begun a few months later, initiated by a painting of trees, *Landscape No. 448* (fig. 61), dated 28 January 1983. That this coincided with a moment of unusual creativity in the artist's career is suggested by the close juxtaposition of dates on several subsequent works of particular interest: 8 March (*No. 454,* fig. 62), 21 March (*No. 464,* fig. 63), 29 March (*No. 466,* fig. 21), 12 April (*No. 472,*

59

Landscape No. 429. April 1982, with color added in 1985. Hanging scroll, ink and color on paper. 40 x 28¾ in (101.6 x 73.0 cm).
Collection of Mr. and Mrs. Chuck Chang.

Inscribed
"*Jen-hsü* [1982], 4th month. Wang Chi-ch'ien."

Artist's Seals
Ch'ung-shu niao-chi (no. 12, lower left); *Wang Chi-ch'ien hsi* (right)

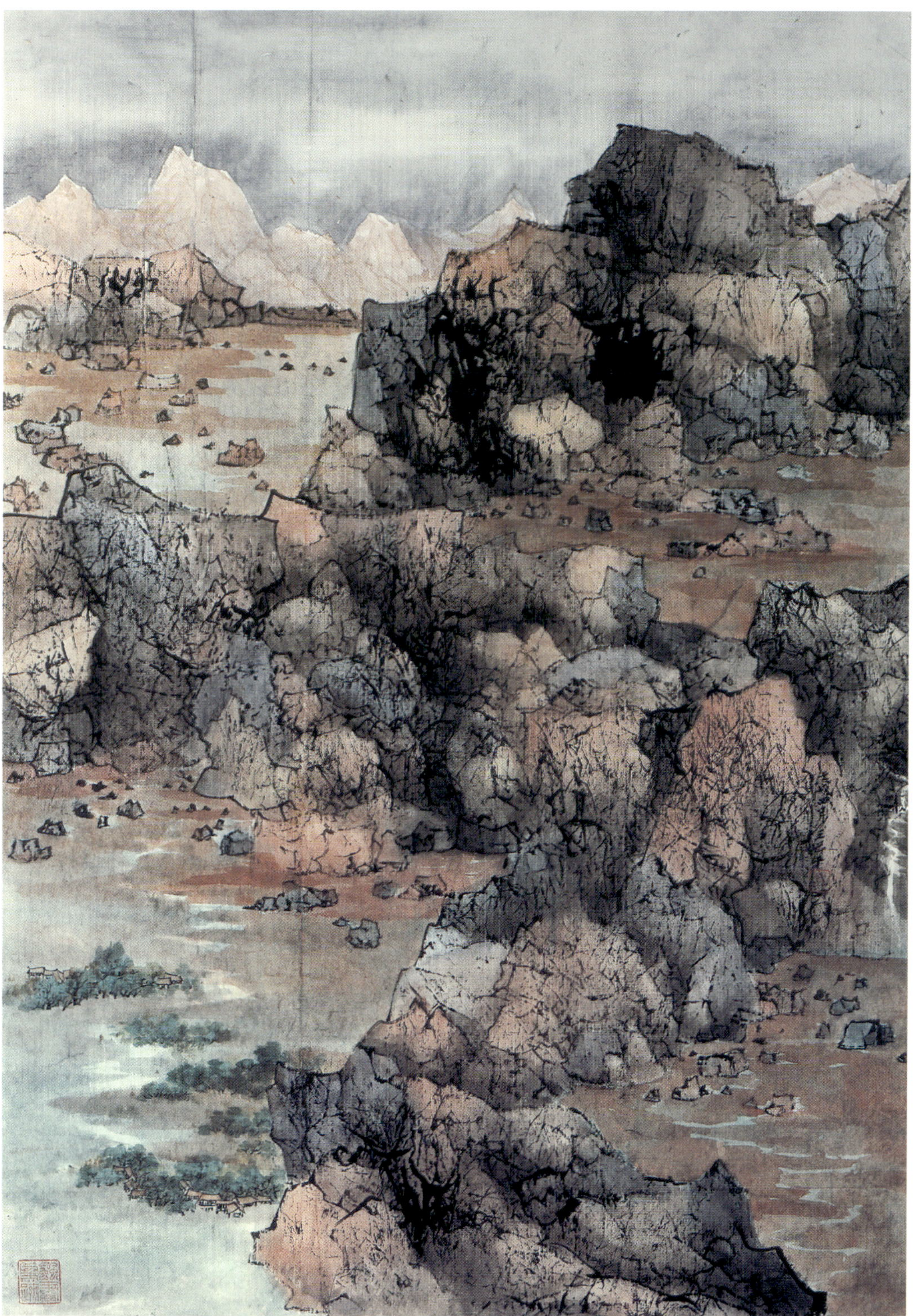

fig. 64), 15 April (*No. 473*, fig. 65), 27 April (*No. 474*, fig. 66), 7 May (*No. 475*, fig. 52)—in all, nine major works painted in only fourteen weeks, and other fine works might also have been included (some of which, like *Landscape No. 450*, fig. 13, done on 25 February, differed stylistically from this group). This moment of heightened creativity also coincided with C. C. Wang's period of recovery from the nearly fatal surgery discussed in the first chapter of this essay, and it deserves repeating that this was a time of withdrawal from virtually all activity other than painting, when (in his daughter's words) he was "in a dreamy state, not alert to the outside world…totally open, totally elusive, like the clouds in the sky," when "all the debris was cleared away and his whole being was completely true to itself."

Aesthetically, the works of this group are distinctly not decorative in intent, although their prominent use of color is a significant stylistic ingredient and although they might satisfy the most serious of decorative tastes; neither are they primarily traditionalistic, although important historical references are sometimes present. Rather, they represent the most highly personal and original of all the artist's work, the most thorough transformation of his scholarly tastes into a modern idiom, yet stern and uncompromising in their artistic values. Technically, these works are distinguished by the application of color not only to the front but, more importantly, to the back of the painting. Aside from black ink and white pigment, the palette was often limited to a single color, most often blue or red. Forms were reduced to severe, often flat patterns.

The inspiration for this technique came from Sung dynasty bird-and-flower painting and figure painting, in which the appearance of colors on the front of the silk was frequently sharpened by the application of certain complementary colors to the back. Sung back-painting was done only on silk; it was limited in scope to details, and it was carefully coordinated with painting on the front side. In contrast to this, C. C. Wang's back-painting is done on paper and the pigments are broadly applied, relating to larger forms, or even applied as an allover wash, requiring thick or repeated applications. The process is laborious and slow, sometimes taking as much as a week for each painting. The strength of the color depends on a variety of factors, including the painting paper, its thickness and irregularities, and the thickness of the pigments on the front side, which impede the emergence of the color from the back.

C. C. Wang says of this technique,

The color comes through by gradations. It is not a solid color—some comes through, some doesn't come through. It has a modern sense. It produces natural markings and gives a natural feeling. I'm not sure what it's going to come out like, because where the pigment goes through the paper and where it doesn't go through is very hard to control.

It is clear from this that the artist feels he has found a second major technique for producing accidental effects, for once again relinquishing some of the control over his work (the perfect solution for an artist who senses he may be becoming too skillful). In these paintings, the artist usually works in a sequence of front-back-front, with a final application on either or both sides that is a spontaneous and unfettered expression of his own artistic inclination and which gives each painting a unique and irreplicable artistic "signature." In a number of cases, he couples this back-painting with his techniques of impressed texture and folding the painting paper, processes that were somewhat minimized in the immediately preceding years. This adds to the feeling that these works hark back in significant ways to the artist's second phase, not just in technique but in their heightened emphasis on accidental effects. The resulting blend of multilayered, multitextured ink and color is visually magnetic, a textural "event" with little reference to traditional landscape painting except perhaps to Wang Yüan-ch'i's best work in layered colors (fig. 23) or works by Wang Meng in ink alone. C. C. Wang says that subsequently even he cannot always tell just how a certain stroke was made or whether a certain color was applied to the front or back side—"*Sometimes* I can," he says, "if I look carefully." The uncertainty of this pleases him. It confirms that these works are full of accident.

The first painting to use this technique, *Landscape No. 448* (fig. 61), was unusual in its subject matter, although since the early 1970s C. C. Wang had occasionally painted works in which long, applied texture strokes were turned into groves of trees rather than rock formations.[20] In this painting, the artist began work on the front of the paper, using black outlines for the trees. This was followed by a layer of light blue wash placed between the trees "for shadows," then another layer of darker blue. Afterwards, red pigment was slowly soaked through from the back side to the front and a bit more was later used to touch up the front side. Finally, not wanting the entire painting to be so dark, the artist completed it with a broad streak of white pigment across the top, which he feels contributes to a modern, "design-conscious" effect. "When I put the white line on it," he says, "I was just having fun." Even so, the painting appears more serious than playful, the tree branches being angular, sharply pointed, not always clearly readable in the "shadows," and matching the dark, brooding mood of the color in character. C. C. Wang is not altogether satisfied with the painting, which he still finds "incomplete," suggesting that he should perhaps yet do more work on it. Nevertheless, the painting is powerfully, almost painfully, evocative and no less different from its recent predecessors in its somber character than in its technical aspects.

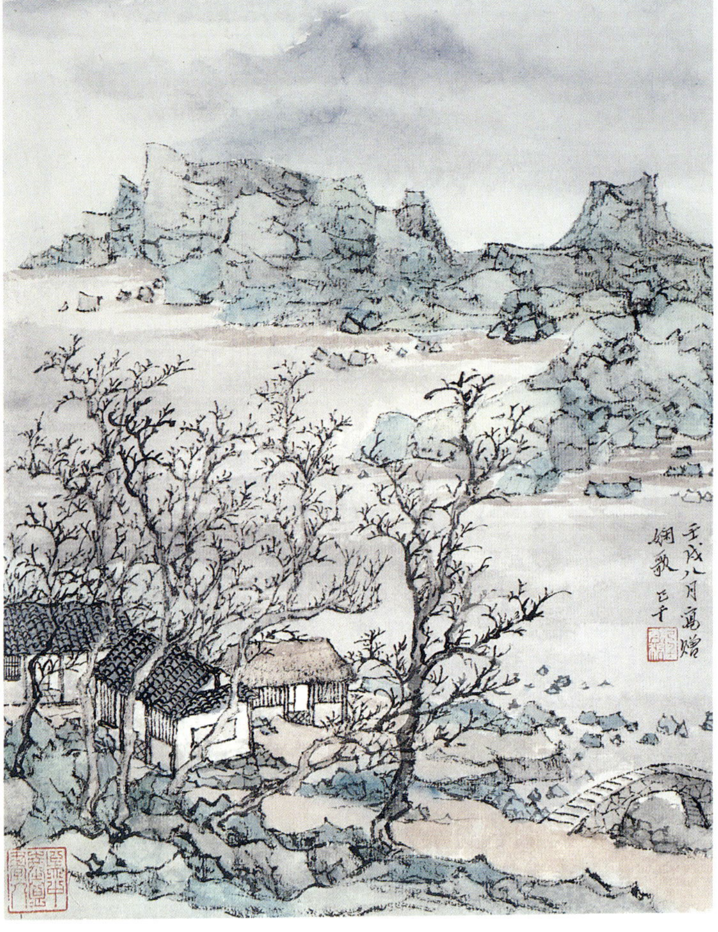

60

Landscape No. 514. August 1982. Hanging scroll, ink and color on paper. 17 x 13¾ in (43.2 x 34.9 cm). Collection of Mrs. Yien-koo Wang King.

Inscribed
"Written in *jen-hsü* [1982], 8th month, to give to Yien-koo. Chi-ch'ien."

Artist's Seals
Chi-ch'ien ch'uang-kao (right); *Wu-chung i hua-jen* (no. 24, lower left)

61

Landscape No. 448. 28 January 1983. Hanging scroll, ink and color on paper. 19¾ x 40 in (50.2 x 101.6 cm). C. C. Wang Family Collection.

Inscribed
"*Kuei-hai* [1983], first month, 28th day. Chi-ch'ien."

Artist's Seal
Yang (lower left)

Exhibited
Taipei Fine Arts Museum, 1984; Hong Kong Arts Centre, 1985; Hong Kong Arts Centre, 1986

20.   See, for example, *Landscape No. 236,* dated February 1973, in ibid., no. 41; and *Landscape No. 447,* dated December 1982 (the immediate predecessor to this painting), in Cahill et al, *C. C. Wang.* For subsequent examples, see *Nos. 485* and *488* in that book.

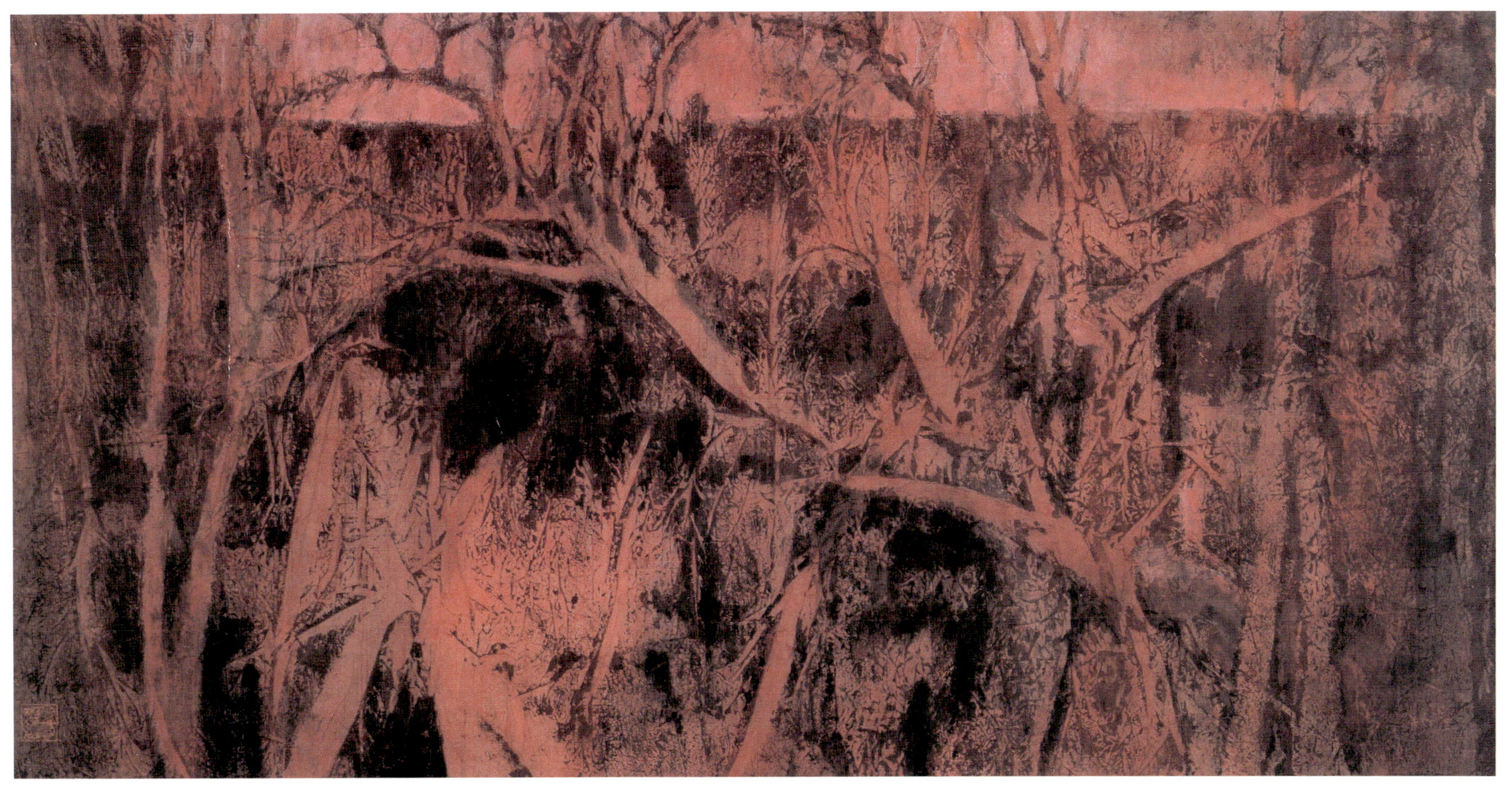

Another work done not long afterwards, *Landscape No. 454* (fig. 62), reveals a similar "design-consciousness" and together with *No. 464* (fig. 63) displays the technical complexity and variety that C. C. Wang's work with back-painting soon acquired. In *No. 454*, the snowy hills were first given their general shape with white pigment, a pearl white casein, applied more thickly along the crests than at the base of the hills. Next, the back side was gradually given a thorough wash of ink mixed with a bit of blue pigment. Penetrating the paper, this darkened the unpainted areas of water and sky as well as the more thinly painted areas such as the base of the distant mountains. Returning to the front side, the few earthen contour lines and the dark outlines of the houses were added in ink, and the tree-filled valley was filled with dark stippling strokes; then a bit of white highlighting was dotted on the trees and washed over the houses. There is an unaffected, understated quality to this painting, an easy naturalness about it, as if it were a real scene casually observed—so much so that its artistic virtues are not appreciated until one reflects that it is drawn totally from the painter's imagination. Particularly effective are the placement and structure of the houses, totally free from any of the mechanical regularity that is sometimes found in the artist's architecture; the varied shapes of his snow-covered hills, so minimally—and seemingly easily—defined; the quality of his brushwork, entirely plain and unpretentious, carrying out its simple task of defining contours without the slightest self-consciousness or even art-historical reference, yet strong, balanced, totally at ease, and uniquely identifiable with the "voice" of C. C. Wang. The window frame, so unlike anything else the artist has ever done, was put on last and came as a complete afterthought. "The window and the scene are different things, unrelated. I just happened to look at a window, my living room window, and then I added the window. In Western watercolor, of course, artists show scenes through a window, but those are real scenes. This is from my imagination." It is only natural to ponder the possible psychological significance of this theme, remembering that it was painted at a time of the artist's confinement to a Manhattan apartment from whose windows no landscape is visible.

The first works that C. C. Wang feels achieved his artistic goals using the technique of painting from the back side are *Landscape Nos. 464* and *466* (figs. 63, 21). In these, back-painting is combined for the first time with the artist's older techniques of impressing textures and folding his painting paper. The composition of *No. 464* is a particularly successful realization of a very traditional Northern Sung Li Ch'eng style, so that the blend of old and new is especially pronounced.

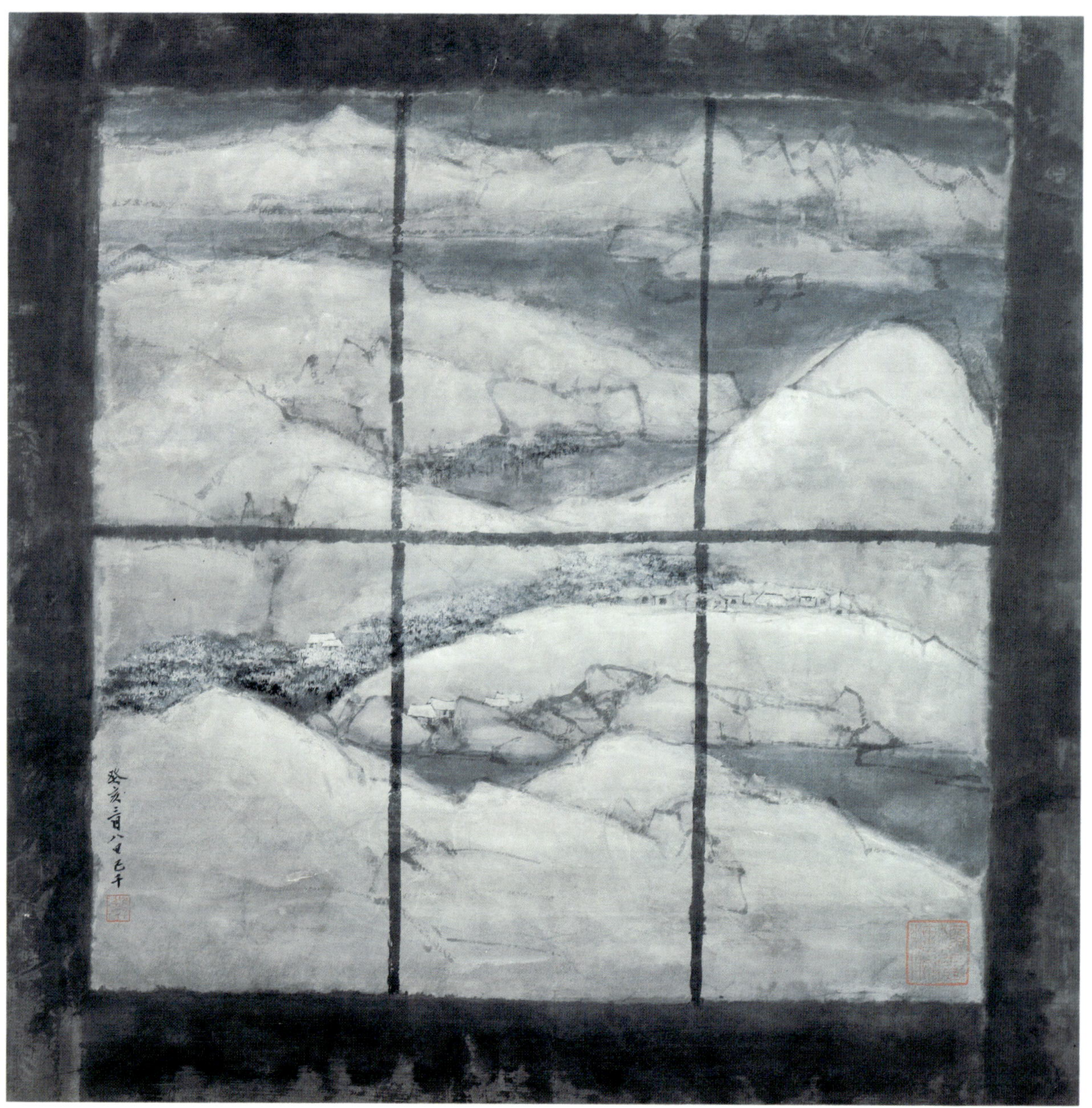

62

Landscape No. 454. 8 March 1983. Hanging scroll, ink and color on paper. 26¼ x 27 in (66.7 x 68.6 cm). C. C. Wang Family Collection.

Inscribed
"*Kuei-hai* [1983], 3rd month, 8th day. Chi-ch'ien."

Artist's Seals
Chi-ch'ien ch'uang-kao (lower left); *Huai-Yün Lou* (no. 26, lower right)

Exhibited
Taipei Fine Arts Museum, 1984; Hong Kong Arts Centre, 1985; Hong Kong Arts Centre, 1986; Birmingham Museum of Art, 1987

Published
Cahill et al., no. 16

63

Landscape No. 464. 21 March 1983. Hanging scroll, ink and color on paper. 26 x 13⅜ in (66.0 x 34.0 cm). Collection of Peter Neaman.

Inscribed
"*Kuei-hai* [1983], 3rd month, 21st day. Chi-ch'ien."

Artist's Seals
Chi-ch'ien ch'uang-kao (left); *Hsiung-chung ch'iu-ho* (lower right)

Published
Cahill et al., no. 27

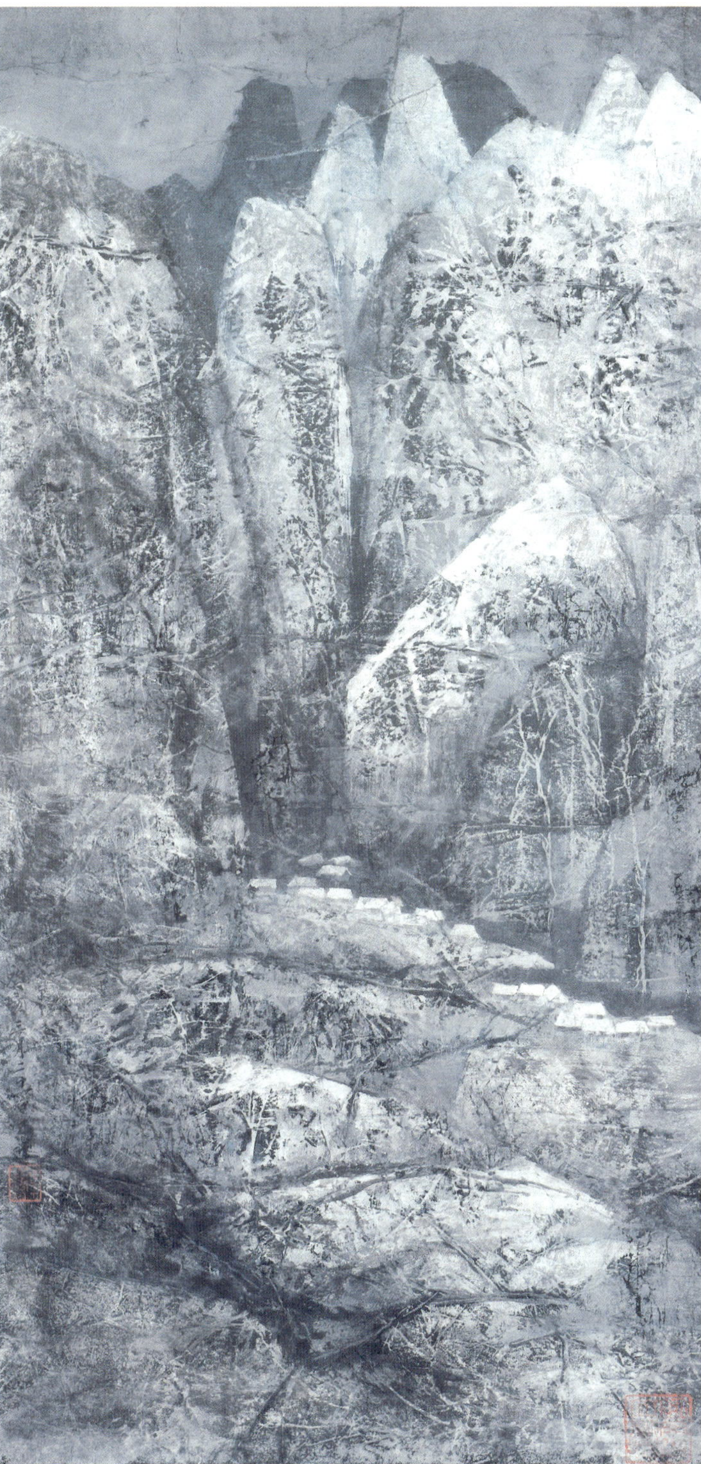

After the painting paper was wrinkled, the front was first textured with crumpled paper and then brushed with blue-black ink. Crevasses were darkened with a blacker ink, particularly those behind the ledge where houses were later to be lodged. The upper tips of distant mountains were also deeply toned and the sky above less deeply so. White casein was then applied to the whole back side of the paper, amplifying the tonal contrasts already established on the front. Where impressed textures blackened the painting surface, little or no white emerged. Where folds in the paper protected the surface from ink, long white streaks emerged. The rounding of the mountain contours and the depth of the crevasses were exaggerated, providing a sense of volumetric solidity and hardened rocky surfaces worthy of the Sung tradition. Afterwards, slight touches were added to the front, primarily ink and white highlights, the artist painting in the houses and imitating with his brush the accidental patterns of his impressed and folded textures. Finally, came the addition of the artist's signature and seals. The name and date, along the left side, blend in with the ink-scarred texture of the rocks like the famous Fan K'uan signature (fig. 16), a rare, early signature from the Sung period, so well concealed that it was "lost" for hundreds of years. In the lower right corner, the artist has impressed his seal, *Hsiung-chung ch'iu-ho:* "Mind landscape."

Landscape No. 466 (fig. 21) is technically similar to *No. 464*, only here the entire landscape was first toned with red. This is initially the most striking feature of the work and a seemingly radical departure from the landscape painting tradition. However, while painted completely red, the work is still essentially monochromatic in the best Sung tradition, red replacing the tan of Sung silk and thus an extension rather than a denial of this tradition (Sung "monochrome" also allowed minor amounts of red and green for architectural and vegetal details). The composition, similarly, seems to play within the tradition, to develop it further, to modernize it.

Structurally, it resembles *No. 464* but represents a closer view of a much smaller area. This view, so minimally defined as to seem abstract and lacking any measurable scale, becomes more comprehensible only after one comes upon the ten or more tiled buildings tucked into the lower left corner. The scene could almost be an enlargement of the upper right quarter of *Landscape No. 464*, including only the uppermost cluster of houses; the difference between these two landscapes could be compared to looking at an actual scene through two different photographic lenses. And although this is but another "mind landscape" with no such contrivances in mind, the brushwork and texture of the second painting also seem more legible, as if seen more closely.

But despite all its technical complexity, contrivance could not be more remote from this painting, which surpasses all earlier C. C. Wang works in artistic naïveté—that most revered concept among his artistic values—and in its modernity. In no other painting does the applied texture look so much like fine brushwork, and in no other painting does the brushwork look so fine. The surface of the painting invites careful, inch by inch scrutiny and pleases the eye with pure, beautiful, abstract form. Everywhere, the markings on the painting appear to be as natural as the marks of dripping water and worm holes eaten into old books, and the painting might deservedly have been impressed with the seals of the artist that record these metaphors for naive perfection, *Wu lou hen* and *Ch'ung-shu niao-chi*. Instead, C. C. Wang has stamped this painting in the lower left corner with the seal, *Wen-ko Kung hou-jen*, "Descendant of Mr. Wen-ko," meaning his ancestor, Wang Ao —and the painting certainly suggests worthy descent from that famous, art-loving Chinese prime minister.

In the spring of 1983, in a span of less than a month, C. C. Wang brought this sequence to a close with a series of four paintings, *Landscape Nos. 472, 473, 474,* and *475* (figs. 52, 64-66), done on 12 April, 15 April, 27 April, and 7 May). All of these works share certain composition similarities and related color schemes, reflecting again the artist's tendency to focus for periods of time on some particular artistic theme while producing variants on it in each successive work. Each of these four landscapes is composed in some variation of the so-called "dragon vein," relatives of the designs already seen in the earlier sequence, *Landscape Nos. 398, 397, 450* (figs. 53, 22, 13), and elsewhere. But unlike their predecessors, they are all vertical in format—as an increased proportion of his works in the past five years have been—which allows less side-to-side movement and thus contributes to a more subdued compositional rhythm. The colors are similarly subdued, each painting hushed by a veil of blues that vary in tone from one work to another. *Landscape Nos. 472* and *475* form a natural pair for comparison by virtue of design, as do *Nos. 473* and *474* (the artist confirms that he worked with these groupings in mind, although not literally intending to produce formal sets). Each pair reveals the artist exploring the particular variables of certain problems and may thereby be contrasted with the other pair; but within each pair, the individual works are bound together as much by alternative solutions as by their similarities.

Landscape Nos. 472 and *475* (figs. 64, 52) are quite similar compositionally and can readily be imagined hanging as a pair. In *No. 472*, the mountains were picked out from the plain paper by impressed and folded textures applied at the beginning of the painting process, and white was first applied to the back side in the second stage; in *No. 475*, which has no applied texture, the mountains were first formed by white paint applied to the front of the painting at the outset. In hue, despite sharing a blue-and-white color base, they differ in terms of the color complement that was added next, yellow-ochre in *No. 472* as opposed to blue-green in *No. 475*. By way of similarity, the dominant blue hue was applied to the back side of both paintings. In *No. 472*, blue was applied only to the part that corresponds to water, the impressed ink texture pattern of the front side being complemented on the back side by alternating white and yellow-ochre areas that provide the mountains their initial form; whereas in *No. 475*, the dark blue ink tone was applied over the entire back side of the painting. In both cases, after the back side had been painted, the mountains were further developed by applying additional color to the front: in *No. 472*, with more white and yellow-ochre, making an impasto over earlier applications of the same colors; in *No. 475*, by using a bit more white over earlier front-side whites that turned blue-gray from the back-painting, then adding pale blue-green pigment. In *No. 475*, two different colors were applied to the back side, the first time the artist had done this.

In sum, the similarities and differences in these paintings are well balanced. Their close match in compositional design is beautifully complemented by variety in tonal contrast—high in *No. 472*, low in *No. 475*—and focus—sharp in *No. 472*, soft in *No. 475*. *Landscape No. 472* glistens like a silvery, moonlit night in icy northern islands, while *No. 475* evokes the soft, moist glow of moonlight along the South China coast. *Landscape No. 472* greatly resembles a printed textile and reminds even its painter of the Chinese batiks that are basic decor throughout his Manhattan apartment.

Landscape No. 472. 12 April 1983. Hanging scroll, ink and color on paper. 39½ x 19½ in (100.3 x 49.5 cm).
C. C. Wang Family Collection.

Inscribed
"*Kuei-hai* [1983], 4th month, 12th day. Chi-ch'ien."

Artist's Seals
Wang Chi-ch'ien hsi (right); *T'ung-hsin wei ni* (lower left)

Exhibited
National Museum of History, Taipei, 1983; United States Embassy, Beijing, 1986-1988

Published
Stanley-Baker, "Closed Cycle," p. 23; Cahill et al., no. 7

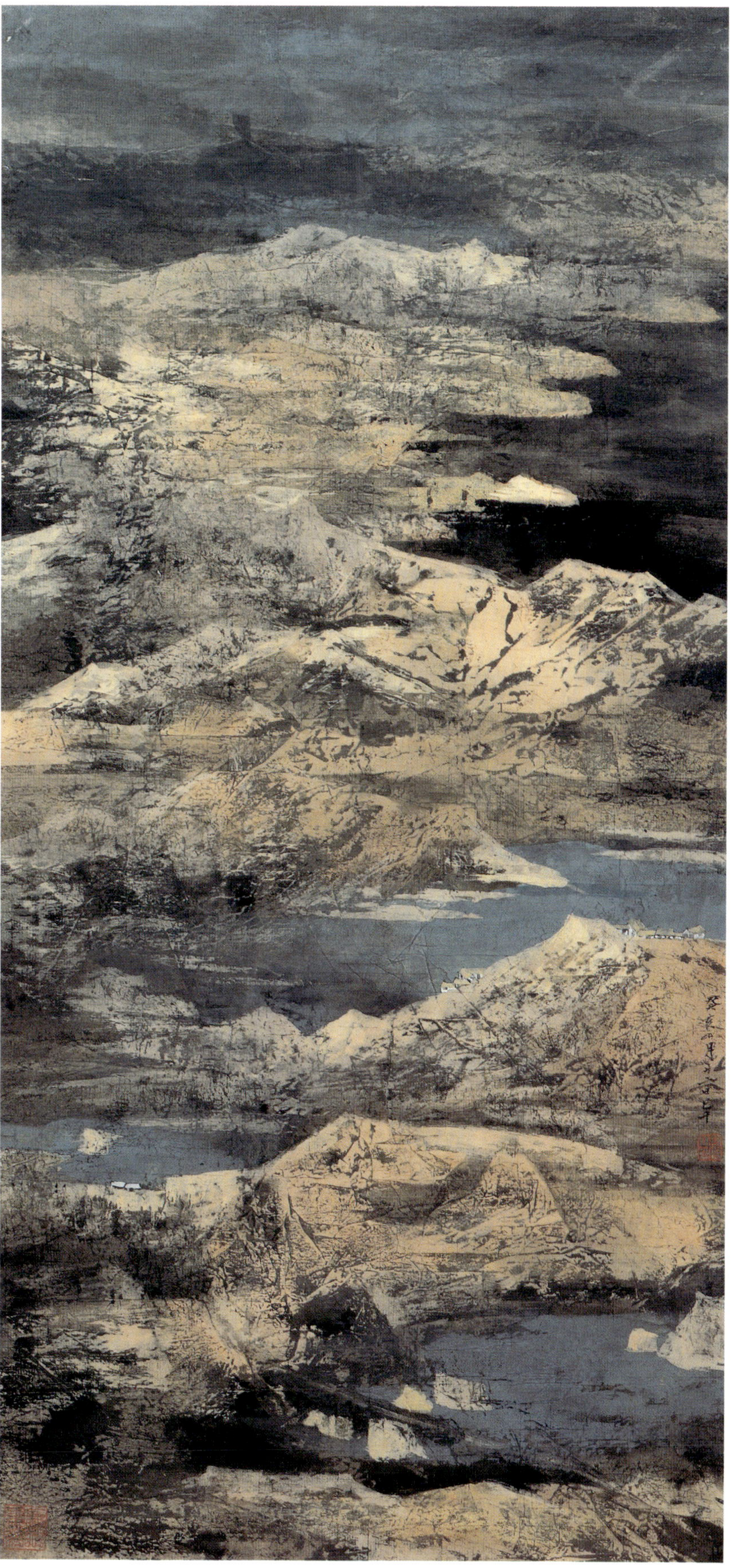

Similarly taken as a pair, the landscapes in *No. 473* and *No. 474* (figs. 65, 66) differ from the previous pair in several regards. Both present a simplification of landscape forms. These forms are more compressed as viewed along the vertical axis, and therefore seem to be set somewhat closer as well as being seen from a slightly lower viewpoint, compared to the striking vertical extension and spectacularly high vantage point of *Nos. 472* and *475*. *Nos. 473* and *474* are simpler in their color schemes, both limited to white and a tonal range of blue. But these two paintings also vary in technique in a manner that parallels the differences between *Nos. 472* and *475:* in *No. 473* (like *No. 472*, the first of its pair to be painted), the mountains were first shaped by impressed and folded ink textures and brushstrokes applied to the front of the paper, and the white casein was first painted on the back; in *No. 474* (like *No. 475*, the second of its pair to be executed), the mountains were first formed by white painted on the front side. In both cases, the blue was applied from the back side, turning the black ink on the front, as well as the white, to blue. In *No. 473*, the landscape setting has been given determinative form and detail, beginning with texture and brushstrokes and concluding with the painting of the houses. Except for a compound of five or six snow-enshrouded huts in the middleground, *No. 474* approaches complete abstraction; lacking any detailed brushwork, it is a fine example of what the Chinese would call "boneless"—an unusual example of this among C. C. Wang's paintings—and a work deeply imbued with his love of naïveté.

C. C. Wang's gradual physical recovery was marked by a return to styles and techniques more typical of his work in the two preceding years. Constrained by the amount of time it consumes, he has done little painting from the back side since this period, although often saying he wishes to do more. Most of his later work leaves behind the extreme abstraction of forms and the haunting, otherworldly feeling of this period. Even the few works in which he returned to the back-painting technique seem rarely to recapture the same profoundly introspective spirit. One later back-painted work is *Landscape No. 483* (fig. 67), from February 1984. If "otherworldly," it still differs considerably from the back-painted works of 1983 in mood: the red and blue mountains, touched with snow and flecked with bits of other colors, are piled up like a magical Taoist fairyland, bright and cheerful in spirit. The artist says their color is derived from the painted Buddhist caves at Tun-huang, direct predecessors to the highly colored Taoist landscapes of T'ang and later times. This painting seems a light-hearted diversion among more weighty landscapes, a reminder of the artist's playful personality. *Landscape 895* (fig. 74), from 1986, perhaps the one painting that *does* recapture the mysterious feeling of its back-painted predecessors, will be discussed shortly.

The paintings done during the later months of 1984 herald an extended period of high productivity—some sixty-five paintings in the twenty-four months from August 1984 to July 1986—and a return to C. C. Wang's traditional techniques, namely the application of brush and texture to the front side of the painting, using ink and sometimes no color at all. But the works of this period are greatly varied and joined more by an artistic maturity common to all than by any specific style. *Landscape No. 510* (fig. 69), painted in August 1984, typifies the artist's refusal to become bound by habit and represents a singular departure from his normal practice, occasioned by a gift of painting paper from his artist-friend, Liu Kuo-sung. Now a senior lecturer at Chinese University of Hong Kong, Liu Kuo-sung has long been one of the leading "expatriate" Chinese painters, a progressive artist deeply involved with textural innovation. One of Liu's favorite techniques is to paint on a specially-prepared mulberry paper with loose, long-staple fibers and afterwards to pull long strands of fiber off of the surface, exposing white streaks of paper beneath the ink. Borrowing Liu's medium and something of his style, C. C. Wang soon produced a landscape that could almost be exhibited as one of Liu's. Viewed from an extremely high vantage point, the composition is organized by three loosely linked rows of serrated peaks—one crossing the lower right corner, one marching horizontally across the center of the painting, one stretched along the upper border—which create two long valleys in their midst. Beneath the arc of the darkest and most prominent of these mountain peaks, near the center of the painting, and enclosed on the other sides by rising slopes and a pale reddish shoreline, is a small near-circle of icy blue water that dominates the entire painting and gives it its name: *Heavenly Lake,* the 6,000-foot high lake in China's northwestern T'ien-shan or Heavenly Mountain range. All along the mountain rows, streaks of exposed paper are etched into the ink by pulled mulberry fibers, leaving marks like the snowy tracks of glaciers headed down the mountain sides.

Never having been to T'ien-shan to see its unique nature, Wang was free to describe it in terms of his own inner nature. While borrowing Liu Kuo-sung's technique and something of his style, this painting is not all Liu. One can see just how much of C. C. Wang remains in this transformation, right down to the strong directional flow of the mountains, by comparing *No. 510* with *Landscape No. 855* (fig. 71). *No. 855* was done six months later in a style and technique more distinctively his own, and while cast entirely in monochrome black and gray, it in turn is structurally comparable to *Landscape Nos. 398* and *450* (figs. 53, 13)—as if they were viewed from a slightly different angle. One might also compare the linear, torn-fiber textural streaks of *Landscape No. 510* to those of his *Landscape No. 1: Clearing Skies After Snow on the Nine Peaks* (fig. 41), from 1968, to gauge just how much of this effect C. C. Wang had already achieved at an earlier date by means of his folded paper techniques. In *Landscape No. 510,* Wang has used Liu Kuo-sung just as he might use Ni Tsan or Wang Yüan-ch'i: as a point of departure for discovering additional variations within his own, now highly-developed landscape painting idiom.

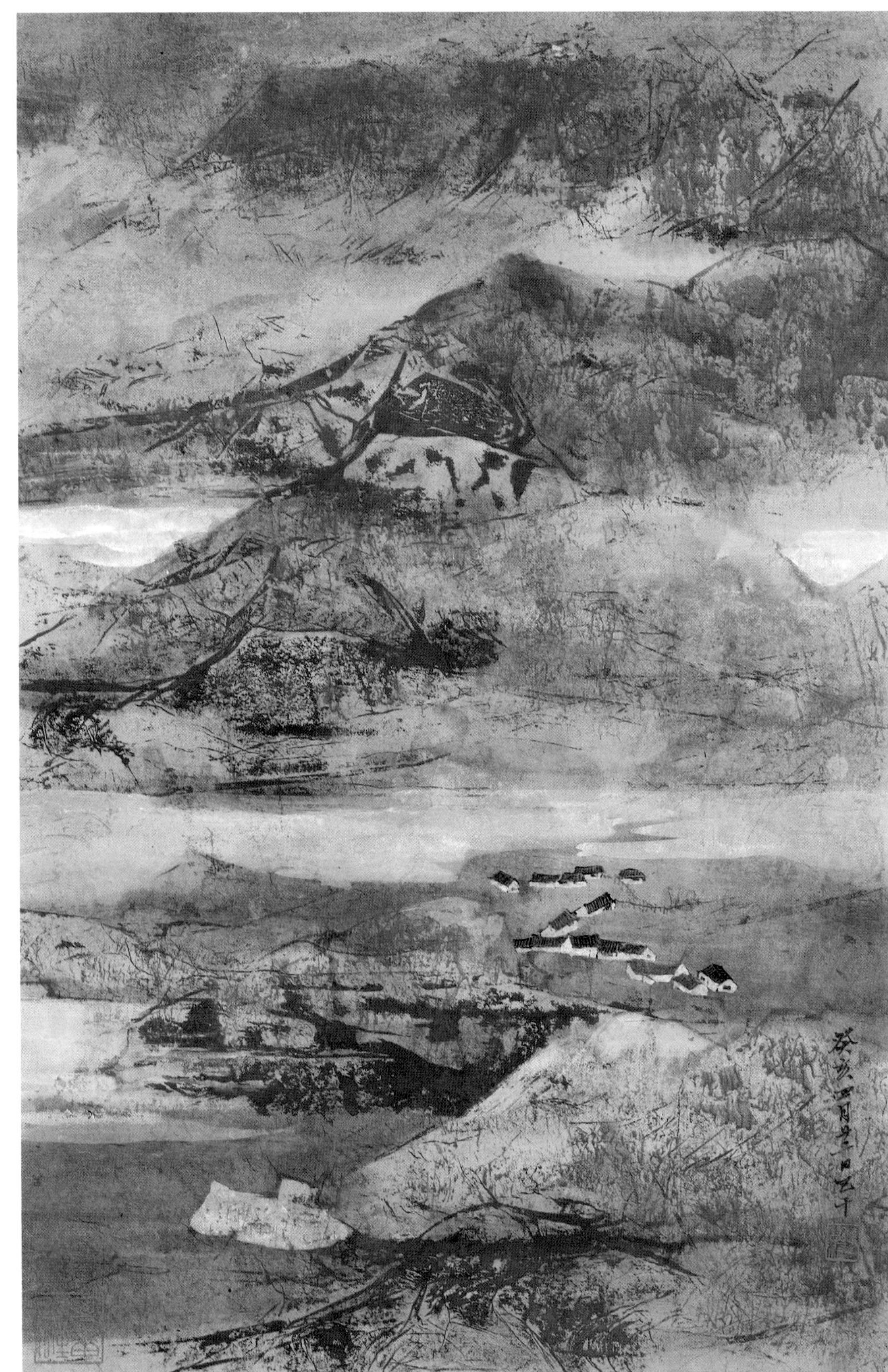

Landscape No. 473. 22 April 1983. Hanging scroll, ink and color on paper. 23½ x 15⅝ in (59.7 x 39.7 cm) C. C. Wang Family Collection.

Inscription
"Kuei-hai [1983], 4th month, 15th day. Chi-ch'ien."

Artist's Seals
Chi-ch'ien ch'uang-kao (lower right); *Hsiung-chung ch'iu-ho* (lower left)

Landscape No. 474. 27 April 1983. Hanging scroll, color on paper. 20¾ x 14¾ in (52.7 x 37.5 cm). C. C. Wang Family Collection.

Inscribed
"Kuei-hai [1983], 4th month, 27th day. Chi-ch'ien."

Artist's Seals
Wang Chi-ch'ien (no. 1, lower right); *Hsiung-chung ch'iu-ho* (lower left)

In *Landscape No. 503* (fig. 68), which follows *Heavenly Lake* by three months, C. C. Wang creates his most remarkable compositional variation of all, simultaneously recapitulating three of the leading compositional motifs set forth over the past two decades. The design of this painting can be read in relation to a number of his "dragon vein" compositions, such as that in *No. 855* and others dating back to his untitled landscape of 1966 (figs. 71, 37)—in this case, a mountain chain that crosses the lower right portion of the painting, swings upward and left, then back to the right across the top of the painting; in this painting, however, it is shown from a low point of view, with objects seen from the side, as in the frontal landscapes of C. C. Wang's "second phase." Seen from this perspective, the foreground chain crosses over the outcropping on the left and completes a compositional circle, or "space-cell," surrounding a bright, rocky depression, the focal center of the painting. This circular arrangement makes evident its relationship to the compositional type seen particularly in the 1960s, such as in the untitled landscape of 1965 and, less obviously, *Landscape No. 76* from 1968 (figs. 36, 39). Finally, the composition is clearly related to that group of "top-heavy" works which began with his *Sailing Boats* of 1964 and continued with *Landscape Nos. 40, 205,* and *241* (figs. 34, 38, 47, 48).

Landscape No. 503 signals the fact that the artist's own best-developed compositions have become as worthy as those of his finest traditional predecessors to provide the basic visual themes for his expanding series of variations on the past. On the other hand, the process of composing traditional variations —which C. C. Wang is certainly quite conscious of—need not be understood, in this case, in terms of his intellectually calculating all the available permutations and solutions inherent within his art and of thereby discovering the possibility of transmuting three of his favorite compositional modes into one; indeed, for him to recognize that such a result had actually taken place, it would have to be pointed out to him first. Rather, the process is a much less conscious one, which in the progress of time finally led the artist to the fortuitous crossing of three compositional pathways, all of them well traveled and intuitively familiar to him but never before seen at one place, in one painting.

If *Landscape No. 503* bears particular comparison to paintings from his "early modern" years, such as *Sailing Boats* of 1964, the untitled landscapes of 1965 and 1966, and *Landscape No. 76* of 1968 (figs. 34, 36, 37, 39), such comparison also demonstrates the extraordinary difference between this early and later art—the irrepressible force of "youth" in a work like *Landscape No. 76*, done at age sixty-one, contrasted with the noble maturity of *No. 503*, painted at the age of seventy-seven. In *Landscape No. 76*, the artist's textures, whether brushed on or applied, spread across the surface of the paper more than into the surface of the mountains, whereas in *No. 503* the texture is so fully integrated with the objects described that the painting must be examined carefully to perceive its artistry. Particularly effective in *No. 503* are the stippling strokes that crown its contour lines with short growth, produced by the brush, yet so

adapted to the artist's applied textures that it is most difficult to
tell which layer of ink represents the transition from impressed
texture to brushwork. This vegetative stubble strongly recalls
Fan K'uan's Sung dynasty masterpiece, *Travelers Among Streams
and Mountains* (fig. 16)—the last word in monumentality—as
does much else about this painting. Also particularly beautiful
are the artist's washes of moderate to light gray, brushed on
over painting paper that has been deeply creased by folding.

The applied texture, even more than the brushwork,
manages in this painting to create surfaces so naturally rocky
or wrapped in vegetation, to describe forms so volumetric
and organized in space, that the painting looks almost
photographic. The artist's mastery of his techniques is set forth
here in a flawless performance. Cast in black to silvery tones
of ink, with carefully coordinated areas of luminosity (that
is to say, unpainted or spared out areas) such as the rocky
depression encircled by these mountains or the towering
monolith to its left, streaked by folds of the painting paper, the
landscape bears comparison with Ansel Adams' powerful
photographic evocations of Yosemite Valley in moonlight.
Yet there is no such photograph, no Ansel Adams in the
artist's consciousness, only the mental transformation of
old techniques, old compositions which he has completely
mastered and turned into new landscape visions. Not reliant
on external landscapes, the mental images of landscapes in
the artist's mind now seem to emerge seamless and fully
formed. The inner nature of the artist seems to have become
undifferentiable from the external nature of the landscape
itself, just as was the case with Fan K'uan. But even Fan K'uan
has "been forgotten." The painting is pure landscape, with no
trace of human existence and little record of artistic precedents.
In the lower left corner of the painting, the artist has impressed
a seal that reads, *Wu jen, wu wo, fei ku, fei jin,* "Not from others,
not from myself, not from the past, not from the present":
in other words, entirely natural, timeless.

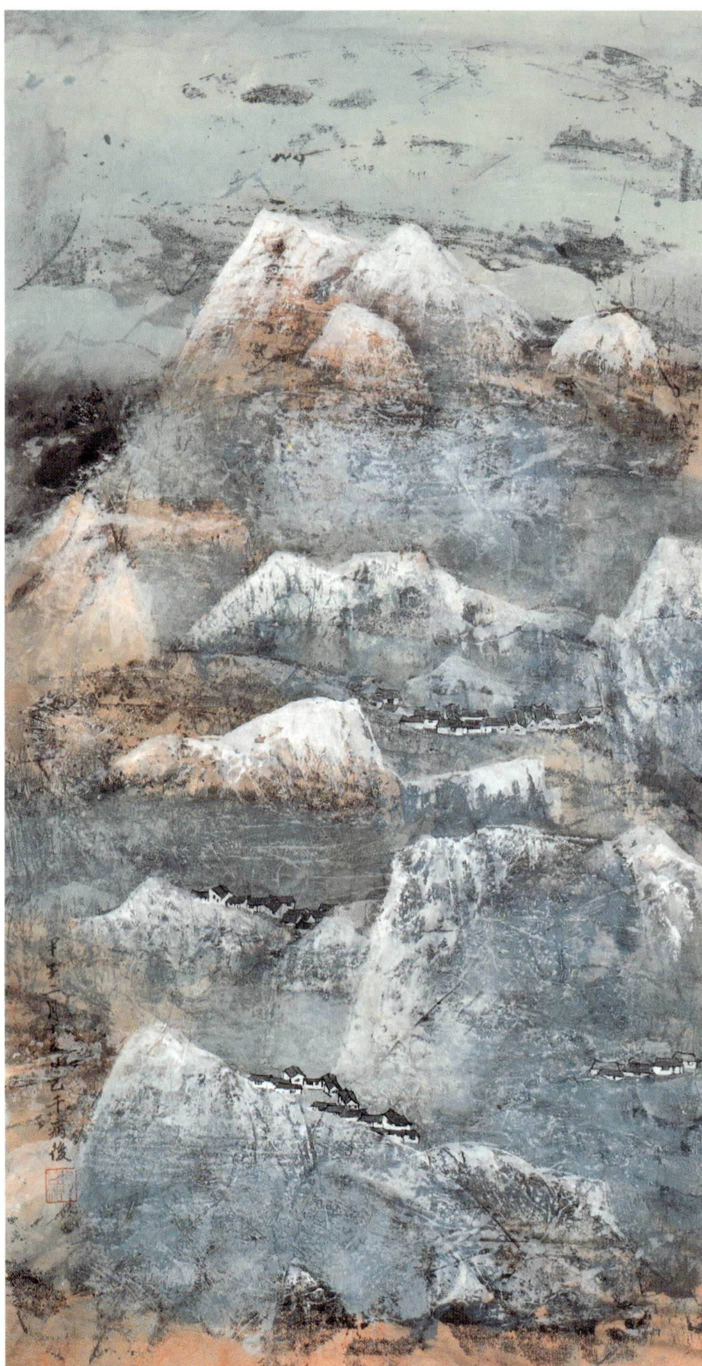

67

Landscape No. 483. 15 February 1984. Hanging
scroll, ink and color on paper. 25⅜ x 13¾ in (64.5 x
34.9 cm).
Collection of Mr. and Mrs. Wayne G. Quasha.

Inscribed
"*Chia-tzu* [1984], 2nd month, 15th day. Chi-ch'ien.
After being ill."

Artist's Seal
Chi-ch'ien ch'uang-kao (lower left)

Exhibited
Hong Kong Arts Centre, 1986

Published
Cahill et al., no. 28

68

Landscape No. 503. 1 November 1984. Hanging
scroll, ink on paper. 25 x 34 in (63.5 x 86.4 cm).
Collection of the Hong Kong Land Company.

Inscribed
"*Chia-tzu* [1984], 11th month, first day. Wang
Chi-ch'ien. Written in San Francisco."

Artist's Seals
Chi-ch'ien yin (lower right); *Wu jen wu wo, fei ku fei jin*
(lower left)

Exhibited
Hong Kong Arts Centre, 1986

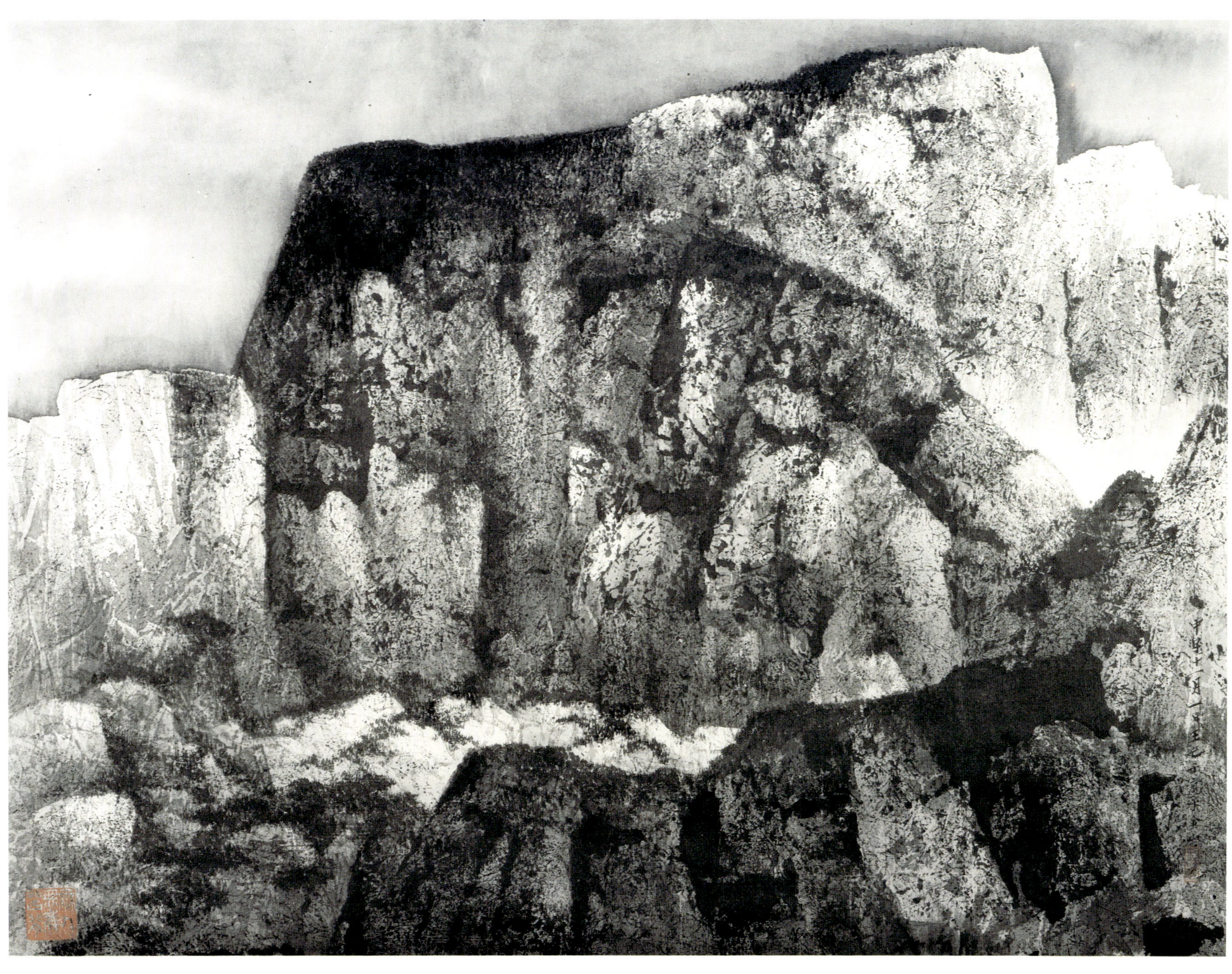

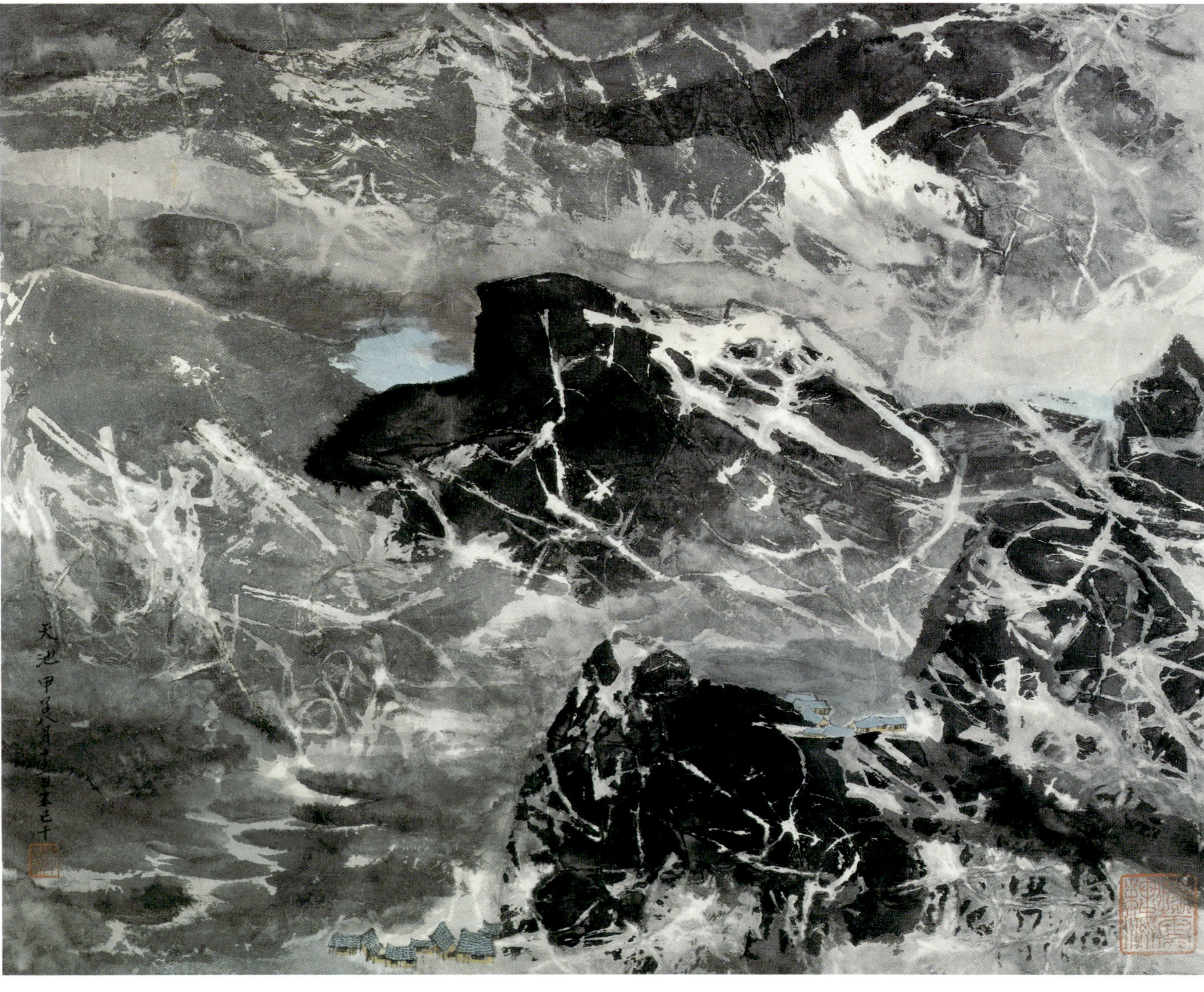

69

Landscape No. 510: Heavenly Lake. 15 August 1984.
Hanging scroll, ink and color on paper. 19½ x 25 in
(49.5 x 63.5 cm).
C. C. Wang Family Collection.

Inscribed
"*The Lake of Heaven. Chia-tzu* [1984], 8th month, 15th
day. Wang Chi-ch'ien."

Artist's Seals
Wang Chi-ch'ien hsi (lower left); *Huai-Yün Lou* (no. 26,
lower right)

70

Landscape No. 856. 17 March 1985. Hanging scroll,
ink and color on paper. 27⅛ x 18 in (68.9 x 45.7 cm).
C. C. Wang Family Collection.

Inscribed
"*I-ch'ou* [1985], 3rd month, 17th day. Wang Chi-ch'ien."

Artist's Seals
Chi-ch'ien ch'uang-kao (right); *Wen-ko i-sun* (lower left)

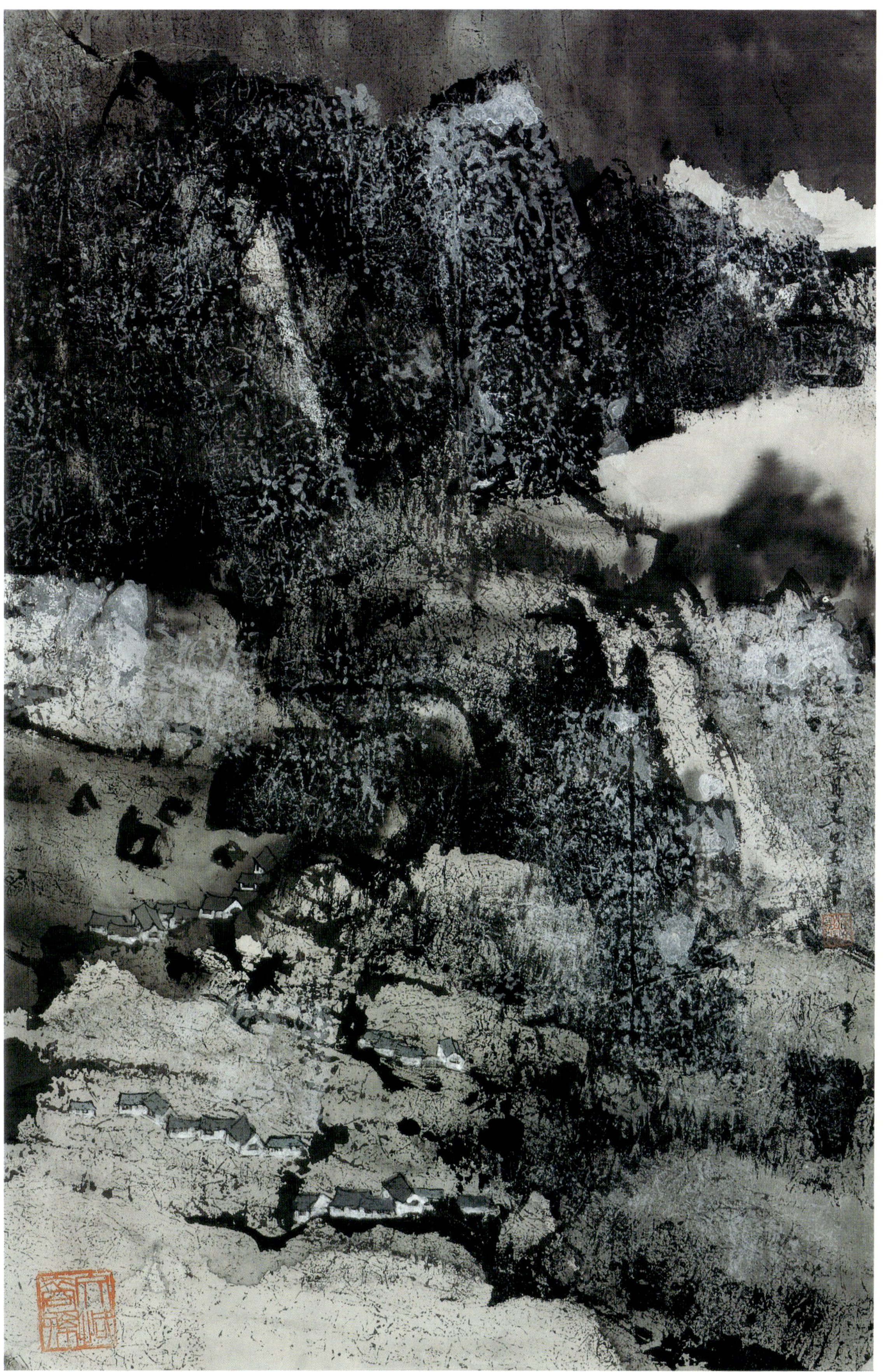

Such an accomplishment only establishes a dilemma for the living artist: how to go on producing more paintings without becoming repetitious or lowering one's standards. Already, he has declared "I don't want to be realistic" and mastered the art of abstraction, well defined by works that range from *Landscape No. 1: Clearing Skies After Snow on the Nine Peaks* to *Landscape No. 466* (figs. 41, 21); yet in this work he has mastered realism. He has already attained success in numerous different styles, poles apart, from works of raw, primitive power (*Landscape No. 112, Clouds in the Mountains of the Immortals,* figs. 40, 42), to ones of stern self-discipline or sober maturity (such as *Landscape Nos. 305, 450,* and *475,* figs. 51, 13, 52), to others that are elegant or beautifully colored (*Nos. 162, 398, 397,* figs. 49, 53, 22) or even self-indulgently "decorative" (*Nos. 419, 420,* figs. 56, 57). Yet the mind of an outstanding artist somehow remains filled with landscapes, and always with some that are new and different. That exhaustion has not threatened C. C. Wang's artistry is attested to by numerous paintings following *Landscape No. 503* over the course of the next two years. One that followed shortly afterwards, in March 1985, *Landscape No. 856* (fig. 70), may be most interesting as an experiment, but it succeeds in a variety of ways. It shows the artist's unflagging boldness in its unusual fusion of composition and tonal structure, in its mirror-like symmetry of darkened tones which dominate the upper portion of the painting, diffusing as they spread downwards, and of lighter tones predominant in the lower section but increasingly submerged in the darker areas above. The applied texture of this painting is no less bold, including not only black ink but layers of gray and even white pigment, while the brushwork is similarly uncompromising. The radical thrust of the landscape's forms toward the lower right of the painting creates a dynamic environment for this expression of dramatic artistic forces.

Two other paintings from 1985—*Landscape Nos. 851* and *881* (figs. 72, 73)—are of more conservative vintage than this last example and more closely related to the artist's other paintings. Both bear comparison with the masterful *No. 503* (fig. 68) and a number of other works already considered, for it is now through such comparisons that the artist's transforming abilities can best be understood. The first of this pair, *Landscape No. 851,* from April 1985, is back-painted, and its patterned water, an inky black with white tracery, suggests a lineal descent from *Landscape Nos. 398, 397,* and *450* (figs. 53, 22, 13). But its "dragon vein" compositional type, tightly bound within a vertical format, is more reminiscent of the dark blue landscapes, *Nos. 472* and *473* (figs. 64, 52)—although unlike theirs (or any other example before it), the coils of the dragon seem to have been cut into segments, no longer connected. The result is a receding series of earthen curtains, each one varied in shape, size, and disposition, and each used like a blank screen for the display of the artist's textural effects.

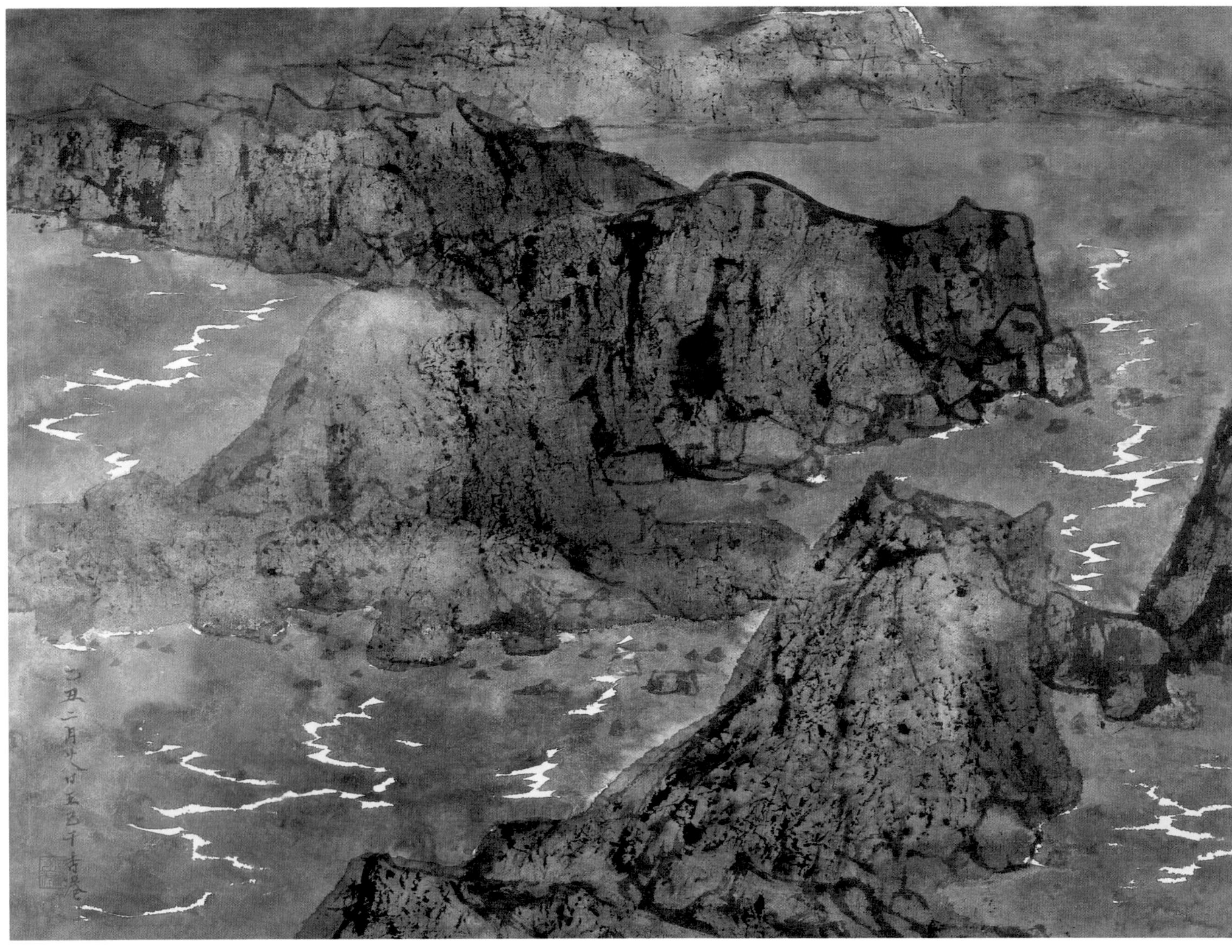

Landscape No. 855. 18 February 1985. Hanging scroll, ink on paper. 19 x 25³⁄₁₆ in (48.2 x 64 cm). C. C. Wang Family Collection.

Inscribed
"*I-ch'ou* [1985], 2nd month, 18th day. Wang Chi-ch'ien in Hong Kong."

Artist's Seal
Chi-ch'ien ch'uang-kao (lower left)

Exhibited
Birmingham Museum of Art, 1987

72

Landscape No. 851. 15 April 1985. Hanging scroll, ink and color on paper. 35⅝ x 23¹³⁄₁₆ in (90.5 x 60.5 cm). C. C. Wang Family Collection.

Inscribed
"*I-ch'ou nien* [1985], 4th month, 15th day. Chi-ch'ien."

Artist's Seals
Wang Chi-ch'ien hsi (lower right); *Ch'ung-shu niao-chi* (no. 25, lower left)

Exhibited
Hong Kong Arts Centre, 1986; Birmingham Museum of Art, 1987

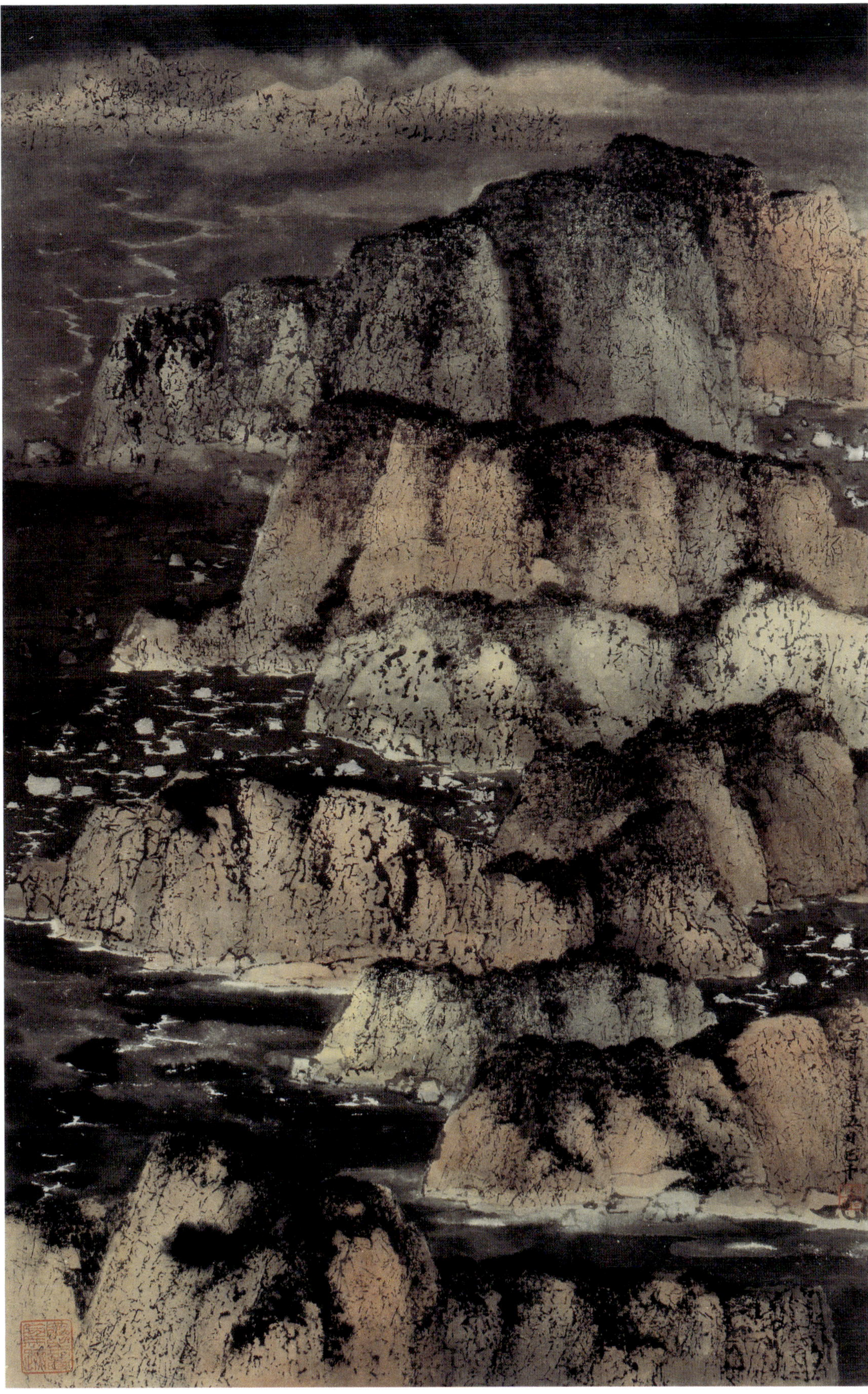

Like *Landscape Nos. 472* and *473*, *No. 851* was begun with the application of inked textures on the front of the paper, after which white pigment was painted on the back in accordance with these patterned areas, giving the mountains their form. One of the beautiful features of the painting is the subtly varied color that appears from ridge to ridge, resulting from the artist having followed his use of white with further back-painting in yellow and ochre, tonally enriched by the addition of a variegated gray wash to the front of the painting. Unlike *Nos. 472, 473,* or any other back-painted examples, however, the waters here were not painted their inky black until after the back side was done, which enabled the artist to hold in reserve the long trails of white which streak the plateau and the small white patches or chunks of rock which tend to define this area as tidal flats and link it to yet another family of works, including *Nos. 398, 397, 450,* and *855* (figs. 53, 22, 13, 71). One more group to which this highly inbred work must be related stems from *Landscape No. 503* (fig. 68) and, before it, *No. 425* (fig. 58). A comparison of the uppermost ridge of this landscape with that in *No. 503* shows the derivation here from the massive rockery found in that work. Among the varieties of texture in *No. 851* is the same dry, finely stippled brushstroke for vegetation that accompanies this particular kind of rockery in *Nos. 503* and *425.*

The second painting of this pair is *Landscape No. 881:
Clearing After Snow on the Nine Peaks* (fig. 73), painted in San
Francisco on 12 December 1985. At first, it may hardly seem
related to *No. 503*, let alone to *No. 851*. But a comparison of the
upper ridges of all three paintings shows their relationship.
No. 881 is very much a detail, almost as if cut out of the upper
right quarter of *No. 503*—although it must be reemphasized
that all these images are set forth spontaneously by the artist
and reflect persistent modes of imagination rather than
mechanical transformations of other paintings. *No. 881* is not
intended to be as powerful, as dramatic or magnificent a
landscape as *No. 503*. It is a softer, more conservative landscape,
more scholarly in taste and painted under the gentle influence
of Tung Yüan (fig. 9). Its forms are rounder, less monolithic:
the mountain sides are subtly but repeatedly ridged and the
upper contours are gently fragmented, composed of rounded
earthen clusters (like alum rocks), best seen on the darker,
nearby ridge. The sides and ridges of the mountains are also
more gently shaded by pale washes, brushwork, and impressed
texture strokes that look more like brushwork than usual. The
mist, the "mountain's breath," is puffier and more palpable. A
soft snow has begun to fall—a sprinkling of white pigment over
the dark surface.

The composition of the painting is scarcely dynamic, and
everything is stabilized by shapes and tones, the V-shape of the
lower ridge holding the Y-shape of the upper mountains
in balance, the dark and heavy supporting the light.
The gathered mist that helps to separate the nearby and
middleground mountains creates a tonal focus for the painting
that is balanced and stable, even if not literally centered. The
landscape is also hospitably populated: silhouetted against this
mist, a row of houses lines the contour of the lower ridge,
claiming the best view of the mountains beyond and of the
valley in between. The modernity of C. C. Wang's painting style
is suppressed in this "old-fashioned" work, and despite links to
more "progressive" paintings, it is more in the company of
other conservative works such as *Landscape No. 429* (fig. 59)
from this latest phase of his development. This painting is now
in the municipal museum of C. C. Wang's home town, the
Suchou Museum.

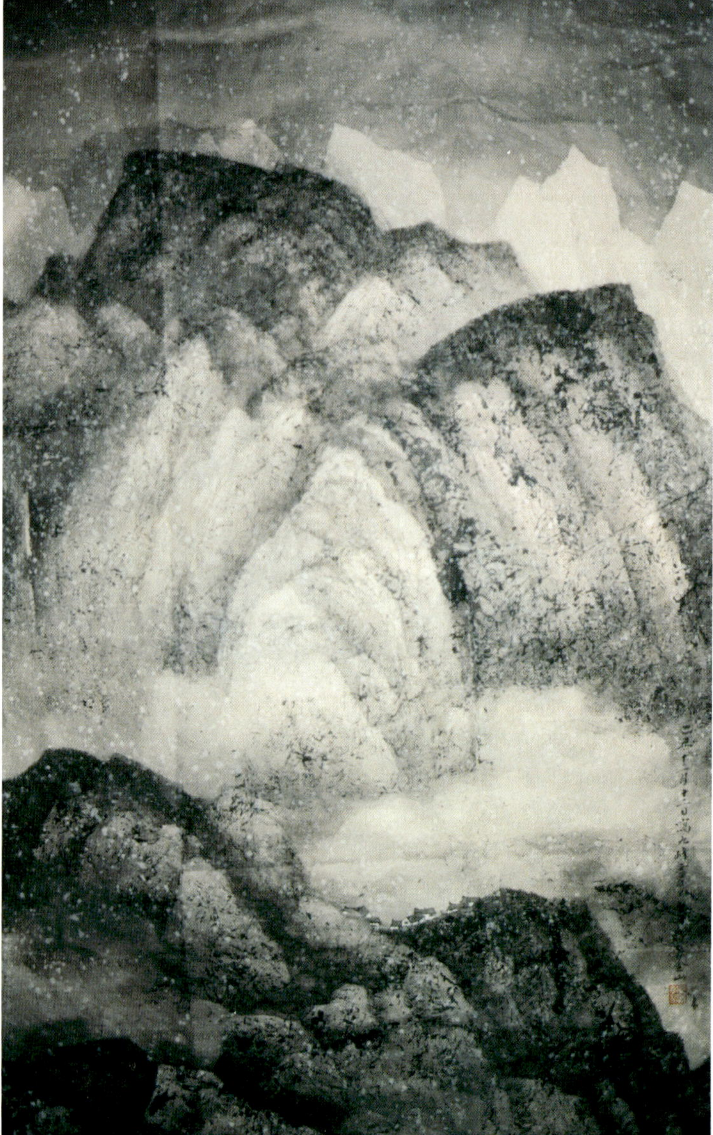

**Landscape No. 881: Clearing After Snow on the
Nine Peaks.** 12 December 1985. Hanging scroll, ink
on paper. 25 x 38 in (63.5 x 96.5 cm).
Suzhou Museum.

Inscribed
"Written in *i-ch'ou* [1985], 12th month, 12th day.
Clearing After Snow on the Nine Peaks. Chi-ch'ien, while a
guest in San Francisco."

Artist's Seal
Chi-ch'ien ch'uang-kao (lower right)

Exhibited
Shanghai Art Academy, 1986

74

Landscape No. 895. 10 April 1986. Hanging scroll,
ink and color on paper. 36 x 19½ in (91.4 x 49.5 cm).
C. C. Wang Family Collection.

Inscribed
"*Ping-yin* [1986], 4th month, 10th day. Wang
Chi-ch'ien."

Artist's Seal
Wang Chi-ch'ien hsi (right)

Exhibited
Hong Kong Arts Centre, 1986; Birmingham Museum
of Art, 1987

21.   Illustrated in Laurence Sickman and Alexander
Soper, *The Art and Architecture of China* (Baltimore:
Penguin Books, 1971), pl. 241.

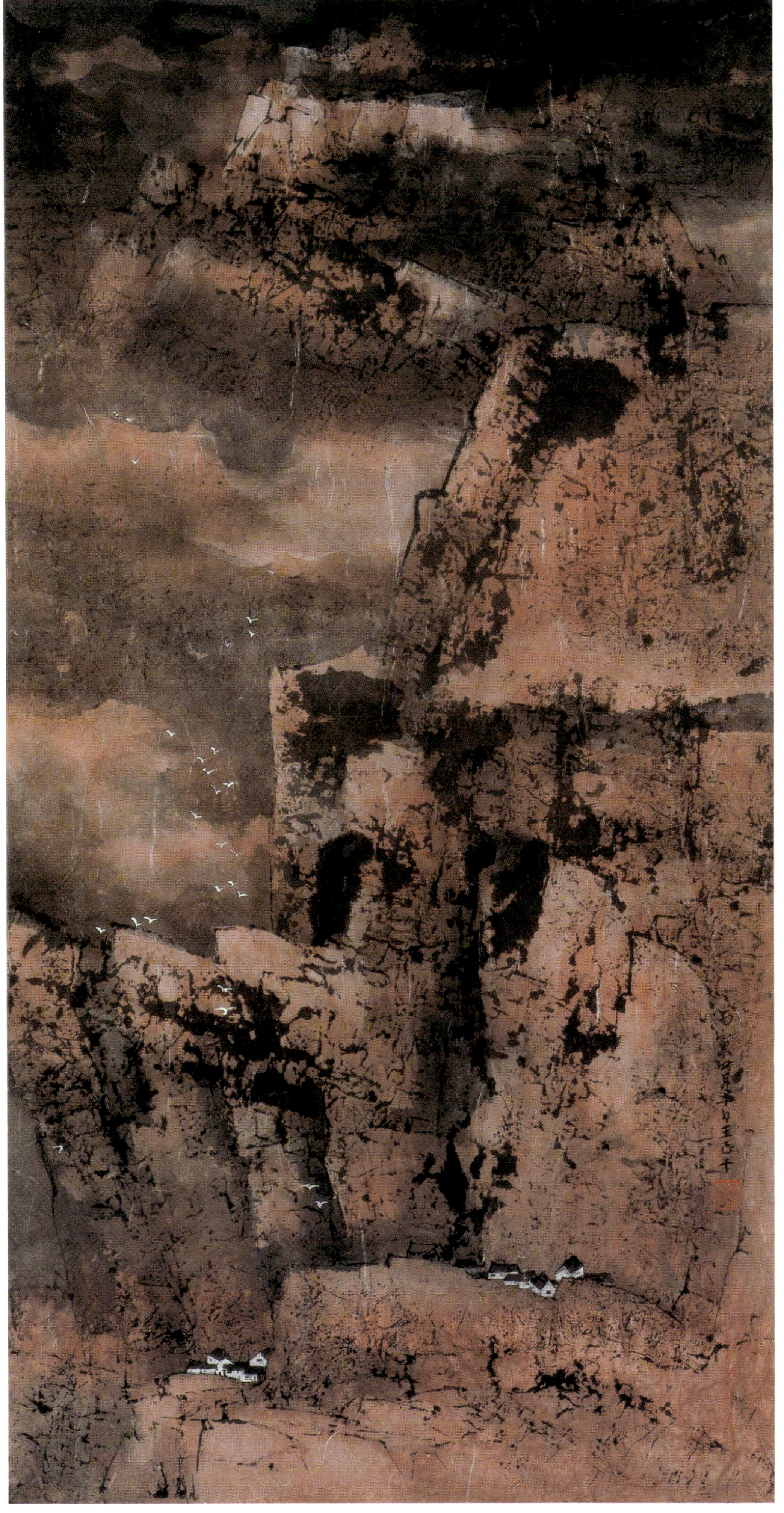

The notion of two paintings—like *Landscape No. 503* and *No. 881*—displaying a far and near view of the same scene and allowing the painter to focus on different aspects of the same artistic problem is recognized by C. C. Wang as valid. One such pair in which he acknowledges this is *Landscape Nos. 464* and *466* (figs. 63, 21), already discussed. Two other paintings in which this is acknowledged are *Landscape No. 888* (fig. 20), painted on 14 December 1985, in San Francisco, just two days after *No. 881*, and *No. 895*, dated 10 April 1986 (fig. 74). The highest mountain crest in *No. 888* displays a superficial similarity to that in *Landscape No. 503* (fig. 68), but the slight traces of pale brushwork that outline the peaks, the looseness of the impressed texture, and the fragmentation of the mountain forms all derive from another source, as do other aspects of the painting. This brushwork has a bit of Ni Tsan's style (fig. 5) in the lightly touched corners, angular and pointed, similar to earlier paintings such as *Landscape Nos. 398* and *450* (figs. 53, 13). Other aspects of the painting suggest the style of Ni Tsan as modified by a 17th-century follower, Hung-jen: the somewhat unstable mountain forms, often drawn in at the base, top-heavy, and tilted on top; the fragmentation of compositional parts, with thin mountain ridges stacked up in a receding series like dominoes; and the vegetation used to line the nearer mountain contours, made of vertical striations and occasional branching systems.[21] Like Hung-jen, C. C. Wang has painted a landscape which—despite its vertical format, and however lofty its forms and spacious their arrangement— remains light and airy in feeling rather than truly monumental, with a certain playful insubstantiality that is well in accord with the taste of China's later scholar-painters. Yet whatever historical sources can be envisioned, always the traditional forms and brushwork are altered in ways that make them C. C. Wang's. Certainly, Hung-jen used no applied texture strokes, no darkened waters streaked with white, nor a half-dozen other features that link this work more closely with C. C. Wang's other works in other modes than with anything ever done by Hung-jen, and which eliminate even the slightest possibility of confusing this for a Hung-jen painting. The artist now has all his historical models only barely in mind, if at all, while painting, and his present consciousness of Hung-jen as an inspiration may have appeared upon completing the work.

The tilted forms and thin faceting of *Landscape No. 895* (fig. 74) suggest that the landscape type seen from afar in *No. 888* is related to the one shown closer up and in greater detail in this painting. This whole landscape, for example, can be compared to the upper left corner of *No. 888*. And yet this painting is actually considerably more monumental in effect—indeed, in terms of spaciousness rather than bulk, it is one of the most monumental of all C. C. Wang's paintings. Clustered houses, clinging to a few level spots on steep, bare-sided mountains, are shown from high above with no trace of access to them. A flight of birds rises from this area to a still loftier realm, dominated by two peaks that crown the painting and tower over the clouds below. Whether the farther of these two peaks is taller or shorter than the nearby peak, connected to it or remotely

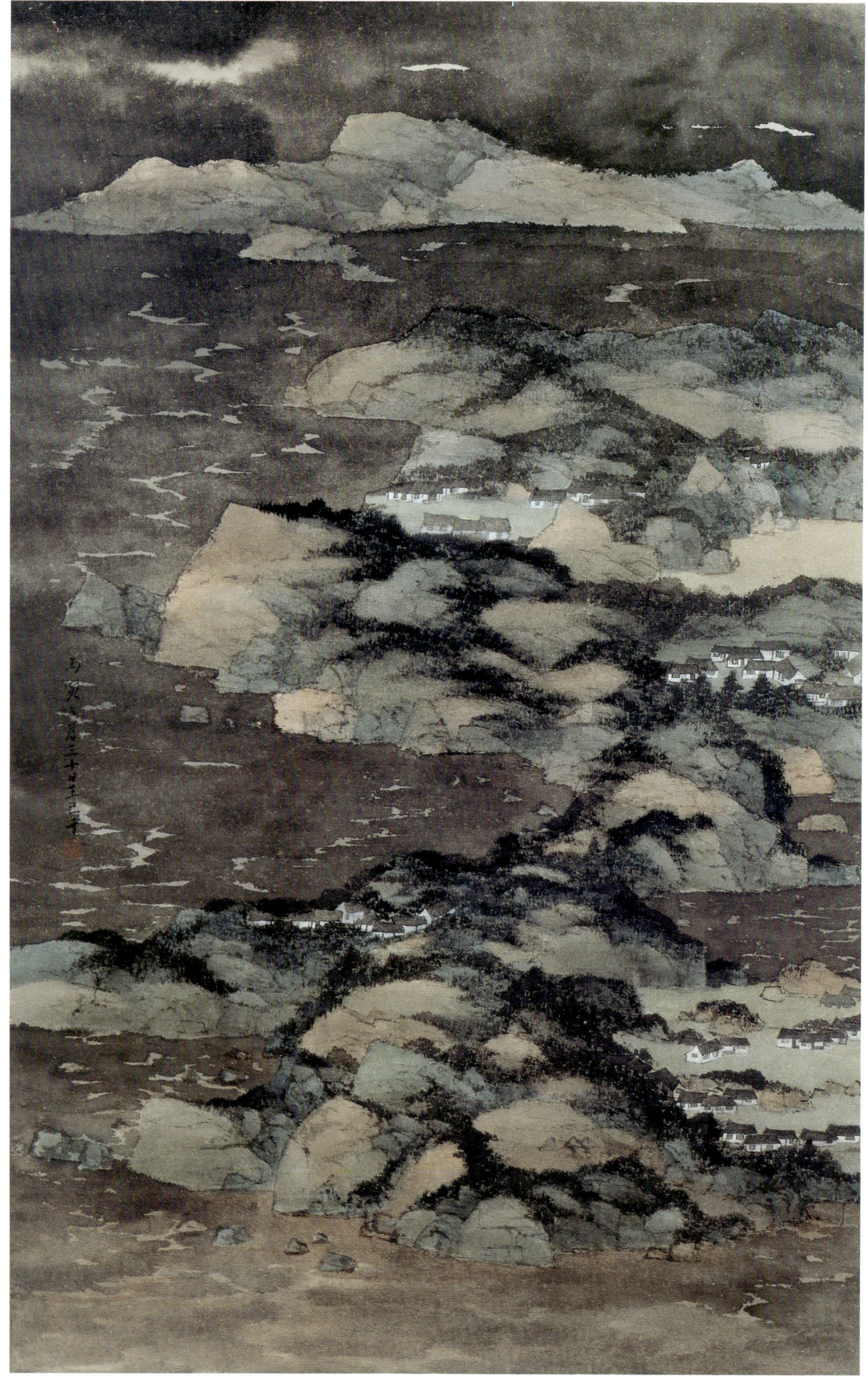

Landscape No. 882. 30 March 1986. Hanging scroll, ink and color on paper. 25 x 38 in (63.5 x 96.5 cm). Private Collection.

Inscribed
"*Ping-yin* [1986], 3rd month, 30th day. Wang Chi-ch'ien."

Artist's Seal
Wang Chi-ch'ien yin (left)

Exhibited
Hong Kong Arts Centre, 1986; Birmingham Museum of Art, 1987

isolated, varies according to the perspective and scale one applies to this scene, which is left intriguingly ambiguous. The sheer verticality of these rugged forms and the untenability of the viewer's suspended position might otherwise make this remote landscape threatening. But the artist's use of color—painting the entire landscape red from the back side and applying elegant touches of white to the houses, the soaring birds, and faint vertical streamers of floating mist like one actually finds at extremely high altitudes—seems to transform the painting into a fairyland, albeit one more somber, darkly mysterious, and compelling than the bright and thoroughly childlike fairyland of *Landscape No. 483* (fig. 67). While possibly a vision that could only be viewed in magical flight, the lofty perch from which this landscape is shown presents such a hypnotic image that at best it surpasses reality and transcends the need for comparison with it, or at least it recalls such remarkable vantage points as those at Mount Huang, where one is never sure of correct perspective and where impossible scenes such as this, architecture and all, really do exist.

One of the paintings done after *Landscape No. 503* (fig. 68) which seems most different from it and yet, like it, represents the artist's very best work is *Landscape No. 882,* dated 30 March 1986 (fig. 75). More than any other painting of the 1980s, it directs its focus to the artist's earliest training: in technique, it uses only the brush, and there is neither applied texture nor painting from the back side; in taste, it is as self-restrained and softly understated as any painting by the artist's esteemed teacher, Wu Hu-fan. C. C. Wang talks about this painting in terms of its "naturalness" and its "naïveté," and so forth, but he perhaps described it best when he simply called the painting "soft as cotton candy." The compositional design of *No. 882* owes much to Chu Ta (fig. 17) and to Wang Yüan-ch'i's "dragon vein" (fig. 23), and its close compositional resemblance to *Landscape Nos. 472* and *475* (figs. 64, 52) should be evident. Indeed, this painting is so close in design to the latter two that the artist might well invoke the traditional excuse that a well-executed landscape has no need for compositional originality. As in the two earlier examples, the potentially dramatic rhythm of such a composition is subdued by the vertical format of the painting. The form of the rocks and the brushwork relate to Ni Tsan at his softest and most fully rounded (as in *Pine Pavilion, Mountain Colors,* fig. 5, the longest held of C. C. Wang's early paintings).

Like many of his paintings in the 1980s, this is distinguished by its colors. Strands of ochre, indigo blue, light yellow-green, and gray ink, with points of white, are woven into the composition like a brocade. This merging of layered color with compositional structure is particularly reminiscent of Wang Yüan-ch'i (fig. 23). A lovely ochre-rose color serves as a warm overpainting for the entire work. The brushwork approaches the artist's very best, yet it is far more restrained and less obvious in its virtues than in other superior examples such as *Landscape No. 466* (fig. 21). Brushstrokes are fully rounded and unassertive, avoiding any dramatic movement of the brush. The softly dotted foliage they describe, together with the flat,

pale green meadows spread throughout the landscape, recommend this as a gentle and fertile land, while the proliferation of comfortably placed and neatly kept houses (approximately fifty in number) suggests that others have found it a fine place to live. In contrast to *Landscape No. 895,* which seems designed to create in the viewer an urge to soar past magnificent but rugged mountains, this painting offers a tempting place to settle down. It is executed with unusual thoroughness and took the artist more than a full week to complete.

In its visual qualities as well as its techniques, *Landscape No. 882* seems to weave together the beginning and the end of the artist's career, to express his modernism in a most traditional Chinese manner. Were his venerated teacher, Wu Hu-fan, able to select any one painting by his pupil, this might well be the one. It is perhaps the one landscape that best encompasses the full span of C. C. Wang's artistic journey, from East to West, from traditionalism to modernity, a span of ten thousand miles, and ten thousand volumes.

Impressions of all available seals that appear on paintings in this book. Seals are reproduced actual size and are arranged accordingly.

Alphabetical listing

1
Wang Chi-ch'ien
Wang Chi-ch'ien

2
Wang Chi-ch'ien yin
"Seal of Wang Chi-ch'ien"

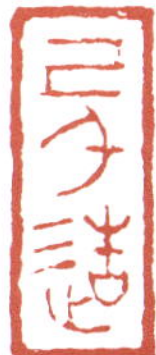

3
Chi-ch'ien tsao
"Created by Chi-ch'ien"

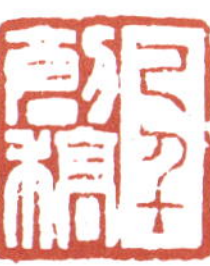

4
Chi-ch'ien ch'uang-kao
"Invented by Chi-ch'ien"

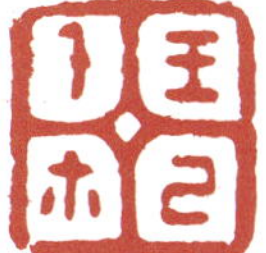

5
Wang Chi-ch'ien hsi
"Seal of Wang Chi-ch'ien"

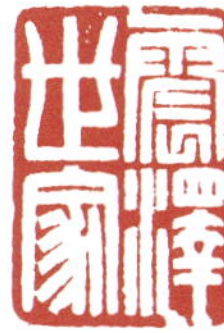

6
Chen-tse shih-chia
"From Chen-tse's [Lake T'ai's] family of distinguished officials"

長季
壽遷

7

Chi-ch'ien ch'ang-shou
"Long life to Chi-ch'ien"

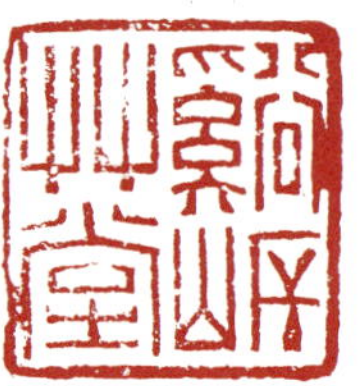

草溪
堂岸

8

Hsi-an Ts'ao-t'ang
"Thatched Hut by the Riverbank"

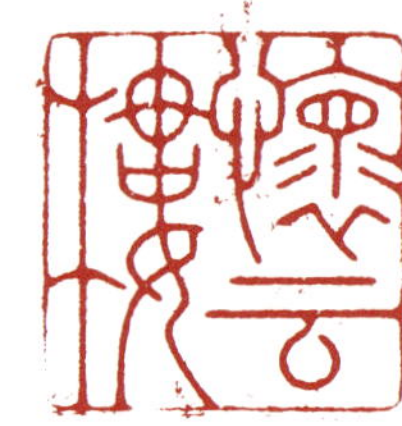

懷雲
樓

9

Huai-Yün Lou
"The Hall Where [Ni] Yün[-lin] is Treasured"

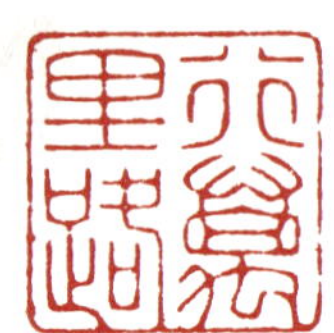

里行
路萬

10

Hsing wan li lu
"Travel ten thousand miles"

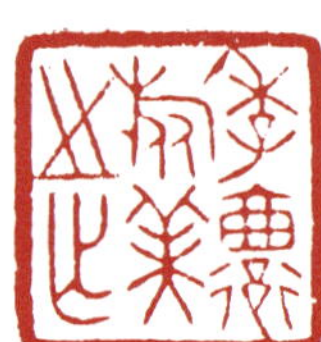

之旅季
作美遷

11

Chi-ch'ien lü Mei chih-tso
"Done by Chi-ch'ien in America"

鳥蟲
迹書

12

Ch'ung-shu niao-chi
"Wormy books and bird tracks"

未童
泯心

13

T'ung-hsin wei ni
"Heart of a child, unobscured"

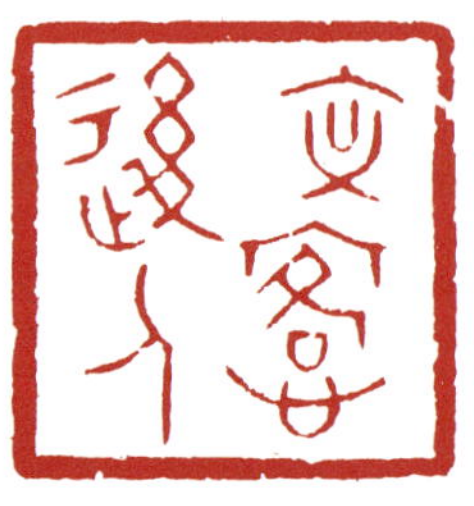

文恪
後公
人

14

Wen-ko Kung hou-jen
"Descendant of Mr. Wen-ko [Wang Ao]"

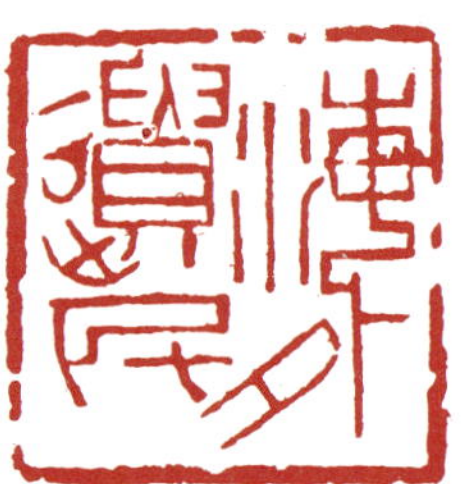

遺海
民外

15

Hai-wai i-min
"Overseas exile"

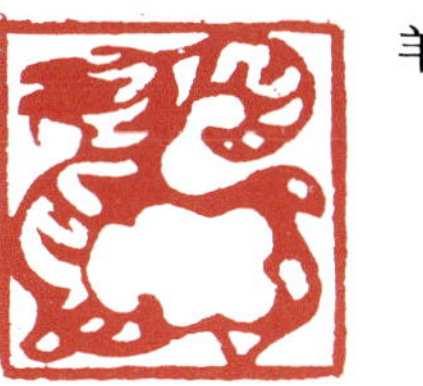

16
Yang
"Ram" [the artist's zodiac sign]

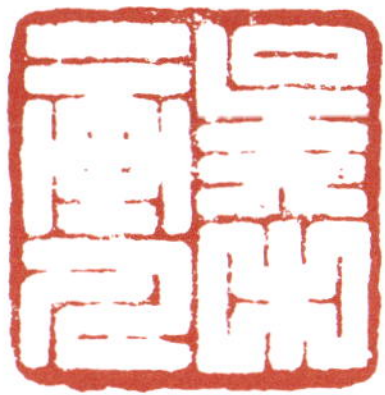

17
Wu-chung i hua-jen
"One painter from Wu"

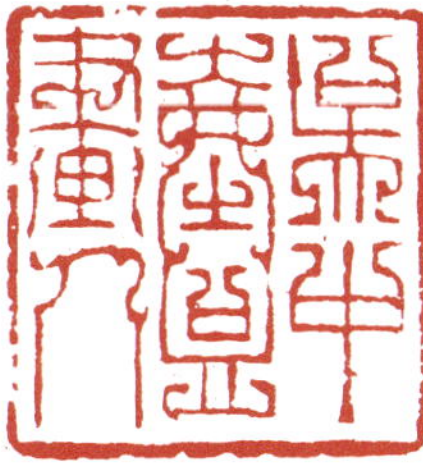

18
Wu-chung i hua-jen
"One painter from Wu"

19
Hsiung-chung ch'iu-ho
"Mind landscapes"

20
Chi-ch'ien hsin-ching
"From the imagination of Chi-ch'ien"

21
Fei Nan fei Pei, i ku i chin
"Neither Southern nor Northern School, both ancient and modern"

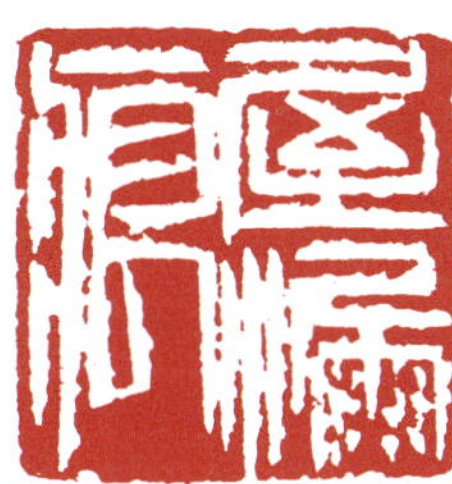

22
Wu lou hen
"Stains from a leaky roof"

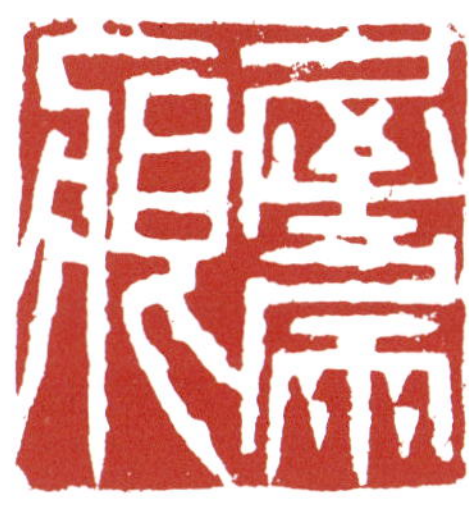

23
Wu lou hen
"Stains from a leaky roof"

24
Wu jen wu wo, fei ku fei chin
"Not [derived] from others, not from myself, not from the past, not from the present."

鳥蟲
迹書

25
Ch'ung-shu niao-chi
"Wormy books and bird tracks"

懷雲
樓

26
Huai-Yün Lou
"The Hall Where [Ni] Yün[-lin] is Treasured"

裔文
孫恪

27
Wen-ko i-sun
"Descendant of Wen Ko [Wang Ao]"

人邨石
家裏橋

28
Shih-ch'iao-ts'un li jen-chia
"From the family of Shih-ch'iao Village"

拾偶
得然

29
Ou-jan shih-te
"Gotten by accident"

象得
外之

30
Te chih hsiang wai
"Obtained from beyond the realm of appearances"

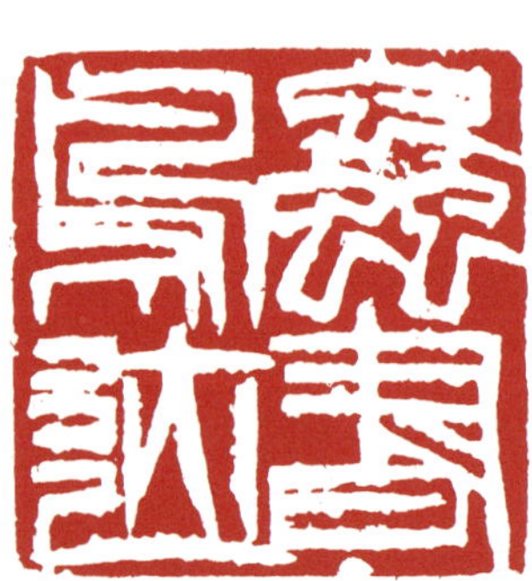

鳥蟲
迹書

31
Ch'ung-shu niao-chi
"Wormy books and bird tracks"

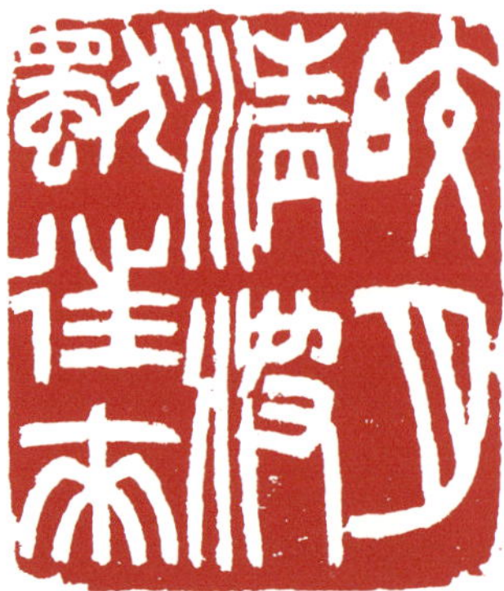

獨清皎
往波月
來

32
Chiao-yüeh ch'ing-po tu wang-lai
"Beneath the bright moon, on clear waves, traveling alone"

寶武
堂

33
Pao-Wu T'ang
"Seal of the Hall Where Wu [Tsung-yüan] is Treasured"

Barnhart, Richard. *Along the Border of Heaven: Sung and Yüan Paintings from the C. C. Wang Family Collection* New York: Metropolitan Museum of Art, 1983.

————. "Recent Paintings by C. C. Wang." *Oriental Art,* N.S. 19, no. 4 (Winter, 1973), pp. 459-460.

Byrd, Jennifer S. [Joan Stanley-Baker]. "C. C. Wang, The Last Literatus." *Asian Pacific Quarterly* 7, no. 1 (Summer, 1974), pp. 1-15.

Cahill, James, C. C. Wang, Lynn King, and Kao Mayching. *C. C. Wang: Landscape Paintings.* Hong Kong: Hsi An T'ang, distributed by the University of Washington Press, Seattle, 1986. (Introduction by James Cahill also published in *Mei-shu-chia* 53 (December, 1986), pp. 4-8.)

Chang, Arnold. "The Landscape Painting of Wang Jiqian [Wang Chi-ch'ien]: A Modern Dialogue with the Ancients." *Orientations,* 14, no. 1 (January, 1983), pp. 26-39.

————. "Modern Expressions of the Literati Aesthetic in Chinese Painting." *Orientations,* 17, no. 3 (August, 1986), pp. 33-43.

————. *Painting in the People's Republic of China: The Politics of Style.* Boulder: Westview Press, 1980.

————, and Brad Davis. *The Mountain Retreat: Landscape in Modern Chinese Painting.* Aspen: The Aspen Art Museum, 1986.

Contag, Victoria, and Chi-ch'üan Wang. *Maler- und Sammler-Stempel aus der Ming- und Ch'ing-Zeit, Ming Ch'ing hua-chia yin-chien.* Shanghai: Commercial Press, 1940.

————. *Seals of Chinese Painters and Collectors of the Ming and Ch'ing Dynasties.* Hong Kong: Hong Kong University Press, Translation of first edition with supplement, 1966.

Fong, Wen. *Summer Mountains: The Timeless Landscape.* New York: Metropolitan Museum of Art, 1975.

————, and Marilyn Fu. *Sung and Yuan Paintings.* New York: Metropolitan Museum of Art, 1973.

Hsü, Hsiao-hu [Joan Stanley-Baker]. "Hua-yü lu." *Ku-kung wen-wu yüeh-k'an* 13 (April, 1984), 15-29 (June, 1984-July, 1985).

Kao, Mayching. "China's Response to the West in Art, 1898-1937." Ph. D. diss., Stanford University, 1972.

Katz, Lois, and C. C. Wang. *The Landscapes of C. C. Wang: Mountains of the Mind.* New York: AMS Foundation, 1977.

Laing, Ellen. *An Index to Reproductions of Paintings by 20th-Century Chinese Artists.* Eugene: University of Oregon Asian Studies Program, 1984.

Li, Chu-tsing. *Trends in Modern Chinese Painting (The C. A. Drenowatz Collection).* Ascona: Artibus Asiae, 1979.

Moss, Hugh. *The Experience of Art: 20th Century Chinese Paintings From the Shuisongshi Shanfang Collection.* Hong Kong: Adamans International, Ltd., 1983.

————. *Some Recent Developments in 20th Century Chinese Painting: A Personal View.* Hong Kong: Umbrella, 1982.

Phoenix Art Museum. *The Modern Spirit in Chinese Painting: Selections from the Jeanette Shambaugh Elliott Collection,* text by Wai-fong Anita Siu. 1985.

Stanley-Baker, Joan [Hsü Hsiao-hu]. "A Closed Cycle in Chinese Art." *Free China Review* 36, no. 7 (July, 1986), pp. 10-27.

Sullivan, Michael. *Chinese Art in the 20th Century.* Berkeley: University of California Press, 1959.

Wang, C. C. *Album Leaves from the Sung and Yüan Dynasties.* New York: China Institute in America, 1970.

————. *Authenticated Works from the Collection of Chang Ts'ung-yü.* New York: C. T. Loo and Co., 1948.

————. "Introduction to Chinese Painting." *Archives of the Chinese Art Society of America,* 2 (1947), pp. 21-27.

————. "Ni Yün-lin sheng-p'ing chi shih-wen (The Life and Writings of Ni Tsan)." *National Palace Museum Quarterly* 1, no. 2 (Winter, 1966), pp. 29-42. (Chinese with English summary.)

————. "Ni Yün-lin chih hua (The Paintings of Ni Tsan)." *National Palace Museum Quarterly,* 1, no. 3 (Spring, 1967), pp. 15-46. (Chinese with English summary.)

————, and Li Lin-ts'an. "Wang Meng ti 'Hua-hsi Yü-yin T'u' (A Study of Wang Meng's Masterpiece, 'Hermit Fisherman on the Hua Stream')." *National Palace Museum Quarterly,* 1, no. 1 (Autumn, 1966), pp. 63-68. (Chinese with English summary.)

Weatherby, Meredith, ed., Hsü Hsiao-hu [Joan Stanley-Baker], James Cahill, Alfred Frankenstein, and Michael Chacko Daniels. *Mountains of the Mind: The Landscape Painting of Wang Chi-ch'ien.* New York: Walker/Weatherhill, 1970.

Note on the Captions of Paintings by C. C. Wang

The numbering system by which most of these landscapes are identified was not adopted by the artist until 1972 and does not correspond in many cases to the precise order in which paintings were completed. In 1985, the system was revised, and there are no works numbered between 525 and 850.

Although using the Chinese cyclical system to indicate years, the artist's numbering of the months typically accords with the months of the Western calendar and he changes the cyclical date in January.

The seals on these paintings are illustrated and translated in the appendix, unless indicated otherwise; numbers are given when more than one version of a seal is reproduced.

Inscriptions have been translated, not transliterated, with the exception of year names, and punctuation has been provided.

Citations for publications, if not listed in full in the captions, may be found in the Bibliography.

In the dimensions given here, height precedes width.

Historical Paintings

Figure 9, page 40
Tung Yüan (active c. 975), attributed to. *The Riverbank*. **Late 10th century.** Hanging scroll, ink and color on silk. 87¼ x 43¼ in (221.6 x 109.9 cm). C. C. Wang Family Collection.

Figure 8, page 33
Ch'ü Ting (active c. 1023-1056). attributed to. *Summer Mountains* (section). **Late 10th–early 11th century.** Handscroll, ink and color on silk. 17¾ x 45¼ in (45.1 x 114.9 cm). The Metropolitan Museum of Art, Gift of the Douglas Dillon Fund, 1973.

Figure 16, page 50
Fan K'uan (c. 960-c. 1030). *Travelers Among Streams and Mountains*. **Early 11th century.** Hanging scroll, ink and color on silk. 61 x 29¼ in (154.9 x 74.3 cm). National Palace Museum, Taipei, Taiwan, Republic of China.

Figure 3, page 20
Wang Meng (1301-1385). *A Quiet Life in a Wooded Glen.***1361.** Hanging scroll, ink and colors on paper. 60 x 25³⁄₁₆ in (152.4 x 64.1 cm). Art Institute of Chicago, Kate S. Buckingham Fund.

Figure 5, page 22; Figure 12, page 45 (detail)
Ni Tsan (1301-1374). *Pine Pavilion, Mountain Scenery.* **1372.** Hanging scroll, ink on paper. 40 x 17¼ in (101.6 x 43.8 cm). C. C. Wang Family Collection.

Figure 10, page 41
Tung Ch'i-ch'ang (1556-1636). *Painting Wang Wei's Poetic Feeling.* **1621.** Hanging scroll, ink on paper. 42⅞ x 19⁵⁄₁₆ in (109 x 49 cm). C. C. Wang Family Collection.

Figure 6, page 24
Kung Hsien (c. 1618-1689). *A Thousand Peaks and Myriad Ravines.* **c. 1670.** Hanging scroll, ink on paper. 24⁷⁄₁₆ x 39⅜ in (62 x 100 cm). Rietberg Museum, Zürich, Charles A. Drenowatz Collection.

Figure 11, page 43
Tao-chi (1642-c. 1707). **"Rainstorm," from** *Album for Taoist Yü.* **c. 1695.** Album leaf, ink on paper. 9½ x 11 in (24.1 x 27.9 cm). C. C. Wang Family Collection.

Figure 19, page 54
Tao-chi (1642-c. 1707). **"Hut at the Foot of Mountains," from** *Album for Taoist Yü.* **c. 1695.** 9½ x 11 in (24.1 x 27.9 cm). C. C. Wang Family Collection.

Figure 17, page 52
Chu Ta (1626-c. 1705). *Landscape.* **Late 17th century.** Hanging scroll, ink and colors on paper. 69¹¹⁄₁₆ x 36⅝ in (177 x 93 cm). C. C. Wang Family Collection.

Figure 23, page 58
Wang Yüan-ch'i (1642-1715). *The Wang River Villa* (section). **1711.** Handscroll, ink and colors on paper. 14¹⁄₁₆ x 214⅜ in (35.7 x 545.1 cm). The Metropolitan Museum of Art, Gift of Douglas Dillon Fund, 1977.

Figure 1, page 14
Wu Hu-fan (1894-1968). **"Spring," painted in the style of Huang Kung-wang, section of** *Handscroll in the Style of Four Yüan Masters.* **1933.** Handscroll, ink and color on paper. 5½ x 46¾ in (14.0 x 118.6 cm). C. C. Wang Family Collection.

Paintings by C. C. Wang

1930s

Figure 2, page 14

"Landscape After Mi Fu," from *Ink-play by Shuang-wu.* **1932.** Album leaf, ink on paper. 6⅛ x 9¹⁄₁₆ in (15.5 x 23 cm). Collection of Mr. Chun-hua Lee.

Figure 25, page 62

"Landscape After Lu Kuang," from *Ink-play by Shuang-wu.* **1932.** Album leaf, ink on paper. 6⅛ x 9¹⁄₁₆ in (15.5 x 23 cm). Collection of Mr. Chun-hua Lee.

Figure 26, page 63

Landscape After Wang Shih-min. **Mid-1930s.** Hanging scroll, ink on paper. 37⅜ x 17⅞ in (95 x 45.4 cm). Collection of Brad Davis and Janis Provisor.

1940s

Figure 4, page 20

Landscape After Wang Meng. **1940s.** Hanging scroll, ink and color on paper. 42 x 19¾ in (106.7 x 50.2 cm). Collection of Arnold Chang.

Figure 27, page 65

Fisherman's Boat on Evening Waves, After Wu Chen. **Early 1940s.** Album leaf, ink on paper. 17³⁄₁₆ x 13¼ in (43.7 x 33.6 cm). Shuisongshi Shanfang Collection.

Figure 28, page 65

Landscape. **Summer 1943.** Hanging scroll, ink and light color on paper. 30 x 11⅝ in (76.2 x 29.5 cm). Private Collection.

Figure 29, page 66

Landscape in the Manner of Hsia Kuei. **November/ December 1946.** Folding fan, ink on paper. 9½ x 19⅞ in (24.0 x 50.5 cm). C. C. Wang Family Collection.

1950s

Figure 31, page 68

Still Life. **1956.** Casein on wood panel. 26 x 40 in (66.0 x 101.6 cm). Private Collection.

Figure 24, page 60

Lotus. **May 1958.** Hanging scroll, ink on paper. 24½ x 19½ in (62.2 x 49.5 cm). Collection of Mr. and Mrs. Frank Cho.

1960s

Figure 30, page 67

Apples. **Autumn 1960.** Hanging scroll, ink on paper. 36⅞ x 17⅞ in (96.2 x 45.3 cm). Ching Yüan Chai Collection, On Extended Loan to the University Art Museum, University of California, Berkeley.

Figure 34, page 72

Sailing Boats and Misty Mountains. **July 1964.** Hanging scroll, ink and color on paper. 15¾ x 23⅝ in (40 x 60 cm). Rietberg Museum, Zürich, Charles A. Drenowatz Collection.

Figure 35, page 73

Flowing Water in Spring River. **August 1964.** Hanging scroll, ink and color on paper. 15⅜ x 22¹³⁄₁₆ in (39 x 58 cm). Rietberg Museum, Zürich, Charles A. Drenowatz Collection.

Figure 36, page 74

Landscape. **1965.** Hanging scroll, ink and color on paper. Dimensions unknown. Collection unknown.

Figure 7, page 27

Vase and Brushes. **1966.** Hanging scroll, ink on paper. 34 x 17¾ in (86.4 x 45.1 cm). Collection of Mr. and Mrs. Frank Cho.

Figure 33, page 70

River Village in a Rainy Dawn. **1966.** Hanging scroll, ink and color on paper. 18⅞ x 25³⁄₁₆ in (48 x 64 cm). Ching Yüan Chai Collection, On Extended Loan to the University Art Museum, University of California, Berkeley.

Figure 37, page 75

Landscape. **March 1966.** Hanging scroll, ink and color on paper. Dimensions unknown. Collection unknown.

Figure 41, page 81

Landscape No. 1: Clearing Skies After Snow on the Nine Peaks. **1968.** Hanging scroll, ink on paper. 47⁷⁄₁₆ x 22¼ in (120.5 x 56.5 cm). Collection unknown.

Figure 42, page 81

Clouds in the Mountains of the Immortals. **1968.** Hanging scroll, ink on paper. 38⅜ x 24¹³⁄₁₆ in (97.5 x 63 cm). Collection unknown.

Figure 38, page 77

Landscape No. 40. **21 December 1968.** Hanging scroll, ink on paper. 17¼ x 22⁷⁄₁₆ in (43.75 x 57 cm). C. C. Wang Family Collection.

Figure 32, page 68

Landscape No. 284. **1963-69.** Hanging scroll, ink and color on paper. 17³⁄₁₆ x 26 in (44.5 x 66.1 cm). Private Collection.

Figure 39, page 78

Landscape No. 76. **1969.** Hanging scroll, ink and color on paper. 21³⁄₁₆ x 36³⁄₁₆ in (61.4 x 91.9 cm). C. C. Wang Family Collection.

Figure 40, page 79

Landscape No. 112. **March 1969.** Hanging scroll, ink and color on paper. 24½ x 36 in (62.2 x 91.5 cm). C. C. Wang Family Collection.

Figure 43, page 83

Landscape No. 104. **August 1969.** Hanging scroll, ink and color on paper. 18⅝ x 24¾ in (47.3 x 62.9 cm). Private Collection.

1970s

Figure 49, page 89

Landscape No. 162: Heavenly Pond and Stone Cliff. **April 1972.** Hanging scroll, ink and color on paper. 34¼ x 23 in (87 x 58.4 cm). Phoenix Art Museum, Gift of Jeanette Shambaugh Elliott.

Figure 15, page 49

Landscape No. 170. **April 1972.** Hanging scroll, ink and color on paper. 22¹⁄₁₆ x 28⅛ in (56.1 x 71.5 cm). Collection of Mr. James Stark.

Figure 46, page 87

Landscape No. 188. **June 1972.** Hanging scroll, ink and color on paper. 24 x 29¹⁵⁄₁₆ in (61 x 76 cm). Collection of Mr. and Mrs. Frank Cho.

Figure 47, page 87

Landscape No. 205. **December 1972.** Hanging scroll, ink and color on paper. 23¹¹⁄₁₆ x 29¾ in (60.2 x 75.6 cm). Private Collection.

Figure 44, page 83

Landscape No. 240: The Spring of the Immortals. **Spring 1973.** Hanging scroll, ink and color on paper. 24⅝ x 35⅜ in (62.6 x 90 cm). Gift of Kenneth and Yien-koo King, Herbert F. Johnson Museum of Art, Cornell University, Ithaca, New York.

Figure 48, page 88

Landscape No. 241. **November 1973.** Hanging scroll, ink and color on paper. 22¹³⁄₁₆ x 35⅝ in (58 x 90.4 cm). Private Collection.

Figure 51, page 91

Landscape No. 305. **July 1974.** Hanging scroll, ink and color on paper. 35½ x 24 in (90.1 x 61 cm). C. C. Wang Family Collection.

Figure 50, page 90

Landscape No. 239. **September 1974.** Hanging scroll, ink and color on paper. 31¹³⁄₁₆ x 23⅝ in (80.8 x 60 cm). Private Collection.

Figure 45, page 84

Landscape No. 334. **July 1975.** Hanging scroll, ink and color on paper. 23⅝ x 35¹⁄₁₆ in (60 x 89.1 cm). C. C. Wang Family Collection.

1980s

Figure 54, page 96

Landscape No. 369. **July 1980.** Hanging scroll, ink and color on paper. 13¼ x 23⅝ in (33.7 x 60.0 cm). Qing Xing Zhai Collection.

Figure 53, page 95

Landscape No. 398, with figures by Ch'eng Shih-fa. **February 1981.** Hanging scroll, ink and color on paper. 23½ x 33¼ in (59.7 x 84.5 cm). Private Collection.

Figure 22, page 57

Landscape No. 397. **August 1981.** Hanging scroll, ink and color on paper. 24 x 34 in (61.0 x 86.4 cm). Private Collection.

Figure 58, page 101

Landscape No. 425. **May 1982.** Hanging scroll, ink and color on paper. 28⅝ x 40¾ in (72.7 x 103.5 cm). Ching Yüan Chai Collection, On Extended Loan to the University Art Museum, University of California, Berkeley.

Figure 55, page 98

Landscape No. 418. **June 1982.** Hanging scroll, ink and color on paper. 29 x 39¼ in (73.7 x 99.7 cm). Private Collection.

Figure 57, page 100

Landscape No. 420. **24 July 1982.** Hanging scroll, ink and color on paper. 28¾ x 19¾ in (73.0 x 50.2 cm). Private Collection.

Figure 60, page 104
Landscape No. 514. **August 1982.** Hanging scroll, ink and color on paper. 17 x 13¾ in (43.2 x 34.9 cm). Collection of Mrs. Yien-koo Wang King.

Figure 56, page 99
Landscape No. 419. **12 August 1982.** Hanging scroll, ink and color on paper. 23 x 32 in (58.4 x 81.3 cm) Private Collection.

Figure 61, page 105
Landscape No. 448. **28 January 1983.** Hanging scroll, ink and color on paper. 19¾ x 40 in (50.2 x 101.6 cm). C. C. Wang Family Collection.

Figure 13, page 46
Landscape No. 450. **25 February 1983.** Hanging scroll, ink and color on paper. 23¼ x 32 in (59.1 x 81.3 cm). C. C. Wang Family Collection.

Figure 62, page 106
Landscape No. 454. **8 March 1983.** Hanging scroll, ink and color on paper. 26¼ x 27 in (66.7 x 68.6 cm). C. C. Wang Family Collection.

Figure 63, page 107
Landscape No. 464. **21 March 1983.** Hanging scroll, ink and color on paper. 26 x 13⅜ in (66.0 x 34.0 cm). Collection of Peter Neaman.

Figure 21, page 56
Landscape No. 466. **29 March 1983.** Hanging scroll, ink and color on paper. 27 x 13⅛ in (68.6 x 33.3 cm). Collection of Joan Stanley-Baker.

Figure 64, page 109
Landscape No. 472. **12 April 1983.** Hanging scroll, ink and color on paper. 39½ x 19½ in (100.3 x 49.5 cm). C. C. Wang Family Collection.

Figure 65, page 110
Landscape No. 473. **22 April 1983.** Hanging scroll, ink and color on paper. 23½ x 15⅝ in (59.7 x 39.7 cm) C. C. Wang Family Collection.

Figure 66, page 111
Landscape No. 474. **27 April 1983.** Hanging scroll, color on paper. 20¾ x 14¾ in (52.7 x 37.5 cm). C. C. Wang Family Collection.

Figure 52, page 92
Landscape No. 475. **7 May 1983.** Hanging scroll, ink and color on paper. 40 x 20 in (101.6 x 50.8 cm). Collection of Mrs. Yien-koo Wang King.

Figure 67, page 112
Landscape No. 483. **15 February 1984.** Hanging scroll, ink and color on paper. 25⅜ x 13¾ in (64.5 x 34.9 cm). Collection of Mr. and Mrs. Wayne G. Quasha.

Figure 69, page 114
Landscape No. 510: Heavenly Lake. **15 August 1984.** Hanging scroll, ink and color on paper. 19½ x 25 in (49.5 x 63.5 cm). C. C. Wang Family Collection.

Figure 68, page 113
Landscape No. 503. **1 November 1984.** Hanging scroll, ink on paper. 25 x 34 in (63.5 x 86.4 cm). Collection of the Hong Kong Land Company.

Figure 59, page 103
Landscape No. 429. **April 1982–1985.** Hanging scroll, ink and color on paper. 40 x 28¾ in (101.6 x 73.0 cm). Collection of Mr. and Mrs. Chuck Chang.

Figure 71, page 116
Landscape No. 855. **18 February 1985.** Hanging scroll, ink on paper. 19 x 25³⁄₁₆ in (48.2 x 64 cm). C. C. Wang Family Collection.

Figure 70, page 115
Landscape No. 856. **17 March 1985.** Hanging scroll, ink and color on paper. 27⅛ x 18 in (68.9 x 45.7 cm). C. C. Wang Family Collection.

Figure 72, page 117
Landscape No. 851. **15 April 1985.** Hanging scroll, ink and color on paper. 35⅝ x 23¹³⁄₁₆ in (90.5 x 60.5 cm). C. C. Wang Family Collection.

Figure 73, page 118
Landscape No. 881: Clearing After Snow on the Nine Peaks. **12 December 1985.** Hanging scroll, ink on paper. 25 x 38 in (63.5 x 96.5 cm). Suzhou Museum.

Figure 20, page 55
Landscape No. 888. **14 December 1985.** Hanging scroll, ink on paper. 38¼ x 25 in (97.2 x 63.5 cm). C. C. Wang Family Collection.

Figure 75, page 120
Landscape No. 882. **30 March 1986.** Hanging scroll, ink and color on paper. 25 x 38 in (63.5 x 96.5 cm). Private Collection.

Figure 74, page 119
Landscape No. 895. **10 April 1986.** Hanging scroll, ink and color on paper. 36 x 19½ in (91.4 x 49.5 cm). C. C. Wang Family Collection.

Figure 18, page 53
Landscape No. 910. **22 July 1986.** Hanging scroll, ink and color on paper. 24⅜ x 24⅜ in (62 x 62 cm). Collection of Jean and Sun-chang Lo.

Figure 14, page 48
Landscape No. 970. **9 February 1987.** Hanging scroll, ink on paper. 48⅜ x 18⅛ in (122 x 46 cm). Collection of Jean and Sun-chang Lo.

Index